UNANSWERED QUESTIONS

UNANSWERED

Nazi Germany and

QUESTIONS

the Genocide of the Jews

edited by **François Furet**

Schocken Books

New York

FIRST AMERICAN EDITION

Translation Copyright © 1989 by Schocken Books Inc.

All rights reserved under International
and Pan-American Copyright Conventions.
Published in the United States by Schocken Books Inc., New York,
and simultaneously in Canada by Random House of Canada Limited, Toronto.
Distributed by Pantheon Books, a division of Random House, Inc., New York.
Originally published in France as
L'allemagne nazie et le génocide juif, by Éditions du Seuil.
Copyright © November 1985 by Éditions du Seuil.

Library of Congress Cataloging-in-Publication Data

Allemagne nazie et le génocide juif. English.
Unanswered questions.

Translation of: L'Allemagne nazie et le génocide juif.
Includes index.
1. Holocaust, Jewish (1939–1945)—Congresses.
2. Antisemitism—Germany—Congresses.   3. Holocaust, Jewish (1939–1945)
—Historiography—Congresses.
I. Furet, François, 1927–   . II. Title.
D804.3.A4413 1989   940.53'15'03924   88-42613
ISBN 0-8052-4051-9
ISBN 0-8052-0908-5 (pbk.)

Manufactured in the United States of America

24689753

CONTENTS

PREFACE

This book is, in one respect, incomplete, as it lacks the name of the man who should have written its preface: Raymond Aron. At my request, Raymond Aron had agreed to share with me the chair of the colloquium sessions which resulted in these essays. That was in 1982. He was also scheduled to present a summing-up at the end of the meetings. But sadly he died the year before, and today I can but inscribe his name at the head of this book, in recognition of all that he contributed to it. As always, intelligence and a truthful spirit were his bywords in the meetings he commented upon, discussing his own views on the different contributions.

Our initial idea was quite simple. We knew that it was time, even high time, almost forty years after World War II, to collect in a single volume what specialists had discovered about one of the most tragic episodes of that war: the genocide of the Jews by the Nazis. Like many others, I had been surprised and shocked by the efforts of small partisan groups to cast doubt upon the veracity of the facts, or to banalize their import. But indignation does not constitute knowledge: it may even be an obstacle to knowledge, like prejudgment of materials or partisanship. Therefore, it was necessary to let some people speak who had devoted their principal efforts to historical research on nazism, World War II, and the "final solution of the Jewish problem." As the professional jargon puts it, the time had come for summing up the "state of the question." Hence, the initiative of a colloquium organized by the École des Hautes Études en Sciences Sociales (School for Advanced Studies in the Social Sciences) at the beginning of July 1982. Most of the participants were foreign specialists. The historiography of the genocide of the Jews is, in effect, dominated by contributions from Germany, the United States, and Israel. Even so, there have been some pioneers in France, such as Léon Poliakov. Therefore, with a few exceptions, we find in this book all the historians who have reconstructed, explicated, and interpreted Hitler's policy of exterminating the Jews of Europe. We should also take note of their disagreements, which are significant. Finally, we may adumbrate what is known and what remains to be known, what is certain and what uncertain, and the scope and limitations of various interpretations.

By its very excess, nazism remains, forty years after its fall, a sort of enigma for historical rationality. The "Final Solution," which is nazism's culmination point, remains the horrifying embodiment of this mystery. If the present volume may help to account for it, in the fullest sense of the term—that is, to work out possible explications for the questions it raises—it will have fulfilled its aim.

François Furet

École des Hautes Études en Sciences Sociales

P.S.: A last word to thank those who made possible the colloquium where this book originated, by covering its costs: the Ministry of Industry and Research, and the Fondation du judaïsme (Jewish Foundation). Let this note express the acknowledgments of all the participating historians to these institutions for what we owe them.

UNANSWERED QUESTIONS

I

From Anti-Semitism to Extermination

*A Historiographical Study of Nazi Policies Toward the Jews and an Essay in Interpretation**

SAUL FRIEDLÄNDER

Over the past decades, the volume of recorded history dealing with the extermination of the Jews of Europe has reached considerable proportions. This applies equally to the history of the roots of Nazi anti-Semitism and its development, of Nazi policies toward the Jews, of the "Final Solution" as such, or the attitudes and reactions of German society, the neutrals, or the Allies during the war, of the Church, of Western society in general, and also of the victims, the Jews, as they faced the growing peril and the ultimate catastrophe. Studies and publications have multiplied, historical approaches have evolved and changed with time.[1] Today, in fact, one can perceive clearly distinct ways of considering these issues—one could almost speak of different schools of thought.

As far as Nazi anti-Semitism and the policies of the Third Reich toward the Jews are concerned—the only aspect of the problem which will be considered here—any global evaluation of the historical studies published since the end of the war cannot but aim at answering one

* I wish to thank my friends and colleagues Yehuda Bauer, Dov Kulka, Hans Mommsen, Dina Porath, and Aharon Weiss for their help at various stages of the preparation of this paper. For earlier presentations of some of the issues dealt with in this paper, see Saul Friedländer, "Some Aspects of the Historical Significance of the Holocaust," *Jerusalem Quarterly*, no. 1, Fall 1976; "De l'Antisémitisme à l'Extermination: Esquisse Historiographique," *Le débat*, no. 21, September 1982; for the final section, under the heading "Some Comments," see also my Introduction to Gerald L. Fleming, *Hitler and the Final Solution* (Berkeley, 1984).

3

central question. Do these studies make it possible to insert the events under consideration into the framework of a global and coherent historical explanation, or do they provide only very fragmentary insights, which do not lend themselves to a significant synthesis and, ultimately, to an overall understanding? In other words, does what Isaac Deutscher wrote some fifteen years ago still apply today?

> For the historian who attempts to understand the holocaust of the Jews, the most important obstacle is the absolutely unique character of this catastrophe. It is not only a matter of time and of historical perspective. I doubt that in a thousand years people will better understand Hitler, Auschwitz, Majdanek and Treblinka than we do today. Will they have a better historical perspective? It may be, on the contrary, that posterity will understand all that even less than we do.[2]

Or should we accept instead the interpretation given some years ago by Raymond Aron?

> As for the genocide . . . I would say that its apparent irrationality results from a false perspective. Hitler had proclaimed many times, particularly on the first day of the war, that the Jews would not survive a war which they, according to him, had initiated. . . . If one is prepared to admit that the liquidation of the Jews, the Jewish poison, the corrupting blood, was Hitler's primary aim, the industrial organization of death becomes rational as a means toward this end, genocide. Instrumental rationality is amoral by its very nature, or morally neutral. Once the genocide had been established as the aim, the materials, the men, and mostly the means of transportation needed for this enterprise had to be diverted from the logistics of the armed forces.[3]

These two opposing positions are the implicit foundation of the historiography of our subject. But, insofar as the more specific evaluation of this historiography is concerned, one can consider it at two different levels of analysis: that of the global interpretations of nazism, and that of the more limited but no less controversial interpretation of the anti-Jewish measures taken by the Nazis, considered from the viewpoint of their concrete evolution and internal dynamics. We shall discuss the issues of the global level in brief, and approach the controversies over the origins and development of concrete policies in somewhat greater detail.

Anti-Semitism in the Global Interpretations of Nazism

At the level of global interpretations of nazism, one can distinguish between three major approaches: explanations drawn mostly from Ger-

4

man history; those using the concept of "fascism"; and those which consider National Socialism as a facet of "totalitarianism."[4] Within each of these approaches we find more or less systematic attempts to integrate Nazi anti-Semitism into the general explanatory framework. We shall briefly mention some of these attempts.

The first of these approaches, that which explains nazism as being mainly the result of a specific German national evolution beginning, for most historians, in the nineteenth century, sometimes places German anti-Semitism at the very core of its interpretation (some of these interpretations, in fact, take German anti-Semitism, German racial or "*völkisch*" thinking, as a starting point of what is either an explicit or an implicit interpretation of the roots of National Socialism).[5]

That Nazi anti-Semitism cannot be explained without this national background goes almost without saying. However, the difficulty lies in assessing the significance of those roots, the relative importance of the *völkisch* ideology, and the place of anti-Semitic themes and attitudes within German society, be it during the Wilhelmine period or under the Weimar Republic. Only such an assessment, linked to the various studies of German public opinion and the Jews under the Third Reich, would allow us to understand the possible interaction between the Nazi drive against the Jews and German society. The roots of Hitler's own ideology are essential in an interpretation of Nazi policies. However, an evaluation of the explicit or implicit support given to his policies concerning the Jews, at various levels of the population, is another aspect necessary for the interpretation, one directly linked to the question of the national roots of anti-Semitism and their relative importance. The available studies on this crucial matter may lead to quite different conclusions.

First of all, in assessing the importance of German anti-Semitism at the end of the nineteenth century and up to World War I, one has to take into account recent studies on France which reveal very similar themes, attitudes, and initiatives of various anti-Jewish groups.[6] This implies having to look for a specific German evolution during the war years and the Weimar Republic; but the precise importance of the diffusion of anti-Semitism in German society during this period remains unclear. We don't have an overall systematic study of the subject. The many studies dealing with aspects of the issue do not provide an entirely coherent picture. We know, for instance, that the German anti-Semitic parties disappeared on the eve of the war,[7] and that anti-Semitic themes decreased at the outset of the hostilities. We are also aware of the subsequent sharp increase in anti-Jewish agitation between 1916 and 1924.[8] The significance of anti-Semitism during the decisive period of the early

5

1930s is less than clear. According to William Sheridan Allen's study of the rise of nazism in a small town near Hanover, it played only a minor role,[9] but it seems more significant in other regions.[10] Regional differences appear to be an important element of the interpretation,[11] as we shall notice when we deal with public opinion and the Jews under the Third Reich.[12] One conclusion at least seems plausible from the information that has been gathered about German anti-Semitism prior to 1933: extreme racial anti-Semitism in its Austrian or German garb certainly fed Hitler's ideology and that of the "true believers" within the Nazi Party,[13] but it offered latent rather than active support to the policies against the Jews, which unfolded from 1933 on, as far as its prevalence among the general population is concerned. In fact, as we shall see, for some historians there isn't even a necessary link between Hitler's ideology and the unfolding of the anti-Jewish policies of the Nazis to their ultimate end. Acceptance of this view would exclude the ideological roots of nazism as an explanation for the development of Nazi policies toward the Jews.

Some of the studies which minimize the role of the national ideological background tend to stress the importance of *traditional social structures* (the bureaucracy, the army, the judiciary) in the development of Nazi policies, but the function of the *traditional* element in the evolution of the anti-Jewish policies is not always clearly explained.[14] All in all, few of the global interpretations of nazism completely dismiss the national background in dealing with the Nazis' anti-Jewish policies, but the importance of that background is often difficult to assess.

Of all the generalizing interpretations of nazism, the one which places the Hitlerian phenomenon within the wider category of "fascism" still remains the most current.[15] It has a Marxist and a non-Marxist version, and in both cases Nazi anti-Semitism, because of its singularity, represents a serious obstacle to this particular type of generalization. Many theoreticians of fascism solve the problem by disregarding it completely: their theories circumvent the obstacle and more or less avoid mentioning it (except for a few words, when necessary).[16] Others do recognize the difficulty, but nonetheless look for the common ground of fascism, "the fascist minimum."[17] Finally, there are those who have tried to integrate Nazi anti-Semitism into the framework of their general theory.

The inclusion of Nazi anti-Semitism within the framework of a non-Marxist theory of fascism can adopt three different focal points: reducing it to a more fundamental ideological characteristic; explaining it through

6

the particular inner dynamics of fascist parties and regimes; and comparing it with similar attitudes toward outside groups evident in other fascist movements and regimes.

Ernst Nolte, in his monumental study *Three Faces of Fascism*, makes the most systematic attempt to reduce Hitlerian anti-Semitism to the common ideological denominator of all fascist movements: anti-Marxism. For Nolte, Nazi anti-Semitism was but the extreme form of the antibolshevism of "radical fascists":

> Hitler always succumbed to an ungovernable passion on the subject of bolshevism. He regarded it as the most radical form of Jewish genocide ever known. . . . According to Eckhart's book, Hitler had specified another bolshevism ahead of Lenin's as an origin—that of Moses![18]

Nolte's quotations give the impression that Hitler's anti-Judaism determined his antibolshevism, rather than the other way around.

A recent publication of all the early texts of Hitler, up to *Mein Kampf*, allows a better evaluation of the relative importance of anti-Judaism and anti-Marxism. References to the Jews are approximately three times more numerous than those related to bolshevism, communism, or Marxism.[19] This brings us back to the obvious difference between National Socialism and other types of fascism: in nazism, anti-Semitism occupies a central and particular place. And in fact the Jews, not the Marxists, were the target of both Hitler's first, and last, ideological statements. While the Soviet Union and the European Communist parties were temporary allies between 1939 and 1941, and the idea of a separate peace with Stalin was frequently discussed toward the end of the war, any "arrangement" with the Jews was absolutely unthinkable from Hitler's viewpoint. Finally, we have the most explicit statement, from Martin Bormann, on the relation between anti-Judaism and anti-Marxism:

> National-Socialist doctrine is entirely anti-Jewish, which means anti-Communist and anti-Christian. Everything is linked within National Socialism and everything aims at the fight against Judaism.[20]

Racial anti-Semitism—we reach now the second approach to an interpretation of Nazi anti-Semitism within the framework of fascism—existed in Germany since the end of the nineteenth century. Its transformation from the stage of hazy theory to that of systematic policy required structural conditions which, according to Hans Mommsen, for instance, are those of fascist regimes:

7

It is not enough to consider [Nazi anti-Semitism] as a more radical variety [of preexisting tendencies]. . . . One has to inquire into the structural conditions which allowed it not to remain at the level of propaganda declarations or at that of outbursts of "savage" radicalism.[21]

To explain these necessary conditions, Mommsen refers to the structure of the Nazi Party and of the Nazi system. This structure, in his opinion, is typical of fascist parties and regimes: a direct link between the various dignitaries and the supreme leader, but vaguely defined areas of authority and therefore constant rivalries and internal fights creating a process of "cumulative radicalization."[22] In that sense, the fight to control "Jewish affairs" led to a growing radicalization in this field, which would explain the "Final Solution" as an ultimate outcome of the internal dynamics of a fascist regime.[23] We will later revert to the problems posed by the "cumulative radicalization" theory. Suffice it to say here that even if we admit the existence of such a process within the Nazi regime and the explanation offered by Mommsen, we hardly notice it in the only other full-fledged fascist regime, that of Italy. As far as Italy is concerned, one could possibly speak of "cumulative radicalization" up to 1939, and of "cumulative moderation" (at least within the party) from 1939 to 1943, when Mussolini was dismissed with the help of the Fascist Grand Council (the short-lived Salo "Republic" being a direct Nazi product).

Finally, an attempt has been made to compare Nazi anti-Semitism with the racism of Italian fascists toward the Africans, the Slavs (Trieste, Fiume), and the Germans of South Tyrol, the difference in degree being explained by the war situation.[24] One may wonder why Italy at war did not attain the same results as Germany and, all in all, question the seriousness of this kind of comparison for the sake of maintaining a unified concept of fascism. In fact, as Karl Dietrich Bracher has written:

A general theory of fascism will always remain questionable when confronted with this problem [Nazi anti-Semitism and the extermination of the Jews]. . . . While [Italian] fascism centred around the quest of the strong state, *Stato Totalitario*, as the basis of a renewed *Impero Romano*, Hitler's basic notion was the primary role of the race, the racist foundation of a future empire, for which the organization of a strong state was no more than instrumental—never an end in itself.[25]

In the Marxist conception of nazism as fascism, Nazi anti-Semitism is assigned an even less coherent place than in the non-Marxist theory of fascism. First of all, it includes political propaganda camouflaged as

8

history: in a certain Soviet "historical" rendition of the last twenty years, the Nazis are found on the same side of the barricades as the Zionists, against their common victim, the Jewish masses. The aim of the Nazis does not matter; that of the Zionists is simple: to collaborate in the extermination of the majority in order to allow a small minority to reach the shores of Palestine and help in the creation of the Zionist state.[26]

On another level the Marxist view of fascism tries very systematically to insert Nazi racism and even the extermination of the Jews into the framework of an ideological orthodoxy. Within this framework the "Final Solution" cannot but be the result of the planned policy of heavy industry, thereby reaping enormous benefits (by the exploitation of a slave-labor force, constantly renewable according to needs, and by the confiscation of Jewish property, etc.). This position, often found in East German historical writing,[27] does not take into account the obvious fact that the extermination of European Jewry deprived German war industries and the German war economy in general of a considerable labor force, and in the Eastern territories in particular, of crucially important skilled manpower.[28] The "Final Solution" meant a loss for the German war economy, which was compensated only to a very small degree by the partial exploitation of Jewish slave labor and the property seized from the victims.[29]

Another Marxist approach consists of interpreting the persecution of the Jews as a method used by the Nazis, and therefore by German capital, to deflect the attention of the masses from the absence of any significant social change and from the endemic crises of the system. In this context anti-Semitism would be fulfilling the same role as external aggression, that of a necessary derivative. But here again, the thesis contradicts the most obvious facts. One knows today that the social transformation wrought by nazism was much more important than was thought immediately after the war.[30] One is also aware, as we shall later show in some detail, that the public was not particularly enthusiastic about the anti-Jewish persecutions.[31] And, as far as the ultimate stage of these policies—the extermination—is concerned, it certainly was not aimed at deflecting anybody's attention, as it was kept absolutely secret.[32]

"Totalitarianism" is the third major approach for a global interpretation of nazism. As a matter of fact, "fascism" and "totalitarianism" are not opposite concepts: Italian fascism proclaimed itself "totalitarian" from the very outset. However, the contemporary analysis of nazism tends to consider these concepts as representing opposite outlooks. In essence, fascism implies the centrality of ideology (anti-Marxism and

9

antiliberalism), and totalitarianism the centrality of the instruments of control and domination, as such. Thus, contrary ideological systems could appear more similar than opposed (Stalinist Russia and Nazi Germany).[33]

At first glance, totalitarianism seems to offer a better global explanation of Nazi policies toward the Jews than does fascism, for instance, but the difficulties soon become apparent in this case too. The interpretation within the framework of totalitarianism can use two main themes. According to the first theme, it is not a fundamental ideological motivation, but rather the will for total domination over individuals and groups that drives the totalitarian system to oppress its victims and to choose them accordingly. When control requires it, the destruction of this or that group is decided upon indifferently. The enemy to be annihilated becomes a functional element within the system of total domination—in order to terrorize a whole population or to galvanize its energy, any one group, then another, may be chosen in a more or less arbitrary way.[34]

The bureaucratic machinery is the most efficient instrument of totalitarian power and terror; bureaucracy with its banal servants whose only ambition is to fulfill their task as efficiently as possible; bureaucracy which, once set in motion, can lead from the most elementary identification measures to total extermination.[35] The most diverse studies confirm the crucial role of German bureaucracy in the persecution and destruction of the Jews, e.g., Raul Hilberg's classic work, Hannah Arendt's essay on Adolf Eichmann, H. G. Adler's study of the deportation of the Jews of Germany, Christopher Browning's research on the role of the German Foreign Office in the destruction process, or Joseph Walk's compendium of the laws and decrees dealing with or relating to the Jews during the Nazi regime.[36]

But the "totalitarian" interpretation of the anti-Jewish policies of the Nazis also faces major difficulties, the main ones being the centrality of anti-Jewish ideology for the leaders of the party, and the nonfunctionality of the enemy within the Nazi system.

There is no need to state once again how deep-seated Hitler's anti-Semitic passion was and what an essential role his anti-Jewishness played within his entire ideological system.[37] The same could be said of Goebbels and Himmler,[38] as well as of an important part of the Nazi elite. "In the theory and the method of mass extermination," writes Karl Dietrich Bracher, himself a proponent of the "totalitarian" interpretation of nazism, "the racist ideology of National Socialism had become an aim in

10

itself."[39] If that is so, then the interpretation of the Nazi persecution of Jews within the framework of totalitarianism confronts a major difficulty. The classical theory of totalitarianism, as presented by Hannah Arendt in the early 1950s, postulates a growing ideological emptiness as one penetrates into the center of the system—the totalitarian leader supposedly does not believe in his ideology; ideology is merely used to control and mobilize the masses or, at best, the outer periphery of the totalitarian party.[40] The Nazi system does not correspond to this model as far as the role of anti-Semitic ideology was concerned. Moreover, if anti-Semitic ideology was of central importance to Hitler and part of the leadership of the party, then the explanation of the persecution and extermination of the Jews must be sought outside the constitutive elements of the totalitarian system: *the totalitarian framework is the means of destruction, not its basic explanation*.

Moreover, the centrality and autonomy of the anti-Jewish ideology in nazism resulted in a situation where the "enemy" was not a functional concept[41] and could not be replaced, at will, by another target. The Jewish enemy was the prime unchangeable target, exterminated in utter secrecy, a sacred aim and not an instrument for the achievement of some other end.

Considering these various approaches, it seems that no global interpretation of nazism can integrate Nazi anti-Semitism and Nazi policies toward the Jews without encountering major problems. *In fact, Nazi anti-Semitism and Nazi policies toward the Jews place a question mark on the validity of the main global interpretations of Nazism*.

Nazi Policies: The Contending Approaches

Most historians do not work at the level of global interpretations but at that of the concrete interpretation of facts within their immediate context, of decisions in relation to one another, of a policy in terms of its internal coherence. Since the end of the 1960s, the historiography of National Socialism at this level, in the Federal Republic in particular but in other Western countries too, has tended to adopt two opposite positions: "intentionalism" and "functionalism."[42]

For the intentionalists there is a direct relationship between ideology, planning, and policy decisions in the Third Reich. As for the absolute centrality of the supreme leader, Adolf Hitler, it is obvious to such a degree that Klaus Hildebrand claims: "One should not talk about National Socialism but about Hitlerism."[43] The functionalist position, on the other hand, implies that there is no necessary relationship between the ideological basis and the political initiatives of the Nazis. It holds that decisions are functionally linked to each other and to a given state of the political context, that through the constant interaction of various semiautonomous agencies the role of the supreme decision-maker may sometimes be quite limited, and that his decisions often take on the aspect of planned policy only from the vantage of hindsight.[44] We have the image of a system in which every crucial decision depends on the will of Adolf Hitler on the one hand, and that of a more or less anarchic polycracy on the other hand.

The opposition between these two theses appears with particular clarity in terms of their interpretations of Nazi policies toward the Jews. For the intentionalists there is, first of all, continuity between the ideology of the 1920s and the final extermination. This linear approach is strongly underlined in Ernst Nolte's *Three Faces of Fascism*, where the author shows that in Hitler's system the Jews, the carriers of bolshevism and, more generally, of all the antinatural forces, had to be annihilated in order to save humanity.[45] Their extermination is the obvious corollary of ideology in Eberhard Jäckel's study of Hitler's *Weltanschauung*:

> Whether it is possible or not to establish a link between the use of gas during the First World War and the gas chambers of World War II, there is no doubt that Hitler's anti-Semitism, as presented in *Mein Kampf*, was marked by war. It was born from the war, it needed war-like methods and had to be realized in wartime; it was therefore logical that this anti-Semitism would find, during the next war, which anyhow was foreseen from the very beginning, its bloody climax.[46]

Sometimes the thesis of a direct link between the initial ideology and ultimate policies finds an even more extreme expression. In Gerald Fleming's recent book, *Hitler and the Final Solution*, the declarations attributed to the young Hitler by his friend, August Kubiczek, are directly related to his annihilation orders during World War II. Fleming states:

> There is a direct way leading from the remark made by Adolf Hitler, the student at the Realschule in Linz, to the friend of his youth, August Kubiczek, "this doesn't belong to Linz," as both were walking in the Bethlehemstrasse by the small synagogue, to the Führer's declaration on October 21, 1941, ". . . if we exterminate this pest, we shall accomplish something for humanity, the meaning of which cannot even be

12

grasped by our men out there. . . ." A direct way lead[s] from Hitler's anti-Semitism in its Linz formulation of the years 1904–1907 to the first mass executions of German Jews in Fort IX in Kovno on the 25th and 29th of November, as well as on the 30th of November, 1941, at 8:15 in the morning, in the forest of Rumbuli near Riga. . . .[47]

Few historians, even among the staunchest intentionalists, would accept such an extreme linear thesis. But even if the intermediary stages between Hitler's early anti-Semitism and his final policies toward the Jews were numerous and complex, Fleming's position is helpful on one essential point. It reminds us of the implacable aspect of Hitler's anti-Semitism, of its deep and early roots, as well as of its obsessional character. Any attempt to deny that it was an essential factor in the later extermination policies calls for at least as much explanation as the view considering it as a major impetus.

To prove their point, the intentionalists can cite the distinct and rapid succession of stages in Nazi anti-Jewish policies (as well as in other fields, foreign policy being perhaps the most telling example):

The National-Socialist program called for the disenfranchisement of all Jews; anti-Semitic activities were part of its early history. Once in power, the Nazis began the systematic organization of the persecution of Jews. No tactical considerations were allowed to interfere substantially with instituting the boycott of Jews, expelling them from public life, making them subject to special laws, and finally annihilating them.[48]

In addition to discerning a continuity between Hitler's ideology and his policies and pointing to a rapid succession of stages, the intentionalists sometimes assume technical planning. The "euthanasia" program at the beginning of the war, for example, could represent a technical preparation for the "Final Solution." In any event, killing by gas on a small scale certainly led to the idea of using it for mass extermination: "The method that was later used for the mass extermination of Jews by gas was then tried from the very beginning of 1940, during the extermination of people interned in psychiatric institutions, within the framework of the *Aktion* called 'T4.'"[49]

The major issue which separates the two approaches is that of the actual order to implement the extermination. For those historians who believe there was planning and premeditation, Hitler must have given an order to exterminate the Jews of Europe, one way or another, sometime in the spring or early summer of 1941. For the functionalists, such an

13

order may have been given much later on in the course of events, but in all probability was never issued at all.

For a presentation of the intentionalist position relating to Hitler's order, let us consider the following statement of Helmut Krausnick:

> What is certain is that the nearer Hitler's plan to overthrow Russia as the last possible enemy on the continent of Europe approached maturity, the more he became obsessed with the idea—with which he had been toying as a "final solution" for a long time—of wiping out the Jews in the territories under his control. It cannot have been later than March 1941, when he openly declared his intention of having the political commissars of the Red Army shot, that he issued his secret decree—which never appeared in writing though it was mentioned verbally on several occasions—that the Jews should be eliminated. . . .[50]

The possibility that such an order was issued in the spring of 1941 is made even more plausible by a series of additional concurring indications. At the same time, the Einsatzgruppen (special SS task forces) were instructed to exterminate the Jews in occupied Soviet territory, and a "certain final solution of the Jewish problem" was mentioned in a Reich Main Security Office circular forbidding further Jewish emigration from Belgium and France.[51] Alternatively, the order could have been given in the early summer of 1941, shortly after the German attack on Russia, when Göring instructed Heydrich to prepare the "total solution of the Jewish problem in all the territories under German control."[52]

No historian today believes that such an order was issued in writing. In its oral form it could have been either a clear instruction passed on to Göring or Himmler, or, more probably, a broad hint understood by everybody. In any event, the intentionalist historians believe that a signal must have come from Hitler to set the "Final Solution" in motion.

For the functionalists, most of the basic tenets of the intentionalist position are improbable. Let us recall, first of all, the common denominator of all functionalist interpretations: the Nazi system was to a great extent chaotic, and major decisions were often the result of the most diverse pressures, without any imperative central planning, forecasting, or clear orders given from the top indicating the aim and means of execution of a given policy.

Within the functionalist mode of interpretation, the existence of a strong anti-Semitic ideology is not denied, but its link to policies is considered to be indirect at most. For Martin Broszat, for instance, Nazi anti-Semitism had essentially a general mobilizing aim—it was a "fighting symbol," not a direct source of action. It did lead to the "Final Solution," in a way by chance, because slogans so often repeated ultimately had to be carried out:

> The stereotypical negative aims were from the beginning the only concrete element around which the Nazi "extremism of the middle" could unite itself, that which allowed it to keep the illusion of a community of action. . . .[53] The selection of negative ideological aims during the power seizure and during the later development of the Third Reich . . . meant simultaneously an increasing radicalization, a growing perfection and institutionalization of inhumanity and persecution. . . . But, this process of discrimination could not go on indefinitely. In consequence, the "movement" had ultimately to end in the "final solution." . . . The phraseology had ultimately to take itself on its word and what had objectively been only an ideological instrument for the mobilization of fighting readiness, what had had a sense only in terms of belief in the future, had to be literally realized. . . . The secret extermination of the Jews, with which anti-Semitism as a propaganda instrument was also logically brought to an end, concretized the insane confusion between a fighting symbol and a final aim. . . .[54]

If in Broszat's view ideology leads indirectly to the "Final Solution" through confusing a mobilizing symbol with a concrete aim, for Hans Mommsen the lack of relation between ideology and policies is even greater:

> In present-day research the conception is still held that from the beginning Hitler gave a concrete sense to the extermination of the Jews and set it as an ultimate aim. The carefully collected utterances of the future dictator on this issue certainly do not confirm this in any necessary way. . . .[55]

According to Mommsen, Hitler's declarations are no different from those made by any radical anti-Semite since the later part of the nineteenth century, and as far as his actions during the 1920s are concerned, they rather show restraint.[56] Mommsen does not deny Hitler's hatred of the Jews, but, in his opinion, this hatred was not necessarily the origin of the various measures taken. In fact, he states, "whenever he [Hitler] was confronted with concrete alternatives, he used to act not as an extremist, but to give preference to the less radical solution."[57] We will revert to these various points. Let us now consider some aspects of the function-

15

alist interpretation of the course of anti-Jewish policies under the Third Reich.

In the words of Karl Schleunes:

> During the early years of the Third Reich, no one in the Nazi movement, from the Führer down, had defined what the substance of a solution to the Jewish problem might be. . . . Only in the broadest sense are the anti-Semitic premises of National Socialism useful in explaining the course which a wide variety of Jewish policies eventually took.[58]

Uwe Dietrich Adam, after following in detail the anti-Jewish measures of the 1930s in which, he claims, no clear direction is to be found until 1938—when the SS took over and furthered a systematic emigration policy—reaches a first general conclusion:

> One cannot speak of a coordinated and planned policy toward the Jews . . . a global plan concerning the nature, content, and scope of the persecution of the Jews never existed; it is even highly probable that the mass extermination was not an aim that Hitler had set *a priori* and that he tried to achieve.[59]

As an example of this total lack of planning during the 1930s, Mommsen mentions the Nuremberg Laws of 1935. According to him, a foreign-policy declaration concerning the Abyssinian conflict was to be delivered by Hitler at the Party Congress which opened on September 10. This project was abandoned on September 13 at the request of Foreign Minister Konstantin von Neurath, and it was only then, two days before the closing session of the Congress, that Hitler hastily had the racial laws prepared.[60]

With regard to the crucial events of 1941, the functionalist interpretation is diametrically opposed to the one presented by the intentionalists. In Adam's view the extermination of the Jews in occupied Soviet territory was not necessarily part of a global extermination plan. It was only between September and December of that year, following the situation created by the deportations of Jews from the Reich to the ghettos of the east on the one hand, and the stalled German offensive in Russia on the other, that Hitler decided to replace the "territorial solution" of the Jewish problem with global extermination.[61]

Broszat adopts Adam's general description of the 1941 events, but he takes the argument one step further. Whereas Adam concedes that Hitler must have ordered the global extermination of European Jewry some time in the fall of 1941, Broszat believes that such an order probably

16

never existed. The "Final Solution," Broszat suggests, was the result of a series of local initiatives aimed at solving local problems (the chaotic situation in the ghettos); it only gradually developed into an overall action:

> It thus seems that the liquidation of the Jews began not solely as the result of an ostensible will for extermination but also as a "way out" of a blind alley into which the Nazis had maneuvered themselves. The practice of liquidation, once initiated and established, gained predominance and evolved in the end into a comprehensive "program."
>
> This interpretation cannot be verified with absolute certainty but in the light of circumstances, which cannot be discussed here in detail, it seems more plausible than the assumption that there was a general secret order for the extermination of the Jews in the summer of 1941.

In a footnote to the above lines, Broszat adds: "It appears to me that there was no overall order concerning the extermination of the Jews and that the program of extermination developed through individual actions and then gradually attained its institutional and factual character in the spring of 1942 after the construction of the extermination camps in Poland."[62]

In Broszat's presentation, Hitler's anti-Jewish ideology is not denied, but, as we have already seen, its direct relation to policies is questioned. According to Mommsen, ideology is even more independent of the dynamics of destruction, which can be explained much better in the context of the previously mentioned process of "cumulative radicalization" resulting from the constant competition between various Nazi agencies, and representing the overall fight for positions of power within the system:

> . . . to prevent Jewish property from falling into the hands of the Gau organizations as a result of wildcat "aryanization," Göring, following the November Pogrom . . . gave orders for aryanization by the state; the departments involved hastily busied themselves with supporting legislation, even if only to retain their share of responsibility. The impossible situation created by the material and social dispossession of the Jews caused individual Gauleiters to resort to deportations, regardless of consequences, a move bitterly resisted by the departments concerned. However, the result was not the replacement of deportation by a politically "acceptable" solution, but, on the contrary, the systematic mass murder of the Jews, which no one had previously imagined possible—the most radical solution, and incidentally, one which coincided with Hitler's own wishes.[63]

17

In Mommsen's interpretation, Hitler's role in the implementation of anti-Jewish policies and the execution of the "Final Solution" is particularly minimized:

> Hitler hardly dealt with the concrete realization of the anti-Semitic program; his occasional interventions do not point to any practical conception and they lay in the line of more extreme reprisals. It is the propagandist aspect which remains for him, as usual, in the foreground. . . .[64]

As for the absence of planning, even the Wannsee Conference of January 1942, usually considered as having established the main operational directives for the global extermination of European Jewry, appears in Mommsen's presentation as rather hazy in this respect.[65]

Some Comments

It may be tempting to seek a synthesis between the intentionalist and functionalist positions.[66] In fact, functionalism, which stresses the dynamics of a system rather than the central role of a leader, in many ways fits better within the mainstream of modern historiography.[67] The image it offers of nazism is more "normal," easier to explain: any group can stumble haphazardly, step-by-step, into the most extreme criminal behavior. Beyond the sociological theory of polycracy and administrative chaos, functionalism confronts us, implicitly, with Hannah Arendt's thesis of the "banality of evil." Functionalists can claim, quite correctly, that their position implies a much broader spread of responsibility for the crimes committed than that recognized by the opposite position which considers Hitler as the prime mover and the only authority.[68] On the other hand, the intentionalist position implies a key element: premeditation. Planning and premeditation at the top lead, of necessity, to planning and premeditation at various levels of the hierarchy and to no less awareness of the events within the various agencies involved than is implied by the functionalist position.

At the more concrete level of historical inquiry, functionalism has undoubtedly added greatly to our understanding of the chaotic nature of the Nazi system and the complex interactions surrounding various decisions. However, as has been pointed out, while correcting past interpretations which may have been too simple, it went to the opposite extreme by trying to stress autonomous processes to such a degree that the role of

Hitler was almost eliminated.[69] Some of the functionalist arguments are bolstered by the somewhat obvious fact that even in a monolithic system decisions are constantly subjected to the pressure of the most varied internal and external factors, and that no policy can unfold without false starts, hesitations, tactical adaptations, etc. This becomes even more evident if we admit that the Nazi regime was anything but monolithic in its internal structure. Moreover, as Hans Heinrich Wilhelm has mentioned, the führer's orders were followed but not always without hesitation, the more so because Hitler himself, although set on a line of action, would still continue to muse quite openly about alternative ways of attaining his goal.[70] Thus the impression of improvisation and haphazardness—the mainstay of the functionalist approach—is created.

Nevertheless, it appears that the available evidence strengthens the traditional, intentionalist position, at least insofar as anti-Jewish policies and the "Final Solution" are concerned. In the matters which obsessed Hitler, those forming the core of his system—conquest of the *Lebensraum*, as well as the all-embracing fight against the Jews—his intervention is felt at all crucial stages, and his declared policies were ultimately carried out, notwithstanding hesitations and obstacles.

Within the limited framework of this historiographical essay, any detailed discussion of the various arguments presented by both sides is impossible. Of necessity, only a few comments will be ventured in response to some of the points presented above. I shall deal with some arguments concerning Hitler's personality and the function of his ideology; a few aspects of Nazi anti-Jewish policies during the 1930s; and, finally, with the discussion concerning the course of events in 1941 and Hitler's direct involvement in the "Final Solution."

In discussing Hitler's anti-Semitism and his role in the anti-Jewish policies of the Nazi regime, many of the historians mentioned here have tried to present an explicit or implicit psychological portrait of the dictator.[71] None of these authors deny Hitler's fanatic anti-Semitism and many stress its pathological aspect. Martin Broszat ranks among those who place the strongest emphasis on the pathological form of Hitler's hatred of the Jews and stress the fact that the more Hitler sensed that the military confrontation was lost, the more he pushed forward what had become the "real" war for him.[72] There is an obvious element of contradiction between the description of such a basic obsessive hatred on the one hand and Broszat's main thesis concerning the "genesis of the Final Solution" and the absence of an order from Hitler on the other. Why would such a pathological Jew-hater shy away from giving an order of total extermination? How could he let his subordinates be in sole charge of what was, according to Broszat himself, his main obsession?

Hans Mommsen tries to avoid this logical pitfall not by denying Hitler's fanatic anti-Semitism but by presenting a rather complex psychological picture which one could sum up more or less as follows: Firstly, and this relates to earlier texts by Mommsen, Hitler often did not impose his will, but was something of a "weak dictator."[73] In "Die Realisierung des Utopischen," this weakness appears in another form. In many fields Hitler did not avoid decisions, but on the contrary we often witness, according to Mommsen, a kind of "forward flight."[74] But this did not apply in the case of the Jewish question, on which, for some mysterious reason, Hitler constantly presented his position in chiliastic terms[75] and hesitated to confront his ideological make-believe world with political and social reality (*Hitler . . . scheute davon zuruck, die ideologische Scheinwelt, in der er lebte, mit der politischen und sozialen Realität zu konfrontieren*). This would explain his noninvolvement in the decisions concerning the extermination of the Jews:

> Confronted with the real consequences of the extermination of the Jews, Hitler did not react differently from his subordinates—he tried not to take notice of it or to repress it (*Konfrontiert mit den realen Konsequenzen der Judenvernichtung, reagierte Hitler nicht anders als seine Unterführer—er suchte diese nicht wahrzunehmen oder zu verdrängen*).[76]

The extermination process unfolded through the inner dynamics of the system, as we have already mentioned, and through Himmler's fanatic ambition to realize Hitler's apocalyptic dreams here and now.[77] In this way the fanatic dreamer remains a fanatic, but, being a dreamer, he is hardly involved in the actual decisions concerning the extermination itself. This explanation runs into difficulty because it fails to take into account known facts about Hitler's personal involvement in the "Final Solution." We shall come back to this later on. However, one may well ask why, for instance, did Hitler request to be kept informed regularly of the operations of the Einsatzgruppen on Soviet territory[78] and why, on December 21, 1942, was Report No. 51 sent to him by Himmler? It deals with the Einsatzgruppen operations on Soviet territory over the period August through November 1942, and it mentions the execution of 363,211 Jews (according to a note by Hitler's adjutant, Pfeiffer, the report was submitted to Hitler on December 31, 1942).[79] One also wonders why we have direct orders from Hitler to execute the Jews remaining in

20

the Rovno district in the Ukraine in 1942.[80] And, finally, if Hitler shied away from confronting his ideological dreamworld with reality, if he repressed the knowledge of the extermination of the Jews or avoided it for any number of psychological reasons, then one wonders why in his ultimate political declaration, the testament written on April 29, 1945, on the eve of his death, he boasted of this very extermination as the greatest service rendered by National Socialism to humanity.[81] In more general terms the discrepancy between Hitler's absolute ruthlessness concerning the unleashing of the war, the killing of the mentally ill, the orders given about the type of annihilation war to be fought in Russia, and so forth, and his presumed fear of facing reality as far as the extermination of the Jews was concerned, does not carry conviction.

If we move from Hitler's personality to the function of his anti-Semitic ideology as described by Broszat, that is, as an essentially instrumental, mobilizing ideology,[82] we encounter the same kind of difficulty as previously mentioned. Why would such an obsessive Jew-hater not wish, first and foremost, to implement his anti-Jewish ideology? Why wouldn't that ideology lead to a concrete aim, to a concrete policy? But beyond this logical point, the question arises: whom should this mobilizing ideology have mobilized? The general population? The party members?

As far as the general population is concerned, we know today that although anti-Jewish prejudices were widespread and although the anti-Jewish policies of the regime did not significantly affect attitudes even within German opposition circles,[83] these measures did not evoke general enthusiasm. From the Nazi viewpoint the reaction patterns to their anti-Semitism must have been considered mixed at best. Otto Dov Kulka's studies of this issue reveal important regional variations, but some predominant aspects nevertheless emerge: a dislike of disorderly anti-Jewish measures and, therefore, a preference for an orderly, "legal" solution (the Nuremberg Laws), but mostly growing depersonalization, passivity, and inertia.[84] Ian Kershaw's study, more specifically centered on Bavaria, shows a greater reticence on the part of the population:

> The permanent radicalization of the anti-Jewish policies of the regime can hardly be said, on the evidence we have considered, to have been the product of, or to have corresponded to, the strong demands of popular opinion. It led in 1935 and 1938 to a drop in prestige for the Party, which might even have had repercussions for Hitler's own nimbus had he been seen to have supported and sided with the radicals. The radicalization of the negative dynamism, which formed the driving-force

21

of the Nazi Party, found remarkably little echo in the mass of the population. Popular opinion, largely indifferent and infused with a latent anti-Jewish feeling further bolstered by propaganda, provided the climate within which spiraling Nazi aggression towards Jews could take place unchallenged. But it did not provoke the radicalization in the first place.[85]

Whatever the nuances of public-opinion reactions may have been, it soon must have become clear to the Nazi Party, well informed by the police and the SD (SS Security Service) about the state of mind of the population, that anti-Semitism had no major mobilizing effect and could even have its drawbacks. There remains, therefore, the question of the mobilization of the party itself.

That anti-Jewish actions were an outlet for party radicals, in the spring of 1933, the spring and summer of 1935, and in November 1938, is well documented today.[86] But was this outlet fostered by the leadership? Were those outbursts encouraged by Hitler? The documentation seems to prove the contrary: in 1933, in connection with the expulsion of the Jews from the civil service, and mostly in connection with their expulsion from the legal profession, Hitler opposed the demands of the radicals, siding with the more restrained proposal of the Ministry of Justice.[87] In 1935 the Nuremberg Laws were proclaimed, *inter alia* to put an end to the agitation of the radicals.[88] In his speech to party district chiefs at Ordensburg-Vogelsang, on April 29, 1937, Hitler warned the radicals not to demand of him steps in Jewish matters which he had not carefully planned beforehand.[89]

In November 1938, after the disastrous consequences of the *Kristallnacht* became obvious, Hitler definitively took Jewish matters out of the hands of the party radicals and transferred them to the Göring-Himmler-Heydrich triumvirate,[90] true radicals indeed, but who did not need anti-Semitism as an outlet, or anti-Jewish initiatives in order to be "mobilized."[91]

▬

Nazi anti-Jewish policies of the 1930s do indeed indicate the absence of any precise preestablished plan at the outset and the necessity to act according to a somewhat loose strategy, owing to internal and external difficulties. However, a general aim is quite evident: the segregation of Jews from German society and their expulsion (by voluntary or forced emigration) from German territory. The points of the party program of February 1920 which deal with the Jewish question were, in fact, being

22

implemented. Ideology expresses itself in concrete measures; there was no backtracking whatsoever. Since we are speaking of an aim and a policy, the problem of Hitler's direct involvement is of importance.[92] To reach a firmer conclusion concerning this involvement, we would need a study of the 1930s similar to that carried out by Gerald L. Fleming on the period of the war and the "Final Solution." As such a study does not exist (the importance of the general works on Nazi anti-Jewish policies during that period notwithstanding), let us limit ourselves here to a few remarks.

On March 26, 1933, Hitler summoned Goebbels to Berchtesgaden to discuss preparations for the anti-Jewish boycott of April 1. Two days later he again spoke of the forthcoming event with his propaganda minister, indicating what themes should be used in the first substantial anti-Jewish initiative of the new regime.[93] With regard to the discussion on the civil-service law and the legal-profession law, we have already noted what Hitler's general stand was; according to Uwe Adam, Hitler probably participated in this discussion, which took place on March 31 or April 1, 1933.[94] As for the exclusion of the Jews from the legal profession, his rejection of the demands of the radicals is on record.[95] In fact, we see that throughout 1933 Hitler kept control of the rhythm of the anti-Jewish measures taken, accepting the initiative of a boycott as desired by the radicals, but opposing the extreme measures they urged later, in view of the global political situation.

The Nuremberg Laws are at the heart of the argument over Hitler's interventions during the 1930s. We have seen Mommsen's account, the gist of which was presented already in Bernhard Lösener's report: *the laws were prepared at the very last moment*, because the issues which were supposed to be dealt with by Hitler at the closing session of the Party Congress were abandoned two days before the final meeting.[96] In fact, reexamination of the sources shows that the racial laws had been in preparation for several months, and that they were discussed at the ministerial level and with Hitler himself. On August 30, 1935, their forthcoming promulgation at the September Party Congress was even reported in the foreign press.[97]

As to Hitler's attentiveness to even the smallest details relating to anti-Jewish policies, one could mention his last-minute deletion of the crucial words "this law applies to full Jews only," when announcing the Law for the Protection of German Blood and Honor before the Reichstag on September 15, 1935.[98] One could also point out that during the *Anschluss*, it was Hitler himself who conceived of forbidding Austrian

Jewish civil servants from taking the new loyalty oaths made to him personally.[99] Finally, one could indicate that on November 9, 1938, when Ernst vom Rath's death was announced, a Hitler-Goebbels meeting probably took place prior to the unleashing of the anti-Jewish pogrom. But as far as the main arguments dealing with the evolution of the anti-Jewish policies are concerned, the decisive period is obviously that of the war.

As we have indicated, the general aim during the years 1933–39 seems to have been segregation and expulsion. The outbreak of the war was followed by a necessary interval of groping for a new solution in view of the entirely new circumstances.[100] Finally, in the year 1941, when the hesitations seem to come to an end, is that which confronts the historian with the most crucial questions.

Martin Broszat stresses that none of Hitler's principal aides, when interrogated after the war, had any recollection of a verbal order for the overall extermination of the Jews. Moreover, entries in Goebbels's unpublished diaries, when referring to the Jewish problem during the summer and fall of 1941, often allude to an evacuation to camps in Russian territory, but do not mention any extermination order. Finally, still in terms of documentary evidence, Broszat cites, *inter alia*, the controversy between Himmler and SS Brigadier General Übelhör, in charge of the Łódź ghetto. At the beginning of October 1941, Übelhör strongly objected to deportations from the Reich to Łódź, because of the overstrained capacity of the ghetto. This controversy would be meaningless if extermination had already been decided upon.[101]

These arguments have been answered by Christopher Browning. He points out that after the war, Himmler and Heydrich, the main architects of the "Final Solution," were not available for interrogation, and Göring, fighting for his life, would certainly not have admitted that he furthered a global extermination order. The Goebbels diaries were a poor source at best, as Goebbels was known to have been deliberately excluded from Jewish affairs after November 1938 by Göring, Himmler, and Heydrich. On the other hand, a series of references to the preparation, during the summer and fall of 1941, of the "Final Solution" was omitted by Broszat—for instance, after the war both Rudolf Höss, former commander of Auschwitz, and Adolf Eichmann referred to overall extermination plans being worked out during that period. As for the treatment which, according to Broszat, was envisaged for the Jews transferred to the east (death by hunger, overwork, exposure to cold, etc.), it was not very different from an extermination plan. Finally, Göring's order to

Heydrich of July 31, 1941, signifies a global preparation which necessarily entailed exploring various possible methods, hesitations and sudden initiatives, which together may, for a few months, have given the impression of chaos that Broszat takes as a sign of the total lack of planning.[102] But let us turn to the sequence of events as such.

Until the fall of 1941 only the Soviet Jews were systematically exterminated. Adam and Broszat do not regard these exterminations as being necessarily linked to the "Final Solution," although, as Browning points out, the exterminations on Soviet territory represent a manifest "qualitative" change in Nazi policies toward the Jews. Moreover, in the fall of 1941 deportations from the Reich began, mostly to Łódź, Kovno, Minsk, and Riga. Some of the deportees sent to Riga and Łódź were murdered on the spot, near Riga and in the Chełmno (Kulmhof) extermination camp near Łódź (local Jews were included in these killings). It would seem that we are now confronted with the stages of an overall plan, as the extermination process includes Jews transported from Germany to the killing sites. However, as mentioned before, Broszat interprets these killings as having been necessitated by local considerations (the deportations from the Reich increased the overcrowding in the ghettos and the Jews could not be sent further east, because the Wehrmacht's advance in Russia was slowing down). He adds that the very chaotic aspect of the deportations, due to Hitler's sudden desire to see the Reich cleared of Jews as soon as possible, seems to preclude any systematic planning of an extermination process.

In fact, however, the Riga exterminations were not a local improvisation. On November 10, 1941, Heinrich Lohse, the *Reichskommissar* for the Baltic countries, was advised by Himmler, through SS General Friedrich Jeckeln, that these exterminations were to be carried out on his (Himmler's) orders, in accordance with the führer's wishes ("Tell Lohse that it is my order, which is also the Führer's wish"—"*Sagen Sie dem Lohse es ist mein Befehl, was auch Führers Wunsch ist*"[103]). Clearly, then, this is no local initiative, but to all purposes, an initiative from Hitler.

The evidence relating to the onset of the Chełmno exterminations is more complex. Broszat reminds us that the idea of exterminating some of the Łódź ghetto Jews in an attempt to solve the problem of overcrowding was already discussed among local SS officers and with the Reich Main Security Office as early as July 1941, when no general plan for the "Final Solution" could yet have existed.[104] Isn't it possible that the exterminations of the fall resulted from the same kind of consideration, developed at a rather low echelon?

25

In March 1944, according to Gerald Fleming, Wartheland Gauleiter Arthur Greiser (whose domain included Łódź and Chełmno) proudly reported to his führer that practically all the Wartheland Jews had been exterminated (mostly in Chełmno). On November 21, 1942, Greiser informed Himmler that when he had met Hitler he was instructed to "act according to his own judgment" as far as the Jews were concerned. Greiser had had two meetings with Hitler, the first on October 1, 1942, and the second on November 8 of the same year.[105]

Greisler's report to Hitler in 1944 clearly indicates that Hitler's statements of October or November 1942 were well understood. On the other hand, as we know, Greiser had initiated the exterminations in Chełmno a year before those meetings. If he had received the same kind of order as Lohse did in the fall of 1941, Hitler's words, a year later, would not make sense. Two possible explanations, of wider significance, come to mind. Either Greiser, or for that matter, Übelhör in Łódź, was not informed of the general plan at that early stage, or—and this could explain Heydrich's own hesitations about the fate of Spanish Jews in France in October of the same year (a case used by Mommsen to challenge the hypothesis of an existing order for general extermination[106])—*the manifold concrete situations, as would be the case throughout the following years, led to limited contradictory decisions, notwithstanding the general plan of extermination.*

If one moves from individual cases to the general context, the whole picture becomes much more obvious. During the second half of 1941, the Einsatzgruppen exterminated nearly one million Jews in the Soviet Union; 11,000 stateless Jews expelled from Hungary were exterminated at Kamenets-Podolsk during the last days of August 1941; in November, mass killing of Jews deported from the Reich started in Riga and in December the first extermination center, that of Chełmno near Łódź, was set in action. All emigration of Jews from occupied Europe was forbidden (order of October 23, 1941), and construction work on the Bełżec extermination camp in the General Government had commenced. It is also commonly mentioned that in the early fall of the same year the first experiments in killing with Zyklon B gas took place at Auschwitz, this method of liquidation being used mainly on Soviet officers. In view of these converging elements the existence of an overall plan for the extermination of the Jews of Europe, by the fall of 1941, can hardly be questioned any longer: the groping phase had come to an end and the general framework of the "Final Solution" was becoming apparent.

It is within the same context, as much as by itself, that the intent of

26

the Wannsee Conference—where on January 20, 1942, Heydrich presented to the assembled representatives of various ministries and SS agencies the outline of the "Final Solution"—seems to be unmistakable. The establishment of extermination camps in the General Government in the following months eliminates any possible remaining doubt or vagueness about what was meant at Wannsee.[107]

Moreover, what logic dictates, direct evidence confirms. At his trial in Jerusalem, Adolf Eichmann—who was technical organizer of the conference and attended its meetings—was asked by the president of the tribunal what the general sense of the discussion was. He answered: "One spoke of killing, of elimination, of annihilation" (*Es wurde von Töten und Eliminieren und Vernichten gesprochen*).[108]

If we admit that the intent of the Wannsee Conference is unmistakable, if we recall that in his opening remarks Heydrich referred not only to the order given him by Göring, but also to Hitler's agreement to start evacuating the Jews to the east, this can only mean one thing: Hitler agreed to the extermination plan. One can hardly believe that Heydrich would present an extermination plan to a whole array of high-ranking civil servants if Hitler had intended a *bona fide* evacuation plan.

The conference was first set for December 9, 1941 (later postponed to January 20, 1942). One has to assume, therefore, that the preparation of the scheme presented by Heydrich must have taken several months, and it seems likely that Hitler's "agreement" was expressed some time in the summer of 1941, at the latest. And Hitler's "agreement," like Hitler's "wish," actually means Hitler's "order," with no necessity for a formal decree. Finally, from an early interrogation of Rudolf Höss undertaken by the British authorities at the time of his arrest, it now appears that when he wrote in his prison memoirs about having heard of an order for the global extermination of the Jews in the summer of 1941, he was not mistaken about the date, as was often thought. It seems that Höss met Himmler in June 1941 and heard from him about a Hitler order to prepare for a general extermination of the Jews.[109]

Höss's testimony fits in with the material collected by Gerald Fleming and with the various references to an order from Hitler, coming from the most diverse sources. When in August 1941 Otto Bradfisch, head of Einsatzkommando 8 operating in the Minsk region, asked Himmler who bore responsibility for the executions, Himmler answered, "The orders come from Hitler and, as such, have force of law."[110] A year later, when SS General Gottlob Berger, speaking on behalf of the Ministry for the East, suggested that a more exact definition of the term "Jew" should be provided, Himmler rejected the very idea of further definition, which would only impose limitations, and added:

> The occupied eastern territories will be freed of Jews (*judenfrei*). The Führer has laid on my shoulders the execution of this very difficult order. Nobody can take the responsibility away from me anyway, and I therefore forbid any interference.[111]

During the first half of 1944, Himmler made reference to the very difficult führer order concerning the "Final Solution" in no less than four different speeches (January 26, May 5, May 24, and June 21), three of which were delivered before large audiences of senior Wehrmacht officers.[112] According to the testimony of SS Judge Konrad Morgen, when Christian Wirth's special sections were dispatched to the General Government to help Odilo Globocnik in the extermination process, "Himmler is supposed to have of asked each of them to swear an oath of silence and to have told them: 'I have to expect of you superhuman acts of inhumanity. But it is the Führer's will.'"[113]

At the end of December 1941, Bernhard Lösener, adviser on Jewish affairs at the Ministry of the Interior, informed Undersecretary Wilhelm Stuckart that because of the extermination of the Jews in the Riga region, news of which had reached him, he could not remain in his position. Stuckart replied: "Don't you know that these things happen according to the highest orders?"[114] In May 1942, Reinhard Heydrich, the head of the Reich Main Security Office and newly appointed protector of Bohemia and Moravia, and several Abwehr officers met in Prague. In the course of a very heated discussion on the exterminations, Heydrich stated that the Reich Main Security Office was not responsible for the killings; they were being executed on the personal orders of the führer.[115]

As mentioned before, on August 1, 1941, Gestapo Chief Heinrich Müller sent the following order to the heads of the four Einsatzgruppen: "Regular reports have to be submitted to the Führer concerning the work of the Einsatzgruppen in the East" (*Dem Führer sollen von hier aus lfd. Berichte über die Arbeit der Einsatzgruppen im Osten vorgelegt werden*).[116] We have noted that in December 1942 Report No. 51 was sent by Himmler to Hitler. It deals with the operations of the Einsatzgruppen in Soviet territory for the period August through November 1942, and mentions "363,211 Jews executed" (the report was submitted to Hitler on December 31, according to a note by his adjutant, Pfeiffer).[117] During the same month, Himmler noted: "Point (3) Jews . . . to be eliminated, Jews in

28

France, 600–700,000, to be eliminated" (*Juden . . . abschaffen, Juden in Frankreich, 600—700,000, abschaffen*).[118] In fact, in terms of statistics, Himmler was to be better informed at the end of December, when the SS inspector for statistics, Richard Korherr, prepared for him a complete and accurate report on the course of the "Final Solution." In April 1943 the report, updated to March 31 of that year and condensed to six and a half pages, was ready for the führer. Typed on the special "führer-type-writer" (which had extra-large letters), the report was submitted to Hitler some time before mid-April 1943.[119] According to Eichmann's testimony, when the report was returned to the Reich Main Security Office, it bore the following note: "The Führer has seen. To be destroyed. H.H.[i.e., Heinrich Himmler]."[120]

Here we must consider the strange contradictions of Nazi camouflage of the "Final Solution." Richard Korherr was asked to delete the word *Sonderbehandlung* (special treatment), which appeared in his report; Rudolf Brandt, Himmler's personal assistant, wrote to Korherr:

> He [Himmler] wishes that in no place should one speak of a "special treatment of the Jews" (*dass an keiner Stelle von "Sonderbehandlung der Juden" gesprochen wird*). On page nine, point four, the formulation should therefore be as follows: "Transportation of Jews from the Eastern Provinces to the Russian East: they passed through the camps in the General Government . . . through the camps in the Warthegau" ("*Transportierung von Juden aus den Ostprovinzen nach dem russischen Osten: Es wurden durchgeschleust durch die Lager im Generalgouvernement . . . durch die Lager im Warthegau*"). Another formulation is not allowed. I am sending you back the copy of the report already marked by the *Reichsführer SS*, with the demand that page nine be changed accordingly and the report be sent back again.[121]

One wonders about the inconsistency of the attempts at camouflage. On the one hand, even the code word *Sonderbehandlung* was eliminated from the report sent to Hitler; on the other hand, Himmler referred on several occasions to Hitler's orders when speaking about the total extermination of the Jews. Or, even more paradoxical: in a document sent to Hitler himself, no reference to the "Final Solution" is permitted; but in speeches delivered to wide audiences (not only SS officers, but also regular officers of the Wehrmacht), Himmler quite blatantly refers to Hitler's orders.

It may well be that in the case of the Korherr report the explanation is provided by an instruction issued somewhat later, on July 11, 1943, by the head of the Party Chancellery, Martin Bormann, whereby "in agreement with the Führer, the 'Final Solution' should in no way be mentioned in any document relating to the Jewish question: mention should only be made of Jews being sent to work."[122]

Nevertheless, the inconsistency remains. In 1942, in no less than four speeches (January 1, January 30, February 24, and November 8), Hitler himself hinted darkly that his prophecy about the extermination of the Jews in the event of a world war was being fulfilled.[123] In April 1943 he more or less admitted to the extermination in his talks with the Rumanian chief of state, Ion Antonescu, and the Hungarian regent, Admiral Miklós Horthy.[124] In one of his last talks, on February 13, and in the political testament he wrote on the eve of his death, he boasted about it quite emphatically.

There is, finally, indirect evidence of Hitler's attention to the extermination process. For example, Odilo Globocnik, the Higher SS and Police leader in charge of the four extermination camps established in the General Government during 1942, visited the Reich Chancellery in the autumn of that year. A note by Himmler referring to a conference with Hitler on October 7, 1942, bears the following annotation: "Situation in the General Government. Globus [Globocnik's nickname was 'Globus']."[125] The subject of the conference thus becomes evident.

On April 13, 1943, a proposal to promote Christian Wirth (Globocnik's right-hand man and a specialist in killing by gas—first the mentally ill and then the Jews) to the rank of SS Sturmbannführer (captain) was submitted to the Main Personnel Office of the SS. The file notes that since the beginning of the war Wirth has been "on a special mission by order of the Führer."[126]

That Hitler could have been unaware of the "Final Solution" up to 1943, as suggested by David Irving,[127] goes against all evidence; that he gave an oral order for the overall extermination of the Jews of Europe some time in the spring or summer of 1941 is highly probable, but cannot be proved with absolute certainty on the basis of existing documents. We have seen, however, that he was kept informed of the extermination process and made ad hoc interventions in it.

On the limited level of the analysis of Nazi policies, the resolution of the debate between various approaches appears possible. On the level of global historical interpretation, however, the real difficulties remain. The historian who is not encumbered with ideological or conceptual blinkers can readily recognize that it is Nazi anti-Semitism and the anti-

Jewish policies of the Third Reich that gave nazism an essential part of its *sui generis* character. We have noted that the explanation based on the course of German history leaves many questions unanswered, and that "fascism" and "totalitarianism" are hardly adequate categories, in view of the centrality of Hitler's anti-Semitic drive. The consideration of nazism as a "political religion" could eventually offer us a better grasp of some of the issues raised here, if inquiry in that direction is further developed.[128] In fact, the very difficulty of integrating the "Final Solution" into the framework of global interpretations of nazism has led some historians into the paradoxical position of stressing the absolute centrality of Hitler's racist ideology within the Nazi system and then continuing the interpretation of the main issues posed by nazism without taking the policies against the Jews into account. [129] All this may well lead us to the conclusion that the destruction of European Jewry poses a problem which historical analysis and understanding may not be able to overcome.

At most one can speak of the emergence, unique to date, of a messianic faith and an apocalyptic vision of history at the heart of the political, bureaucratic, and technological system of an advanced industrial society. Yet here again, the image is false—there was no mass movement with respect to the Jews, nor even a crusade of a fanatic sect. Bureaucracy occupied center stage, a bureaucracy indifferent to the destruction, but driven by its leader who, in turn, was moved by the most intense of convictions.

The historian's paralysis arises from the simultaneity and the interaction of entirely heterogeneous phenomena: messianic fanaticism and bureaucratic structures, pathological impulses and administrative decrees, archaic attitudes within an advanced industrial society.

We know the details of what occurred, we are aware of the sequence of events and their probable interaction, but the profound dynamics of the phenomenon evades us. And what likewise escapes us is the almost immediate disintegration of the political, institutional, and legal structures of Germany, as well as the surrender of the moral forces that by their very nature ought to have been important obstacles to the Nazis in Germany, in other European countries, and in the entire Western world.

2

The Written Matter
and the Spoken Word
On the Gap Between Pre-1914
and Nazi Anti-Semitism

SHULAMIT VOLKOV

I

Almost without exception, general histories of National Socialism and especially of the Nazi policies concerning the "Jewish question" begin with the story of nineteenth-century anti-Semitism. Conversely, most works on anti-Semitism in pre-Nazi Germany see in it a prelude to the Holocaust. Modern German history is then scrutinized for the manifestations of anti-Semitism, always unique in their radicalism and pregnant with destructive implications. For some, continuity is established by perceiving the history of anti-Semitism as a circular phenomenon, a series of historical repetitions, reenacting in different guises one permanent, central theme. For others, the link is made through the paradigm of a dynamic process, an acceleration inevitably culminating in catastrophe. The fanaticism and finality of the Nazi case is always acknowledged, but it is rarely studied apart from its so-called "origins."

Historians are, of course, repeatedly confronted with the issue of continuity versus change, and it would be banal to repeat the simple truth that these are always bound together. Nevertheless, the balance is perpetually a matter of controversy; and the balance normally established between continuity and change in the case before us is, I believe, inadequate. By practically obliterating the elements of novelty and overestimating the forces of continuity, we have too often obscured important issues. Both the study of the pre-Nazi tradition of German anti-Semitism and the issue of the Nazi attitudes and behavior toward the Jews have thus been forced into preconceived patterns, missing, so it appears to me, much of the essence of historical developments. It is the proper balance between continuity and change, permanence and novelty, that must be sought; and it is this balance that I would here like to try and redress—yet once again.

The stress on permanence and continuity is especially evident among Jewish historians.[1] The most extreme position was taken by Benzion Dinur, writing during the Second World War and perhaps before the magnitude of the Holocaust had been fully realized. In "Exiles and Annihilation," Dinur offered a circular view of Jewish history, in which each center of Jewish life and culture was in its turn destroyed, only to be reconstituted elsewhere—another heir to an awesome tradition, a link in a perpetual chain. Within this view the Holocaust repeated, admittedly in a modern and unusually efficient manner, the pattern of the past.[2] For Shmuel Ettinger, the explanation of the permanence of anti-Semitism lies not in the uniqueness of Jewish history, but in the existence of a Jewish stereotype as a permanent feature of Western culture. Reappearing in times of crisis, it transforms a latent hatred into the various forms of active persecution.[3] Salo Baron, to take another example, used both the permanent peculiarity of Jewish status among the nations and the others' inevitable "dislike of the unlike" in his "theory of anti-semitism."[4] In all these versions Nazi performance, despite its totality and scope, is yet another chapter in the history of anti-Jewish measures—a modern version of old pogroms, expulsions, mass executions.

Other historians prefer development, dynamism, growth, to repetition and permanence. For Yaakov Talmon, Nazi anti-Semitism was not yet another anti-Semitic episode but the culmination of a long development. He traced the links between Richard Wagner and Houston Stewart Chamberlain on the one hand, and Alfred Rosenberg or Adolf Hitler on the other, and followed the intensification of anti-Jewish sentiments and the ripening of the "exterminatory ideology." It was the development of a radical ideology which, according to him, systematized the wishes and the ideas of the anti-Semites and made them a basis for the eventual Nazi policy of annihilation. In his last book, Talmon restated in a slightly different form his diagnosis of over twenty-five years ago: anti-Semitism,

he concluded, was a "centuries-old neurosis culminating in a demonic
and murderous madness."[5]

Using a culturally more diffused view, taking into account more than
the highlights of the anti-Semitic literary ideology, George Mosse too
presented the Nazi case as the end result of a long acceleration. Anti-
Semitism, he explained, was the center of the "German Ideology," an
institutionalized part of the *völkisch* movement, and finally the basic reality of nazism. Conversely, National Socialism was a fulfillment of a
promise, the realization of a dream.[6] Yaakov Katz, in a recent book
on anti-Semitism, reached a similar conclusion, despite some reservations and an explicit admission of unease. The theories of racial anti-
Semitism, he finally agreed, "helped to consolidate ideas by making clear
thought of them, transforming them into a plan of execution, eventually
carried out by the Nazis."[7]

The sense of self-evidence, characterizing these presentations of the
link between pre-Nazi anti-Semitism and the extermination of the European Jews is also prevalent among historians outside the Zionist tradition. These, however, usually pay only lip service to the age-old tradition
of anti-Semitism in Christian Europe, and concentrate instead on the
period beginning in the 1870s.[8] Typical, and by now of textbook significance, are Paul Massing's *Rehearsal for Destruction*, and Peter Pulzer's
history of *Political Antisemitism in Germany and Austria*; but even Hannah Arendt, pointedly stressing the uniqueness of what she introduced
as "modern anti-Semitism," does not draw a clear line between it and the
Nazi phenomenon.[9] In her *Origins of Totalitarianism* she examined the
general nature of anti-Semitism in postemancipation modern Europe,
presenting it clearly as a prelude to nazism. The by now standard work
of Helmut Krausnick on the persecution of the Jews in the Third Reich
opens characteristically with a review of pre-Nazi anti-Semitism in imperial Germany.[10] Thus, while sometimes rejecting the search for roots
in the very remote past, most historians accept, almost intuitively, the
"origins thesis."

Let me begin my critique of these positions by quoting at some length
from Marc Bloch's *Métier d'historien:*

> Naturellement chère à des hommes qui font du passé leur principal
> sujet de recherche, l'explication du plus proche par le plus lointain a
> parfois dominé nos études jusqu'à l'hypnose. Sous la forme la plus car-
> actéristique, cette idole de la tribu des historiens a un nom: c'est la

35

(obsession)

hantise des origines. . . . Mais le mot est inquiétant parce qu'il est équivoque. Signifie-t-il simplement "commencements"? Il sera à peu près clair. Sous réserve, cependant, que pour la plupart des réalités historiques, al notion même de ce point initial demeure singulièrement fuyants. . . . Par origines entendra-t-on au contraire les causes? Il n'y aura alors plus d'autres difficultés que celles qui, constamment (et plus encore, sans doute, dans les sciences de l'homme) sont, par nature, inhérents aux recherches causales. Mais entre les deux sens s'établit, fréquemment, une contamination d'autant plus redoutable qu'elle n'est pas, en général, tres clairement sentie. Dans le vocabulaire courant, les origines sont un commencement qui explique. Pis encore: qui suffit à expliquer. Là est l'ambiguité, là est le danger.[11]

In the post-1945 historiography, German anti-Semitism before 1914 has become "a beginning which explains," and too often, indeed, "a beginning which is a complete explanation." It is presented as a necessary condition for the Nazi 'Final Solution,' and sometimes, though usually not explicitly, as a necessary and sufficient condition—"a complete explanation" in Marc Bloch's terminology.

Allow me to approach the problem from this perspective. In what follows I would like to argue that while on the basis of demonstrable continuity pre-Nazi antisemitism can serve as a useful *background* to the National Socialist rise to power and the Nazi Jewish policies, it should not be construed as an *explanation*, let alone a *complete explanation*, of these phenomena. The Nazi policy of extermination took shape during the years of the Second World War and never before, within the bounds of the Third German Reich and not elsewhere. If pre-Nazi German anti-Semitism actually brought it about, it must have been in itself significantly different from all previous forms of anti-Semitism, and unique for its time and its place. But what was novel in the anti-Semitism of late nineteenth- and early twentieth-century Germany, I would attempt to argue, was time specific and grew out of the particular needs and problems of that era. It had little relevance for later events, and in comparison with the contemporary French case even its characteristic features seem to lose much of their uniqueness. Pre-Nazi anti-Semitism in Germany, in all its peculiarities, was more akin to the French version of the time than to the later Nazi positions. It can, therefore, serve as a loose "beginning" for National Socialism but not as an explanation for it, as its background but not as its cause. A special "turnabout of meaning," a growth of a new language, and an all-important transition from words into action was required in moving from Marr, Stöcker, and Dühring to

36

Hitler, Goebbels, and Himmler.[12] The explanation of nazism, therefore, I believe, lies not in the analysis of its so-called origins, but in a fuller and better understanding of its total present.

II

In order to present nineteenth-century anti-Semitism in Germany as a "beginning" of Nazi anti-Semitism, the establishment of any kind of continuity is sufficient. Nazi anti-Semitism ought to be shown as touching somehow upon the last link in the chain of earlier forms of anti-Jewish manifestations, through personal contacts, organizational developments, or some apparent ideological borrowing. All these have been exposed by historians, with a fair amount of success. In the realm of ideas historians showed the affinity between Hitler's diatribes against the Jews and the pronouncements of men from Paul de Lagarde to Heinrich Class. It will probably remain unclear how much of these men's works was actually read by Hitler, though his early reliance on Theodor Fritsch is presumably certain. Operating within the postwar context, Hitler employed some new, if not original, themes, especially concerning the links between Jews and bolshevism, or Jews and the revolution in Germany. But with some shifts in emphasis, old anti-Semitic claims and prejudices were all there too. His was a mixture not unlike those dished out to the Munich crowd by other anti-Semitic orators.[13]

From a wider perspective too, a line of continuous development is not difficult to establish. The old anti-Semitic political parties were virtually extinct on the eve of the First World War. But anti-Semitism in associations and trade societies, in student organizations and in groups of organized officials, teachers, lawyers, or medical doctors, was rampant. This socially diffused form of anti-Semitism, characteristic of the prewar years, can be seen as an early stage in the preparation of popular support of, and compliance with, first the vigorous anti-Jewish tone of the early Nazi propaganda and then with later Nazi actions.[14]

But once this kind of continuity is established, the thread begins to unravel. With similar methods the line of development can easily be traced back to earlier periods and other national environments. Why not, after all, go back to the time of the Black Death or to the writings of Martin Luther? And through the mood of pietism, why not stretch the line to the many-sided manifestations of anti-Semitism in nineteenth-century German society? And what about the often latent, but occasionally erupting, anti-Semitism elsewhere in Europe? Are these not all chapters in the long story of the rise of nazism?

Historians of anti-Semitism do indeed look back to the distant past and beyond the borders of Germany.[15] If the search is for a *beginning*, there is then little justification in stopping at the establishment of the Bismarckian Reich or in remaining within its borders. If, however, *a beginning* is to be made *an explanation*, then a thousand years of such a beginning, spread across an entire continent, is particularly inappropriate for the task. If modern pre-Nazi anti-Semitism is to become the *explanation* of the unique horrors of the Holocaust, not merely its prolonged prelude, then it must be shown as a phenomenon *sui generis*. If German anti-Semitism before the First World War is to *explain* the unequaled case of Auschwitz, then it must itself be perceived as unique—both in relation to previous anti-Jewish manifestations and in comparison with contemporary anti-Semitism elsewhere. History must seek to account not just—perhaps not even primarily—for the very existence of situations or the actual occurrence of events, but for their existence or occurrence *then and there*.

Much of the historiography of nineteenth-century anti-Semitism strives, indeed, to establish the uniqueness of this so-called "modern anti-Semitism." Hannah Arendt went so far as to consider the disregard of its peculiarities a cause for the blindness of Jews and non-Jews alike in the face of the approaching Nazi danger.[16] But while for Arendt change resulted from the transformed position of emancipated Jews within the new context of the modern nation-states, most historians diagnose the new beginning in the mid-1870s, when anti-Semitism presumably began to show two new traits: it became a platform for political organization, and it was ideologically transformed by the introduction of racial theory. From Stöcker, Böckel and Ahlwardt, through Zimmermann and Förster, modern anti-Semitism was operating as a political force, used for the mobilization of the social elements responsive to its manipulation. With Gobineau, Chamberlain, and the biologists, it was finally able to dispense with its religious rationale, and pose as a modern, scientifically based theory, with legitimate constitutional, social, and political implications.

Now, without extensively going into the matter, I would like to suggest that not much can be made of the novelty of modern anti-Semitism on these two counts. A political though not a strictly party-political use of anti-Semitism was widespread before the 1870s, both in Germany and elsewhere. In an important and little-known book on 1848, Yaakov Toury has conclusively shown the force of *political* anti-Semitism during the months of this mid-century revolution.[17] Though anti-Semitism at the time was spontaneous and popular, and did not reach the organizational form of a proper political party, its political usefulness was never in doubt after the turbulent revolutionary experience.[18] Neither did political parties in their full modern sense exist under the particular constitutional arrangement of imperial Germany. None of the then existing parties, including the so-called anti-Semitic parties, was entirely devoted to the Jewish issue, and all were willing to employ the anti-Semitic idiom to attract potential voters.[19]

Furthermore, it is sobering to remember that the small anti-Semitic parties, all taken together, constituted less than 2.5 percent of the electorate in 1893, and less than 2 percent by 1907, the two peak years of their success. The parties themselves have been grossly overestimated by historians, partly due to the slanted perspective of the post-Nazi era, and partly because of the often eccentric and scandalous behavior of their leading figures.[20] Anti-Semitism in various social associations and half-political groups was far more important for the fabric of social life in imperial Germany, and of greater importance for later developments. But anti-Semitism in these forms was not essentially different from its varied manifestations throughout the century, and indeed even before. Anti-Semitism, diffused in the various social elements and expressed in their organizations, was not new in the immediate prewar years, nor was it unique to Germany.

Second, racism is often cited as a peculiar trait of German anti-Semitism beginning with the last quarter of the nineteenth century—a central heritage to be absorbed by nazism. But as in the case of the anti-Semitic political parties, this aspect too has grown out of proportion. Racism, as a biologically founded social theory, claiming the support of modern science, was indeed a novelty of these years, but its importance for the development of contemporary anti-Semitism was overestimated. A reexamination of the writings of the main ideologues of anti-Semitism—and here we are primarily dealing with matters of ideology—throws grave doubts on the significance of the purely racial element for their thought processes and the essence of their message. It is true that the vocabulary of anti-Semitism had been changing, but only rarely did this entail a corresponding change in content.[21] It was Marc Bloch, again, who commented that, to the great despair of the historian, "les hommes n'ont pas coutume, chaque fois qu'ils changent de moeurs, de changer de vocabulaire."[22] But to add further confusion, men also often preserve their customs while changing their vocabulary.

Richard Wagner is an interesting case in point. Wagner's writings are

39

diffused with nationalist-racist concepts. In an interesting interpretation of his anti-Jewish works, Yaakov Katz has recently reargued that, despite this usage, Wagner was never a true racist, though he clearly was an extreme and venomous anti-Semite. He apparently was willing to consider, albeit grudgingly, the possibility of the eventual assimilation of the Jews in their environment, thus not sharing a belief in the basic tenet of racism: the incurable, permanent, inborn inferiority of the Jew. But Wagner, like the majority of the anti-Semitic ideologues, was not a systematic thinker. He adopted the racist vocabulary when it suited his purpose, and abandoned it as he saw fit.[23] This was the way racism was used by other anti-Semites throughout the century: it was no more than a useful instrument for them, an additional weapon in their arsenal of anti-Jewish arguments—a convenient but not indispensable substitute for the outdated categories of religion.

Among the anti-Semites, Lagarde explicitly ridiculed the idea of race as "a crude form of materialism, scientifically meaningless."[24] But for the others, too, moral and cultural questions seemed always to have been more crucial than the racial-biological perspective. Even Eugen Düring, who in the title of his main anti-Semitic publication claimed to treat the Jewish question as a racial problem, used the term quite arbitrarily. *Volk, Nation,* and *Kultur* were all used by him interchangeably with *Rasse,* and his application of the term *Judenhaftigkeit* virtually emptied the racial argument of all meaning.[25] Wilhelm Marr and Otto Glagau too occasionally vented their rage against the "*verjudeten*" elements in German society, as despicable and as dangerous as the real, "racial" Jews.[26] Finally, here is a passage from the 1910 edition of Theodor Fritsch's *Antisemiten-Katechismus,* the main handbook of the presumably new type of racial anti-Semites:

> Es ist also eine oberflächliche und irreführende Auffassung, wenn die Gegnerschaft gegen das Judentum als der Ausfluss eines *blöden Glaubens- und Rassenhasses* dargestellt wird, während es sich in Wahrheit um eine selbstlose, von den höchsten Idealen getragene Abwehr gegen einen *Feind der Menschlichkeit, Gesittung und Kultur* handelt.[27]

III

The uniqueness of late nineteenth-century and early twentieth-century anti-Semitism lies neither in its forms of political organization nor in its ideological characteristics. The novel elements in the anti-Semitism of this period depended upon the particular needs and difficulties of the time. The significantly new aspects of this anti-Semitism were the roles which it had grown to fulfill within the social, political, and cultural systems of imperial Germany. Its functions developed in response to the main issues of late nineteenth-century Germany, and were time-specific—to be explained only by an analysis of the context in which they had emerged.

First, anti-Semitism played a constitutive role in the definition of the German self-image, and in rebuilding a German sense of identity after the crisis of unification. A series of basically internal wars, and a reshuffling of borders and constitutional structures created the need for a new type of integration. In the new Bismarckian Reich, anti-Semitism was a welcome weapon in welding together the geographically, historically, and socially disparate elements of the German nation. It is, therefore, hardly surprising that the most influential representative of the new anti-Semitism was Heinrich von Treitschke, the fervent nationalist and prominent spokesman of German unity under the power domination and the class rule of Prussian Junkerdom. Treitschke was above all concerned to achieve an internal cohesion in Germany, based on a common consciousness of a unique nationality and culture. He did not hesitate to use anti-Jewish sentiments for the task. Thus, he warned against the undue influence of *Judentum* on "our national life," and the approach of a "*Zeitalter deutsch-jüdischer Mischkultur.*" He called for the creation of a "*gekräftigtes Nationalgefühl,*" rejecting any form of "Doppelnationalität," particularly that of the "Jewish-cosmopolitan" type.[28]

These themes, bound up with Treitschke's contempt for parliamentarism and democratization, had a lasting effect upon a generation of students who were later to become the leadership of the nationalist-imperialist, and almost invariably anti-Semitic, movement in the early years of the twentieth century.[29] That was a time of another crisis of self-consciousness and national identity, clumsily covered up by a pompous and irresponsible *Weltpolitik.* At that time, once again, anti-Semitism proved its usefulness as a convenient tool for integration, a complementary sentiment to national pride, an effective addition to a communal sense of uniqueness and superiority.[30]

Second, anti-Semitism channeled a growing social malaise and discontent engendered by rapid industrialization and the disappointment with the liberal-capitalist economic system. This was particularly needed following the crash of 1873 and during the following period of deflation and instability up to the mid 1890s.[31] Presenting the Jew as the corrupter of capitalism, and the real destructive force behind liberalism, the new economic order could be attacked without fear of revolution and without inciting class struggle or civil strife. Otto Glagau, who coined the slogan *"Die soziale Frage ist die Judenfrage,"* was second in popularity and influence only to Treitschke. Adolf Stöcker, an eager imitator, was soon to roam the streets of Berlin with a similar message. At a time of economic insecurity and social disorientation it was such slogans that appealed to the German urban *Mittelstand*, and provided it with a proper target for venting its anxiety and rage.[32]

Third, anti-Semitism had a political role to fulfill too. Many prominent anti-Semites in Bismarckian Germany were trustworthy conservatives, though Stöcker's tactics in Berlin were always suspect in Bismarck's eyes, and even the old kaiser, whose court chaplain Stöcker was for some years, remained cautious and aloof. But the anti-Semitic movement of this early period also included a group of ex-liberals, sometimes even old radicals, with a revolutionary past. Wilhelm Marr was an old forty-eighter, but Glagau and Henrici too had had a previous liberal record. These men represented a considerable segment of German society, especially from among the *Mittelstand*, who were by this time seeking a new political allegiance. After the events of 1848 craftsmasters, shopkeepers, small officials, and perhaps also elements of rural Germany, tended to combine political liberalism with a set of clearly antiliberal economic demands. The prosperity of the third quarter of the century made this combination tenable, though it was always problematic. But with the economic reversal of the 1870s, these men increasingly distanced themselves from liberalism, usually of the left-wing version, to which they had been loyal for decades. The "social" or "reform" parties, practically all anti-Semitic splinter groups, often managed to enter into the political gap. They offered an anti-industrial and antimodern platform, without being temperamentally conservative, aristocratic, or elitist. Later in the century, when the anti-Semitic parliamentary representatives joined the conservative block in German politics, they were once more merely reflecting the shift in the electorate. By the late nineteenth century, the established conservative party was striving to appear as a popular movement, belatedly responding to the needs of a new political age. Where the Conservatives could only do a half-job, the Bund der Landwirte, using different tactics and aggressively flaunting its anti-Semitism, proved fully successful. Adopting nationalism, with its anti-Semitic overtones, the conservative forces in Germany managed to attract much of the previously liberal, even left-wing, *Mittelstand* electorate. Anti-Semitism played a major role in this restructuring of German politics, helping to introduce new social and ideological elements into the traditional German right.[33]

Fourth, and finally, anti-Semitism had a unique cultural position in Wilhelmine Germany. It had gradually become *a code* for the overall *Weltanschauung* and style of the right. In a situation of cultural polarization developing in Germany in the late nineteenth and the early twentieth century, anti-Semitism became a sign of belonging. The expression of anti-Jewish sentiment, even occasionally by Jews, indicated the adherence to "Germanic culture" and a rejection of everything that stood opposed to it at the other end of the evolving cultural spectrum. Even more: opposition to anti-Semitism clearly identified individuals and groups in the camp of democratization, parliamentarianism, and often also with cultural and economic modernism.[34] Indeed, socialists, who were not previously slow in attacking Jews, became increasingly careful with the application of these tactics. Social Democracy may not have been successful in weeding out anti-Semitism from among its membership, but its public stand on the matter, from the early 1890s onward, was quite unequivocal.[35] Anti-Semitism was not merely an element in the overall political worldview of the right in Germany, but became a communication signal within the overall political culture of the Reich. It served a unique function in defining the borderline between the two opposing camps which dominated its public life.

These four specific functions of anti-Semitism in the Second Reich gave it its peculiar modern character. Their time-specific nature, however, restrict their significance to the period under consideration. They can be used for understanding the surge of anti-Semitism in the postwar years only by adjusting them, often quite radically, to the entirely different circumstances in Weimar Germany. Perhaps more problematic still is the rarely admitted, but easily apparent, similarity between the functions of anti-Semitism in Wilhemine Germany and in France of the Third Republic. The explanatory power of the foregoing functional analysis for later events is further reduced by the comparison—this time not along a time axis but across the geographical border between Germany and France.

IV

French anti-Semitism has received far less attention from historians than its German counterpart. We still have no complementary volume to Robert Byrnes's *Antisemitism in Modern France*, which covers the years up to the Dreyfus Affair; and only a few monographs treat this subject in depth.[36] The spread of anti-Semitism outside the immediate political sphere and the realm of journalism, in social organizations and trade societies, at the local level and the margins of society, all that is only marginally discussed by French historians.[37] General books mention, of course, Édouard Drumont and his astounding public success and tell the story of the Dreyfus case. But one cannot help wondering how slanted the picture of the past has become through the perspective of later events.

It is beyond my competence and not entirely necessary for my purpose to go into the specific details of the French history of anti-Semitism. It is sufficient to mention here that since the early part of the nineteenth century anti-Semitism in France had developed on both the left and the right, and that on both extremes of the political spectrum it was, in a way, always grafted upon the widespread anti-Jewish, Catholic sentiment. French anti-Semitism of the latter part of the century, however, in its form and content alike, can easily be defined in terms reminiscent of the German case: it is characterized by an introduction of new ideological elements, by new organizational experiments, and above all by its particular functions in the public life of the French Republic before the onset of the First World War.

The ideological novelty, on a European scale, indeed, came from the pen of Édouard Drumont. *La France Juive* (1886) won more popularity, and gained more serious treatment in well-placed circles than anything produced by the German anti-Semites at the time.[38] In its cultural prestige it could only be compared with Houston S. Chamberlain's *Grundlagen des neunzehnten Jahrhunderts* (Foundations of the Nineteenth Century) (1899), and perhaps with Langbehn's *Rembrandt als Erzieher* (Rembrandt as Educator) (1890). None of these, however, enjoyed the popularity of Drumont's treatise, none such a good press, and none so lenient a historiography. While most of the anti-Semitic literature was spurned by the German educated elite, Drumont was discussed in the best Parisian papers, and read, even studied, by some of the outstanding French intellectuals.[39] Nevertheless, Drumont's book suffers from all the shortcomings typical of the works of his German contemporaries. *La France Juive* is a confused, eclectic, and boring book. Its popularity was clearly due to the response it had managed to draw from various social elements in France. It had appealed to them all, expressing the whole range of their fears and anxieties, reflecting the general malaise prevalent in these transitional years of the Third Republic.

44

With the success of Drumont's book there was also a reprinting of some of the French and German anti-Semitic "classics," such as Alphonse Toussenel's *Juifs, rois de l'époque* (1845), and Augustus Rohling's *Der Talmudjude* (1873). New anti-Semitic writers appeared on the scene, eager to make their fortunes, and pleased to exploit the obviously sympathetic reading public.[40] But the French anti-Semitic literature of these years somehow managed to preserve a reputation for remaining essentially nonracist. The racist elements in the works of Drumont, Maurice Barrès, and Charles Maurras have all been naturally observed, but for all three, it was repeatedly indicated, the moral, the social, and the cultural aspects of anti-Semitism were always of greater importance than the radical-biological perspective. This, however, as I have attempted to indicate, was also the position of the leading German anti-Semites. Count Gobineau, it has been recently reasserted, was far better known in France than had been previously assumed; Hippolyte Taine supplied an original French version for social racism; and racial anthropology had some of its main protagonists in France.[41]

Anti-Semitic political parties, of the kind known from the German experience, did not exist in the Third Republic, but here too the comparison with Germany is illuminating. The Ligue Antisémitique Française, while not a proper political party, nevertheless gained an unequaled prominence in France in the late 1890s. It aggressively pushed its candidates in municipal and national elections; and a group of anti-Semitic delegates in the Chamber was not very effective, yet easily recognizable. By 1898 an anti-Semitic bill managed to receive close to two hundred votes in an early reading, exploiting the hostile atmosphere immediately after the publication of Émile Zola's *J'accuse*.[42] The Ligue's showing in urban constituencies was particularly impressive, and in January and February of 1898 it managed to organize, or at least encourage, some sixty anti-Jewish riots throughout France, many in some of its main urban centers. These became real pogroms only in Algeria, but in France, too, much damage was done and the Jewish population was thoroughly intimidated. The political potential of a populist anti-Semitic movement in France was further demonstrated by the Marquis de Morès, operating in the early 1890s, especially in the Ist Paris *arrondissement*, and later by Jules Guérin in the popular XIXth. By the peak year of 1898, the Ligue and its satellites carried on intensive street agitation, organized parades, and tried its hand at all kinds of propaganda.[43]

These were perhaps meager successes, but they were not so entirely unimpressive in comparison with the German performance. In fact, the German parties never managed to attract as much public support as the

45

anti-Semitic anti-Dreyfusards did at the turn of the century. One suspects that more complete studies of anti-Semitism in French social organizations, among artisans, white-collar employees, shopkeepers, and the professions would have shown a spread of anti-Semitic attitudes not unlike that characteristic of Germany at the time. Stephen Wilson's excellent analysis of the lists of contributors to the *Monument Henry,* published periodically by *La Libre Parole* from December 1898 to January 1899, suggests that the social composition of anti-Semites in late nineteenth-century France was essentially similar to that in Germany, with a somewhat clearer emphasis on elements of the working class and, understandably, on the lower Catholic priesthood. Otherwise, in France too one can identify army officers, small employers, students, and members of the professions as the most highly overrepresented groups among the anti-Semites.[44]

The spread of anti-Semitism in Germany might have been somewhat wider than in France. The French movement, however, had had an unequaled one-time peak at the height of the Dreyfus Affair, never to be regained until the Nazi period in Germany and the Vichy period in France.

Beyond the ideological and social-organizational aspects of anti-Semitism, all of its functions observed in Germany between 1870 and 1911 reappear when we turn to examine the French case. Anti-Semitism was an integral component of the new French right-wing nationalism that asserted itself from the early 1880s. In France too the Jew as a foreigner, a non-Frenchman, an outsider, provided a useful symbol of negation of all that was presumably purely authentically, and uniquely, French and diffused with the special signs of national greatness and promise. Anti-Semitism appeared, as for instance on the left wing of the Boulangist movement, when an effort was made to enlist the workers and lower-middle-class elements to the support of the Union Générale—obliterating class differences for the sake of a united, glorious France. In Drumont's and Barrès's writings anti-Semitism was turned into a major unifying element, and it became an indispensable part of Maurras's "integral nationalism."[45]

France did not face the complex identity crisis which was imposed upon Germany by the Bismarckian unification-from-above. Nevertheless, it was engaged during the latter years of the century in an internal controversy, often real strife, over the meaning of its modern nationalism. Similarly, France did not have to tackle the rapid pace of industrial development characteristic of the German economic growth during the second half of the nineteenth century. But she too was seeking ways to deal with the implications of a new, emerging national market and the unmistakable symptoms of industrial capitalism. Thus, anti-Semitism, in France as in Germany, played a role in the channeling of socioeconomic dissatisfaction and resentment engendered by the economic transformations and social restructuring of these years. This is all too well known to be repeated at length. Suffice is to mention the surge of anti-Semitic sentiments following the collapse of the Union Générale in 1882, and the increasingly anti-Semitic tone of the Catholic newspaper La Croix, gradually to become the most outspoken mouthpiece for the anti-industrial, anticapitalist, antimodern reaction in France. Among the anti-Semitic literary stars too, the social theme was and remained prominent throughout. It was Drumont, once again, who gave an early French version to it: "L'antisémitisme"—he proclaimed—"n'a jamais été une question réligieuse, il a toujours été une question économique et sociale."[46]

Furthermore, the role of anti-Semitism in the political transformation of late nineteenth-century France was parallel to its corresponding role in Germany. As an element of new nationalism, it operated with it to "transform from Left to Right a whole combination of ideas, sentiments and values henceforth considered the birthright of Radicalism."[47] Between 1879 and 1899, explains the historian of the French right, René Rémond, the left center in French politics moved slowly and by degrees to the right, making for an important change in the political map of the country. While the newly created right mostly used the arsenal of political ideas and ideals borrowed from the tradition of the two empires, only one new element was added—anti-Semitism. It was anti-Semitism which, in France too, helped reshape the social, not merely the ideological, composition of the main political camps in the country. Finally, French anti-Semitism seems to have become in France as in Germany a culture code, a sign of belonging. Even if the controversy during the Dreyfus Affair was not primarily a matter of justice versus patriotism, or generally an argument over principles, the struggle itself crystallized the two main blocks in French politics, style, and culture. On the one hand, the antirepublican right was regrouping its forces and testing its muscles. On the other, the republicans were joining hands despite deep internal divisions. The case of the socialists, in France as in Germany, is particularly instructive. In the late 1880s, anti-Semitism was still widely diffused across the social and political spectrum of France. La Revue socialiste published a series of anti-Semitic articles dealing with the Jewish question as late as 1887–89, though it opened its columns to opposite views too. The Blanquist and Proudhonist traditions of the socialist left in France were heavy with anti-Semitic material. But as anti-Semitism became increasingly an identity card for the new revolutionary, antirepublican right, the socialists began to distance themselves from it. By 1892 their line became clearly opposed to anti-Semitism, though their position on the Dreyfus case was still equivocal. It was only in 1898, after the public appearance of Zola on the Dreyfusards' side, and as the specter of the Ligue in the streets of Paris was becoming increasingly alarming, that the socialists came out finally for revision. But from that point onward they seemed to have grasped the overall political, indeed cultural, meaning of anti-Semitism, and they acted accordingly.[48] The Dreyfus Affair made this last function of anti-Semitism unquestionably clear, in a more overt and outspoken manner than had ever been the case in Germany.

V

Two points of diversity are often mentioned when French anti-Semitism is compared with its contemporary German counterpart. First, the fact that the French Jewish population was considerably smaller than the German Jewish one; and second, that France was then, unlike Germany, a republic, traditionally and structurally better equipped to guard against anti-Semitism. Other elements may be added; above all, the unique French path to industrialization. But these two do seem to be of special significance. By 1900 the French Jewish community numbered 80,000 members only, while their number in Germany, in proportion to the general population, was five times as large.[49] And after all, the French Republic did come out victorious at the end of the Dreyfus Affair, reasserting its faith in liberty, equality, and fraternity. Though the battle over Dreyfus may have indeed ended as it did despite, and not because of, the pressure of public opinion and the press, the very fact of victory imbued nationalists and anti-Semites with bitterness and a sense of impotence that seemed never to be erased, even after the upheavals of two world wars. Reversely, it gave the republican forces a consciousness of their responsibility and power, as well as the necessary self confidence to continue the battle. It certainly gave the French Jewish community a lasting faith in the benevolence of French civilization.[50]

Germany never experienced such a test case, and we shall never know how she would have reacted. But it is instructive to remember that

48

many in Germany at the time of the Affair saw in it a proof of the inferiority of the French system, and even the Jews expressed the concern
of the better-situated brother. Anti-Semitism in such extreme and overt
forms, they believed, was not respectable in Wilhelmine Germany,
though it was almost self-evident in mild, latent forms. In the few riots
against Jews at that time, in Neustettin (1881), Xanten (1891), and
Konitz (1900), the state authorities proved entirely reliable in using
troops to provide protection, and the courts handed out stiff sentences
to the rioters. In the Reichstag the anti-Semites never managed to get
their various bills beyond the initial parliamentary stage and were often
ridiculed there and laughed at.[51] In his memoirs, Heinrich Class recalled
that the Alldeutscher Verband had not been anti-Semitic until *he* was
nominated its president in 1908.[52] According to a detailed study of the
predecessors of the postwar Schutz- und Trutzbund, the leadership of the
ADV had to tread carefully on the anti-Semitic issue as late as 1913,
because this clearly had no public resonance, even among its prospective
members. Only in 1916, with the early war crises, did it openly launch
an anti-Semitic campaign, reaching its high point in the summer of
1918.[53]

It is also interesting to observe the reactions to Class's 1912 book
Wenn ich der Kaiser wär. The book included a comprehensive critique of
the government's domestic and foreign policies and an overall plan for
an alternative—reformist and imperialist. Some twenty-five thousand
copies were printed by the spring of 1914, but there was much criticism
of its anti-Semitic part. The conservative, right-wing Reichspartei, some
big-business groups, and even the *Verein deutscher Studenten*, known for
its anti-Jewish stand, regarded these demands as unrealistic, immoder-
ate, impossible, though admittedly not undesirable.[54] Somewhat later,
the highest government echelons took the chance of reacting to similar
proposals, presented as a memorandum by a close associate of Class, one
cavalry officer Konstantin Gebsattel. This was a moderate document according to the standards of ADV, and both Chancellor Theobald von
Bethmann-Hollweg and the kaiser agreed to comment upon it. As to its
anti-Semitic points, protested Bethmann-Hollweg, it was impossible
even "*sich mit solchen Gedanken ernsthaft auseinanderzusetzen.*" The kaiser called these proposals "childish," insisting that such ideas went
against the best interests of the German state, and "*uns auf den Zustand
vor 100 Jahren zurückwerfen und zugleich aus der Reihe der Kulturnati-
onen ausscheiden würden.*"

Thus, even that leadership, which continuously toyed with ideas of

49

a *Staatsstreich* to solve domestic problems, and a war of aggression to solve international tensions, recoiled from taking actual anti-Semitic ac-tion, and considered those suggested "*im ganzen phantastisch.*"[55] The leadership feared the revolutionary implications of anti-Semitism, it is true, but it was also apparently aware of its incommensurability with the most minimal standards of existing civilization. The picture is similar to that disclosed in France: in both countries a widespread anti-Jewish sen-timent, a popular demand for anti-Semitic literature, and compliance with certain kinds of social discrimination, combined with an avoidance of any practical public anti-Jewish measure. Beyond the socially diffused antipathy toward Jews, the main legacy of prewar radical anti-Semitism, in Germany as well as in France, was a written, literary one. From the very beginning Hitler sensed its basic irrelevance to his kind of anti-Semitism, and consciously set out to surpass its very premises.

VI

With the possible exception of Adolf Stöcker, the politicians of late nineteenth- and early twentieth-century German anti-Semitism quickly moved from the streets and the public rally to the parliamentary halls, where they were drawn into impotent Reichstag speech-making. They dissipated their energy in internal strife and showed no talent for carrying out any of their grandiose schemes. In fact, neither the politicians nor the ideologues of the movement had any real plan of action. Stöcker and Treitschke repeatedly assured their respective audiences that they had no intention of going back on emancipation.[56] Marr and Glagau occasion-ally toyed with the idea of restrictive legal measures to cut down Jewish influence on the German economy and in Germany's public life. But neither they nor their younger and more practical heirs in the organized anti-Semitic movement had any conception of the kind of desirable or feasible action needed to bring such measures about. Among the early ideologues, only Eugen Düring somewhat expanded upon his proposals for the solution of the "Jewish question," and even hinted at the inevi-tability of physical extermination. But he too buried his suggestions in the last chapter of his anti-Semitic book, which was unusually confused even for this "master" of anti-Semitic prose. Essentially, Düring was far too pessimistic to busy himself with drawing practical blueprints. No European government, he argued, was in a position to act against the Jews, and no suggested solution could therefore be applied. One was left to wage only a personal struggle, he concluded, a war of "enlightenment and self-defense."[57] He too was primarily busy reediting his old anti-Semitic opus or expanding and attempting new versions of it. Together with other anti-Semites, he was thrown back on written matter, attempting to gain as many *converts* as possible among the reading public, not to recruit *soldiers* for an actual battle.

In Wilhelmine Germany anti-Semitism was a part of the written culture. But this was a culture of paradoxes. It included the bureaucratic Potsdam style and the romantic style of Wagnerian grandeur.[58] It also gave rise, despite the authoritarianism of the regime and the pressure of its censor, to Theodor Fontane's moderate tone, and to Thomas Mann's reflective elegance. Moreover, this was a culture which served, to use George Steiner's phrase, as "the real homeland of the Jews."[59] Marr, Friedrich Lange, and even Lagarde remained always bitter and frustrated at its margin. Witness the continuous attacks on the Jewish intellectual and literary man, and the diatribes against Heinrich Heine and Ludwig Börne repeated by every anti-Semite from Wagner in the middle of the century to Fritsch at its close. The verbal aggression of these men gives the impression of a public ritual: the preoccupation with the same themes, the return to the same historical and personal examples, the hammering of the same complaints. The written comments, added by the contributors to the *Monument Henry* in France during the Dreyfus Affair were observed to have had the object and the function of *a liturgy.* Theirs was "*une réaction de type magique,*" serving an end in itself, not meant to lead to further action.[60] Much of the anti-Semitic verbiage in Germany of that time was all of the same kind.

Hitler had no use for this verbiage. Already in *Mein Kampf* he extensively explained the superiority of the spoken word over written matter. All world-shaking events, he argued, have been brought about not by "*Geschriebenes,*" but by "*das gesprochene Wort.*"[61] His two examples were the exploits of the French Revolution and the effectiveness of Marxism. In both cases he was at pains to show it was oratory and not ideology, propaganda and not ideas, which won the day. In passing, as was often his habit, he poured scorn on the German "*Tintenritter,*" and the highly educated but entirely purposeless "*Schreibseele.*" Written matter, always smacking of intellectualism, was despised and ridiculed by him. He himself wrote extensively only once, when the speaker's platform was forcibly denied him, and *Mein Kampf* remained, to borrow his own term, a book "*das geredet ist.*"[62]

Striving for power, it was Goebbels the speech-maker who quickly became second only to Hitler himself within the Nazi Party. Men like Alfred Rosenberg were considered harmless but useless. Hitler never actually read his *Mythos des 20. Jahrhunderts*, though he claimed to have been versed in the earlier anti-Semitic literature. His admiration, however, was saved for the great rabble-rouser of *fin de siècle* Vienna, Karl Lueger, and his anti-Semitism was clearly picked up in conversations, in beer halls, and on street corners. He was converted to anti-Semitism by the spoken word, and he knew he could best transmit it by the same medium. And in his case the medium was indeed the message.[63]

Nazism was a spoken culture. Its language was all speech, with no literary dimensions, no privacy, no individuality. It was the language of demagogy, of declamations and shouts, with flags flying in the wind and the swastika constantly before one's eyes.[64] It was a culture in which verbal aggression was *not a substitute for action but a preparation for it*. In contrast to the language of Wilhelmine Germany, this was a medium which in all seriousness meant to lead to the glorious deed. In his so-called "*grundlegende Rede über den Antisemitismus*," Hitler sounded his faith in final victory, when "*endlich der Tag kommt, an dem unsere Worte schweigen und die Tat beginnt.*"[65] Thus, the spoken word too was merely a tool for action, a practical instrument for bringing it about. Hitler's rhetoric forced a transformation of meaning even upon the substance of anti-Semitism. He may have not had a clear plan for handling the Jews if and when he would seize power in Germany, but his anti-Semitism was, from the very beginning, entirely and consciously, a matter of action. It turned the old written stuff into a new kind of material—explosive, dangerous, leading inexorably to catastrophe. The change came gradually and almost imperceptibly. Contemporaries were easily fooled by it; historians too often ignore it.

The old, tenacious tradition of European antipathy for the Jews no doubt contributed to the choice of the Jews as a target for persecution, and to the preparation of the crowds of onlookers throughout Europe to accept passively the reality of the Holocaust in their midst. The anti-Semitism of the pre-1914 years helped preserve this tradition and adapted it to the modern social and political context. It was as such of great significance in shaping the particular human environment at the time. But the murderous acts of the Nazis were of a different category and sprang from different sources. The prose of the prewar anti-Semites was as remote from the marching SS troops as is the normal verbal aggression of small children from the rare assaults of youngsters upon their elders. The final act of violence must be understood by the specific details of the case, not by reference to some commonly observed pattern of human behavior. Nazism too, I believe, can best be studied through its own dynamism and character, not by reliance upon its "beginnings." Here is how Marc Bloch concluded his chapter on the "idol of origins":

> Jamais, en un mot, un phénomène historique ne s'explique pleinement en dehors de l'étude de son moment. Cela est vrai de toutes les étapes de l'évolution. De celle où nous vivons comme des autres. Le proverbe arabe l'a dit avant nous: "Les hommes ressemblent plus à leur temps qu'à leur pères." Pour avoir oublié cette sagesse orientale, l'étude du passé s'est parfois discrédite.[66]

3

Retracing the Twisted Road
*Nazi Policies
Toward German Jews, 1933–1939*

KARL A. SCHLEUNES

It is nearly fifty years ago that Adolf Hitler and his National Socialists came to power in Germany. It is more than forty that SS Einsatzgruppen began their sweeps through western Russia in search of Jews to kill,
that a conference was convened at the Wannsee in Berlin to extend that
search through all of Europe, and that the first gassings of Jews were
begun at Chełmno in Poland. This summer (1982) it is exactly forty
years ago that Rudolf Höss, the commandant at Auschwitz, hit upon
Zyklon B as the ultimate agent in effecting what the Nazis were beginning to call their "final solution to the Jewish problem."

No one of the questions surrounding this Final Solution has been
fully settled. Vico once thought it "a truth beyond question" that a world
made by men would for that reason be one that "men could come to
know."[1] That principle, so enriching to the enterprise of explaining the
human past, has in our day run head-on into the reality of Auschwitz, a
world clearly created by men, but one that still confounds their capacities
to know, or to understand, how it came to be. Descartes's doubts about
our capacity to know ourselves, doubts Vico was at pains to dispel, seem
to have been vindicated by Auschwitz.

Some of the questions regarding Auschwitz are beyond settling
simply because they are rooted in metaphysical assumptions. Others that

54

once appeared settled are—for reasons good and ill—being reopened. Still others need to be reopened because new evidence has come to light.

The major questions—short of the one about how such things are possible—can be grouped into those that probe the mysterious reaches of anti-Semitism, those that investigate the historical uniqueness of the effort to destroy an entire people, those that treat the matter of what contemporaries, German and non-German, knew about what was going on, and those that consider whether Hitler (or any other Nazi leader) knew from the outset what the objectives of Nazi Jewish policy were to be. It is to the last of these questions that this essay is addressed.

Did Hitler know, when he became chancellor in 1933, what he hoped to accomplish concerning the Jewish question? Was Auschwitz the product of such a clearly conceived design? Or did Hitler, as some suggest, have his objectives defined even before 1933? As early as 1919, after all, before joining the German Workers' Party, Hitler had communicated to one of his superiors his views on the Jewish problem and his belief that a "rational anti-Semitism" must have as its fixed goal the "removal of the Jews altogether."[2] By 1924, when he wrote Mein Kampf, he was clearly in possession of a full-blown racist Weltanschauung that had anti-Semitism as its centerpiece. Even the gassing of Jews is mentioned in Mein Kampf. If, during the world war, Hitler wrote, Germany had placed "twelve or fifteen thousand . . . Hebrew corrupters of the people under poisonous gas," so they might have suffered at home what hundreds of thousands of German soldiers endured on the battlefield, the sacrifices at the front "would not have been in vain."[3]

The view that Hitler knew from the outset, possibly as early as 1919, what the outline of a Jewish policy should be, has been most fully and persuasively argued by Lucy Dawidowicz, principally in her book The War Against the Jews, 1933–1945 (1975). To support her case she cites Hitler's 1919 letter, appropriate passages from Mein Kampf, and numerous other references Hitler made to Jews before he was made chancellor. Each one of these utterances, she argues, "prefigures the political realities of the German dictatorship under Hitler. . . ."[4] When these prefigurations are placed in light of Hitler's subsequent warning on January 30, 1939, that if Jews should "succeed in plunging the nations once more into a world war," the result would be "the annihilation of the Jewish race in Europe,"[5] the argument that the "Final Solution" was the inevitable culmination of a grand design becomes all the more persuasive.

Was the road to Auschwitz in fact that clearly charted? If so, it would be one of the few objectives the Nazis ever managed to pursue both clearly and consistently. Is it not possible that hindsight allows us to see a clarity and a design where they did not exist? There seems to be a moral level, to be sure, upon which the horrors of Auschwitz demand that they be preceded by such clarity and design. Possibly a degree of comfort may even be extracted from the horrors, if their evil can be shown to have signaled itself fully beforehand. Yet, would the horror be in the least diminished if it should turn out to have been the product of something other than a long-standing policy? Would Nazi anti-Semitism be rendered any less monstrous if the road to Auschwitz was something other than direct? There is a danger, as Martin Broszat points out, in making the Final Solution into a "metahistorical" phenomenon.[6] At best, it can serve to diminish our obligation to support the answers to those questions we do ask; at worst, it can serve to diminish the need to ask the questions themselves.

Did Hitler, or anyone else in the Nazi leadership, know in January 1933, or even before then, what the objectives of a Jewish policy should be? The evidence suggests that he did not, and that no one else did either. There was, to be sure, the anti-Jewish rhetoric that had been a central theme of Nazi propaganda from the beginning. Without "the Jew," Hitler's own *Weltanschauung* could not have held together. "In whatever direction one follows Hitler's train of thought," Alan Bullock has said, "sooner or later one encounters the Satanic figure of the Jew."[7] Many Nazis, though not all of them, shared Hitler's brutal anti-Semitism. From it came the energy that eventually propelled the Nazis toward Auschwitz, but in 1933, to say nothing of 1919 or 1925, no one yet imagined where that energy might lead.

In reference to the first six years of Hitler's rule, one cannot speak of a Nazi Jewish policy. Instead, one must speak of many Jewish policies, no one of them truly official, no one of them coordinated with the others, and many of them pursued in contradiction to each of the others. Not until 1939, in the aftermath of difficulties produced by the Reichskristallnacht, is there brought into Jewish policy a measure of coordination that reflects clearly the intervention of Adolf Hitler. Until then Jewish policy had been the object of extraordinary contention within the Nazi leadership, the object of internal power struggles that resembled nothing so much as they did jungle warfare.[8] It was a warfare in which the fittest prevailed. By 1939 that had proved to be Heinrich Himmler and his various police agencies, particularly the SS and its SD adjunct. Left by the wayside were such other contenders as the SA, various economic

officials, Interior Minister Wilhelm Frick, Joseph Goebbels, Alfred Rosenberg, and a host of others. That there was a struggle for control over
Jewish policy is evidence confirming the lack of Hitler's direction; that
the struggle was such a bitter one is evidence confirming the importance
of anti-Semitism to him and to the Nazis.

Given their commitment to anti-Semitism, it is surprising that they
had no clear plans about how to handle the Jewish question when they
came to power in 1933. Until 1929, of course, the NSDAP (Nazi Party)
had been little more than a noisy fringe group on the German right wing.
Plans for being in power were necessarily subordinate to plans for acquiring it. By late 1929, however, electoral successes in communal and *Land*
elections, together with the national publicity Hitler gained in the
Young Plan plebiscite campaign that same year, set the stage for the
extraordinary success in the Reichstag elections of September 1930. Suddenly, the Nazis, with their 6.5 million votes and 107 seats in the Reichstag, had become the second largest party in the republic. This was the
setting in which Gregor Strasser, second to Hitler in the party leadership, observed that "we are actually conducting a struggle for power without knowing exactly what we would do with it, if we should get it."[9]

At Strasser's instigation in late 1929 there was established an agency
within the party, the Organizationsabteilung II (OA II), that was
charged with making "intellectual preparations for the future National
Socialist state."[10] In a technical sense, though not a political one, the
OA II was to function as a shadow cabinet, producing "detailed program-
matic statements"[11] and training the experts who might some day be
called upon to run government ministries. Some of the plans produced
in the OA II did eventually become the basis for policy. Walther Darré,
who headed its agriculture section, used the OA II as the base for for-
mulating an agricultural program rooted in blood and soil. Hans Frank
used the legal section to draw up plans that were later helpful in reshaping the legal system along *völkisch* lines.

Nothing of a comparable nature was produced regarding Jewish policy. The few plans that were made had little effect upon what ultimately
happened. Their authors, obscure when they joined the OA II, played
almost no role in the eventual execution of any sort of policy. Such plans
as were made were largely the work of the pro-Nazi bureaucrat, Dr. Helmut Nicolai, and his aide, Ernst von Heydebrand. They proposed that
Jews be subjected to certain "racially hygienic" measures and that they
be locked out of the professions. Some of their proposals did in fact

prefigure the later Nuremberg Laws.[12] More significant, or so it seemed at the time, was Nicolai's recommendation to the NSDAP regarding its strategy on the Jewish question.

> Should the NSDAP receive an absolute majority, Jews will be deprived of their rights by legal process. If, however, the NSDAP receives power only through a coalition, the rights of German Jews will be undermined through administrative means.[13]

This was not yet the imagination that produced Auschwitz.

There is no reason to believe that Hitler ever took the slightest note of what Nicolai and Heydebrand proposed. The OA II itself was brought more closely under Strasser's own wing in June 1932, only to be disbanded in December when he himself defected from the party. A successor commission was appointed under the leadership of Rudolf Hess, but it had even less influence than did its predecessor.[14] Hitler was obviously in no mood to delegate authority in Jewish affairs.

The nature of Nazi ideology made it possible, of course, to forecast what the Nazis should do if and when they came to power. In May 1932, Herman Göring, then the chief Nazi delegate in the Reichstag, attempted to explain to the Italian journalist Pietro Solari what it was that the Nazis eventually would do to the Jews. All Göring could do, however, was to draw the conclusions made necessary by National Socialism's anti-Semitic premises. Marriages between Jews and Germans would no longer be tolerated, he said. Jews who had settled in Germany since 1914 would be expelled. Any Jew who had insulted the German nation was to be punished. Jews were to be removed from their commanding positions in the press, the theater, the cinema, the schools, and the universities, as well as from "every office, every honor, every position from which they can exercise their destructive antinational, international . . . influence to the detriment of the German people." Göring foresaw only one exception: "The decent Jewish merchant who is willing to stay in Germany as an alien protected under the law will be allowed to pursue his business undisturbed."[15]

When the Nazis did come to power some eight months later, Jewish policy did not receive the immediate priority that ideological considerations might lead one to suspect. As a result, there were soon many Jewish policies. No one was in charge and so it would remain until January 1939, when Hitler empowered Göring to commission Reinhard Heydrich and the SS to coordinate the expulsion of Jews from the German Reich.

As soon as it became clear that Hitler was not going to place anyone

58

in charge of Jewish policy, its control became the object of bitter rivalry. The rivals were numerous. Those most clearly associated with ideological matters naturally thought their claims to be the strongest. Alfred Rosenberg, the editor of the *Völkischer Beobachter* and the self-styled ideologist of the movement, was particularly eager to be heard on racial matters. Without an institutional base in the new state apparatus, however, and since not even Hitler took his ideological views seriously, Rosenberg was soon hopelessly outclassed by the competition. Another contender, at least by virtue of his reputation as a Jew-baiter, was Julius Streicher, editor of the notoriously scurrilous *Der Stürmer*. But Streicher was a man of limited abilities. His role in Jewish policy came to be confined largely to fanning the flames of race hatred.

A more serious candidate for control over Jewish policy was the party's chief propagandist, Joseph Goebbels, whom Hitler named propaganda minister in March 1933. Goebbels was extremely ambitious, able, and hardworking. As propaganda minister he thought it only proper that the "Jewish press," as represented in the publishing firms of Mosse, Ullstein, and Sonnemann, should come under his control. Equally serious as a candidate was Ernst Röhm, the head of the SA. Röhm, in addition to being an impassioned racist, took all the tenets of National Socialism seriously and had the advantage of being backed by several hundred thousand storm troopers. He also had a long and friendly association with Hitler.

Another contender, though less powerful politically than Röhm or Goebbels, was Wilhelm Frick, the interior minister in Hitler's cabinet. Frick, like Röhm, had a longstanding association with Hitler. As a legal official in Munich's police department in the early 1920s, he had been one of Hitler's earliest protectors. He had also been the first Nazi to hold high public office when in 1930 he became interior minister in Thuringia. Now, as interior minister for the Reich, he was better positioned than anyone else to implement those anti-Jewish measures that had been proposed in the OA II by Nicolai and Heydebrand.

Perhaps the most serious candidate for major influence of any sort in the new Reich was Hermann Göring, already the Prussian minister of the interior and therefore in control of a sizable police force. From this Prussian base Göring organized the dreaded Gestapo. In due course Hitler was also to make him aviation minister, commissioner of the Four-Year Plan, and Reich counselor for defense, as well as using him as his chief troubleshooter. Göring also happened to be an extremely able combatant in the warfare going on under the führer's nose.

59

There is no suspense, of course, as to who it was that finally gained control over Jewish policy. No one of those who appeared in 1933 to be the most likely to succeed, with the exception of Göring, was ever to establish himself as a dominant figure in its making or its execution. Instead, that policy came to be almost entirely within the purview of Heinrich Himmler (and by extension, Reinhard Heydrich) and his SS. It is worth emphasizing that in 1933 neither Himmler nor his SS appeared destined for great influence in Hitler's Reich. They were then still fully subordinate to the powerful Ernst Röhm and his SA. Himmler, moreover, had for a long time been associated with Gregor Strasser, a connection that did not augur well for him in the wake of Strasser's defection from the party. Yet the story of Jewish policy in the Third Reich became, in large part, the story of the rise of the SS and of Heinrich Himmler. It is a rise that appears more likely in retrospect than it did in prospect.

Nonetheless, the story of Jewish policy during the 1930s must recount also the failures of the other contenders to establish their claims. That no one was clearly in charge of Jewish policy was evident in the many policies that were pursued in the early days of the Reich. The orderly, "legal" direction proposed by bureaucrats like Nicolai was evident in the series of discriminatory laws promulgated in April 1933. By introducing the Aryan paragraph, this April legislation served to limit the number of Jews in the civil service, in the legal and medical professions, in the schools and universities, and led to the dismissal of some eight hundred "non-Aryans" from their academic positions in the universities.[16] Every minister during these early days created its own "Jewish Section" (*Judenreferat*) in order to administer the discriminatory legislation.[17] In Frick's Interior Ministry it was Dr. Nicolai who was named to head the Jewish Section.[18]

The niceties of legal action, no matter how discriminatory, were totally inadequate for containing the anti-Semitic energies unleashed by Hitler's seizure of power. Röhm's SA saw in Hitler's chancellorship the license for unrestrained action against its enemies, and particularly against the Jews. In the face of the SA's terrorization campaign during the first months of 1933, thousands of Jews fled Germany in panic. Local SA units, eager for blood and spoil, initiated their own campaigns of boycott and violence all over Germany. Jewish lawyers, judges, medical doctors, and other professionals, along with Jewish businessmen and shopkeepers, were victims of these boycotts and beatings. Hitler himself found the SA's actions embarrassing, not out of any newfound sympathy for Jews, but because they undermined his vitally important image as the restorer of stability and order. To curtail SA hoodlums, SS units were sometimes called in to maintain order.[19] More important, after consulting Propaganda Minister Goebbels, Hitler tried to steer SA energies toward a more limited, though officially sponsored, nationwide boycott of Jews. Julius Streicher, leader of the most rabid anti-Semites, was named to head the boycott planning commission. Heinrich Himmler was made a member. Ernst Röhm was not.[20]

By any measure the Nazis themselves were able to devise, the Streicher-led boycott, begun on Saturday, April 1, 1933, was a failure. Lack of public enthusiasm severely disappointed the boycott's organizers. Moreover, it was obvious immediately that the boycott created more problems than it solved. Any interference with economic activity could serve only to increase the number of business failures and add to the already large numbers of unemployed. With the Nazis now bearing the responsibility for the German economy, Hitler could ill afford to add to its problems. In fact, if he hoped to hold on to power, he would have to acquire at least the image of having contributed to their solution. The boycott, originally scheduled to go on indefinitely, was canceled the same day it began. Publicly it was heralded as a great success. Privately, Nazi leaders recognized what one of them called "the many failures of our recent Saturday boycott."[21]

The same considerations that undermined the boycott also thwarted Nazi hopes for the expropriation, or "Aryanization," of Jewish businesses. Jewish shopkeepers and tradesmen were the most immediately vulnerable to Nazi pressures. One estimate has it that during the first two years of Nazi rule at least 75,000 of them were put out of business.[22] The larger and more complex a supposedly "Jewish firm" was, however, the more likely, at least until 1938, that it would be able to resist Aryanization. Joseph Goebbels's ambitions were several times frustrated by other economic realities as well. From the outset he had his eye on several large Jewish firms in Leipzig which specialized in publishing music and German literature for foreign markets. His efforts in 1934 to gain control of these firms and place them under the supervision of the cultural section of his ministry failed when Economics Minister Hjalmar Schacht pointed out the importance of these firms in earning foreign exchange.[23] At the same time, Goebbels's attempts to acquire control over the Berlin publishing houses of Mosse and Ullstein failed when he was outmaneuvered by Max Amann, head of the official Nazi Party publishing house Eher Verlag, who managed to persuade Hitler to have these properties trans-

ferred directly into the party's hands. By the time systematic Aryanization of Jewish businesses resumed in late 1937, Goebbels had been all
but eliminated from the competition for control over Jewish policy.

Hitler's own hand in Jewish policy during these early years appears
only as a restraining one, as in the case of his ordering a halt in 1933 to
SA initiatives, or a steering one, as in the case of his deciding for Amann
and against Goebbels in the Mosse and Ullstein expropriations. A solution to the Jewish problem in the sense of there being mounted a concentrated and centrally coordinated policy did not yet have a sufficiently
high priority for Hitler to place someone clearly in charge; neither did
he contribute specific ideas as to what a solution might actually entail.
It is instructive to contrast Hitler's involvement in the Jewish question
during these early years with his concern for building the autobahn network. To accomplish the latter, he accorded in 1934 full and special
authority to Fritz Todt, inspector-general of the German road and high-
way system, and committed to him men and matériel in numbers sufficient to accomplish the task.[24] The objective was clear from the outset.
In contrast, matters concerning Jews became increasingly murky after
early 1934.

Nazi radicals were furiously unhappy about what they saw to be the
lack of any Jewish policy. "Please tell me in what form it is still possible
. . . to carry on anti-Semitic actions and propaganda," one of them
complained to Streicher after the cancellation of the Saturday boycott.[25]
Neither was there after April 1933 much movement evident on the legislative or administrative fronts. The discriminatory legislation of early
1933 in no sense went to the heart of what most Nazis considered to be
the Jewish problem. Simply to exclude Jews from certain professions, or
to limit their numbers in the schools and universities, while it struck
hard at the Jews, did little to further the biological separation demanded
by a racially defined anti-Semitism. The entire Nazi ideological structure
rested on the belief that the Jew was evil because of his blood. The
promise of the Twenty-Five Points, of *Mein Kampf,* indeed of all of modern anti-Semitism, had been to end race-mixing. As mentioned before,
Göring had only recently reiterated that promise to Solari, telling him
that under the Nazis, "naturally, marriages between Germans and Jews
will not be tolerated."[26] But they were tolerated and continued to be so
on into 1935. Racist radicals were extremely frustrated by these examples
of what Julius Streicher liked to call "racial treason."[27] Under pressure
from local Nazis, or under their own volition, state marriage officials

62

sometimes refused licenses to "racially mixed" couples, or otherwise warned them that their marriage was inadvisable. Some couples in turn, because the marriages were still legal, would resort to court action, thereby adding to the confusion. Pressures mounted upon Interior Minister Frick to issue a directive to guide local officials. Already in November 1933 the German Medical Association under Reich Medical Leader Dr. Gerhardt Wagner had launched a campaign urging an immediate ban on marriages between Aryans and Jews. At first, Frick resisted such pressures, pointing out reluctantly that Germany's reputation abroad could ill afford what would be perceived as a Nazi assault upon a basic human right.[28] Only in early 1935 did he begin to relent.

A solution to this biological dimension of the Jewish problem was not reached until the promulgation in September 1935 of the Nuremberg Laws. The Law for the Protection of German Blood and Honor finally forbade "marriages between Jews and citizens of the state with German or related blood." Extramarital relations between such persons were likewise declared illegal. The Nuremberg Laws did represent a solution of sorts to the Jewish problem. Their provision for a second-class, noncitizen status for Jews satisfied those willing to have Jews placed in what was in many respects a return to the "tolerated Jew" (*Schutzjude*) status of the seventeenth and eighteenth centuries. Most important, the process of biological separation had finally begun. Many Jews themselves hoped that the Nuremberg Laws, by clarifying the situation, might become the legal foundation for a continued, if circumscribed, existence in Germany.

Rather than provide the foundation for such a solution to the Jewish problem, however, the Nuremberg Laws merely marked the end of the pseudolegal phase of the Nazis' persecution of the Jews. For many Nazis the continued existence of Jews in Germany, no matter how circumscribed, was still intolerable. They now took their turn in trying to effect a Jewish policy.

Words like "emigration" and "expulsion" had long been part of the Nazis' anti-Semitic vocabulary. The idea of expelling Jews is one of the oldest weapons in the arsenal of their enemies, one reaching back to the expulsions during the Middle Ages from England, France, Spain, and many of the German states. That the thought might occur again to modern-day anti-Semites hardly occasions surprise. Many Jews had already fled Germany during the early stages of Hitler's *Gleichschaltung*, most of them to neighboring countries like France, Belgium, or England, but in 1934, during the lull following the first storm, many of them were forced by economic necessity to return to Germany. Their return made immediate to the Nazis the question of their permanent emigration—or expulsion.

Legally, emigration of any sort was a concern of the Interior Ministry. As it turned out, it was the matter that brought the SS to prominence in Jewish affairs. It also provided the springboard for the rise to influence of Heinrich Himmler. Himmler had very early accumulated a number of important titles, among them police president of Munich, commander of the Bavarian Political Police, and inspector of the Prussian Gestapo, but it was Hitler's decimation of the SA leadership in June 1934 that finally gave the SS its full independence. Two years later, in June 1936, over Frick's objection[29] Hitler also made Himmler chief of the German Police, giving him control over every police agency in the party and the state.

The SS had begun sizing up the Jewish problem and considering possible solutions at least by 1934, for in the summer of that year it produced its first "Situation Report—Jewish Question."[30] For the first time mention was made of organizing a massive emigration of Jews from Germany. It had occurred to the SS that to support Zionist sentiment among Jews could serve to encourage their departure.

The SS was not to gain full control over Jewish emigration (and therefore over Jewish policy) until 1939 when Hitler commissioned it to organize the emigration of Jews from the entire Reich. It gained that control, however, because it had "earned" it by virtue of having organized, within six months after the *Anschluss of Austria*, the emigration of nearly one-quarter of Austria's Jews. Such successes the system rewarded.

The success of the Austrian operation can be credited to the work of Adolf Eichmann, a minor SD official hired in 1934. It is the emergence of Eichmann as an important figure in Jewish policy that provides some of the most persuasive evidence that the Final Solution was not the result of a long-standing grand design. Before joining the SD, Eichmann had been little more than an unsuccessful oil salesman, and not, apparently, seriously anti-Semitic.[31] Within a year he had become the SD's resident "Jewish expert" and involved in a number of schemes to organize the mass emigration of Jews.

The early emigration schemes concocted by the SS were all failures in the eyes of the Nazis. Of the half million or so Jews in Germany in 1933 when Hitler came to power, some 350,000 remained at the end of 1938.[32] Their attachment to Germany, economic conditions abroad, and the hope that the Nazi storm might blow over, left many Jews reluctant to leave. Then, too, emigration was made difficult by the extremely tight restrictions the Nazi government placed upon the movement of financial resources out of Germany. Obviously, top-level priority had not yet been accorded to solving the Jewish problem by way of emigration. Moreover, some of the emigration schemes concocted by the SS can only be described as harebrained. Eichmann himself was associated with one in 1936 that recommended the purchase of an uninhabited province in Ecuador which was then supposed to serve as the destination for Germany's Jewish emigrants.[33]

Paradoxically, there were also anti-Semitic reasons for questioning the efficacy of emigration as a solution to the Jewish problem, particularly if that emigration was directed toward Palestine. In 1937 the British government's Peel Commission raised the possibility of dividing Britain's Palestine mandate into separate Jewish and Arab states. The specter of a sovereign Jewish state gave some Nazis second thoughts about encouraging Zionism. Ribbentrop, for one, warned Hitler about the dangers that might emanate from such a "Jewish Vatican."[34] Eichmann, for the same reason, had seen an advantage in the Ecuador scheme. South America, he believed, would be large enough to withstand the introduction of a "Jewish infection."[35]

As late as January 1938 an SD report on the Jewish situation sounded discouraging. Emigration in 1937 was back down to 1934 levels, and there was now the added uncertainty about its efficacy as a solution to the problem. The recent upsurge in Aryanization of Jewish businesses, prompted by Göring, also cut off a major source of funds to support Jews in their emigration. There was hardly an aspect of the several Jewish policies in early 1938 to which the Nazi observer could look with satisfaction. On top of that the policies themselves seemed to be without coherent direction.

All that was to change during the course of 1938, beginning in March with the annexation of Austria. The annexation brought an additional 200,000 Jews under Nazi control. At first glance these additional Jews seemed only to complicate matters. On the one hand, more Jews were added to the Reich than had emigrated from it during the previous five years; yet on the other, Austria also offered the opportunity for experimentation. None of the rivalries that hindered the making of a coherent policy at home were as yet institutionalized in Austria. Austria could be made a laboratory in which to test methods for solving the Jewish problem.

65

The story of the Austrian experiment, the brainchild of the SD's "Jewish expert," Adolf Eichmann, is too well known to need recounting here. Suffice it to say, the Central Office for Jewish Emigration which he established in Vienna to centralize control over the entire emigration process managed within six months to force the emigration of 50,000 Austrian Jews, more than twice as many as had emigrated from Germany proper in all of the previous year.

Within the old Germany, Jewish policy also took a new direction during 1938. Early in the year, Göring, who had emerged by 1937 as Hitler's chief troubleshooter in addition to having gained vast powers in economic affairs, began an assault on the narrow foothold Jews still maintained in the German economy. Aryanization of Jewish-owned firms began to proceed at a pace for which radical Nazis had been hoping since 1933. In mid-1937 already Martin Bormann had told a meeting of Nazi gauleiters that "Göring intends to have a fundamental cleaning up of the Jewish question."[36] By April of the next year some 6,000 Jewish businesses had been Aryanized, another 11,000 were on the verge of Aryanization, and 15,000 had been liquidated altogether.[37] In June 1938 a series of decrees supplementary to the Nuremberg Laws began to bar from practice the remaining Jewish medical doctors, lawyers, patent agents, dentists, pharmacists, and so on.[38]

It was the effort to expel foreign Jews from the Reich, however, that induced the great crisis in Jewish policy of 1938, the resolution of which clarified both its control and direction. Such expulsions had been promised long ago in the party program of 1920. Altogether, there were well over 70,000 foreign Jews resident in Germany, the vast majority of them from Poland, but some also from the Soviet Union. In February, Himmler ordered that the expulsion of Soviet Jews be carried out within ten days, notwithstanding the fact that such an operation was impossible in so short a time. Finally, after having been granted several extensions, Soviet Jews were simply rounded up in May and sent to concentration camps in preparation, said the SS, for their "emigration" to the Soviet Union.

Nazi persecutions reached unprecedented fury in the summer of 1938 on other fronts as well. In June some 1,500 German Jews were rounded up for allegedly "antisocial" and criminal behavior and sent to Buchenwald. Wholesale terrorization of Jews had become the order of the day, wrote Bella Fromm from Berlin. In Nuremberg Julius Streicher was contemplating razing a local synagogue and erecting in its place a museum devoted to advancing the cause of anti-Semitism.[39]

66

The most dramatic occurrence of the year was undoubtedly the nationwide pogrom on the night of November 9–10, an action that, because of the large amount of broken glass it produced, was immediately dubbed the *Reichskristallnacht* (Night of Crystal) by Berlin wits. Synagogues all over Germany were set on fire. Insurance officials estimated property damage at 25 million marks; Heydrich thought it should probably be set at "several hundred million."[40] Thousands of Jews were beaten up, arrested, and sent off to Buchenwald and Sachsenhausen. The pogrom had been triggered by the assassination of a German embassy official in Paris by a young Jewish student, an act that in turn had been set off by German efforts to expel the 70,000 Polish Jews to their homeland. The Polish government's refusal to accept them had left thousands of Jews stranded for days on the border between German and Polish anti-Semitism. Among them were the parents of the young assassin.

The Night of Crystal was the kind of anti-Semitic orgy for which Nazi ruffians had been yearning since 1933. It was also to be their last independent action. The pogrom had been set into motion by Joseph Goebbels, much to the resentment of people like Göring and Himmler, who preferred to conduct these persecutions themselves, and to do so in a manner less rowdy and more controlled. Göring complained that the damage of the Kristallnacht hurt German insurance companies more than it did the Jews. Nothing that Göring was hoping to accomplish in solving the Jewish problem had been advanced by the pogrom.

Hitler apparently felt the same way. He and Göring spent the two days following the pogrom closeted with each other, assessing the state of Jewish policy. No protocol of these talks was made, yet it is clear that they were decisive. Göring emerged from the talks on November 12 to announce that the führer had issued an order "requesting that the Jewish question be now, once and for all, coordinated or solved in one way or another."[41]

That Göring had been placed in charge of Jewish policy is clear from the way he conducted the meeting called to consider the effects of the Kristallnacht. The meeting was held in Göring's own Aviation Ministry headquarters. Over a hundred people attended, among them Goebbels, Heydrich, Frick, Economics Minister Walther Funk, and a representative of the German insurance companies. Göring used the meeting as a forum to announce the conclusions reached during his discussions with Hitler. Goebbels was castigated for encouraging the pogrom; the insurance companies were ordered to pay for the damage and, to prevent Jews from profiting, the payments were to be confiscated immediately by the state.

Germany's Jews, he declared, were to have imposed upon them a fine of 1 billion marks for having provoked the righteous anger of the German people. Göring announced also that henceforth he would be in control of the entire process of expropriating Jewish property. No one talked that way without having Hitler's approval.

Any lingering doubts about Göring's authority were removed when a month later, on December 14, he sent a letter to all Reich officials informing them that he had taken charge of Jewish policy:

> To secure the necessary unity in the handling of the Jewish question, upon which rests the handling of economic matters, I am asking that all decrees and other important orders touching upon Jewish matters be cleared through my office and have my approval. Remind all of the officials under your authority that absolutely no independent initiatives on the Jewish question are to be undertaken.[42]

There was a great deal of talk in late 1938 and early 1939 about a solution to the Jewish problem being imminent. "The problem will soon be solved," Hitler told South Africa's minister for defense, Oswald Pirow, on November 24, 1938.[43] To Czech Foreign Minister Frantisek Chvalkovsky a few weeks later, he said: "We are going to destroy the Jews. They are not going to get away with what they did on 9 November 1918. The day of reckoning has come."[44] And on January 30, 1939, he made his forecast to the Reichstag that war, if it should come, would lead to "the annihilation of the Jewish race in Europe."

Did Hitler mean actual physical annihilation? Probably not yet, although the viciousness of his rhetoric certainly served to bring that day nearer. Eberhard Jäckel has pointed out that Hitler did not mean physical killing every time he used the word "extermination."[45] There is a wealth of evidence to indicate that throughout 1939 the Nazis still saw a Germany rendered *judenrein* ("cleansed of Jews") by emigration as their vision of a solution to the Jewish problem. On January 24, 1939, one week before Hitler's much quoted Reichstag speech, Göring had commissioned Reinhard Heydrich to coordinate the accelerated emigration of Jews from Germany.[46] Heydrich had been at the meeting in the Aviation Ministry following the Kristallnacht and used the opportunity to boast about the successes Eichmann had achieved in organizing emigration from Austria. Eichmann's techniques were now to be employed also in Germany. From within the SS, Heydrich appointed Gestapo official Heinrich Müller to direct the new Central Office for Jewish Emigration. Offices

68

similar to the one Eichmann had established in Vienna were to be created in Berlin, Breslau, Frankfurt, and Hamburg.[47]

Göring's commission to Heydrich was followed the next day by a dispatch sent to all German diplomatic missions requesting their cooperation so as to "speed up the emigration of all Jews living in the territories of the Reich," as this had become, the message concluded, "the ultimate aim of Jewish policy."[48] The emphasis upon emigration was everywhere evident. At a press conference on February 7 Alfred Rosenberg alluded to the possibility of the eventual emigration from Europe of perhaps as many as 15 million Jews.[49]

While Heydrich and Müller were eventually able to show record emigration figures for 1939, they were no longer able to see their successes as much of a contribution to solving the Jewish problem. Nearly 80,000 Jews left Germany during the course of the year; yet by June, Heydrich was complaining that emigration was not proceeding satisfactorily. To Himmler he cited in explanation "the failure to organize effectively the Central Offices for Emigration" and "the growing tendency for other countries to lock their doors against immigration."[50] He might have added that the annexation on March 15 of "Rump" Czechoslovakia had by itself added more Jews than could be expelled from Germany during the entire year. Eichmann was immediately dispatched from Vienna to organize emigration in Prague,[51] but to little avail.

Emigration schemes that had been unable to keep pace with Hitler's peacetime acquisitions fell apart almost completely with the outbreak of war in September 1939. The war was larger than Hitler had anticipated, involving an unexpected front in the west, as well as one to the east. One more emigration scheme, the so-called Madagascar Plan, did briefly dominate Jewish policy in the period immediately following the outbreak of war. Originating in the Foreign Office,[52] the plan called for the settling of Jews from Nazi-controlled Europe in this French protectorate. Briefly stated, the scheme called for France to cede Madagascar, thereby making it available for Jewish immigration. The settlement in turn was to be financed by Jewish assets the Nazis would seize in Europe. Himmler and Heydrich found the idea acceptable because Madagascar was to be governed by the SS. Nothing came of the plan.[53] The war virtually precluded its success or that of any other emigration scheme. Not only was the war larger than expected, but it also transformed dramatically the nature of the Jewish problem. The conquest of Poland brought at least 3 million Jews into the Nazi orbit. Their emigration or expulsion, Rosenberg's grandiose visions notwithstanding, was out of the question.

The radicalizing effect of war must also be taken into consideration in accounting for the new direction taken in Jewish policy after 1939. War simplifies perceptions and brutalizes them. To Nazi ideologues war meant that the ultimate conflict between the superior and inferior races had finally been joined. Goebbels's propaganda was to make much of the point that the war pitted Aryans against non-Aryans in a struggle to the death. That such a war was seen immediately as an opportunity for strengthening Aryan racial purity is apparent in Hitler's appointment in October 1939 of Himmler as Reich commissioner for the strengthening of Germandom. As Goebbels was to point out in reference to Jewish policy, "A whole series of possibilities presents itself for us in wartime that would be denied us in peacetime."[54]

On balance, Nazi Jewish policies from 1933 through 1939 are less ones that prefigure the Final Solution, at least in a conscious sense, than they are policies that the Nazis themselves saw as failures. What the Nazis had managed in their first six years of power was to undo an emancipation that had been more than a century in the making. One by one, they had peeled back the layers of an assimilation that had been building up since the early nineteenth century. By September 1939 Jews remaining in Germany were excluded from the universities and schools, from the professions, and from the economy. Prohibited from visiting theaters, museums, and concerts; banned from going to swimming pools or attending sporting events; forced to adopt Jewish-sounding names; prevented from possessing driver's licenses, telephones, and radios, they were physically and psychologically separated from the surrounding German culture to whose making they had contributed so much. If this was not a solution to the Jewish problem, there were now those who, behind the curtain of war, saw other possibilities.

4

Relations Between Jews and Non-Jews in Eastern Europe Between the Two World Wars

EZRA MENDELSOHN

This paper will raise, and will try to answer, the following questions: What was the impact of the establishment, after World War I, of the new nation-states of eastern Europe and of the Soviet Union on Jewish-Gentile relations? Can the interwar years be justly regarded as a kind of prelude to the Holocaust, in the sense that government actions and the views of leading politicians prepared the masses for the Nazi policy of the war years? Was there a major distinction between the policy toward Jews in Communist Russia and in capitalist eastern Europe? And finally, did the Jewish condition and Jewish behavior have a significant influence on the degree of anti-Semitism?

On the face of it, the new order in post–World War I eastern Europe did not appear to strike at the Jewish interest. On the contrary. The February revolution brought emancipation to Russian Jewry. The millions of former Russian Jewish subjects who were now inhabitants of Poland, Romania, Lithuania, Latvia, and Estonia, were also declared equal before the law. Romanian Jewry, the vast majority of those whose members did not enjoy citizenship rights before the war, was finally emancipated.[1] Moreover, in some cases Jews were recognized as a national minority and were awarded collective national rights, something greatly desired by the modern Jewish national parties which now came, in east-

71

ern Europe if not in the Soviet Union, to dominate Jewish public life. The fact that Poland had only reluctantly put its signature to the Minorities Treaty did not overly worry some optimistic Jewish politicians, who proclaimed in 1919 the beginning of a "new era" in Polish-Jewish relations.[2] In Lithuania, Jewish leaders were certain that they would be allowed to create new and imposing institutions of Jewish national autonomy unknown since the days of the "Council of the Four Lands" in medieval Poland-Lithuania.[3] In many regions Jewish politicians, not long ago unknown leaders of small underground or semilegal groups, were actively courted by non-Jewish leaders. The granting of civic and national rights, and the new feeling of political power, was a heady experience for east European Jewry, which in the old tsarist empire was a despised and oppressed minority and which in Habsburg Austria-Hungary was emancipated but not recognized as a national minority.

There were other reasons for Jews to welcome the emergence of the new nation-states of eastern Europe. The nature of such "peasant states" as Lithuania and Latvia, and the peculiar conditions in such provinces as Bukovina, Transylvania, and the Polish *kresy* (eastern borderlands), where cultural vacuums came into existence, were perceived (rightly) as likely to lead to an unprecedented flourishing of Jewish national culture and politics.[4] And the fact that nearly all of the new states were, at least in the beginning, democratic and pluralistic, meant that Jewish politicians, educators, journalists, and writers would be working under favorable conditions unknown in the prewar Russian Empire. Finally, many Jews believed that the creation of conservative, capitalist countries in which traditional elites played a major role was also a positive development, since it seemed to pose no danger to the essentially conservative, religious Jewish society.[5] In short, the new eastern Europe seemed to offer something to most, if not all, types of Jews—to the nationalists and to the "assimilationists," to secularists and to the Orthodox. Above all, it offered hopes for new alliances between the Jews and the newly triumphant masters of the region—the Czechs, the Lithuanians, the Latvians, the Romanians, and even the Poles.

In Soviet Russia, of course, the situation was quite different, but here too there was cause for Jewish enthusiasm. True, the new regime was violently antibourgeois and antireligious, and no ethnic group was as bourgeois or as religious as the Jews. But it was also committed to the struggle against anti-Semitism and embraced the doctrine of careers open to talent (so long as one toed the party line). The number of prominent Jews engaged in building the new Soviet order, unparalleled in anti-

Communist eastern Europe, indicated that there was ample room for an alliance between the more modernized groups within Russian Jewry and communism. If such an alliance implied the need to distance oneself from traditional Judaism and traditional economic behavior, this was regarded by many as a legitimate price to pay for equality. Moreover, if many Jewish organizations now found themselves outside the law, a new collective identity—secular and based on Yiddish culture—was actually encouraged by the government and by its Jewish arm, the Yevsektsia. No wonder then that so many Jews so fervently identified with the new regime.[6]

And yet, despite voices of optimism in the capitals of eastern Europe, from Prague to Moscow, there was from the very beginning of the interwar period no lack of indications that all was not well with Jewish-Gentile relations in a region where, after all, anti-Semitic traditions going back to the Middle Ages were generally stronger than in the west. So far as non-Communist eastern Europe is concerned, it was evident already in 1918–19 that the dramatic triumph of integral nationalism constituted a grave danger to the Jewish communities. The new or semi-new states of the region gained their legitimacy by virtue of the all-conquering doctrine of nationalism, and virtually all were dominated by elites who were convinced that the new states' raison d'être was to further the interests (however defined) of the dominant ethnic group. Such slogans as "Poland for the Poles" and "Romania for the Romanians" were extremely popular and perfectly natural. Why else, after all, had these peoples shed their blood during the years of war and national insurrection? Such sentiments coexisted uneasily with the multinational character of most of the new states—Poland was one-third non-Polish, Romania more than one-fourth non-Romanian, and so forth. But the leaders of the new states, with the possible exception of Tomáš Masaryk, had no intention of sharing the resources of their countries, which were meager enough to begin with, with the national minorities, who were often regarded as traitors dedicated to revision of the postwar territorial settlement. Thus the 4 million Ukrainians in Poland, the 1.5 million Hungarians in Romania, and the Polish minority in Lithuania were seen as potential fifth columnists and were often treated as such. Everywhere in the region national tensions ran high, feeding chauvinistic tendencies on the part of the dominant nations and representing a constant source of instability.[7]

The implications of all this for the Jewish minority were clear from the outset. In Europe in general, extreme nationalism was almost invariably accompanied by anti-Semitism, and this was especially the case in eastern Europe. The triumph of integral nationalism meant, almost automatically, the triumph of anti-Semitism. "Poland for the Poles" was obviously an anti-Semitic slogan, just as it was an anti-Ukrainian slogan. It meant that the Polish state had no intention of honoring any commitments it might have made to national Jewish rights (why should the Polish state fund Hebrew or Yiddish schools?) and it also meant that the Jews, like the other national minorities, would not be regarded as truly equal citizens of the state. There was yet another important implication—namely, that even those Jews who wanted to become Poles by nationality and to identify themselves as such would not be allowed to do so. Integral nationalism of the type triumphant in postwar eastern Europe was definitely of the exclusivist type. Very few leading Polish, Romanian, and Hungarian politicians were prepared to regard the Jews as an assimilable element.[8]

Also ominous, from the Jewish point of view, were certain aspects of the new territorial settlement in eastern Europe. There were examples of the transfer of Jews from relatively benevolent to very hostile environments (in Bukovina, the most striking example of all, but also in Galicia and Transylvania). It was often the case in these and other regions that the Jews, caught between conflicting national movements, came to be identified in their new political environment as supporters of the national enemy. This was the case in those Lithuanian areas attached in Poland, where the Jews were regarded as being pro-Lithuanian; in Poznań, where Jews were identified with the German enemy; and in Slovakia, where Jews were regarded as being pro-Hungarian. This was also true in the new areas annexed by Romania, where Jews were perceived as being pro-Magyar (in Transylvania), pro-German (in Bukovina), and pro-Bolshevik (in Bessarabia).[9]

The devastation, class warfare, and foreign invasions which characterized the immediate postwar situation were also ominous developments so far as the minorities, and perhaps especially the Jews, were concerned. The Communist threat to the conservative regimes of eastern Europe was everywhere identified with the "Jewish menace" in Hungary in 1919, when the Jews made up so high a percentage of the leadership within the short-lived Communist regime; in Poland in 1920, where Jews were accused of welcoming the invading Bolshevik forces: and in Romania, whose problematic province of Bessarabia was seen as a bridgehead of "Jewish bolshevism." Civil strife, widespread suffering, and invasions did not guide the new states of the region toward tolerance and pluralism.

74

The reverse was the case. And if this was true in those states which by all standards had greatly profited from the new territorial settlement, so much more was it true of the losers, of which Hungary was the prime example.[10]

Underlying the national and social conflicts of the immediate post-war period were severe structural weaknesses in the new states, weaknesses which also augured ill for the Jewish minority. Nowhere in the region, again with the possible exception of Czechoslovakia, was there a deep-seated liberal, tolerant, pluralistic political tradition, and the socialist left, which was not philo-Semitic but was nevertheless usually committed to the campaign against anti-Semitism, was weak and divided. The social elites which ran the new states, including the landowning and clerical elements, were for the most part historically very anti-Semitic. No less important was the economic backwardness of the region, accentuated by the five years of war and the collapse of the Austrian and Russian markets. In such circumstances the economically high visible and highly vulnerable Jewish minority could easily be singled out as the main target by local nationalists who wanted to cleanse the economy of "foreign domination" and assist in the creation of a new, "native" middle class.[11]

It is generally the case that the Jewish minority, in order to flourish, requires the existence of tolerant, liberal, stable, and economically viable regimes and societies. None of these characteristics were much in evidence in most of the states in non-Communist eastern Europe. Nor were they in evidence in Soviet Russia. But there the triumph, at least in the short run, of internationalist communism rather than integral nationalism, the destruction of traditional elites, and the commitment to dynamic economic growth at all costs, created an environment favorable to the particular (though not to the collective) Jewish interest. The division of eastern Europe into Communist and non-Communist zones was of great moment to the Jewish population and led, by the end of our period, to the creation of something approaching a "western-type" Jewry in the Communist zone. I shall return to this point later on.

Given the above-described general atmosphere in eastern Europe, it should come as no surprise that there was a great deal of anti-Jewish violence. In 1918 through 1920 there were a number of bloody anti-Jewish riots in Poland, including pogroms in such cities as Lvov and Vilna which had, in the prewar period, never experienced such disturbances.[12] In Hungary, where there had been during the old regime scarcely any pogroms on the Russian model, a "white terror" directed against the left and the Jews (generally regarded as synonymous) broke out during 1919–20.[13] There were anti-Semitic incidents too in such regions as Bohemia, Slovakia, and Lithuania.[14] And, of course, worst of all, there was the slaughter of thousands of Jews in the hotly contested Ukraine.[15] These events constituted a clear warning to the Jewish population, and in many cases destroyed the confidence within the Jewish community that the establishment of the new order in eastern Europe signaled the coming of better times. "Poland, we who are about to die salute you," we read in the Jewish press in Poland in 1919, and similar statements and sentiments are easy to locate.[16] I would interpret the events of 1918 through 1920 as the first round in the anti-Jewish campaign of the interwar years. These events, far more than the promises inscribed in the various democratic constitutions and in the Minorities Treaty, reflected the reality of the new east European environment so far as the Jews were concerned.

Let me turn now to a brief discussion of several case studies of Jewish-Gentile relations in eastern Europe in the interwar period, beginning with the extraordinarily interesting and symptomatic example of Hungary. Before World War I, Hungary was justly regarded as a kind of "paradise for the Jews." The Hungarian "liberal" old regime regarded the Jews as loyal Magyars in the bitter struggle for Hungarian domination in the multinational empire and as invaluable partners in the economic modernization of the land. Popular and political anti-Semitism was officially opposed by the political elite, which was chiefly composed of the great magnate families. Thanks to this unique set of circumstances, Jews prospered as nowhere else in eastern Europe, and came to play a remarkable, unprecedented role in commerce, industry, the professions, and intellectual life.[17] Indeed, in Hungary there was more truth to the familiar accusation of "Jewish domination" than anywhere else in the region. And it comes as no surprise that Hungarian Jewry was nearly unanimous in its condemnation of modern Jewish nationalism and in its deeply felt attachment to the Hungarian nation, culture, and political leadership. After the war everything changed. Violent anti-Semitism erupted during the white terror, and in 1920 Hungary became the first country in the new eastern Europe to introduce anti-Jewish legislation—the notorious *numerus clausus* law. The "restoration" of the 1920s brought with it a certain relaxation of tensions, but the old Jewish-magnate alliance, which was expressed in a basically pro-Jewish policy on the part of the elite, was not reconstructed. In 1932 an avowedly anti-Jewish regime under the leadership of Gyula Gömbös took power, and beginning with

1938 a series of anti-Jewish laws brought about the official abolition of Jewish emancipation won in 1868 and the relegation of the Jewish minority to the status of a despised and humiliated racial minority.[18]

How is this dramatic turnabout in Jewish-Gentile relations to be explained? Its most fundamental cause was the clearly terrible national trauma suffered by the Hungarian nation, which upset forever the stability of the old regime and brought forth new social and political forces based on a new, exclusive nationalist worldview and bent on revision both of the Trianon Treaty and of the traditional Hungarian social and political order. Other causes are also easy to identify—the overwhelmingly "Jewish" nature of Béla Kun's regime, the transformation of Hungary into a nation-state which no longer needed its Jewish citizens to write "Hungarian" on census returns, and the economic crisis accentuated by the loss of empire and by the influx of numerous Hungarians from the lost territories. The prosperous Jewish minority, regarded as an ally by the confident magnates of the old regime, now came to be regarded as the enemy by extreme Hungarian nationalists intent on purging Hungarian society of "non-Hungarian" elements generally regarded as responsible for the terrible social dislocations of the 1918–20 period. As the interwar period progressed, these extreme nationalists grew more and more powerful.

Interwar Hungary was characterized by the fateful political struggle between what might be termed the "moderate" right and the extreme right (the left, totally discredited by the revolutionary events of 1918–19, was virtually nonexistent). The "moderates" were represented by such leaders as Istvan Bethlen, symbol of the restoration of the 1920s, and by the regent Horthy. These men were, to be sure, out-and-out revisionists and fierce anti-Communists, but they strongly opposed extremist behavior, were often prowestern, and so far as the Jewish question was concerned, were willing to distinguish between "good Hungarian Jews," loyal Magyar citizens, and "bad Jews," who were often identified with the so-called "Galician invasion" which had brought to Hungary undesirable east European Jews of the sort who supported Béla Kun.[19] These moderate men were challenged from the right by a new force in Hungarian politics, almost unknown before the war—populist, anti–old regime, antiurban (meaning anti-Budapest), chauvinistic, and extreme revisionist. The leader of this camp was the above-mentioned Gömbös, who in 1933 became the first foreign prime minister to visit the newly elected Chancellor Hitler in Berlin.

In the decisive struggle between the moderate right and the extreme right, the Jewish question played a cardinal role. The moderates, while often perceived as protectors of the Jews, were prepared to sacrifice the Jewish interest, at least to some extent, in order to mollify the extremists, who vociferously demanded the curtailment of Jewish rights and the "Magyarization" of the economy. The Jews themselves, or at least their official leaders, were obliged to accept the sacrifice, having nowhere else to turn save to the moderates grouped around Horthy. Thus, the 1920 *numerus clausus* law, passed by the moderates under pressure from below, was "accepted" by the Jews as a necessary concession which, so they hoped and so they were promised, would be eventually repealed.

During the 1930s the contest between the radical right and moderate right tilted toward the radicals. The economic depression and the emerging alliance with Nazi Germany, the only European power which appeared able and willing to enforce revision of the hated Trianon Treaty, fed the growing radical-right movement, whose leader, as we have noted, was made prime minister in 1932. Gömbös turned out to be less anti-Jewish than was originally feared, but the handwriting was on the wall. It is no accident that the real turning point, 1938, the year of the first anti-Jewish law, was also the year in which the revision of Trianon was begun with the German-arbitrated return of parts of Slovakia and Subcarpathian Ruthenia. The Hungarian moderates were not entirely routed until 1944, when Hungarian fascism rose to power with the help of Nazi bayonets, but their desire to protect the Jews, while not disappearing altogether, grew ever weaker. The assimilated, prosperous, loyal Magyar Jews of the pre-1914 era had been reduced, by 1944, to a terrorized minority bereft of legal protection.[20]

Let me try to summarize the factors which led to the inexorable deterioration of the Jewish condition in Hungary: a national and social trauma of unprecedented dimensions; the decline of the pro-Jewish old-regime establishment; the rise of the extreme nationalistic right inspired (but not created) by Nazi Germany and aided by the economic crisis; the contest between the moderate and radical right in which the Jewish interest was constantly sacrificed. The Jews themselves, no less assimilated and patriotic at the end of our period than at its beginning, could only cling to the moderates for support, but these men proved of little assistance.[21] In short, Hungary serves as a remarkable example of how the new environment of the interwar years served to transform what was a "paradise for the Jews" into something of a Jewish hell.

The case of interwar Poland, with the largest of all east European Jewish populations, was in some ways rather different from that of Hungary. Here there was no drastic contrast to the prewar period so far as Jewish-Gentile relations were concerned. The immediate prewar period in all three of the partitioned areas witnessed a deterioration of Jewish-Polish relations.[22] In all these regions, in contrast to prewar Hungary, Polish nationalism bore a distinctly anti-Semitic cast, best expressed by Roman Dmowski's powerful National Democratic Party. The new Polish state maintained this tradition. Indeed, now that the Poles had obtained full independence at last, they were in a position to implement an anti-Jewish policy which had been, at least to some extent, most notably in Galicia, blunted by the partitioning powers.

It is true that Poland, on the face of things, was in a happier situation than Hungary. The Poles were among the biggest winners of all the peoples of eastern Europe in the postwar period, having established against all odds a strong, relatively cohesive state with few burning territorial ambitions and an interest in maintaining the status quo. Nonetheless, in many ways Poland's interwar development was not unlike that of the other states of the region, including Hungary. Here too the reigning ideology was exclusivist nationalism, and here too those groups not belonging to the dominant nationality (Ukrainians, Belorussians, Jews, and Germans, who together constituted about one-third of the population) were from the very beginning regarded as disloyal and dangerous elements. Here too the political elite, with the possible exception of the socialist leaders, who at any rate were largely excluded from power, believed that the Poles had shed their blood in order to establish an exclusive Polish nation-state, and that the Poles should be the only beneficiaries of the new order. In Poland, as in the other states of the region, liberalism and pluralism were fragile growths under constant attack in the wake of the devastation of war, violent clashes with the minorities, foreign invasion which characterized the early years of the state, and economic crisis.

In the Polish context, Marshal Józef Piłsudski represented the forces of the moderate right, protecting to some extent the minorities and particularly the Jews from the forces of the extreme right. But during the 1930s, which were characterized by severe economic depression and growing social tensions, the marshal and his followers within the Sanacja were challenged by the radical right. As in Hungary, so in Poland the contest between the moderate and the extreme right (represented by the Endecja and its more radical offshoots) raised the Jewish question to new heights of intensity.[23]

Polish Jewry, mostly lower-middle-class and proletarian, Orthodox, and unassimilated, was more vulnerable to the anti-Jewish campaign than was Hungarian Jewry. From the very outset of the interwar period Jews were rigorously excluded from all sectors of the economy over which the state had control. Heavy taxes on the urban sector and the law prohibiting work on Sunday also struck at the Jewish interest, as did the unofficial but effective *numerus clausus* at Polish universities and high schools.[24] Already in the 1920s Jewish leaders spoke, with some exaggeration, of the "economic extermination" of Polish Jewry, and by the 1930s it was customary to speak of the new Jewish generation as consisting of "youths without a future."[25] Quite early on Jews began to look back with nostalgia, if not to Czarist Russia, then at least to the times of Franz Josef, when Galician Jewry enjoyed equality and was able to enter both institutions of higher learning and the bureaucracy. The obvious contrast between the Jewish condition in prewar Galicia, part of a relatively tolerant multinational empire, and the Jewish experience in interwar Polish Galicia, when the nation-state ruled supreme, illustrates how the new order in eastern Europe was inimical to the Jewish interest.

The 1930s in Poland witnessed a dramatic escalation of the anti-Jewish campaign. The political and clerical leaders agreed that the Jews would have to leave Poland, and they also agreed that almost any means aimed at weakening the Jewish "domination" of the economy was justified. The boycott against Jewish shops was renewed, and numerous anti-Jewish disturbances occurred.[26] No explicitly anti-Jewish legislation was passed, but by the late 1930s a politically unstable and socially turbulent Polish state had made it clear that it had totally abandoned the democratic and tolerant prescriptions of its 1921 constitution.

Let me now turn very briefly to the interesting and instructive case of Lithuania, Poland's small neighbor to the north which had, most unexpectedly, received independence as a consequence of the Great War. In sharp contrast to Poland, the prognosis regarding Jewish-Gentile relations in this new state was very good. The Lithuanians, unlike the Poles, Hungarians, and Romanians, were a small and weak nationality which felt the need for allies from any conceivable direction, including the large Lithuanian Jewish community. The Jews, for their part, regarded the Lithuanians, with justice, as bearers of a less anti-Semitic tradition than the Poles, Russians, and Ukrainians, and welcomed the idea of a Jewish-Lithuanian alliance dedicated to the establishment of a large Lithuanian state with its capital in Vilna.[27] Such a state did not, in fact, come into being, but in the small "Kaunas Lithuania" Jews were granted not only emancipation but also a remarkable degree of national

autonomy, including the right to a minister for Jewish affairs in the government and complex institutions of representation. It appeared to many
that Lithuania was well on the way to becoming what Jews had hoped
would emerge elsewhere in the region—a true "state of nationalities"
rather than a narrowly defined nation-state of the intolerant Polish,
Hungarian, or Romanian type.

And yet, while the Jews were surely better off in Lithuania than in
Poland, here too the tolerant, pluralistic settlement of the immediate
postwar period did not last. Lithuania also moved quickly to the right,
the institutions of Jewish autonomy were rapidly dismantled, instances
of anti-Semitism increased, and the Jewish economic condition deterio-
rated.[28] In Lithuania, as elsewhere, the atmosphere grew more and more
nationalistic, less tolerant, less pleasant for the national minorities. The
special conditions of the Lithuanian national movement may have dictated a friendly attitude toward the Jewish minority in the early 1920s,
but in the last analysis the difference between Poland and Lithuania
proved to be one of degree, not of kind.

The real exception in eastern Europe was Czechoslovakia. To be
sure, there was a strong anti-Semitic tradition in the Czech lands, and
an even stronger one in Slovakia, where Jews were regarded not only as
economic oppressors but as faithful allies of the Magyars. And yet Czechoslovak Jewry during the interwar period was surely justified in regarding
itself as uniquely privileged, and as enjoying an excellent relationship
with the regime. The ruling elite in this state refrained from using anti-
Semitism as a weapon in the internal political struggle. It was only after
Munich, during the short-lived Second Republic, which existed under
highly abnormal conditions, that anti-Semitism came to the fore.[29]

Why was Czechoslovakia the great exception? Two major factors
were at work here. For one thing, the Czechs possessed a much stronger
liberal political tradition than their neighbors in eastern Europe, a tradition which grew up in the Hapsburg empire. It is worthy of note that
Masaryk, who exemplified this liberal tradition, was the only great interwar east European politician who was actually friendly to the Jews' aspirations both for true equality and for national renaissance.[30] Second,
Czechoslovakia was an economic success—it was considerably richer
than its neighbors to the west, and the stability which derived from a
strong economy was certainly a blessing for the Jewish minority, among
other reasons because it helped to prevent the emergence of a strong
fascist movement.[31] It is true, of course, that not all the national minorities were delighted with Czech predominance in the new state, and one

can certainly exaggerate the degree to which the country was an island of democracy and toleration in the chaotic, nationalistic, east European sea. Nevertheless, so long as Masaryk and his allies remained in positions of influence, the "Czech-Jewish alliance" forged in 1918 proved much more effective and beneficial to both sides than the "Lithuanian-Jewish alliance" formed with such enthusiasm in the same year.

Finally, a word on the Soviet Union and its large Jewish minority. No greater contrast to bourgeois, liberal, capitalist Czechoslovakia can be imagined, and yet, as I have already mentioned, this totalitarian state was also a favorable environment for individual Jews, if not for Jewry in the collective. During the interwar period the Soviet Union was not an anti-Semitic state, and for much of the time it actively combated anti-Semitism.[32] Thanks to this fact, to the dynamic economic growth of the country, and to the desperate need for capable people to run the new, extensive bureaucracy, numerous Jews began that process of upward mobility which was, in the long run, to transform Russian Jewry from a lower-middle-class and proletarian community into a professional and middle-class group, on the pattern of west European and American rather than of Polish Jewry.[33] The interwar Soviet experience demonstrates that Jews are capable of flourishing even in despotic regimes, so long as these regimes do not violate the ideology of careers open to talent. The danger, of course, is that sooner or later such regimes, for one reason or another, tend to turn against religious and national minorities, as in fact happened in the Soviet Union during and after World War II. This more recent and tragic chapter in the history of Soviet Jewry lies outside the scope of this paper.

In conclusion, let me return to the questions posed at the outset. I have argued here that during the interwar period non-Communist eastern Europe was a uniquely hostile environment for Jews as individuals, though it was certainly a favorable one so far as autonomous Jewish culture and politics was concerned. The deterioration of the Jews' condition was not the result of the rise of nazism, although the latter event certainly had a great impact. By the 1930s it was clear to the citizens of most east European countries that the Jews were second-class citizens, possessing few if any rights, legitimate targets for organized attacks; in this sense the interwar period did, in my view, constitute a prelude to the Holocaust, although it is no less true that the Poles, Hungarians, Romanians, and other ruling nationalities of the region did not foresee or promote a Nazi-type policy, preferring to encourage mass emigration and gradual elimination of Jews from economic and cultural life.[34] The

basic causes of this uniquely hostile environment were the extreme nationalistic atmosphere, the social and national upheavals in the immediate postwar period, the near total failure of democracy and liberalism,
and the collapse of the economy in the 1930s. In Soviet Russia, on the
other hand, special conditions deriving from Bolshevik ideology and
practice created a temporarily favorable environment for Jews, while at
the same time stifling collective Jewish activities in the religious, cultural, and political arenas.

I would add, finally, that the obvious fact that there existed different
types of Jewish communities in eastern Europe had little impact on the
nature of Jewish-Gentile relations. The highly acculturated and mostly
assimilated Jewish community of Hungary was regarded with more hatred
than the wholly unacculturated and unassimilated Jewish community of
Lithuania. Soviet Jews were largely unacculturated at the beginning of
the interwar period, but this was not held against them, and the favorable environment in that country induced them to Russify very rapidly.
It is possible that the relatively small, middle-class, and acculturated
nature of Bohemian-Moravian Jewry had something to do with failure of
anti-Semitism to become a major political factor in that region, but I
would place far more emphasis on the external environment than on
Jewish characteristics and behavior. The triumph of unbridled nationalism after World War I and the rapid decline of democracy was perhaps
not an unadulterated disaster for the Jews—it certainly strengthened
Jewish political movements such as Zionism, which now became a truly
mass movement for the first time. But it had a disastrous effect on Jewish-
Gentile relations in the countries of mass Jewish settlement in eastern
Europe, and it helped pave the way for Nazi mass murder.

5

Nazi Actions Concerning the Jews Between the Beginning of World War II and the German Attack on the USSR

UWE DIETRICH ADAM

I

The topic of this essay constitutes a period of special interest in conjunction with one of the colloquium's objectives—the question as to the origin and development of this most extraordinary case of genocide. Even before the outbreak of the war, elimination of German Jews from political, cultural, economic, and professional spheres had already been accomplished as anticipated in the Nazi Party platform. Thus, the period between September 1939 and June 1941, the latter marking the stopping of German troops outside Moscow, can also be regarded as a succession of steps that ended with the "Final Solution." However, even the chronological placing of an order to carry out the "Final Solution" constitutes a classic dating problem in both German and world history. Here I am not referring to that literature in which the massacres are made innocuous or are denied altogether;[1] neither do I intend to delve into the literature that does not take Hitler, but rather Himmler, as the initiator and executor of the "Final Solution."[2] By the same token, I shall not concern myself further with the conjecture that Hitler may have sought the Jews' physical extermination as the ultimate racist objective even as early as the end of the First World War or the days of *Mein Kampf,* and pursued this systematically and over the course of a long period of time.[3] I agree with the overwhelming majority of historians that an order to wipe out the Jews under German control, in whatever form it may have taken, was not given or even planned until the beginning of the war.

Since it has not been possible so far to give documentary proof of such an order and, judging from the sources tried until now, it does not appear likely that such proof will ever turn up, the job is left to the historian to determine a more accurate date for such an order through interpretation. Since this is being done by different methods and hypotheses, we have a considerable range of opinion as to the time at which a decision of Hitler's could have been given. One estimate places the conception of the "Final Solution" in the time of Landsberg (Jäckel, Dawidowicz),[4] others fix the time as March 1941 (Krausnick) or July 1941 (Wilbert, Browning),[5] and another indicates late autumn 1941 (Adam, Broszat).[6]

Neither the legislative nor the administrative steps taken by the Third Reich itself against the Jews may be considered appropriate means of answering the question as to the possible date for an extermination order. But if one is familiar with the institutional structure of the Reich after the war broke out, knowing which steps were taken narrows down the possibilities for interpretation and even provides grounds for the elimination of certain dates or the confirmation of other ones with a greater degree of certainty. If one does not confine such a study to the dates at which these steps were made official, but instead includes their genesis in the decision-making process, then one may arrive at indications of the development of Nazi policy toward the Jews.

Other problem areas such as the following have intentionally been excluded from this paper: type and extent of any plans for extermination, or the connection between the ideological components in Hitler's thinking and practical implementations of them.

The term "measure" shall be used in this paper to mean any political, administrative, or legal command with an implicit claim to universal applicability.

II

At the moment of the German attack on Poland, the so-called "Jewish problem" was resolved as far as the party program of the NSDAP (Nazi Party) and the early protagonists of a "völkisch" law were concerned. German Jews had been expelled from all public offices, and were also excluded from every occupation subject to national supervision or regulation. These occupational prohibitions (*Berufsverbote*) were so numerous that Jews had only two alternatives: they could either work for members of their own faith or live from their fortunes. The economic and professional measures found their consummation in the decrees immediately following the Reichskristallnacht.

The withdrawal of all employment possibilities, the seizure of Jewish property, and the strictly exercised control over their investments were among the primary aims of the NSDAP from the beginning and were put into effect before the outbreak of the war.

Other important parts of the party program—the prohibition of "mixed marriages" (*Mischehen*) between Jews and "Aryans," and lower civil and legal status for Jews—were put into effect in the Nuremberg Laws of 1935. For any transgression against these sanctions, Jews were subject to especially harsh criminal laws that were gradually extended throughout the whole private and public sphere.

If it is possible to summarize most of the measures in a general Nazi Party policy against the Jews, we find one dominant and repeated goal: the separation of "Aryans" and Jews. That political and racial target of party ideology—the elimination of the Jews from the German *Volkskor-per*—was achieved in 1938. By official order of the authorities, a curfew could be imposed on Jews and they could be forbidden to enter certain areas.[7] In 1939 in the "*Gesetz über Mietverhältnisse mit Juden,*" the government passed a law creating all prerequisites necessary to force Jewish people to dwell in certain regions or houses.[8] It is really no overstatement to assert that the so-called "Jewish power" or influence was broken before the outbreak of the war.

III

The first known endeavors of German officials regarding the "Jewish question" after the beginning of the war were aimed at preventing any possible connection between "Aryans" and Jews under the conditions of war. On September 1, 1939, a prearranged emergency measure fixed the conditions to be imposed on the already mostly segregated groups: the common use of air-raid shelters was not to be allowed. In subsequent decrees, the Jews were ordered to take care of their own air-raid protection.[9]

These first measures were accompanied by the efforts of various government institutions to fix special times Jews were allowed to leave their homes. On September 10, 1939, the Reichsführer-SS (RFSS; Heinrich Himmler) established an obligatory curfew for the entire Reich.[10] Some community administrations also started to limit the time during which Jews were allowed to purchase food. Since September 1939, Jews had been allowed to purchase their provisions only in specially designated shops, and since January 1940 their ration cards had been marked with a J. They were not allowed to shop in Berlin, for example, before 3:30 P.M.[11]

Otherwise, freedom of movement was not further restricted until being dramatically curtailed on September 1, 1941, in the *Polizeiverordnung über die Kennzeichnung der Juden* (Police Decree for the Marking of Jews).[12] It not only required every Jewish person who had reached the age of seven to wear a "Jewish star" in public, but also prohibited Jews from leaving their community without the written permission of the local police. From the moment the decree was published (we shall return later to the decision-making process leading up to it), it was obvious that policy toward Jews had taken a new turn. Other decisions emphasize this change.

To enforce the *Polizeiverordnung,* the minister of transportation and the Reich Main Security Office (RSHA) regulated transit in the following months by specifying the means and manner of transportation open to Jews. These were gradually restricted by the RSHA and eliminated altogether in March 1942.[13]

In the area of food and clothing, which had been rationed for everyone immediately after the outbreak of the war, Jews received visibly worse treatment starting in December 1939. They received smaller special rations of meat and fat products, and the sale of cocoa and chocolate products to them was completely forbidden.[14] As the war continued, special rations were shortened more and more. Jews received no textiles, shoes, or leather goods because they were not eligible for cloth ration cards after January 1940. A minor food cutback in August 1941 was followed in September 1942 by the permanent cancellation of all rations for meat, eggs, milk and milk products, tobacco, and tropical fruits. Jewish children's rations were shortened in the same way.[15]

Besides all restrictions on freedom of movement and the shortening of food rations, in the first months of the war the regime hit the Jews particularly hard in the field of communications. A sign of the changing power relationships among Reich authorities concerned with the Jewish question was already visible in September 1939. While the ministries conferred about a decree concerning the confiscation of all radios belonging to Jews, the RFSS, less interested in such administrative discussion, "suddenly" ordered the Gestapo to confiscate the radios on September 23, 1939. The Jews were forbidden to buy new ones.[16] Before the end of the second year of the war, they were deprived of the last possibilities of communication inside their ghettolike environment. Effective September 30, 1939, all telephones used by Jews were disconnected; few exceptions were permitted.[17]

The exploitation of the labor power of the Jews, who had been mostly unemployed, was both an economic and an ideological problem. Economic pragmatists fought for a comprehensive labor program, while the ideologically convinced racial dogmatists were afraid of renewed and increased contact between "Aryans" and Jews and that the Security Police would lose effective control of the Jews. This struggle influenced the measures of the regime significantly.

After the minister of the interior pointed out the possibility of deploying Jewish labor in a secret directive in October 1939, the question was immediately raised as to whether there were not other possibilities. While the ministries concerned began to consider this question, the minister of labor affirmed his intention to increase the use of the Jewish work force.[18]

The first effort by the Ministry of Labor concerning a special status for working Jews, a draft of a decree submitted in April 1940 to the Council of Ministers for the Defense of the Reich, was laid aside by the Reich Chancellery and by Göring in his capacity as Plenipotentiary for the Four-Year Plan (Beauftragter für den Vierjahresplan, BVP). Although Göring had agreed to take charge of the affair, he chose not to do so and the labor minister was forced to take things into his own hands. In a proclamation of June 3, 1940, he ordered that Jews no longer be granted certain employment or social benefits.[19] The minister in charge maintained that his proclamation did not interfere with the legal employment guarantees and that Jews were only denied certain social advantages.

In late autumn of 1940, the Gestapo began to register all unemployed able-bodied Jews between the ages of eighteen and fifty-five in a special work program. This measure again affected the legal status of the forced laborers. The party commission called the Stellvertreter des Führers (StdF), headed by Martin Bormann, submitted "urgent wishes" to the labor minister, which led to a denial of wages and exclusion from Labor

Court jurisdiction. During an interministerial conference held on January 8, 1941, nearly all participating ministers, especially the BVP, opposed these plans and refused to consent to them. They insisted on a general codification of special Jewish labor laws, which would have been an impossible undertaking in the face of the complex legal factors involved. The differences between the ministers could not be resolved.[20] Finally, a nonbinding program was agreed upon: Jews had to take any job assigned to them by the employment offices, and the employer-employee relationship was to be "*sui generis,*" disregarding the regulations in effect. For the rest, the minister of labor and the StdF realized that nothing further could be done against the opposition of other ministers and the BVP, so the labor minister published his proclamation of June 1940 unchanged as a provisional decree on February 19, 1941.[21]

Still, the minister felt himself caught between two sides and tried to reach a compromise which would satisfy the StdF also. In March 1941 he informed the Reich ministers that he did not intend to refuse Jews the right to wages and other labor benefits, but wanted to fulfill the request of the StdF to exclude them from the jurisdiction of the Labor Court. The first result of this letter was a sharp protest by the minister of justice, who wished to retain the procedure of examining and enforcing the social rights of Jews.[22]

During the following months, in the spring of 1941, the proponents of the pragmatic and the ideological positions clashed over special labor regulations for Jews. On January 8, 1941, Heydrich had ordered the deportation of 90,000 Jews from the Warthegau into the General Government. Because of the lack of transportation and the resistance of Governor-General Hans Frank, only 17,000 were arrested and deported. The Reich governor of the Warthegau, Arthur Greiser, eager to remove "his" Jews under any circumstances, evidently approached Göring and offered him more than 70,000 Jews to be used as forced laborers in the Reich. Göring, obviously a man not bound to sentiments of racial ideology if he was able to raise production, accepted the offer and gave a secret order to the commissioner for the defense of the Reich (Reichsverteidigungskommissar) to eliminate all obstacles preventing the employment of Jews. Following this order, the labor minister gave instructions to the offices under his jurisdiction concerning the employment, transportation, and separate accommodations of these Jews and pointed out that, due to the general situation, Germany could not afford not to employ these workers.[23]

This decision, dictated by the requirements of the war, to address the

"Jewish question" in a more rational way, taking into account the conditions of war but guaranteeing some legal protection and a certain amount of remuneration, was stopped quickly and brutally. In April 1941, Hitler prohibited the employment of foreign Jews in Germany.[24]

Meanwhile, the labor minister and the BVP took another six months to unite on a common policy. It was another compromise. On October 3, 1941, the BVP signed the *Verordnung über die Beschäftigung von Juden* (Decree Concerning the Employment of Jews), which declared in vague terms that Jews were in an "employment relationship of a special kind." The labor minister, who had been authorized to issue this decree, the fulfillment of the demands of the StdF from late autumn of 1940, published the new order on October 31, 1941. Essentially, it repeated the regulations which had been published in June 1940, but contained some important new restrictions: Jews were not entitled to sick pay, and vacations were unpaid. Any arrangements for social welfare or old-age pensions were forbidden. Jewish laborers no longer fell under the protection of labor rights, and Jewish children were no longer protected by juvenile laws.[25]

There was some discussion in late autumn of 1941 as to whether and to what extent this decree should be valid in the newly incorporated eastern regions of Germany. The representative of the labor ministry did not succeed in defending the position of his ministry that the decree referred to all Jews working in "free employment." It is noteworthy that the decree was not extended to cover the occupied and incorporated zones of former Poland.[26]

Without a doubt, the decree of the labor minister of October 31, 1941, on the employment of Jews meant a dramatic change in Jewish policy. If we compare the rights of a Jewish worker in June 1940 and in October 1941, we see that his legal status was weakening. The minister tried to regulate the employment of Jews in a last, almost comical effort on December 19, 1941. He asked all bureaus under him to protect Jewish workers against molestation by the Gestapo.[27] A month later during the Wannsee Conference, Heydrich proclaimed the real goal: destruction by labor.

An even more interesting example of the measures against the Jews is the *Polizeiverordnung über die Kennzeichnung der Juden* of September 1, 1941, mentioned above.[28] The origin and history of this decree are informative in many respects on the development of anti-Jewish policy during the war years.

A first proposal to identify the Jews in public with special symbols was made by Heydrich on November 12, 1938. At the conference following the Reichskristallnacht, the chief of the Security Police suggested a special mark for the better identification of Jews. Heydrich's proposal was nothing but a countermove to Göring's suggestion to place Jews in ghettos.[29] Hitler had to decide now between two proposals, either to build ghettos—as Göring wanted—or to mark every Jew. Heydrich was opposed to ghettos because he doubted the use of fencing off these areas from their surroundings. Hitler himself turned down both plans during a gauleiter conference on December 6, 1938.[30]

As was already the case in certain regions, it was ordered by the governer-general of Poland on November 23, 1939, that all Jews were to wear the so-called "Jewish star" (*Judenstern*) on a band around their right arm in public. The gauleiter of Saxony, Albert Mutschmann, wanted to introduce a similar measure for the Jews of the Reich and applied to the minister of the interior. The minister denied this request at once, pointing to Hitler's decision. In August 1940 the minister received confirmation of Hitler's negative position on this question.[31]

In 1941 the question suddenly received new importance. Independently of each other, certain authorities had become active. In April 1941, Goebbels expressed his consent for such plans and informed the public that he had given the instructions to his civil servants to create a badge so that every Jew of Berlin would be marked. Karl-Hermann Frank, secretary of state in the Protectorate of Bohemia and Moravia, asked the Reich Chancellory in June 1941 for permission to mark the Jews of his region. The Chancellory replied that the führer had forbidden the marking of Jews living within the boundaries of the Reich, and that it would be impossible to institute in Bohemia-Moravia a measure like that in the General Government.[32]

At the same time, the RSHA was also active on this question. At a conference on August 15, Adolf Eichmann informed the other ministries about the efforts of his police bureaucracy. He announced to his colleagues that he had sent a corresponding request to Reichsmarschall Göring, who insisted that Hitler had the final authority. Eichmann added that nothing could be done by the RSHA to gain access to Bormann, who could deliver a decree directly to Hitler.[33]

In the meantime, Goebbels succeeded in asserting that the responsibility for this question lay in his ministry. His state secretary invited all participating ministries to a conference at which all aspects of the Jewish question were to be discussed. In addition to certain discriminatory measures confining the lives of the Jews, he also proposed marking them with an identifying symbol.

Although the representatives of the BVP and the Ministry of the Interior insisted on their fundamental right to rule on this question, the only result was a comment by the secretary of propaganda that his ministry was responsible for resolving every issue which threatened to disturb the common order. Therefore, he proposed to submit a report to Hitler on the bad influence of the Jews.[34] The representative of the Interior Ministry recognized at once that a report from Goebbels would constitute the final decision on the marking of Jews. While he was attempting to convince his minister to exclude at least the mixed marriages (*Mischehen*), he was informed that Goebbels had already spoken to Hitler. Hitler had basically agreed to all the plans, especially those to mark the Jews in the *Altreich* (Germany within the boundaries of 1937), which was a prerequisite for all other measures.[35]

The Ministry of the Interior, truly convinced that responsibility had shifted to the Ministry of the Propaganda, was still busy attempting to participate in the realization of the decree.[36] At the end of August 1941 the ministry heard with amazement that the responsibility of working out a draft had suddenly been given to the RSHA. Heydrich's police authority prepared the draft with such speed that the Interior Ministry barely succeeded in inserting a special exception for certain privileged mixed marriages before the decree was signed on September 1, 1941. The decree not only forced all Jews over six years old to wear a Star of David in public but also to give back any medals of honor, orders, or decorations they had received.[37]

IV

All tax disadvantages for Jews, even those from before the war, were retained and intensified. In 1939, with few exceptions, Jews fell into the highest tax bracket. This special taxation was increased by special laws throughout the following years. The finance minister aggravated the existing inequality in an edict of February 10, 1940, which denied any tax deductions or exemptions to Poles and Jews.[38] In the same month the minister planned a special tax for the Czechs and Poles, but extended it under pressure from the StdF to include Jews too. He abandoned his plan and limited his edict to Polish people living within the Reich after the

Foreign Ministry criticized the equal treatment of Poles, Czechs, and Jews.[39] As a "Christmas gift," so to speak, the finance minister extended this special tax to Jews in an edict of December 24, 1941. This meant a 15 percent increase in income taxes.[40]

The relatively protracted period that can be observed between the first discussion of anti-Jewish measures and their final legal settlement can be explained not only by the anarchic decision-making process in the Third Reich, but also as the expression of a common uncertainty about the guiding political principles of Nazi Jewish policy. In this context the *Kriegsschädenverordnung* (Decree Concerning War Damages) of November 30, 1940,[41] is a very good example of the slow-working and almost hesitant legislative process we have already described. This decree provided for financial compensation for property damages caused by the war, but was to be applied to Jews according to special directions. Indeed, the interior minister assumed that Jews were permitted to file requests for compensation.[42] A definite regulation of the treatment of Jews was not reached until July 1941, when a very short decree ordered that Jews were not permitted to apply for or receive compensation for war damages.[43]

It is impossible to recognize deeper political intention or calculation in this or in most other legal decisions. Shortsighted considerations, offices which thought themselves powerful enough to force through an issue, an accidental or intentional utterance by Hitler—these and other imponderables formed and characterized the anti-Jewish policy to a large degree. The lack of unity and the erratic shifts in this legislation were influenced not least of all by the fact that there existed no central authority able to coordinate, administer, or direct all the anti-Jewish measures. Even though the RSHA claimed authority in this matter from 1938 until 1941, when it was, in fact, responsible for it, its influence on Jewish policy was not complete until events (i.e., the war) rendered its original plans for the treatment of the Jewish question obsolete.

Before the beginning of the war, the Security Service (SD) in particular argued vehemently for a "solution to the Jewish question" by emigration and even obtained Hitler's approval in February 1938.[44] The establishment of the Zentralstelle für jüdische Auswanderung (Central Agency for Jewish Emigration) in January 1939 gave Heydrich a voice in the determination of Jewish policy on the ministerial level. Heydrich pushed the emigration plans of the SD quickly and had his first substantial success in July 1939 when he founded the Reichsvereinigung der Juden in Deutschland (Reich Association of Jews in Germany).[45] Because the Reichsvereinigung was subordinate to the RSHA, he not only succeeded in gaining control over the important Jewish cultural associations, but also became the ultimate authority in all financial and organizational questions of Jewish emigration. But the chief of the RSHA had not reckoned with the anarchic structure of the Third Reich. From 1939 on, the RSHA was forced to lead a constant battle against numerous institutions which laid claims on the property of the Reichsvereinigung.[46] The result of this struggle was that, whereas Heydrich's representative Adolf Eichmann was able to achieve astonishing emigration figures first in Vienna and later in Prague with draconian measures and unhindered by quarreling Reich authorities, there were still more than 180,000 Jews living in the *Altreich* in September 1939.

After the outbreak of the war, we may assume that the policy of the RSHA was in accord with Hitler's intentions to produce a "*judenreines Deutschland*" (Germany purified of Jews) as quickly as possible. This theory is supported by the attempts to push the emigration of Jews, even during the first years of the war. But Hitler's irrational attitude toward the Jews, with his decisions dependent on incalculable aims and the increasing success of his war policy, doubtlessly influenced his personal troops—the SS—and therefore the center of his *Weltanschauungstruppe*, the SD and the RSHA. If we examine the policy of the RSHA more closely, even though it seems incomprehensible at first glance, we recognize that the RSHA tried to realize its emigration policy and at the same time to be Hitler's executor in all questions of *Weltanschauung*.[47] This is the root of the difficulties in analyzing the policy of the RSHA; this institution's policy-making is only an example of the entire general policy of irrationalism in the Third Reich. After all, the SS and especially the RSHA and Heydrich were trapped in an ideology which above all corresponded to the structure in which they were living.

The RSHA followed Hitler's lead in entertaining the belief—which went back to the führer's army days—that the Jews were capable of weakening and destroying the people's defenses. Because Himmler and Heydrich as well as the SS as a whole were bound to Hitler's pathological fear of the Jews as the "enemy inside," they tried to subject their policy to the will of the führer. It was undoubtedly on an order given by Hitler that Himmler personally commanded in October 1939 that every Jew who seemed suspicious and not totally progovernment be arrested and taken to a concentration camp.[48] And surely it was in keeping with this intention in April 1940 that Himmler prohibited the release of any Jewish prisoner for the duration of the war.[49] On the other hand, the RSHA attempted to secure the urgent treatment of the emigration problem. It is true that the emigration fee increased steadily, but at the same time the RSHA worked to weaken the regulation on currency.[50] Contrary to all legal restrictions, the RSHA even permitted the employment of Jews in agriculture "in order to facilitate the emigration of Jews and to give them a professional education."[51]

The RSHA was also able to weaken or abolish a large number of special tax and currency-limitation regulations for the Jews. In December 1940 it succeeded in convincing the Reichswirtschaftsminister to throw all his regulations overboard and to direct his currency and revenue offices and to speed up financial procedures in all emigration cases.[52]

The general purpose of solving the "Jewish question" was still visible in May 1941 when the RSHA tried to obtain a general emigration clause from Göring, an order which later was often interpreted incorrectly because of its content and its wording. Göring directed all institutions to facilitate the emigration of Jews from the Reich, including the Protectorate, as far as possible, even during the war. On the other hand, the emigration of Jews from Belgium and France was to be prevented because of the "final solution doubtlessly coming."[53] This deceptive term "final solution" was interpreted by later generations of historians as meaning physical destruction, but at that time it meant only the emigration of Jews to Madagascar.[54]

Not until August 1941 onward was the net around the Jews drawn tighter. The RSHA imposed an emigration prohibition on able-bodied Jews.[55] At the end of August 1941, Eichmann extended the order to all Jews in the areas occupied by Germany. On October 23, 1941, the RSHA informed all police authorities and the SD of Himmler's order to prohibit the emigration of Jews during the war, without exception.[56]

6

The Decision Concerning the Final Solution

CHRISTOPHER R. BROWNING

The decision concerning the Final Solution has been the subject of a wide variety of historical interpretations. The major differences emerge over two related questions: first, the nature of the decision-making process, with particular focus on the role of Hitler and his ideology; and second, the timing of the decision. Such a variety of interpretations warns us, as Martin Broszat has correctly pointed out, that any thesis concerning the origins of the Final Solution is a matter of probability, not certainty.[1] In this light I present the following thesis. The intention of systematically murdering the European Jews was not fixed in Hitler's mind before the war, but crystallized in 1941 after previous solutions proved unworkable and the imminent attack upon Russia raised the prospect of yet another vast increase in the number of Jews within the growing German empire. The Final Solution emerged out of a series of decisions taken that year. In the spring Hitler ordered preparations for the murder of the Russian Jews who would fall into German hands during the coming invasion. That summer, confident of military victory, Hitler instigated the preparation of a plan to extend the killing process to European Jews. In October, although military expectations had not been

Research for this paper was made possible in part by a grant from the Alexander von Humboldt Foundation.

realized, Hitler approved the rough outline of that plan, involving deportation to killing centers that used poison gas. While I wish to give special attention to the arguments and evidence concerning the course of events in the summer and fall of 1941 that I consider so crucial, let us first briefly review the historiography of the issue.

In recent years interpretations of National Socialism have increasingly polarized into two groups aptly designated by Tim Mason as the "intentionalists" and the "functionalists."[2] The former explain the course of Nazi Germany in terms of Hitler's intentions derived from a coherent and consistent ideology and implemented through an all-powerful totalitarian dictatorship. The latter emphasize the anarchical nature of the Nazi state, its internal competition, and the chaotic decision-making process which resulted in continuous improvisation and radicalization. The intentionalists do not deny the polycratic nature of the Nazi state but portray it as the conscious product of Hitler's Machiavellian cunning, cleverly manipulated to realize his fixed intentions. The functionalists do not deny that Hitler played a central role but see this role as a mobilizing and integrating agent. Thus, for them Hitler's limitless hatred of the Jews and his aggressive and destructive impulses gave an overarching unity of purpose and direction to the chaotic Nazi state but only at the cost of constant radicalization culminating in a *Vernichtungskrieg* (war of annihilation) in the east, genocide of the European Jews, and ultimately overwhelming defeat.[3]

These two modes of historical explanation are useful in analyzing the vastly differing interpretations concerning German Jewish policy in general and the decision for the Final Solution in particular. At one extreme the ultraintentionalist Lucy Dawidowicz has argued that as early as 1919 Hitler decided to exterminate the European Jews. Moreover, he knew when the murderous plan would be implemented. The Second World War was to be both the means and the occasion intended by Hitler to carry out his premeditated, genocidal "war against the Jews." While Hitler awaited the predetermined moment to carry out his "grand design," however, he tolerated a meaningless and irrelevant pluralism in Jewish policy in the lower echelons of the state and party.[4]

If Dawidowicz emphasizes the element of Hitler's premeditation and "grand design," Martin Broszat's ultrafunctionalist view of Hitler's role, particularly concerning the decision for the Final Solution, stresses the opposite. In his view Hitler made no ultimate decision and issued no comprehensive order for the Final Solution. Rather, the program of destruction evolved gradually out of a series of separate killing actions in late 1941 and 1942. These local massacres were improvised responses to an impossible situation created by two factors: first, the ideological and political pressure for a judenrein Europe, exerted above all by Hitler; and second, the military failure on the eastern front that caused a lack of both rail transport and reception areas for the Jews who were to be uprooted. Once underway, the killing program gradually became institutionalized and, having proved itself logistically the simplest solution, grew finally into a comprehensive and distinctive program. In this view Hitler was a catalyst but not the decision-maker.[5]

According to Dawidowicz, conception of the Final Solution preceded implementation by twenty-two years; according to Broszat, conception emerged from practice—the act of sporadically killing groups of Jews gave birth to the idea of systematically killing all Jews. A wide variety of interpretations flourishes between these distant poles. For example, Eberhard Jäckel argues that the idea of murdering the Jews crystallized in Hitler's mind around 1924.[6] Emphasizing Hitler's threatening statements of the late 1930s, Karl Dietrich Bracher assumes that the intention was there by then.[7] Andreas Hillgruber and Klaus Hildebrand assert the primacy of ideological causation but do not offer a specific date.[8] Others, not all of them functionalists, have focused on 1941, though within that year a number of possible turning points have been suggested. Léon Poliakov has urged early 1941 as most plausible, and Robert Kempner and Helmut Krausnick have argued for a Hitler decision in the spring, connected with preparations for the invasion of Russia.[9] Raul Hilberg has argued for a summer date, when the mass murder put into practice in Russia beckoned as a European-wide solution available to victorious Germany.[10] Uwe Dietrich Adam supports a fall decision, when the stalled military offensive precluded a "territorial solution" through mass expulsion into Russia.[11] And Sebastian Haffner, certainly no functionalist, argues for early December, when the first premonition of eventual military defeat caused Hitler to seek an irreversible victory over the Jews.[12]

Why can such diversity of interpretation over the nature and timing of the decision for the Final Solution flourish? I would suggest two reasons. The first is one of definition. What is meant by a decision for the Final Solution? For the intentionalist, there were in fact two decisions. The first decision was the point at which the concept of the mass murder of the European Jews took form in Hitler's mind as a fixed goal—the point at which it became a part of his "unalterable program." The second decision was the point at which Hitler considered it opportune and possible to realize this goal. The former was determinative, the latter rela-

98

tively incidental, for once the intention was fixed, Hitler had the power and cunning to realize it eventually. The functionalist makes no such clear distinction between conceptualization and implementation of the Final Solution. Instead, the conception of systematic mass murder and the decision to implement it emerged simultaneously, products of a conjuncture of factors, of which Hitler's vicious anti-Semitism was but one. His ominous and threatening statements were not evidence of clearly held intentions but of an unquenchable hatred of the Jews that would spur a continuing radicalization of Jewish policy through a search and competition for final solutions of the Jewish problem, until the "most final" of all—extermination—emerged. According to the functionalists, Hitler's ideological fixation assured that a "final solution of the Jewish problem" would be sought, but not what specific form it would take.

A second reason for such diversity of interpretation is the lack of documentation. There are no written records of what transpired among Hitler, Himmler, and Heydrich concerning the Final Solution, and none of them survived to testify after the war. Therefore, the decision-making process at the center must be reconstructed by the historian, who extrapolates from events, documents, and testimony originating outside the inner circle. Like the man in Plato's cave, he sees only the reflection and shadows, but not reality. This hazardous process of extrapolation and reconstruction inevitably invites a wide variety of conclusions. Likewise, Hitler's consciousness remains elusive. We cannot know precisely what was in his mind and again must reconstruct from recorded statements. This poses significant problems for the historian dealing with such a conscious political actor—one who could publicly threaten the Jews with destruction in 1939 and privately mention expulsion as late as January 1942.[13] The historian can avail himself of at least three approaches. First, he can through hindsight judge certain of Hitler's statements to be literal and dismiss the rest as conscious duplicity, thus assuring a coherent ideology and consistent but all too clever pattern of behavior on Hitler's part. Second he can interpret many of Hitler's statements more figuratively, as "symbols of struggle" mobilizing and inciting his followers.[14] Finally, he can accept that Hitler experienced uncertainty and changes of mind and mood, and that contradictory statements are evidence of his own confusion.[15] Each of the above three approaches is valid at least in some cases, and thus the scope of possible interpretations is once again very wide.

Within the broad spectrum of interpretation, my thesis might be termed "moderate functionalist." I do not accept the intentionalists' view

99

that the key decision—the conception of the Final Solution as a fixed goal—had already been taken long before the war and merely awaited the opportune moment for implementation. My position does not deny the significance of Hitler's anti-Semitism, only that the intention to murder the Jews had been consciously derived from it well in advance.

Concerning Hitler's anti-Semitism, the following seems no longer in dispute. Psychologically, it was a deeply held obsession. Ideologically, it was the keystone of his *Weltanschauung*. Without his understanding of politics in terms of a "Jewish-Bolshevik" conspiracy and his understanding of history in terms of a social Darwinist struggle of races (in which the Jews played the most diabolical role), the whole edifice would collapse. Finally, Hitler gave expression to this anti-Semitism in violent threats and fantasies of mass murder.[16] Indeed, for a man whose social Darwinism implied the final resolution of any conflict in terms of the survival of one adversary through the "destruction" of the other, and whose anti-Semitism was understood in terms of race, mass murder of the Jews was a "logical" deduction. Granted all this, the relationship between Hitler's anti-Semitism and the origin of the Final Solution still remains controversial.

Even if the Final Solution can be "logically" deduced from Hitler's *Weltanschauung*, it is improbable that Hitler made that deduction before 1941 and consciously pursued the systematic murder of the European Jews as a long-held goal. The assumption of Nazi Jewish policy as the premeditated and logical consequence of Hitler's anti-Semitism cannot be easily reconciled with his actual behavior in the years before 1941. For example, Hitler's views of the Jews as the "November criminals" who caused Germany's defeat in World War I was as fervently held as any of his anti-Jewish allegations. Indeed, the oft-cited passage from *Mein Kampf* lamenting that twelve or fifteen thousand Jews had not been gassed during the war makes far more sense in the context of the stab-in-the-back legend than as a prophecy or intimation of the Final Solution. The "logical" consequence of the thesis of the Jew as wartime traitor should have been a "preventive" massacre of German Jewry before the western offensive or at least before the attack on Russia.

In actual practice Nazi Jewish policy sought a *judenrein* Germany by facilitating and often coercing Jewish emigration. In order to reserve the limited emigration opportunities for German Jews, the Nazis opposed Jewish emigration from elsewhere on the continent. This policy continued until the fall of 1941, when the Nazis prohibited Jewish emigration from Germany and for the first time justified the blocking of Jewish emigration from other countries in terms of preventing their escape from the German grasp. The efforts of the Nazi Jewish experts to facilitate Jewish emigration both before and during the war, as well as their plans for massive resettlement, were not merely tolerated but encouraged by Hitler.[17] It is difficult to reconcile the assumption of a long-held intention to murder the Jews with this behavior. If Hitler knew he was going to murder the Jews, then he was supporting a policy that "favored" German Jews over other European Jews and "rescued" from death many of those he held most responsible for Germany's earlier defeat.

It has been argued that Hitler was merely awaiting the opportune moment to realize his murderous intentions.[18] Not only does that not explain the pursuit of a contradictory policy of emigration in the meantime, it also does not explain the long delay. If Hitler was merely awaiting the outbreak of conflict to pursue his "war against the Jews," why were the millions of Polish Jews in his hands since the fall of 1939 granted a thirty-month "stay of execution"? They were subjected to sporadic massacre and murderous living condiitons but not to systematic extermination until 1942. If Hitler could kill 70,000 to 80,000 Germans through the euthanasia program between 1939 and 1941, why was it not "opportune" to murder several hundred thousand German Jews who constituted an "internal menace" in wartime? It certainly would have occasioned far less opposition than euthanasia. Why was this period not at least used to make preparations and plans for mass extermination, avoiding the clumsy improvisations of 1941? In short, the practice of Nazi Jewish policy until 1941 does not support the thesis of a long-held, fixed intention to murder the European Jews.

Hitler's anti-Semitism is more plausibly seen as the stimulant or spur to a continuous search for an increasingly radical solution to the Jewish question rather than as the source of a logically deduced and long-established "blueprint" for extermination. As the "satanic" figure for Hitler behind all other problems, "the Jew" was the ultimate problem and required an ultimate or final solution. Hitler's anti-Semitism thus constituted an ideological imperative which, given the competitive nature of the Nazi state, played a central role in the evolution of Nazi Jewish policy. The rival Nazi chieftains constantly sought to expand their private empires and vied for Hitler's favor through anticipating and pursuing Hitler's desires. In his function as arbiter, Hitler in turn sought to avoid totally antagonizing or alienating any of his close followers, even the most incompetent among them, such as Rosenberg and Ribbentrop. Thus, when competing Nazis advocated conflicting policies, all plausibly justified in Nazi terminology, Hitler had great difficulty resolving differences. Paralysis and indecision were often the result. When, however, the competition was carried out at the expense of helpless third parties, such as Jews and populations of occupied territories, protected by no countervailing force, radicalization rather than paralysis followed. Hence, it was the conjuncture of Hitler's anti-Semitic obsession, the anarchical and competitive nature of the Nazi state, the vulnerable status of the European Jews, and the war that resulted in the Final Solution.

By 1941 Nazi Jewish policy had reached an impasse. Military and diplomatic success brought millions of Jews into the German sphere, while the already limited possibilities for Jewish emigration were constricted further by the outbreak of war. Germany's self-imposed "Jewish problem" mushroomed while the traditional solution collapsed. Interim solutions of massive resettlement—in Lublin and Madagascar—likewise were not viable. The imminent invasion of Russia posed the same dilemma once again—further territorial conquest meant more Jews. At some point in the spring of 1941, Hitler decided to break this vicious circle.

Overwhelming documentation exists to show that Germany, under Hitler's prodding, planned and prepared for a *Vernichtungskrieg*—a war of destruction, not a conventional war—in Russia. It would be a clash of ideologies and races, not of nation-states.[19] Detailed negotiations between the army and the SS ended in an agreement with the army promising logistical support and conceding freedom of action to small mobile SS units—Einsatzgruppen—charged with "special tasks" behind German lines. All customs and international law concerning war and occupation were to be disregarded. Political commissars were to be executed. German soldiers were not to be held juridically responsible for actions against the civilian population, which was stripped of any shred of legal protection and subject to summary execution and collective reprisal. Mass starvation of millions was the anticipated result of intended economic exploitation. Preparation for responsible care of prisoners of war was totally inadequate. Despite all that is known of German preparations for the invasion of Russia, however, specific documentation concerning the intended fate of the Russian Jews is lacking. Conclusions must be drawn from postwar testimony, circumstantial evidence, and scattered references in later documents. The weight of this evidence supports the conclusion that the decision to exterminate the Russian Jews was taken before the invasion rather than after. It was part of Germany's preinvasion planning, not a policy that emerged only subsequently.[20]

102

Despite minor differences in their accounts, a convincing number of Einsatzgruppe officers testified after the war that they were informed by mid-June, shortly before the invasion, of the extermination task before them. This testimony is confirmed by both the subsequent behavior of the Einsatzgruppen and later documents. They did proceed to murder all Jews—men, women, and children—though initial reports often attempted to portray these massacres as reprisals for partisan activities. Some documents were, however, more blunt. "Specific orders of the Reichsführer-SS" to the Second Cavalry Regiment of the Waffen-SS on August 1, 1941, stated that "all Jews must be shot; Jewish females (*Judenweiber*) driven into the swamps."[21] Walter Stahlecker, the commander of Einsatzgruppe A, submitted a summary report of events through October 15, 1941, which stated:

> It was expected from the start that the Jewish problem in the Ostland would not be solved solely through pogroms. On the other hand the security-police cleansing work had *according to basic orders* [italics mine] the goal of the most complete removal as possible of the Jews [*moeglichst umfassende Beseitigung*]. Extensive executions in the cities and flat lands were therefore carried out through special units.

By mid-October Stahlecker's "extensive executions" had accounted for the killing of 118,430 Jews![22] The last shred of ambiguity is dropped in a report of Sturmbannführer Dr. Rudolf Lange of January 1942: "The goal that Einsatzkommando 2 had in mind *from the beginning* [italics mine] was a radical solution to the Jewish problem through the execution of *all* Jews."[23]

If the decision to murder the Jews of Russia had been taken before the invasion, precisely how and when this decision was reached remains obscure. It is not possible to determine if the initiative was Hitler's or came from someone else, such as Heydrich. Moreover, it is not possible to determine if Hitler's mind was already set by March, when he made clear to the military that the Russian war would not be a conventional war, or if the degree of military compliance tempted him subsequently to expand the circle of intended victims beyond the "Jewish-Bolshevik intelligentsia."[24] The scant documentation does not permit a definitive answer to these questions, merely informed speculation. Several factors suggest a March date, however. When a late-March draft from the negotiations over the Einsatzgruppen in Russia was suddenly pressed into service to cover the jurisdiction of Einsatzgruppen accompanying the German invasion of Yugoslavia and Greece, "Jews and Communists" had to be specifically added to the list of categories of individuals to be "secured." Helmut Krausnick has plausibly argued that the absence of these categories for Russia would indicate that a different fate had already been decided upon for the Russian Jews analogous to the "Commissar Order" being prepared for Russian Communists.[25] Also, after a conference with Hitler on April 2, 1941, Rosenberg ominously noted: "What I do not want to write down today, I will nonetheless never forget."[26]

With the decision to murder the Russian Jews, Hitler broke out of the vicious circle in which each military success brought more Jews under German control. This did not, however, immediately alter German policy toward the Jews on the rest of the continent. Emigration, expulsion, and plans for future resettlement still held sway. In the fall of 1940 Jews from Baden, the Palatinate, and Luxembourg were expelled to unoccupied France, as were Jews from Vienna to Poland in early 1941. In February 1941, Heydrich was still speaking of "sending them [the Jews] off to whatever country will be chosen later on."[27] And the Foreign Office continued to cooperate with the RSHA (Reich Main Security Office) to block Jewish emigration from other countries, so as to monopolize the limited emigration possibilities for Jews from Germany. This policy was reaffirmed as late as May 20, 1941, in a circular signed by Walter Schellenberg, chief of security in the occupied territories, forbidding Jewish emigration from Belgium and France. The old policy of emigration, expulsion, and postwar resettlement was officially dismantled only gradually. In July 1941 the RSHA informed the Foreign Office that no further expulsions to France were intended.[28] In October Jewish emigration from Germany was forbidden. In February 1942 the Foreign Office formally cancelled the Madagascar Plan. Thus, the preparations for the murderous assault upon the Russian Jews did not have immediate repercussions on Nazi Jewish policy elsewhere. The emergence of the Final Solution for the European Jews was a separate process resulting from a separate decision.

This two-decision thesis, postulating a determination for the Final Solution in Europe only after the Einsatzgruppen were already in action in Russia, was first articulated by Raul Hilberg in 1961.[29] If the two-decision thesis has received increasing acceptance among historians (including the intentionalists, although for them simply in terms of a decision for implementation), the debate over the exact date and nature of that second decision has in contrast become increasingly heated. Thus, the remainder of this paper will be devoted to this particular controversy.

104

Hilberg opted for a date no later than July 1941; Uwe Dietrich Adam has argued for a point between September and November; Sebastian Haffner has suggested December; and Martin Broszat has challenged the whole notion of a comprehensive decision on a particular date, and has argued instead for a gradual and unconscious process of escalation. In my opinion the July date of Hilberg is still the most probable, provided that one understands it as merely the point at which Hitler set in motion the planning and preparation which resulted in the Final Solution.

On July 31, 1941, Heydrich received Göring's authorization to prepare a "total solution" (*Gesamtlösung*) of the Jewish question in those territories of Europe under German influence and to coordinate the participation of those organizations whose jurisdictions were touched.[30] The significance of this document is open to debate. Most historians have assumed that it refers to an extermination program. But some have interpreted it in terms of a "comprehensive program for the deportation of the Jews" to Russia and an attempt by Heydrich to strengthen his jurisdictional position to carry out this task.[31] Indeed, the circumstances surrounding the origins of this document are uncertain. In one account Eichmann claimed that he drafted it on Heydrich's instructions, and it was then submitted for Göring's signature. In another account, however, while still assuming that the initiative came from Heydrich, Eichmann admitted: "In any case, how Heydrich received this authorization I do not know."[32]

However uncertain the origins of the July authorization and however vague the phraseology about the fate intended for the Jews, this much is known. It was signed by Göring, who two weeks later expressed the opinion that "the Jews in the territories dominated by Germany had nothing more to seek." Göring did not spell out their fate further, except to say that where Jews had to be allowed to work, it could only be in closely guarded labor camps, and that he preferred that Jews be hung rather than shot, as the latter was too honorable a death. The impending mass resettlement of Jews in Russia was neither mentioned nor implied.[33]

The authorization was received by Heydrich, who already had an authorization signed by Göring for coordinating Jewish emigration, dating from January 1939. When Jewish emigration gave way to plans for massive resettlement, Heydrich had felt no need for a new "charter" and cited the older one when asserting jurisdiction over the emerging Madagascar Plan in 1940.[34] Moreover, Heydrich had just spent the previous months organizing the Einsatzgruppen for the extermination of the Russian Jews, and that murder campaign was now in full swing. The historical context would thus suggest that if indeed Heydrich was the initiator of the July authorization, he did not need it to continue emigration and resettlement activities over which he had long established unchallenged jurisdiction, but rather because he now faced a new and awesome task that dwarfed even the systematic murder campaign of the Einsatzgruppen.

Precisely how and when Heydrich and his immediate superior, Himmler, became aware of their new task, is not and probably never will be known. But given the political structure of the Third Reich, in which rival paladins vied for Hitler's favor and were successful in the degree to which they anticipated and realized his desires, and given the extermination program already underway in Russia, Himmler and Heydrich surely needed little more than a nod from Hitler to perceive that the time had come to extend the killing process to the European Jews. That such a Hitlerian incitement lay behind the July authorization cannot be definitively proven. But the testimony of Rudolph Höss and Adolf Eichmann indicates that at some point in the summer of 1941—whether in July or shortly thereafter is unclear—Himmler and Heydrich began to act on the assumption that Hitler had given them the "green light" to prepare an extermination program.

Höss testified that he was summoned to Berlin in the summer of 1941, where Himmler told him of the führer's order to exterminate all the European Jews. Höss was then visited by Eichmann, who discussed the inadequacies of existing killing methods but could not give him details about the starting date of the exterminations or the gassing technology to be employed. These questions were still unanswered when Höss attended a conference of Eichmann's men in Berlin in November. That same fall Zyklon B gas was used to kill Russian prisoners in Auschwitz, and this gas was selected for the Jewish exterminations that began in early 1942.[35]

Eichmann testified that Heydrich informed him in the late summer of 1941 that the führer had ordered the physical destruction of the Jews. He was then assigned to report on various preparations and killing actions in the east. First, Heydrich sent him to the already informed SS and Police Leader Odilo Globocnik in Poland, who showed him the early construction of one camp (presumably Bełzec) where it was intended to use carbon monoxide from engine exhaust gas. Eichmann remembered the bright fall colors there. He was then sent by Heinrich Müller to Minsk to witness Einsatzgruppe activities. The weather had already turned cold, for he was wearing a long leather coat which was splashed

106

with the brains of a baby held up to him by a desperate mother. Returning through Lemburg (Lvov), Eichmann saw other mass graves from
which blood spouted in little geysers. Finally, Müller sent him to
Chełmno in late December or early January to report on the gas-van
killings that had just begun there. Upon his return he was chided by
Müller for not having precisely timed the killing operation. Though in
court Eichmann denied the Höss account of a fall visit to Auschwitz, in
earlier testimony he admitted to having been sent by Müller to Auschwitz
"at the beginning," where he discussed gassing methods and was shown
the small hut in which Zyklon B pellets had been tested on prisoners.[36]

In September the German Jews were marked. In October further
emigration was forbidden; the first deportations of German Jews to Łódź
occurred; and Slovakia, Croatia, and Rumania were asked to permit the
inclusion of Jews of their citizenship residing in Germany in these deportations just getting underway. In November the 11th Decree of the Reich
Citizenship Law provided for the loss of citizenship and forfeit of property
of Jews residing outside German borders. Such preparatory measures
would admittedly have been necessary whether the German Jews were
fated at this time merely for deportation or extermination. However, a
few documents survive in support of the testimony of Eichmann and Höss
that planning activities in the fall of 1941 now focused on the ultimate
goal of extermination, not just deportation.

On August 28, 1941, Eichmann wrote the Foreign Office and added
to the old formulation "in view of the imminent final solution" the ominous phrase "now in preparation."[37] The timing of the change in phraseology coincides with Eichmann's own account of learning about the
extermination order in late summer. More explicit documents date from
October. A number of Spanish Jews had been arrested and interned in
France, which led the Spanish to suggest the possibility of evacuating all
Spanish Jews in France (some 2,000) to Spanish Morocco. On October
13, Foreign Office Under Secretary Martin Luther urged negotiations in
that direction—a position fully in line with the prevailing policy of
achieving a *judenrein* Europe through the expulsion of the Jews. Four
days later, however, Heydrich's RSHA informed Luther by telephone of
its opposition to the Spanish proposal, as the Spanish government had
neither the will nor the experience effectively to guard the Jews in Morocco. "In addition these Jews would also be too much out of the direct
reach of the *measures for a basic solution to the Jewish question to be
enacted after the war* [italics mine]."[38] The rejection of deportation to
Morocco, combined with the mention of a basic solution to be enacted

after the war which prior removal of the Jews would thwart, indicated that a fundamental shift in Nazi Jewish policy had occurred. Within the SS a *judenfrei* Europe was no longer being pursued through expulsion.

Also in October 1941 Eichmann's associate, Friedrich Suhr, accompanied the Foreign Office Jewish expert, Franz Rademacher, to Belgrade to deal with the Jewish question in Serbia. After the fate of the adult male Jews was settled (they were shot by army firing squad in reprisal for casualties suffered from partisan attacks), Rademacher reported on the women, children, and elderly: "Then as soon as the technical possibility exists within the framework of a total solution of the Jewish question, the Jews will be deported by waterway to the reception camp in the east."[39] Just after learning of plans for a reception camp in the east at a conference attended by one of Eichmann's closest associates, Rademacher received a letter from Paul Wurm, foreign editor of *Der Stürmer*:

> Dear Party Comrade Rademacher!
>
> On my return trip from Berlin I met an old party comrade who works in the east on the settlement of the Jewish question. In the near future many of the Jewish vermin will be exterminated through special measures.[40]

Together these documents would indicate that the Jewish experts coming to and from Berlin in the month of October were aware of plans for a "reception camp" in the east to receive Jews incapable of heavy labor and for "special measures" for extermination. The exact location of the planned reception camp was not clear, though the reference to transport by waterway would suggest that a Danube–Black Sea route to Russia was being considered.

Discussion of both gassing and the creation of new camps for Jews in Russia was recorded on yet another occasion in October by Ostministerium expert on the Jewish question Alfred Wetzel, who met with Eichmann and euthanasia supervisor Viktor Brack.[41] Brack advised the construction of gassing apparatus, presumably gas vans, on the spot because they were not in sufficient supply in the Reich.[42] Brack offered to send his chemist, Dr. Helmut Kallmeyer, to help out. Eichmann confirmed that Jewish camps were about to be set up in Riga and Minsk to receive German Jews. Those capable of labor would be sent "to the east" later, but he saw no reason "why those Jews who are not fit for work should not be removed by the Brack method" in the meantime.

Riga and Minsk were also mentioned as destinations for deported Jews at an October 10 conference in Prague chaired by Heydrich. At this same conference Heydrich noted that "Nebe and Rasch could take in Jews in the camps for Communist prisoners in the theater of operations." Perhaps Heydrich meant Stahlecker and Nebe, the respective Einsatz-gruppe commanders in Riga and Minsk. In any case, the fact that de-ported Jews were to be turned over to the Einsatzgruppe commanders, who were supervising the killing of Jews and Communists, indicates that even in early October Heydrich was not in doubt about the specific fate of these deportees.[43]

These October documents do not yet portray the Final Solution in its definitive form, but they do suggest that frenetic planning was under-way and that key ingredients of the Final Solution—special reception camps for the deported Jews, and gassing—were being discussed among the "Jewish experts" not only in the SS but also in the führer's Chancel-lery, the Foreign Office, and the Ostministerium. These documents thus enhance the credibility of Eichmann and Höss and the contention that a gradually widening circle of Nazi Jewish experts was becoming con-scious that the ultimate goal was no longer resettlement but rather ex-termination.

In addition to documentary evidence and the testimony of Höss and Eichmann, circumstantial evidence should be considered as well. Is it plausible that in October the Nazis were setting in motion a vast program of deportation while still unaware of its implications and undecided about the ultimate fate of the deportees? The SS had already been forced to call off deportations to the Lublin Reservation in the spring of 1940 because limited but indiscriminate deportation of Jews without careful preparation had proved chaotic and unfeasible. There was no desire for a repetition of that fiasco, yet the attempt to resettle Europe's entire Jewish population in Russia would have had far graver consequences. German planners acknowledged openly and frequently that exploitation of Russian food supplies was going to entail the mass starvation of native inhabitants. A meeting of state secretaries on May 2, 1941, noted that "umpteen million people will doubtless starve to death, when we extract what is necessary for us from the country."[44] The *Wirtschaftsstab Ost* (Economic Headquarters for the East) report of May 23, 1941, stated that the population of the northern forest region,

> especially the urban population, will inevitably face a great famine.
> . . . Many tens of millions of people will be superfluous in this area and will die or have to emigrate to Siberia. Attempts to rescue the popula-tion there from famine by drawing upon surpluses from the black earth

region can only be at the expense of provisioning Europe. They endanger Germany's capacity to hold out in the war, they endanger Germany's resistance to blockade. Absolute clarity must prevail in this regard.[45]

The report also noted that the problem of emigration to Siberia would be "extremely difficult" because "rail transportation was out of the question." And in August, Göring "reckoned with great loss of life on nutritional grounds."[46] Was anyone seriously considering a massive influx of additional people into Russia under these circumstances without being clear about the consequences?

When the SS "Jewish experts" began seriously to consider the Madagascar resettlement in the summer of 1940, they produced within two months a neatly printed brochure, complete with table of contents and maps, outlining the future governance and economy of the "superghetto."[47] However fantastic the Madagascar Plan may have been, the planners were men who clearly thought beyond the initial stage of deportation. By 1941 they could have had few illusions about the practical difficulties of solving the Jewish question. It is inconceivable that they spent the autumn of 1941 wrestling with the obstacles to deportation while undecided about the most important problem of all—the disposition of the deportees.

Given the already apparent inadequacies of the Einsatzgruppe operations—their inefficiency, lack of secrecy, and psychological burden on the executioners—and their even greater unsuitability for use outside Russia, the most important problem Himmler and Heydrich faced was how and where to kill the Jews. Ultimately, the Nazi planners solved this problem by merging three already existing programs with which they had prior experience: the concentration-camp system, euthanasia gassing, and Eichmann's speciality of forced emigration and population resettlement. Auschwitz, because of its rail connections, was chosen as one site for a killing center. The possibility of other sites in Russia may have been weighed until the military and transportation situation made this unfeasible. The exact type of gas to be used remained undetermined; in the end, the Polish camps manned by euthanasia personnel retained carbon monoxide while Auschwitz and Maidanek adopted Zyklon B.

When was this solution—deportation to camps equipped with gassing facilities—finally approved? The answer lies in another question: when did the construction of the first death camps and the initial shifting of euthanasia personnel begin? Sonderkommando Lange, headquartered in Posen (Poznań), had been carrying out euthanasia in the incorporated territories in 1940 and 1941. According to the testimony of Lange's chauffeur, in the fall of 1941 Lange drove around the Warthegau in search of a suitable location and then to Berlin. He returned to Chełmno in late October or early November to assemble contingents of SS men and police from Łódź and Posen and to carry out preparatory work on the buildings to be used before the first transport of Jews arrived in December.[48] Testimony of ethnic German inhabitants of Chełmno confirms that in the fall of 1941 SS men came to inspect the town and returned some days later to confiscate many buildings and evict the Polish owners. Some Poles remained to work on renovating "the castle," where the gas vans would be loaded. Several more groups of SS and police also came. "Some weeks" or "one month" later, the first Jewish transports arrived.[49] Since the first transport of Jews was gassed at Chełmno on December 8, the decision to build a death camp near Łódź cannot date beyond mid or late October.

The evidence indicates that a decision concerning Bełżec came at least as early, even though the camp did not become operational until March 1942. Eichmann reported no activity there when he visited in mid-October. Accounts of subsequent events once again confirm the plausibility of his story. According to Polish testimony, three SS men arrived in Bełżec in October and demanded a draft of twenty Polish workmen. They began work on November 1 under the direction of a young ethnic German *Baumeister* from Kattowitz (Katowice), who supervised the construction according to a set of plans. After putting up two barracks and the future gas chamber near the railway siding, the Polish workers were dismissed on December 23. By then, black-uniformed former prisoners-of-war from the Russian army had arrived to carry on the work and to guard seventy Jewish laborers from Lubycza Krolewska and Mosty Male. The latter were subsequently killed in the first test of the gassing facilities in February.[50]

SS Second Lieutenant Josef Oberhauser, initially an employee of the euthanasia program and subsequently adjutant to the inspector of the Polish death camps (Christian Wirth), testified to a similar chronology. He was reassigned to Lublin in October 1941 and arrived in November. His first job consisted of bringing to Bełżec building materials as well as Ukrainian guardsmen from their training camp at Trawniki. He was in no doubt as to what was intended in Bełżec, as the construction supervisor showed him the plans for the gas chamber. By Christmas the initial construction was finished, and Oberhauser became Wirth's liaison to Globocnik. After the first gassing test killed fifty Jewish workers, Wirth went to Berlin for six weeks. Upon his return in March, transports began to arrive.[51]

While many euthanasia personnel were sent from Germany to Russia in the winter of 1941–42 and were not reassigned to the death camps until the spring of 1942, some key personnel were already involved earlier. Not only had Wirth and Oberhauser been sent from Berlin in the fall of 1941, but Brack also dispatched to Lublin his chemist, Dr. Kallmeyer, the man he had unsuccessfully tried to send to Riga in late October. Kallmeyer admitted being sent to Lublin after Christmas, but said no one had had any use for him and he had been quickly ordered back.[52] SS Second Lieutenant Dr. August Becker, on loan from the SS to the euthanasia program since January 1940 for the purpose of delivering bottled carbon monoxide to the euthanasia institutes, testified frankly (when terminally ill and no longer facing trial): "Himmler wanted to use the people released from euthanasia who were experts in gassing, such as myself, in the great gassing program getting underway in the east." Before being assigned in December 1941 to supervise gas vans operating with the Einsatzgruppen in Russia, Becker had already heard talk in Berlin that other members of the euthanasia program were being sent to Lublin to start "something similar," only this time, according to rumor, it would be the Jews.[53]

If the plans for Bełżec were being drawn up by mid-October and work began on November 1, and if Lange was in Berlin making final arrangements for Chełmno in late October and work began there by early November, it is very difficult to avoid the conclusion that sometime in October Hitler had approved the extermination plan he had solicited the previous summer. Certainly, the subsequent behavior of Himmler, Heydrich, and Rosenberg is compatible with this hypothesis. On October 30, Heydrich sent to the Foreign Office the first five "Activity and Situation Reports on the Einsatzgruppen of the Sipo-SD in Russia," which detailed the massacres that had taken place the previous summer. As the Foreign Office copy was often only one of as many as a hundred copies, such information was being widely circulated.[54] Perhaps Heydrich's timing was fortuitous. Or perhaps he was attuning recipients to the "new realities," psychologically preparing them for participation in the Final Solution. On November 11 Himmler told Kersten that "the destruction of the Jews is being planned. . . . Now the destruction of the Jews is imminent."[55] On November 18 Rosenberg gave a "confidential" background report to the German Press and asserted that the Jewish question "can only be solved in a biological extermination (Ausmerzung) of all

(1941)

Jews in Europe."[56] On November 25 in Kovno and November 30 in Riga, deported German Jews were massacred for the first time. On November 29, Heydrich issued his invitations to the Wannsee Conference, originally scheduled for December 9 but postponed until January 20, 1942. And on December 14, Rosenberg recorded a conversation with Hitler: "I took the viewpoint not to speak of the extermination (*Ausrottung*) of the Jews. The Führer approved this attitude. . . ."[57]

For many who had been waiting anxiously for direction from Berlin on the Jewish question, December was a month of resolution. An inquiry from the Reichskommissariat Ostland as to whether all Jews should be liquidated regardless of age, sex, and economic interest was answered from Berlin on December 18: "In the meantime clarity on the Jewish question has been achieved through oral discussion: economic interests are to be disregarded on principle in the settlement of this problem."[58] On December 16 Hans Frank, who had sent his state secretary, Joseph Bühler, to Berlin to find out what was behind the Wannsee invitation, reported to his followers in the General Government that the Polish Jews could not be deported; thus, they would have to liquidate these Jews themselves. He did not know exactly how, but measures should be taken "in connection with the great measures to be discussed in the Reich" to accomplish this task. If unsure of the method, Frank had no doubt of the goal: "*Wir müssen die Juden vernichten.*"[59]

Heydrich's Wannsee Conference invitation of November 29, 1941, contained a copy of Göring's July 31 authorization.[60] At the conference Heydrich invoked not only it but also "previous approval through the Führer."[61] All Jews, Heydrich announced, would be deported to the east for labor. Most would disappear through "natural diminution." The survivors, the hardiest, would be "treated accordingly," for no Jews were to survive "as a germ cell of a new Jewish reconstruction." That the participants were clear that the real goal of the vast deportation program was extermination, not labor, can be seen from the request of State Secretary Bühler of the General Government that the Final Solution begin in Poland because most of the Jews there were already incapable of work.

If the goal and scope of Nazi Jewish policy were no longer in doubt, some aspects of the Final Solution were still unsettled. "Practical experience" of significance to the Final Solution was being gathered, and "possible solutions" were discussed, which Eichmann confirmed to have been a discussion of "killing possibilities."[62] Though the Chełmno gas vans were already operating, and the makeshift facilities at Auschwitz were just being put into operation, apparently it was not until mid-

113

March, with the opening of Bełżec, that the gas chamber passed the final test. The proportion of those to be worked to death and those killed immediately was left open and remained a source of contention throughout. The issues of *Mischlinge* (those who are half-Aryan, half-Jewish) and German Jews in mixed marriages, which took up much of the conference, would never be definitively resolved. Nevertheless, despite these unanswered questions, the extermination of the European Jews as the ultimate goal of Nazi Jewish policy had been revealed to a significantly wider circle in order to assure needed cooperation.

One must not, however, overemphasize the degree of coherency and clarity in the German policy regarding the Jews in this crucial period from the summer of 1941 to the spring of 1942. In addition to the issues still unresolved at the time of the Wannsee Conference, two further factors confused the situation: (1) Hitler's decision to deport German Jews in the fall of 1941 superimposed upon the planners an additional task before the plan for a European-wide solution to the Jewish question and the means of implementing that plan were ready; and (2) the method of transmitting information about policy changes within the Third Reich was very unsystematic, and the process by which people and institutions were initiated into the policy was gradual and irregular. Hence, considerable uncertainty, confusion, and ignorance surrounded the Nazis' Jewish policy in the fall of 1941. This has led some historians to argue that the ultimate aim of that policy was still very much undecided.

Consider, first, the fall deportations from Germany. Göring's July authorization referred to a plan for the entire German sphere of influence in Europe and came at a time when rapid German victory over Russia was still assumed. In August, before such a plan could be devised and expectations of imminent victory were still alive, Hitler resisted pressure from Heydrich and Goebbels and rejected deportations from Germany "during the war."[63] As late as September 13, Eichmann likewise told the Foreign Office that no deportation of Serbian Jews to the General Government or Russia was possible, for not even German Jews could be lodged there.[64] By then, however, prospects of total German victory that fall were fast dimming, and Hitler appears to have made a snap decision reversing himself. On September 14 Rosenberg urged Hitler to approve the immediate deportation of German Jews in retaliation for the Russian deportation of Volga Germans to Siberia. Four days later Himmler informed Arthur Greiser, gauleiter of the Wartheland (Warthegau), of interim deportations to Łódź, because the führer wished to make the Old Reich and the Protectorate of Bohemia and Moravia *judenfrei* as soon as possible, hopefully by the end of the year.[65] Shortly thereafter, Heydrich likewise announced in Prague the führer's wish that insofar as possible the German Jews were to be deported to Łódź, Riga, and Minsk by the end of the year.[66]

Thus, in addition to their efforts to devise a Final Solution to the Jewish question in all Europe, the planners suddenly had to improvise immediate deportations as an interim solution for the Reich. The attempt to carry out these deportations before the death camps now being conceived were built caused difficulties and confusion. German authorities in the reception areas resisted the unwelcome influx, despite assurances that it was all temporary and the Jews would be sent "to the east" in the spring,[67] because these intended way stations did not have the capacity to take on such numbers even for a half year.

The improvised nature and ultimate failure of the fall deportations from Germany have led Martin Broszat and Uwe Adam to conclude that it was precisely this failure that paved the way for the Final Solution. Hitherto, the Germans had thought only of dumping the European Jews into the vast areas to be made accessible by the conquest of Russia. The stalled military campaign blocked this prospect, and deportations backed up as reception capacity in the "transit ghettos" was quickly saturated. With a resettlement program in motion but no place to go, killing emerged as the only alternative. This thesis is attractive and plausible, but the testimony of Höss and Eichmann and the events of October show that the Germans were working on the extermination program even while the deportations were just beginning. Their plans were not the result of the subsequent failure of these deportations.

The chronology of events provides even less support for Sebastian Haffner's contention that the Russian winter offensive, beginning on December 5, 1941, convinced Hitler that the war against Russia was lost, and that he thereupon sought at least to win the war against the Jews. His argument that the Wannsee Conference of January 20, 1942, followed directly from the Russian counteroffensive of December ignores the fact that invitations to the Wannsee Conference had already been issued and several death camps were already under construction in November.

Consider next the issue of the flow of information within the Third Reich. Broszat has argued that the absence of any reference to a specific Hitler order for the Final Solution in the postwar testimony or the surviving diaries of leading Nazis casts doubt upon the existence of a definitive Hitler decision for the Final Solution. The unsystematic and

115

irregular flow of information was, however, a pervasive feature of the political system of the Third Reich. Ignorance about current Jewish policy among some high-ranking Nazis in no way precludes a clear understanding of Hitler's desires among others. The examples of Joseph Goebbels and Joachim von Ribbentrop, the ministers of propaganda and foreign affairs, are most illustrative in this regard. Goebbels had long attempted to play a role in Jewish affairs. His instigation of the Kristallnacht pogrom had led, however, to the centralization of Jewish policy under the rival triumvirate of Göring, Himmler, and Heydrich. In the summer of 1941 Goebbels again sought a role. On August 15 he addressed a meeting at the Propaganda Ministry on the question of marking. After blaming the Jews for everything from the lack of housing to the strawberry shortage in Berlin, he suggested a series of measures: sending the nonworking Jews to Russia, cutting their rations, or, best of all, killing them (*am besten wäre es, diese überhaupt totzuschlagen*)! Basic to any measures, however, was the marking of the Jews, Goebbels argued, and by August 20, he had secured Hitler's agreement to this preparatory measure. Goebbels's attempted power grab was only partially successful, for despite his initiative in this matter, the SS retained jurisdiction over the marking decree that ensued.[68]

While Goebbels may have constantly agitated for a more radical Jewish policy, he was seldom the designer or executor of these policies. Heydrich jealously guarded his prerogatives, and no representative from the Ministry of Propaganda was invited to the Wannsee Conference. Only six weeks later, presumably in connection with the *Mischlinge* conference of March 6 (which one of Goebbels's men did attend), did the Propaganda Ministry receive a report and an expurgated one at that. On March 7, 1942, Goebbels noted in his diary:

> I read a detailed report from the SD and police regarding the final solution of the Jewish question. Any final solution involves a tremendous number of new viewpoints. The Jewish question must be solved within a pan-European frame. There are 11,000,000 Jews still in Europe. They will have to be concentrated later, to begin with, in the East; possibly an island, such as Madagascar, can be assigned to them after the war.[69]

In contrast, the Foreign Office received its copy of the unexpurgated Wannsee Conference protocol (one of thirty) on January 26, and even the low-echelon officials of the Colonial Desk were informed by February 10 that the Madagascar Plan was defunct.[70] Clearly, much about Nazi

116

Jewish policy was being kept from Goebbels, and his first awareness of the Final Solution was recorded only on March 27, 1942, several weeks after Bełzec began operating.[71]

If the intense competition of the Nazi political system caused a very uneven flow of information through the government, as rivals deliberately withheld information from one another, Hitler's informal and irregular manner of governing contributed to the same result. There was no written order for the Final Solution nor any explicit reference to a verbal order other than the assertions of Himmler and Heydrich that they were acting with the führer's approval. Participation in the Final Solution did not result so much from explicit orders systematically disseminated, as through self-recruitment by the zealous and ambitious servants of the Third Reich in response to the impulses and hints they perceived emanating from the centers of power. If a nod from Hitler could set Himmler and Heydrich in motion, others eagerly looked for similar signs. A classic example of self-recruitment by the clever and ambitious coexisting with enduring ignorance on the part of the obtuse is provided by Under Secretary Martin Luther and his boss, Foreign Minister Ribbentrop. Luther was a man with a sensitive hand on the political pulse of the Third Reich. Keenly aware of the signs of change in Nazi Jewish policy in the fall of 1941, Luther quickly closed ranks with his old antagonist, Heydrich, to secure a role for the Foreign Office and prevent a further diminution of its dwindling influence. Invited to the Wannsee Conference, Luther did not inform Ribbentrop of this until the following summer. Even then the foreign minister, though certainly aware of large numbers of Jews being killed (he had received summaries of the Einsatzgruppe reports from Luther), seemed unable to perceive the scope of the Final Solution and the importance Hitler attached to it. Piqued by SS encroachments on his jurisdiction, Ribbentrop temporarily ordered his Foreign Office to cease pressing Germany's allies on the deportation question. Only Hitler's vehemence on the Jewish question during back-to-back visits in September 1942 by the Croatian head of state, Ante Pavelic, and the Romanian deputy prime minister, Mihai Antonescu, sent the obsequious Ribbentrop scurrying to the telephone to cancel this order. However, it was not until the misfired Luther Putsch in February 1943, when Himmler backed Ribbentrop instead of his under secretary, that Ribbentrop finally perceived the political expediency of engaging in personal diplomacy on behalf of the Final Solution.[72]

Thus, the circle of initiates widened in a very unsystematic manner. The cleverest perceived the signs of change and recruited themselves to

117

the new policy. Others were brought in as their services were needed, such as at the Wannsee Conference. Some appear to have been deliberately excluded. And some were simply too stupid or blind to see what was going on. The bizarre result was that lower-ranking officials in certain areas of the government knew more than some top-ranking Nazis elsewhere. Thus, different Nazis, loyal to Hitler, anti-Semitic to the core, could pursue different policies and make contradictory statements regarding the Jews with the full conviction that they acted with the führer's blessing. This was not a state of affairs Hitler sought to correct. Indeed, given his cynical tongue-in-cheek comments during this period, he set the tone and deliberately encouraged a policy of maximum ambiguity.[73] Such confusion has obscured the origins of the Final Solution but ultimately cannot disguise the fact that, from the summer of 1941, Hitler, Göring, Himmler, and Heydrich knew what they were trying to do. The circle of initiates widened steadily if irregularly thereafter.

In conclusion, there was no Hitler order from which the Final Solution sprang full-grown like Athena from the head of Zeus. But sometime in the summer of 1941, probably before Göring's July 31 authorization, Hitler gave Himmler and Heydrich the signal to draw up a destruction plan, the completion of which inevitably involved the exploration of various alternatives, several false starts, and much delay. Considerable "lead time" was needed, for the Nazis were venturing into uncharted territory and attempting the unprecedented; they had no maps to follow. Hence, a seeming ambivalence surrounded Nazi Jewish policy in the late summer and autumn of 1941, which was aggravated by two factors. The first was the decision in mid-September to deport German Jews before the new killing facilities had been devised. The second was the Byzantine style of government in which initiative from above was informal, information was shared irregularly, and uncertainty was often deliberately cultivated. By October, a not unreasonable two or three months after Hitler had given the "green light" to proceed, the pieces were falling together. Many outside the SS were now involved, and the rough outline of a plan involving mass deportation to killing centers using poison gas had emerged. The first concrete steps for implementing this plan—the start of construction of the earliest death camps at Bełżec and Chełmno and the first transfer of euthanasia personnel, both inconceivable without Hitler's approval—were taken by the end of the month. The decision for the Final Solution had been confirmed.

7

The Bureaucracy of Annihilation

RAUL HILBERG

We are, all of us who have thought and written about the Holocaust, accustomed to thinking of this event as unique. There is no concept in all history like the Final Solution. There is no precedent for the almost endless march of millions of men, women, and children into gas chambers. The systematization of this destruction process sets it aside from all else that has ever happened. Yet if we examine this event in detail, observing the progression of small steps day by day, we see much in the destruction of Jewry that is familiar and even commonplace in the context of contemporary institutions and practices. Basically, the Jews were destroyed as a consequence of a multitude of acts performed by a phalanx of functionaries in public offices and private enterprises, and many of these measures, taken one by one, turn out to be bureaucratic, embedded in habit, routine, and tradition. It is almost a case of regarding the whole upheaval in all of its massiveness as something incredible, and then observing the small components and seeing in them very little that one could not expect in a modern society. One can go further and assert that it is the very mundaneness and ordinariness of these everyday official actions which made the destruction process so crass. Never before had the total experience of a modern bureaucracy been applied to such an undertaking. Never before had it produced such a result.

119

The uprooting and annihilation of European Jewry was a multi-pronged operation of a highly decentralized apparatus. This was no perpetration by a single department staffed with specialists in destruction. Germany never had a commissariat of Jewish affairs. The machinery of destruction was the organized German society, its ministries, armed forces, party formations, and industry.[1] In democratic countries we are accustomed to thinking of legislatures as devices that control administrative units, infuse them with power and money, authorize them to undertake action, and by implication, of course, apportion jurisdiction between them. In Nazi Germany there was no legislature that, like the United States Congress, can create an agency and abolish it. In Nazi Germany every organization moved on a track of self-assertion. To some of us this may seem anarchy. How much more remarkable then that this congeries of bureaucratic agencies, these people drawn from every area of expertise, operating without a basic plan, uncoordinated in any central office, nevertheless displayed order, balance, and economy throughout the destruction process.

The apparatus was able to advance unerringly, because there was an inner logic to its measures. A decree defining the term "Jew," expropriations of Jewish property, the physical separation and isolation of the victims, forced labor, deportations, gassings—these were not random moves. The sequence of steps was built in; each was a stage in the development. By 1941 the participating decision-makers themselves became aware that they had been traveling on a determined path. As their assault took on gestalt, its latent structure became manifest. Now they had an overview that allowed them to see a beginning and an end and that prompted them to demand of indigenous administrations in occupied and satellite countries that the "Nuremberg" principle be adopted in the definition of the Jews and that other precedents laid down in Germany be followed in the appropriate order for the accomplishment of a "final solution."[2]

Nothing, however, was simple. Neither the preliminary nor the concluding phases of the destruction process could be traversed without difficulties and complications. The Jewish communities had all been emancipated and they were tied to the Gentile population in countless relationships, from business contacts, partnerships, leases, and employment contracts, to personal friendships and intermarriages. To sever these connections one by one, a variety of measures were necessary, and these actions were taken by specialists who were accountants, lawyers, engineers, or physicians. The questions with which these men were concerned were almost always technical. How was a "Jewish enterprise" to be defined? Where were the borders of a ghetto to be drawn? What was to be the disposition of pension claims belonging to deported Jews? How should bodies be disposed of? These were the problems pondered by the bureaucrats in their memoranda, correspondence, meetings, and discussions. That was the essence of their work.

No organized element of German society was entirely uninvolved in the process of destruction. Yet this very fact, which is virtually an axiom, has been extraordinarily hard to assimilate in descriptions and assessments of the Nazi regime. It is much easier to visualize the role of a propagandist or some practitioner of violence than to appreciate the contribution of a bookkeeper. For this reason the principal spotlight in postwar years has been placed on the SS and the Gestapo. There is some awareness also of the military, particularly where, as in occupied France, it had made itself conspicuous. Similarly unavoidable was the discovery that an enterprise like I. G. Farben had established branches in Auschwitz. Much less well known, however, are the activities of such faceless components of the destructive machine as the Finance Ministry, which engaged in confiscations, or the armed forces network of armament inspectorates, which was concerned with forced labor, or German municipal authorities that directed or participated in the creation and maintenance of ghettos in eastern Europe. Two large bureaucracies have remained all but obscure, even though they operated at the very scene of death: the German railroads and the Order Police. This omission should give us pause.

Trains and street police have been common sights in Europe for more than a century. Of all the agencies of government these two organizations have always been highly visible to every inhabitant of the continent, yet they have been overlooked in the analysis of the Nazi regime. It is as if their very size and ubiquity deflected attention from the lethal operations in which they were so massively engaged. What *was* the function of the German railroads in the annihilation of the Jews? What tasks did the Order Police perform?

Case I: The Indispensability of the Railroads

In the chain of steps that led to the extinction of millions of Jewish victims, the Reichsbahn, as the German railways were known, carried the Jews from many countries and regions of Europe to the death camps which were situated on occupied Polish soil. The Jews were passed from one jurisdiction to another: from the civil or military authorities that had uprooted and concentrated them, to the Security Police, which was in charge of rounding them up, to the Reichsbahn, which transported them to the camps where they were gassed. Reichsbahn operations were a crucial link in this process and their significance is underscored by their magnitude. Camps account for most of the Jewish dead, and almost all of the people deported there were moved by rail. The movement encompassed 3 million Jews.

Of course, these transports were but a small portion of the Reichsbahn's business. At its peak the railway network stretched from Bordeaux to Dnepropetrovsk and points east, and its personnel consisted of a half million civil servants and almost twice as many other employees.[3] In the Reich itself (including Austria, Polish incorporated territory, and the Białystok district), some 130,000 freight cars were being assembled for loading every day.[4] Germany depended on its railroads to carry soldiers and civilians, military cargo and industrial products, throughout the war. A complex functional and territorial division of labor was required to administer these transport programs.

The transport minister, Julius Dorpmüller, held the office from 1937 to the end of the war. The *Staatssekretär* (state secretary) responsible for railways in the ministry was at first Wilhelm Kleinmann and, from the spring of 1942, Albert Ganzenmüller, a young, capable engineer and consummate technocrat who was to transport what Albert Speer was to production.[5] Ganzenmüller's central divisions, labeled E (for *Eisenbahn*, or railway) included E 1 (Traffic and Tariffs), E 2 (Operations), and L (*Landesverteidigung*, or Defense of the Land, meaning military transport). The Traffic Division dealt with financial matters, E 2 with operational considerations, and L with military priorities. Within E 2, the following breakdown should be of interest:[6]

E 2 (Operations)	Max Leibbrand
	(from 1942: Gustav Dilli)
21 (Passenger Trains)	Paul Schnell
211 (Special Trains)	Otto Stange

Stange administered the transport of Jewish deportees. He received the requests for trains from Adolf Eichmann's office in the Security Police and channeled them to financial and operational offices in the Reichsbahn.[7] The position and designation of 211 on the organization chart point to two important features of the deportation process. The first is

that the Jewish deportees were always booked as people, even though
they were carried in box cars. The passenger concept was essential, in
order that the Reichsbahn could collect the fare for each deported Jew
in accordance with applicable tariffs, and to preserve internal prerogatives and divisions of jurisdiction—the passenger specialists would remain in control. The second characteristic of Stange's office is indicated
by the word "special." He dealt only with group transports, each of which
had to be planned.

Passenger trains were either regular (*Regelzüge*), moving at hours
stated in published schedules, or special (*Sonderzüge*), assembled and
dispatched upon demand. Jews were deported in *Sonderzüge* and the procurement and scheduling of such trains was a lengthy and involved procedure that had to be administered at the regional level, particularly in
the Generalbetriebsleitung Ost (General Directorate East), one of three
such *Leitungen* in Nazi Germany. *Ost* was concerned with trains directed
to Poland and occupied areas farther to the east, and hence Jewish transports from large parts of Europe were channeled through this office. An
abbreviated chart of the Generalbetriebsleitung would look as follows:[8]

GENERALBETRIEBSLEITUNG OST	Ernst Emrich
I. (Operations)	Eggert (Mangold)
L	Bebenroth
P (Passenger Schedules)	Fröhlich
PW (Passenger Cars)	Jacobi
II. (Traffic)	Simon (Hartmann)
III. (Main Car Allocation Office for Freight Cars)	Schultz

In this array of officials, it is primarily Wilhelm Fröhlich and Karl Jacobi
who dealt with Jewish train movements. Conferences were called and
dates were fixed for transport programs aggregating forty or fifty trains at
a time: ethnic Germans, Hitler Youth, laborers, Jews—all were on the
same agenda.[9] The actual schedules were written locally, in the Reichsbahndirektionen, or in the Generaldirektion der Ostbahn, the railway
network in central Poland that dispatched Jews on short hauls from ghettos to death camps nearby.[10] The Reichsbahndirektionen were also responsible for the allocations of cars and locomotives. Only then were
transports assembled for the Jews loaded, sealed, dispatched, emptied,
and cleaned, to be filled with new, perhaps altogether different cargoes,
in the circulatory flow. The trains moved slowly and most were over-
loaded. The norm in western Europe or Germany was 1,000 persons per

train.[11] During 1944, transports with Hungarian Jews averaged 3,000.[12] In Poland such numbers were often exceeded. One train, fifty cars long, carried 8,205 Jews from Kolomea to the death camp of Bełżec.[13] Unheated in the winter, stifling in the summer, the cars, filled with men, women, and children, were death traps in themselves. Seldom would a transport arrive without 1 or 2 percent of the deportees having died en route.

One thinks of railroads as providing a service. What they produce is "place utility," and in this case they contributed their industriousness and ingenuity to the possibility of annihilating people, by the thousands at a time, in places where gas chambers had been installed. The Order Police, like the Reichsbahn a major apparatus of the Third Reich, was also needed over a long period of time in a wide geographic area, and its utility manifested itself in several stages of the destruction process, from concentration to killings.

Case II: The Indispensability of the Order Police

Nazi Germany was in essence a "police state," a type of regime that implies limitless power over the population. Under Heinrich Himmler the offices and units of the SS and Police were welded into an organization that was a symbol of much that Nazism stood for: arrests and concentration camps, racism and destruction. The police components of this power structure were grouped under two main offices: Security Police, directed by Reinhard Heydrich, and Order Police, commanded by Kurt Daluege, organized thusly:[14]

SECURITY POLICE (Sicherheitspolizei, or Sipo)
    Gestapo, ca. 40,000 to 50,000 men
    Criminal Police (Kripo), ca. 15,000
ORDER POLICE (Ordnungspolizei, or Orpo)
    Stationary (Einzeldienst), ca. 250,000, including reservists
        Cities: Schutzpolizei (Schupo)
        Rural: (Gendarmerie)
    Units (battalions and regiments), ca. 50,000, including reservists
    Indigenous personnel in occupied territory of the USSR:
        Schutzmannschaft (Schuma), ca. 100,000, including Einzeldienst
            and Schuma battalions
    Other offices (technical services, volunteer fire departments, etc.)

124

Comparing the Security Police and the Order Police, we may note two differences between them. The Security Police, in which the Gestapo was the predominant element, could be regarded as a new institution, whereas the conventional Order Police was old and established in Germany. Security Police—spread out over a continent—were relatively few; Order Police were clearly more numerous. Even so, the Ordnungspolizei was strained by the extent and variety of its assignments.

The Einzeldienst, a term denoting stationary duty that could be performed by a single individual, was significant mainly in the Reich and annexed territories, while mobile formations (battalions and regiments) were important primarily outside of home or incorporated regions. In most of the occupied countries, including France and the General Government of Poland, where German Order Police personnel served only in units, an indigenous police force remained in place to carry out its own tasks and to assist the Germans in theirs.

The areas wrested from the USSR were covered by a thin layer of Order Police, composed of both Einzeldienst and units. Einzeldienst, stationed in large urban centers as well as in many rural zones, reached a total of close to 15,000 at the end of 1942; battalions not fighting at the front contained a similar number of men.[15] To augment this German police establishment, a native Schutzmannschaft was created that, by July 1, 1942, had already grown to 42,708 in Einzeldienst within cities and on the land, and to 33,270 in Schuma battalions.[16] The so-called rural districts in Latvian, Lithuanian, White Russian, and Ukrainian regions included small towns with many Jewish residents as well as villages with purely Baltic or Slavic populations. Such a district (*Gebiet*), generally with around 250,000 inhabitants, was garrisoned by a German Gendarmerie platoon and its native helpers. The fairly typical rural *Gebiet* of Brest-Litovsk in the occupied Ukraine was controlled by 26 Gendarmerie men (15 of them older reservists) and 308 Ukrainian Schuma.[17] If all of these figures appear to be small, they should be juxtaposed with the numerical strength of the Security Police. Gestapo and Criminal Police in the entire occupied USSR were barely a few thousand, and when a Security Police post was placed in a rural area, it would contain around a half dozen men.

The sheer geographic expanse of the Order Police is in fact the principal clue to its function in destructive operations. The Orpo was the ever present stand-by force that could be drawn upon whenever Jews had to be concentrated or killed. In Amsterdam, Order Police contingents were needed to round up Jews for deportation.[18] In eastern Europe, Order

Police guards were posted near the walls and at the gates of ghettos. For example, in Warsaw a company of a police battalion was steadily engaged in ghetto supervision.[19] Similarly, in Riga, 88 Schuma were assigned to this duty.[20] And so on, for hundreds of ghettos. Order Police detachments were also guarding laborers outdoors. One Order Police battalion and seven Schuma battalions were deployed along Durchgangsstrasse IV, a thousand-kilometer road construction project from the Danube estuary to Taganrog, on which many Jews worked and died.[21] Furthermore, Order Police routinely accompanied the special trains to their destinations.[22] To put it simply, what the victim saw from a ghetto fence, a labor camp, or a box car, were the rifles of ordinary policemen.

The Order Police could not be dispensed with in killing operations themselves. A police battalion (the 9th in 1941 and the 3rd in 1942) was divided among the four Einstatzgruppen of the Security Police that followed the German armies into the USSR to shoot Jews and Communists.[23] Two Order Police detachments in Kiev assisted Einsatzkommando 4a of Einsatzgruppe C in the massacre of Babi Yar.[24] An Order Police contingent was similarly engaged in herding Jews to shooting sites near Riga.[25] A Lithuanian Schuma battalion was stationed in MaŁdanek,[26] and German Order Police from Łódź were transferred to the death camp at Chełmno (Kulmhof).[27] Often, officers of the Order Police were all but in charge of the killings. During the summer of 1942, when an attempt was made to annihilate the Jews in each of several dozen rural *Gebiete* of the occupied USSR, the local *Gendarmeriefïührer,* deploying his Germans and native helpers, would surround a small-town ghetto with guards standing approximately twenty meters apart, round up the Jews inside, and supervise the shootings in ditches nearby.[28] To the west of the USSR, in the improvised killing centers of the General Government, Order Police personnel with previous experience in euthanasia operations were serving not only as guards, but also in command. Such was the career of Franz Stangl, commander of Sobibór and, thereafter, Treblinka.[29]

To be sure, neither the railroads nor the Order Police fit any preconceived notion of an ideological vanguard. For that very reason, however, their heavy participation in relentless acts of mass destruction should engage our attention. If nothing else, this history should tell us that if an Adolf Hitler and his Nazi movement of party offices and SS formations were essential for the destruction of the Jews, so was at least in equal measure the readiness—in the fullest sense of the word—of ordinary agencies to engage in the extraordinary tasks inherent in the "Final Solution."

Bureaucratic Preparedness

The all-encompassing readiness for action of the diverse machinery of public and private agencies is one of the key phenomena of the bureaucratic destruction process. It resulted, in the case of several professions, in complete reversals of time-honored roles. An obvious example is furnished by the physicians who performed medical experiments in camps, or who, as public-health officials, urged the creation of hermetically sealed ghettos for the ostensible purpose of preventing the spread of typhus from Jewish inhabitants to the surrounding population, or who, as specialists in psychiatry, administered the euthanasia program, which was transformed in the *General Government* into a network of camps to kill approximately 1.5 million Polish Jews. Indeed, one of the euthanasia physicians, Dr. Irmfried Eberl, was the first commander of Treblinka.[30] A second illustration of such negation is the planning by offices in occupied Poland, labeled "Population and Welfare," of deportations of ghetto Jews to death camps.[31] Yet a third instance of goal transformation may be glimpsed in the efforts of civil engineers or architects to construct the ultimate antithesis of a shelter or home—the concentration camp, especially the installations designed for controlled, efficient mass annihilation.[32]

What prompted such a sprawling bureaucratic machine to involve itself so profoundly in a single direction toward death and more death? There were, of course, leaders who gave orders, for this was, after all, the state that utilized the *Führerprinzip*, the leadership principle. Clearly, if orders had been disregarded or evaded, the destruction of the Jews could not have been carried out.[33] Scarcely less important, however, is the fact that the process could not have been brought to its conclusion if everyone would have had to wait for instructions. Nothing was so crucial as the requirement that the bureaucrat had to understand opportunities and "necessities," that he should act in accordance with perceived imperatives, and most especially so when it was not easy to enunciate them in plainly written words. The German historian Uwe Adam has shown that, already before the war, there was a pronounced tendency to dispense with laws and other formal enactments. Laws (*Gesetze*) most especially were to be held to a minimum. "Implementary decrees" no longer carried into effect the laws to which they referred and, like the 11th Ordinance to the Reich Citizenship Law, which dealt with confiscations, contained entirely new subject matter.[34] Decree-making gave way to government by announcement, as in the case of a Himmler order of December 1938 to deprive Jews of their driver's licenses, which was published, without first appearing in the appropriate legal gazette, in newspapers directly.[35] This administrative evolution continued with more and more reliance on internal directives, first written, then oral. An order by Hitler to annihilate European Jewry was almost certainly given only in oral form.[36] In the final phases, not even orders were needed. Everyone knew what had to be done, and no one was in doubt about directions or goals.

The bureaucracy itself was the source of much that was to transpire. Ideas and initiatives were developed by experts in its ranks. They were submitted as proposals to supervisors and returned as authorizations to their originators. The foremost example is the famous Göring directive, at the end of July 1941, charging Heydrich with organizing the "final solution of the Jewish question" in Europe.[37] It was drafted by Eichmann at the request of Heydrich and presented to Göring ready for signature (untershriftsfertig).[38] Every word, including an opening reference to an earlier directive for expediting Jewish emigration, was carefully chosen. The substantive paragraph, with its euphemism about a final solution, was designed to assure the necessary backing for maximum freedom of action.

Not surprisingly, a constant reliance on bureaucratic initiation eventually brought about the existence of experts accustomed to dealing with Jewish matters in particular. Many agencies had one or more of these specialists: Lösener and Globke in the Interior Ministry, Mödel in the Finance Ministry, Rademacher in the Foreign Office, Wetzel in the Ministry for the Occupied Eastern Territories, Stange in the Reichsbahn, Eichmann in the Security Police. This kind of specialization emerged also in the field. The organization chart of the Finance Office of the Reichcommissar in the Ostland shows an official assigned to Jewish property.[39]

Occasionally, there were enthusiasts who were not constantly preoccupied with Jewish matters in the normal course of their activities, but who would not relinquish an opportunity to go out of their way to leave their imprint on the annihilation process. One of these men was the army's Major General Otto Kohl who, until June 15, 1942, was in charge of transport, civilian and military, in the occupied zone of France.[40] On May 13, 1942, he received an SS captain, the deportation specialist Theodor Dannecker, for an hour and a half, to assure him: "When you tell me 'I want to transport 10,000 or 20,000 Jews from France to the East,' you can count on me to provide the necessary rolling stock and locomotives." Kohl explained that he regarded the rapid solution of the

Jewish question in France as a vital necessity for the army of occupation, and that therefore he would always maintain a radical point of view, even if some people might regard him as "raw."[41] Most participants, however, were aware of the fine line between volunteering one's services, as Kohl had done, and acting, when the time came, in the full use of one's office. Although they avoided an appearance of rawness or reality, they did not have to be goaded to destroy human lives.

Viewing the makeup of the administrative machine as a whole, we must conclude that there was very little prodding or purging of the German bureaucracy. The Reichsbahn or the Order Police could hardly have been pressured in any case. No one but a railroad man could dispatch a train, and no one but the Schutzpolizei and the Gendarmerie could provide police garrisons in the farthest corners of Europe. Within the entire system, internal directives were, if anything, few and sparse. The fact is that the initiators, formulators, and expediters, who at critical junctures moved the bureaucratic machine from one point to the next, came from within that apparatus. Overburdened as they often were, they contributed their share to the destruction of the Jews as a matter of course.

The Preservation of Procedures

Even as the bureaucracy of annihilation consisted in large part of regular personnel in well-established agencies, so the methods of destruction were to a great extent the traditional means of administrative action. Normal procedures were employed also in abnormal situations, as if extreme decisions were not being made, and there were no discernible differences between everyday government functions and the Final Solution.

Let us take the example of setting up a concentration camp. When Auschwitz was being expanded, condemnation proceedings were launched to acquire public and private property with a view to bringing about land transfers,[42] and when barracks were being built and cyanide gas was being procured, the acquisition of materials was subject to the allocation mechanisms of Speer's Ministry for Armaments.[43]

The routines were being followed with even greater perseverance in financial matters. Fiscal integrity was not to be impaired in the destruction process. Once, Heinrich Himmler himself had to consider the case of an SS lieutenant who, in a previous role as a "trustee" of real estate had been obliged to manage the property for the benefit of the Reich until it could be sold to a new owner, but who had "prematurely" terminated leases of Jewish tenants with resulting losses of rent. Had the officer violated his fiduciary responsibility?[44]

A larger quandary faced the German municipal officials of Warsaw after the sudden mass deportations of the ghetto's Jews had begun in July 1942. Utility bills for electricity and gas had not been paid, and how was this debt going to be covered?[45] A similar dilemma was generated for the chief of the Finance Division of the Generalkommissariat Latvia (Dr. Neuendorff) who discovered that taxes owed by dead Jews could not be collected without transfer to his office of money realized from disposals of their confiscated property.[46]

One of the biggest problems was the financing of transport. The Reichsbahn derived its income from clients, that is, people, corporations, or agencies requiring space on its equipment for personal travel or for shipments of cargo. The client for a death train was the Gestapo and the travelers were Jews. The fare, payable by Gestapo offices, was calculated at the passenger rate, third-class, for the number of track kilometers, one way only, with reductions for children. For guards, the round trip price was charged.[47] If at least 400 Jews were deported, group rates were applicable.[48] Arrangements could be made directly or through the official travel bureau (Mitteleuropäisches Reisebüro).[49] The Gestapo, however, had no budget for transport and it would have been awkward to present a bill for the deportations to the Finance Ministry. Accordingly, a policy of "self-financing" was instituted, whereby the funding burden was shifted to authorities in foreign areas where Jewish property had been expropriated or to Jewish communities themselves. In the satellite state of Slovakia, for example, the Foreign Office argued that the Slovak government should pay for the "resettlement," and that, in exchange, the Jews would not be returned.[50] In Germany the Gestapo directed the official Jewish community organization, the Reichsvereinigung der Juden in Deutschland, to collect cash "contributions" from deportees at the point of their departure to help defray the costs of their future existence in the "east."[51] Such levies were deposited in special accounts "W," which the Gestapo could control. The Finance Ministry, which discovered the stratagem, considered it an evasion of the basic principle that only the ministry could collect funds for the Reich and disburse them to agencies as needed, but it acquiesced in the practice.[52] Even more complex was the payment for transports leaving Holland or France, Italy or Greece, for Auschwitz. These trains passed not only through various countries, but also through several currency zones, and in this traversal the balance of payments had to be considered every time a border was crossed.[53] So costly and difficult were all of these funding requirements that, at one point, consideration was given to the possible erection of a death camp in western Germany for Jews from western countries.[54]

"Self-financing" was involved also for projects other than transport, such as the building of the Warsaw ghetto wall. The chairman of the ghetto's Jewish council, Adam Czerniaków, protested to the German ghetto commissar against this burden on the community's treasury, arguing that, since the ghetto had been created for the stated purpose of protecting the non-Jewish population from the spread of epidemics, the assessment was tantamount to asking the pharmacist to pay the bill for the medicine.[55]

The legal procedures and accounting routines were the essential tools of a decentralized apparatus that was attempting to preserve non-Jewish rights at every turn and to balance the books at all times. By these means the bureaucrat would satisfy himself that his actions were appropriate and proper. He could equate correctness with rightness, and accuracy with accountability. The culmination of this way of thinking may be observed in the reporting system, particularly the regular flow of daily, monthly, or annual reports from regional or local offices. Just as there were no special agencies or extraordinary operating funds for the destruction of the Jews, so there was no separate reporting channel or segregated record-keeping in matters of annihilation.[56] Frequently, offices and units in the field would therefore make references to the Final Solution only in long summaries of diverse activities. Such reports, with their markings denoting authorship and distribution, followed a rigid format, maintained a single perspective, and were cast in a laconic, matter-of-fact style. Typical is a sentence from the war diary of the Armament Inspectorate in the Netherlands for November 1942:

> The accelerated implementation of the de-Jewification action by the commander of the Security Police is being accompanied by unavoidable disturbances in fur and clothing enterprises under contract with the armed forces.[57]

For many of these officials, the Jews became a subheading. We see it in rubrics: Wages—Jews, Rations—Jews, Taxes—Jews, Production—Jews. The Jews are absorbed in the daily passage of events, and there is seldom any disconcerting emphasis on their ultimate fate.

Even secrecy could be abandoned in record management. Railroad timetable orders were being dispatched without stamps calling attention

131

to their sensitivity,[58] and in Riga a bureaucrat noted in 1942 that correspondence about the Jewish "estate" (*Nachlass*) in the Trusteeship Division of the German administration of Latvia was no longer classified for security purposes.[59] In a sense, nonlabeling became the ultimate camouflage.

The Perpetrator

What sort of man then was the perpetrator? The very structure and practices of the German bureaucracy should provide us with indications of his character. He valued his competence and efficiency, surmounting innumerable obstacles and adverse conditions. He knew what to do without having to ask for directives. Political platforms and campaigns provide little specific content for bureaucratic action, and Nazi Germany was no different in this respect. The public utterances of leaders and propagandists, the flags, torches, and drums, all these were acts of psychological mobilization which gave theme, form, and pace to the physical measures that were to follow. The bureaucrat, however, was not a creation of the Nazi Party, nor was he an old-fashioned indoctrinated anti-Semite. Julius Streicher's *Stürmer* was not his literature. When the war ended, he would assert that he had never hated Jews, and in any nineteenth-century sense, he did not harbor such feelings in actual fact. He had stood above the small issues to face the larger challenge, though he would not talk in such terms any more than he would have written the word "kill" in an order or report.

Some observers have already recognized that the diffuse machine that destroyed the Jews was staffed by people who would not be recognized for what they were if one talked to them in a living room or some other quiet place. Their social mores were not atypical and their family life and personal concerns were completely commonplace. To one commentator this was "banality." Another, noting the rote manner of bureaucratic action, may find that the most salient trait of German officialdom was a kind of stupefaction, a vast indifference to the nature and consequence of one's acts. Yet we must beware of veneers. There is nothing that appears banal in Eichmann and his many colleagues as soon as they are seen in their acts of destruction. Nor can we describe them as robots when we recall how they deliberated about definitions and classifications, gains and costs. To be sure, they left unsaid much that they thought, for they were breaking barriers and crossing thresholds in ways that bureaucrats seldom attempt. What they did was <u>designed to make history and</u> <u>they were aware of their roles</u> in this undertaking. In the basement of the Nuremberg Traffic Museum, secluded from the gaze of casual visitors, there is a railway map. It shows the network of lines under German control in 1942, the year of its greatest extent.

8

The Gas Chambers

UWE DIETRICH ADAM

Even today certain false ideas and abusive generalizations about the existence, placement, functioning, and "efficiency" of the gas chambers continue to circulate even in reputable historical works, and these lead to confusion and errors. For example, the necessary distinction is not always made between concentration camps and extermination camps. The former, according to SS terminology, served to imprison individuals either temporarily or permanently "by security measures, preventive measures, or reeducative measures." In the spring of 1942 these camps were fifteen in number. The extermination camps *stricto sensu* were four in number and were institutions *sui generis*, independent of concentration camps, conceived and exploited to destroy the greatest possible number of humans in the most rational way.[1]

In the same way, as in all historical analyses, some scientific controversies remain and all the gray areas have not been removed. For instance, historians have proven the difficulty of finding an exact figure for the number of victims of Nazi death installations. These imprecisions and incertitudes have given way to some deliberately false interpretations and allegations that through ideology and propaganda try to deny the existence of the gas chambers. These writers dare to base their theories on the fact that the number of victims differs according to the author, and thus conclude that these massive killings did not happen. It is as if a person denied that the Bastille was taken because historians do not all interpret that event in the same way.[2] Only the enumeration of precise facts can answer such "arguments."

Euthanasia: The First Use of Gas

In April 1915 at Ypres, the Germans first used poison gas. The Allies followed in the practice shortly thereafter. Adolf Hitler, wounded in October 1918, temporarily lost his sight from it, and in *Mein Kampf* he describes the use of that weapon with evident repulsion.[3] He would very soon afterward associate the use of gas and the destiny of his "mortal enemies" in an explosion, often quoted, of anti-Semitic hatred: "If at first, or during the War, we had suddenly placed twelve or fifteen thousand of these Hebrew rotters under the asphyxiating gas that hundreds of thousands of our best German workers of all social levels and professions had to tolerate at the front, then the millions of victims at the front would not have fallen in vain."[4]

In the 1920s the toxicity of carbon monoxide and prussic acid were studied. These were the two gases used in mass exterminations. Carbon monoxide, found notably in auto exhaust, is a colorless, odorless gas, lighter than air. Absorbed in sufficient quantity, it provokes cellular asphyxiation, as the hemoglobin can no longer carry oxygen. Since 1938 the Security Police's Institute for Technical Criminology (KTI) contained a section, VD2, for "chemical and biological analyses." This was directed by a captain in the SS, Dr. Widmann, who experimented in this field.[5] This gas was first used as an instrument of death, using bottled gas or solids, in December 1939 and January 1940. The method of producing it directly from truck exhaust dated from September 1941.[6] The other gas, prussic, or hydrocyanic, acid was at the base of Zyklon B, a powerful insecticide developed in 1923. Provoking a more rapid asphyxiation than carbon monoxide by the reaction of cellular enzymes, it was also first used at Auschwitz in September 1941.

These technical details are not superfluous, for apart from the psychological and moral problems posed by the exterminations, the material problems were not negligible. The three processes of bottled gas, exhaust gas, and Zyklon B would be used successively in euthanasia operations in the eastern territories and finally in the execution of the "Final Solution."

———

In October 1939, Hitler signed the written commands on euthanasia, backdating them September 1, the day the war began.[7] Long premeditated, the operation consisted of suppressing the "beings unworthy of life" (*lebensunwertes Leben*)—namely, the mentally ill. After a brief power struggle the führer's Chancellery, directed by Reichsleiter Philip Bouhler, was charged with the execution, having already taken under its responsibility the euthanasia of handicapped children.[8] In April 1940, an autonomous service was begun, situated in a villa in Berlin-Charlottenberg at 4 Tiergartenstrasse, with the code name "Operation T4." On Hitler's orders, the secret was kept by the protagonists: SS Colonel Viktor Brack, Bouhler's adjunct; Dr. Karl Brandt, Hitler's medical attaché; and ministry adviser Herbert Linden.[9] Given the size of the task, Bouhler and Brack asked for the help of Himmler and the SS, the only partners capable of employing the technical means necessary to rapidly eliminate, without complications, the greatest possible number of victims.

Doubtless as early as October 1939, Arthur Nebe, head of Amt V (ex-Criminal Police) of the Reich Main Security Office (*Reichssicherheitshauptamt*—RSHA) gave the order to the KTI to start testing different means of extermination.[10] After a conference that reunited Nebe, Brack, and Widmann, the final proposal was to use carbon monoxide rather than morphine, scopolamine, or prussic acid.[11] In January 1940, at Brandenburg-Havel Prison, the first trial was held. Six patients were given scopolamine-morphine injections and twenty others were gassed with carbon monoxide. The very clear superiority of the latter method led Brack to decree that asphyxiation by gas would be used in the six "euthanasia institutes" of the Reich.[12]

A bit later the executions begun after this test conformed to the initial experience. Dr. August Becker, chemist of the KTI, responsible for putting the installations into service, gave this account:

> . . .a room analogous to a tiled shower room, measuring about three meters by five, and three meters high. On the periphery were benches, and along the wall, at about ten centimeters from the ground, a gas main about an inch in diameter passed. This pipe was pierced with little holes out of which the carbon monoxide came. The bottles of gas

were kept outside the room and they were blended at the main in order to carry the gas."[13]

The bottles, furnished by the Ludwigshafen factory of I. G. Farben, were delivered by a complex procedure in order not to attract suspicion about such a large consumption of carbon monoxide.[14] Things developed along practically the same lines in all the asylums: after being undressed, the invalids were given a superficial examination and those who had gold teeth were marked with a cross on the back. Then they were led to the gas chambers that resembled shower rooms. A doctor worked the hand lever of the bottle of carbon monoxide and watched the development of asphyxia, which took about twenty minutes. After the room was ventilated, the corpses—once their gold teeth were removed—were consumed by crematoria constructed for this purpose.[15]

Very soon, putting the mentally ill to death began to seem like a mass extermination, conducted like a well-organized industry. Thus, at Hartheim-Linz, 150 invalids were gassed at once.[16] All told, between 1940 and 1941, 71,088 invalids were exterminated.[17]

In April 1940, for the first time, euthanasia exceeded the initial objectives. It was implacably extended to Jewish invalids who until then, on instructions from T4, were refused the "favor of an easy death."[18] In June 1940, 200 mentally ill patients from the asylum of Berlin-Buch were transported to Brandenburg, where they were quickly gassed.[19] Unlike "Aryan" invalids, they were not selected according to the gravity of their handicaps. The fact of being Jewish was enough to condemn them. Starting in September 1940, in every area, Jewish psychiatric patients were united in a single asylum and in December all the mentally ill Jews of the Reich were gathered at Bendorf-Sayn, near Neuwied. From October these invalids, with only a few exceptions, were no longer gassed on Reich territory but were transferred to the General Government of Poland. Their families were notified of their deaths by the "Psychiatric Asylum of Cholm, in Lublin," a nonexistent institution.[20] In fact, it was T4 in Berlin that was responsible for forging the statements of death sent from so-called Cholm. They also printed letters of condolence and other such documents.[21] We do not know anything about the ultimate destiny of these victims and we particularly do not know the precise circumstances of their deaths. It seems that these Jewish invalids were either beaten or shot, or died in the gas trucks.[22]

Among those responsible for euthanasia, SS First Lieutenant Christian Wirth seems to have played an important role, even if, as Reitlinger states, his name "did not appear on any document or letter dealing with euthanasia."[23] Criminal Police inspector in Stuttgart, transferred in November 1939 to the führer's Chancellery, Wirth participated in the first successful attempts at Brandenburg. Sent to the institute at Hartheim in April 1940, "a real bear-garden where disorder reigned,"[24] he distinguished himself there by his organizational abilities. Named in July 1940 as acting commissioner of Criminal Police,[25] it seems that he officially directed the Hartheim Institute from that date. He filled the role of a sort of inspector general of euthanasia establishments, even if one does not find traces of this fact in the documents. Retrospectively, it is certain that the idea of destroying victims in "shower rooms" as well as the forged reports to families of Jewish invalids must be attributed to Wirth.[26] While the role of the institutes of Grafeneck and Hadamar became very quickly known to the public, that of Hartheim worked practically in secret, even after the official halt of euthanasia operations. It was the asylum with the most "efficient" killing rate: 18,269 dead by October 1, 1941.[27]

While Operation T4 unrolled across the territory of the Reich, a similar action began after the occupation of Poland by the Einsatzgruppen, intervention groups dependent on the head of the Security Police and on the SD.[28] Thus it was that SS Captain Herbert Lange used for the first time, from December 17 to 19, 1939, and in January 1940, a mobile gas chamber, to gas the inmates of the Polish asylums of Tiegenhof and Kosten. In this region over 3,600 invalids were gassed in this manner.[29] In East Prussia SS Captain Kurt Eimann on his part had 2,000 invalids shot near Neustadt, beginning in October 1939.[30] These types of actions, parallel to those conducted in the Reich, if they carried the risk of overlapping prerogatives, nevertheless brought some forms of possible collaboration on the levels of men and matériel, and in any event pursued the same goals.

The order to halt the euthanasia operation was given by Hitler on August 24, 1941. In effect, he feared the reactions of the populace after the protests by the Church, notably the archbishop of Münster, Count Clemens August von Galen.

The Gas Trucks

On the eastern front Heydrich gave the verbal order to four Einsatzgruppen to liquidate certain categories of the population. Among them were the "Jews having responsibilities in the Party and the State."[31] Beginning in July and August 1941, these groups concentrated their actions on all Jewish men, then on women and children.[32] Starting in September and October 1941, the collective decisions which made up the "Final Solution" began to be applied, modifying the givens in the plan of extermination.

At the end of August 1941, during a visit to the regional heads of the SS of central and southern Russia, Himmler attended the execution of one hundred Jews not far from Minsk by Einsatzgruppe B, under the orders of SS Major General Arthur Nebe.[33] The truly nightmarish killings were atrocities that had a great effect on Himmler: "Almost fainting, pale, limbs quivering," he only managed by great effort to withstand the sight of the massacre. The same day he asked Nebe to "ponder" a less barbarous way of killing people.[34] Also at Minsk were Dr. Walter Heess, director of the KTI, and Dr. Widmann, whom we already met in Operation T4. After a fruitless experiment with explosives, Widmann had a successful trial with five mental patients at the asylum of Moghilev. He asphyxiated them with gas escaping from a heavy weight, which caused death in thirteen minutes. This was the first time such a technique was used, different from that which used bottles of gas.[35]

It was after this experience that in September 1941, on the order of Heydrich, at the heart of the RSHA, the section of automobile transports (IID3) dependent upon the division of technical affairs (IID) directed by SS Major Walter Rauff attempted with the active collaboration of the KTI to focus on an operational gas truck.[36] After the success achieved by Nebe it was incontestable that this new technique would conquer. It had never before been possible to kill thousands of victims this way. The bottle method posed enormous problems of cost, transportation, and storage. By contrast, the trucks were very mobile and therefore very efficient. And Himmler, after having attended the shooting massacre near Minsk, feared above all for the psychological balance of the executioners: he actually worried that the SS might become brutes. With a sort of perverse pride, he never ceased to emphasize after 1943 that the SS, despite the "difficulty of the task," remain "correct" internally.[37]

SS Captain Friedrich Pradel, head of Section IID3, was in charge of "examining if it was possible to introduce motor exhaust gas into closed vans."[38] Saurer trucks, and Diamond trucks, even smaller, were specially ordered by the Gaubschat Company of Berlin, who built airtight cases on the chassis. To keep the operation a secret, Pradel's men joined the exhaust canisters to the cases, transforming the vehicles into mobile gas chambers.[39] The first trial of this engine was held in the Sachsenhausen concentration camp at the beginning of November 1941. Some Russian prisoners of war were gassed with this engine to the satisfaction of chemists and technicians from the RSHA, who were on the spot.[40] All told, twenty trucks were in service up to June 1942.[41] From November 1941, a truck was assigned to Lange's special commando (Sonderkommando) at Chełmno (Kulmhof) (see below). The others were assigned to Einsatzgruppen that were operating in the USSR, with some eventually going to Yugoslavia and eastern Poland.

In November 1941 one of these trucks was used at Poltava by Sonderkommando 4B, under the orders of SS Captain Paul Blobel. In December 1941 and January 1942, the Jews of Kharkov were gassed with two of these engines.[42] At the beginning of 1942, at Simferopol, Einsatzgruppe D had at its disposal three trucks, a Saurer and two Diamonds, which were used to kill the Jews of Crimea. In the first months of 1942 two trucks were in service in the sector of Group A (Baltic countries), and four in Group B (Belorussia). Group C (Ukraine) disposed of at least five trucks. Across the territory of the USSR then about fifteen trucks were functioning.[43]

These vehicles served to eliminate all persons whom the Third Reich wanted to get rid of. But numerically the Jews constituted the most important category. From the beginning, ignoring the order given by Himmler to kill only women and children with these trucks, prisoners, notably Russians, partisans, the mentally ill, and handicapped children were all exterminated in this manner.[44] The process of the operation was in general always the same. The victims were pushed inside the vehicle, and then asphyxiated, whether on the spot or en route to antitank trenches (or ravines dug for the occasion) into which the bodies were thrown by Jewish auxiliary personnel—themselves generally slaughtered soon afterward—and covered with a thin layer of slaked limestone. The exhaust gas killed in a quarter of an hour, and a group of trucks, working five times a day, permitted the daily killing of from 600 to 900 persons. That is doubtless the explanation of why the SS was dissatisfied with the vehicles and their limited efficacy. In the first place, they did not provide the psychological soothing to killers that Himmler hoped for. It was rather the reverse effect that was produced. The eyewitness report of Blobel's chauffeur gives one instance: "The bodies were soiled and covered with excrement. It was a horrible sight." According to another member of the commando: "Opening the doors, a thick smoke was let out, as a tangle of convulsed bodies fell from the truck. It was a frightful sight."

All the eyewitness reports describe scenes of victims knocking against the walls of the trunks, their cries and their pitiful groans, and finally the movement when it was necessary to detach the bodies by force, tangled and covered with waste. One commando head refused to serve at these gas trucks "because he couldn't ask his men to do such a thing."[45] On the occasion of a trip during which he had inspected the intervention groups and the gas trucks, Dr. August Becker of KTI, who had already participated in euthanasia, signaled "very grave troubles, psychological as much as physiological, for the men who might do this work [unloading the dead and related tasks], if not immediately, then eventually."[46]

Another reason for the SS's dissatisfaction was the limited "output" of these killing engines, an output quite simply insufficient given the considerable numbers of Russian Jews. The gas trucks were not close to rivaling the firing squads of intervention groups. It was thus, for example, that a commando placed under the orders of the head of the SS and the police of southern Russia, SS Lieutenant General Richard Jeckeln, shot more than 20,000 Jews in three days at Kamenets-Podolsk. As for the reinforced Sonderkommando 4A led by Blobel, it succeeded in shooting in two days—September 29 and 30, 1941—over 33,000 Jews of Kiev in the ravine near Babi Yar.[47]

A gas truck was only "useful" if, as in Yugoslavia, it could provide a "sustained effort," that is, to function slowly and without interruption. The Jews of Serbia and Belgrade, who were regrouped at Semlin (Zemun) and whose number in March 1942 oscillated between 5,000 and 5,500, were decimated starting in mid-March 1942 on the orders of Military Chief of Administration Dr. Harald Turner, by means of a "delousing truck acquired from the SD."[48] In April 1942, the number of camp occupants had fallen to 2,974, and at the end of May Dr. Schaefer, commander in chief of the Security Police and of the SD, could announce that in Serbia there was no longer "any Jewish problem."[49] On July 9, 1942, this gas truck was sent to Berlin for an overhaul, from which it left again for Riga with other uses in view. Another gas truck worked in the same way without interruption at Lublin.[50]

If the gas trucks offered the inconvenience of not being constantly on the scene, this was principally due to their technical deficiencies. Dr. Becker, who on orders of the RHSA controlled, inspected, and repaired all the trucks put into service by the intervention groups, wrote a letter to Rauff dated May 16, 1942, in which he laid out a minute inventory of all the faults he had observed. It was generally a question of trivial mishaps, but given the difficulty of sending for spare parts, these quickly put a vehicle out of service.[51]

In a note of July 5, 1942, sent to Rauff, the Automobile Transport Section affirmed that it had, since December 1941, "treated 97,000 persons with three of the trucks in service, without the vehicles having had any breakdowns."[52] But even this positive accounting could not erase the fact that the seven improvements or changes that this note proposed for the vehicles necessitated important changes in their fabrication.

The Gaubschat establishments, whom we can imagine were asked to make these modifications, declared them impossible because of a shortage of personnel and materials. Another firm in Czechoslovakia did not seem as trustworthy.[53] The total number of trucks in service thus remained at twenty. Ten more trucks were to be delivered, but clearly they were never made, doubtless because the SS finally understood that the possibilities of using these engines were limited.[54]

The Gas Trucks of Chełmno (Kulmhof)

The special commando of Herbert Lange, which on December 17, 1939, had made the first operable mobile gas chamber, was one of the first beneficiaries of the RSHA's special trucks. The commando received them shortly after they were installed at Chełmno, a little spot on the Ner River where an unoccupied castle had been requisitioned at the end of October or the beginning of November. It took them only a few weeks to arrange and mark out the "forest camp," situated five kilometers away.[55]

From December 5, 1941, and until just before Christmas, Lange began to gas the neighboring Jews.[56] Clearly, it was a question of "trial and error," to refine the process of extermination. The same month, Adolf Eichmann arrived to make an inspection.[57]

The victims had to undress in a room situated behind the castle. From there they took a stairway leading to the cellar, then a corridor opening on a ramp surrounded by a high stockade of planks. At the very end of the ramp, a gray truck waited. As soon as thirty or forty persons had entered and the truck was filled, the doors were closed. A Polish worker pulled the flexible cord attached to the exhaust canister under the truck. The driver, an SS soldier, ran the motor for ten or fifteen minutes with the truck standing still. Then he drove to the forest, where the bodies were piled in trenches already prepared by a detachment of Jewish workers. Later the bodies would be burned in crematoria.[58]

The sector that furnished the victims of Chełmno was formed principally by the Warthegau, a newly created *Gau* of which Łódź (Litzmannstadt) was the main ghetto.[59] It was under the control of Reich Governor and Gauleiter Arthur Greiser, who put fanatical fury into "getting rid of the Jews" of his territory.[60] The growing overpopulation of Łódź, which also received the Jews coming from the Reich, clearly made him determined to take up the proposition formulated by the head of the SD of Posen (Poznań) in July 1941: "This winter a danger threatens, that is, that the Jews can no longer all be fed. There is occasion for asking seriously if the most humane solution is to liquidate the Jews, by whatever means, but rapidly, in cases where they are unable to work. In any event, this will be a more agreeable solution than letting them die of hunger."[61]

Less than a year later, on May 1, 1942, Greiser wrote to Himmler: "The operation for which, in agreement with SS Lieutenant General Heydrich, head of the Reich Main Security Office (RSHA), you gave your authorization, that is, that the special treatment of about 100,000 Jews from the region placed under my orders, can be achieved in the next two or three months."[62]

It was Lange's experience which doubtless enabled him to be assigned to Chełmno, and permitted such a result. SS Captain Hans Bothmann, who followed him in March 1942, continued to apply his methods. But clearly a serious situation had developed with the trucks. One of them exploded. The RSHA reacted by giving special instructions that "were so well observed that the degree of security has been clearly augmented."[63] During periods of great "abundance," the gas trucks ran a shuttle up to ten times daily between the castle and the forest, which caused them a lot of wear and tear. Every two or three trips, the drivers were replaced.[64]

Approximately 145,500 people were killed this way. At the end of March 1943, Chełmno was dissolved. The last Jewish workers were shot and the crematoria destroyed by explosives.[65] In April 1944, the massacres began again. In order to gas the last survivors of the ghetto of Łódź, Hans Bothmann and a group of his old followers from the SS "Prince Eugene" Division, quickly rebuilt the installations. Unlike the first period, the victims were gassed directly in the forest camp, where two barracks and a crematorium were built. The victims used a corridor bordered with high planks of wood, opening upon an inclined ramp. They were pushed into the gas truck, and afterward a squad of Jews quickly threw the bodies into the crematory ovens.[66] This "more rational process," which avoided the back-and-forth between castle and forest, claimed at least 7,000 lives.[67]

In July 1944, Chełmno ceased its activities once and for all. The Jews of the Łódź ghetto were sent to Auschwitz. The camp was dissolved in January 1945, but not before the Jews from the remaining work teams staged a violent resistance.[68] Herbert Lange was observed one final time in Berlin in April 1945, according to Bothmann. He hanged himself in April 1946 while a prisoner of the British.[69]

Operation Reinhard

After the Wannsee Conference of January 20, 1942, the representative of the governor-general of Poland, Dr. Joseph Bühler, asked "that the Jewish question in this region be resolved as quickly as possible." This request involved 2,284,000 Jews. In response, Operation Reinhard was launched, under the direction of SS Brigadier General Odilo Globocnik, and this led to the construction of the Bełżec, Sobibór, and Treblinka camps. Certain enigmas persist on this subject. Contrary to what most historians believe, it is not certain that this operation was named in memory of Heydrich, who died on July 5, 1942, after an attempt on his life.[70] Similarly, the time lag in construction work is not fully explained: the Bełżec camp opened in November 1941, Sobibór in March 1942, and Treblinka at the end of May and the beginning of June 1942.

Essentially, these camps were conceived in the same way as the euthanasia operations, Christian Wirth's hand being recognizable. They were situated on isolated sites away from important cities, in the middle of thick forests, and were linked by railways. The arrangement was practicable: a platform alongside the railway, a barbed-wire enclosure three meters high covered with tree branches measuring some hundreds of meters in length and width. Outside was the "camp entry" with barracks for the SS. The camp itself was divided into three sectors: Camp I had lodgings and workrooms for Jews doing forced labor. Camp II was reserved for new arrivals, with storage sheds for baggage and the arriving prisoners' valuable objects. Finally, Camp III, connected to the former by a "communication trench," bordered with a high wall and surrounded by another wall, was reserved for exterminations.

The gas chambers were installed in concrete dugouts, a different method from moving trucks. Camp III also included barracks with gas chambers, other barracks where Jewish detainees were lodged, and the mass graves where the victims were thrown.[71]

Christian Wirth was named inspector of the three camps in August 1942. Doubtless, it was Wirth's idea to include a panel with the inscription "Bathroom and Inhalation Rooms," with flowerpots to create an attractive decor, and to have the camp commandant make lulling speeches to the prisoners.

Wirth was named commandant of Bełżec in the last two weeks of December 1941. When the arrangements were completed in February 1942, he began gassing tests on two or three convoys of Jews, each with one hundred persons. He alternated between using carbon monoxide in bottles and exhaust gas from the diesel motors of cars or large trucks (an innovation), clearly seeking to compare the efficiency of the two processes.[72] On March 17, 1942, a regular arrival of convoys began, first from the ghetto and surrounding area of Lublin, then from the Lemberg (Lvov) district. By the end of May 1942, 80,000 Jews had been killed. During this first period, the "output" of Bełżec, with its three gas chambers, was around 150 to 200 victims per chamber per "session."[73]

On a site at the camp's entry, young and vigorous men were separated from the others and designated for Jewish work teams. Old or feeble persons and invalids were immediately led to the trenches of Camp III and slaughtered. As for the rest, after the "reassuring" speech, men were separated from women and children. These were undressed separately in turn and unburdened of valuable objects and clothes. The men were the first to be led by the "communication trench" to the gas chambers.

In another barracks in Camp II, women had their hair cut. Then they were gassed with the children. A commando of Jewish prisoners removed the dead. A special team looked for gold teeth or hidden jewelry. Then the corpses were transported to the mass graves on flat wagons.[74] At regular intervals, Jews on the work teams were killed.

In April 1942, Wirth returned to Sobibór to instruct the camp commandant, Franz Stangl.[75] They proceeded then to experiments in which thirty to forty Jews were gassed. The gas came from the motors of cars or Russian tractors. The chambers were constructed in brick buildings on concrete foundations, an incontestable improvement over Bełżec. Starting in mid-May 1942, the camp was operational. Jews from the Lublin

145

district and from Austria and Czechoslovakia above all were exterminated there. The three gas chambers had a capacity comparable to those
of Bełżec—from 140 to 160 persons each.[76] But far fewer trainloads of
deportees arrived at Sobibór. At the end of June and beginning of July
1942, the saturation of military transports led to a general blockage. Due
to repairs to the railways between Lublin and Chełm, convoys of deportees arrived only occasionally in August.[77]

At this moment Treblinka, constructed last, began to work. It was
situated in the district of Warsaw, but was placed under the authority of
SS and Police Leader Globocnik. Because of the experience at Bełżec
and Sobibór, the three gas chambers were put into a building capable of
airtightness.[78] But the camp installations were too small for the convoys
from the Warsaw ghetto, which had started arriving on July 23, 1942.
Soon the gassing equipment was saturated, and the elimination of
corpses was no longer possible. Decomposing corpses were visible from
the Treblinka railway station, four kilometers away from the camp. Dr.
Stangl was sent by Globocnik from Sobibór to Treblinka to replace Commandant Eberl. Stangl had participated in euthanasia,[79] and was to assist
in this untenable situation. He summed up his first impressions in this
way: "Dante's Hell has become reality here."[80]

The first period in which Treblinka functioned lasted only five weeks,
during which at least 5,000 Jews arrived at the camp. Later, up to 12,000
Jews arrived daily.

THE EXTERMINATION CAMPS OF OPERATION REINHARD

	FIRST PERIOD OF EXTERMINATIONS					SECOND PERIOD OF EXTERMINATIONS			
	Period	Number of gas chambers	Number of persons per chamber	Number of victims	Date of Transfor-mation	Period	Number of gas chambers	Number of persons per chamber	Total number of victims
Bełżec	March 17 to June 1942	3	150–200	100,000	May/June 1942	July 21, 1942 to Jan. 1943	6	200–250	600,000
Sobibór	May 16 to July 1942	3	140–160	90,000	Sept./Oct. 1942	Oct. 1942 to Oct. 1943	6	200–250	240,000
Treblinka	July 23 to Aug. 28, 1942	3	450–600	215,000	Aug./Sept. 1942	Sept. 1942 to Oct. 1943	10	200–250	700,000

In the spring and summer of 1942, the three camps were enlarged through significant alterations. At Bełżec the wooden buildings were replaced by a solid edifice containing six gas chambers. At Treblinka, Stangl and Wirth had another building constructed beside the old one, capable of holding 2,000 persons. The last of the three camps to be transformed was Sobibór, where the barracks with gas chambers were partly demolished, then rebuilt and enlarged. The above diagram indicates the principal arrangements, their dates, and their "output."[81]

One of the questions that the participants in Operation Reinhard asked themselves was if carbon monoxide was efficient enough to attain the goal in mind. Kurt Gerstein, an SS first lieutenant, commanded the disinfection group under the head of the health service of the Waffen-SS. Gerstein was assigned to buy Zyklon B, a product that made motors unnecessary, which meant that the frequent breakdowns could be avoided. Zyklon B gas was first used at Auschwitz (see below). Its usefulness would prove such that Globocnik visited the camp at the beginning of the summer of 1942 to learn about this new technique.[82] Gerstein assuredly took exception to the Nazi methods and did much to make the exterminations known outside of Germany. Nevertheless, until the killing finally stopped, he remained responsible for supplying Zyklon B.[83] In June 1942, Eichmann's adjunct, SS Captain Rolf Günther, requested that Gerstein furnish 100 kilograms of prussic acid (Zyklon B) for an ultrasecret mission.

In August, Gerstein, Günther, and Private Pfannenstiel returned to Lublin, where Globocnik described the situation to them. He defined Gerstein's task in these terms: "Another, far more important mission is your duty: it consists of achieving the reconversion of our gas chambers, which currently work with exhaust gas from diesel engines, until they can function with something quicker and more efficacious. I believe prussic acid is foremost."[84]

On August 17, 1942, Gerstein attended a demonstration of extermination with carbon monoxide in the new installations at Bełżec.[85] As an express fact, the diesel engines started up only after "2 hours and 49 minutes," according to the chronometer that Gerstein held. However, for reasons that remain inexplicable, Wirth asked Gerstein, despite this defeat, not to "propose any modification of the installations and to leave the system as it was, since it is working itself in perfectly."[86] Gerstein tried to bury Zyklon B. However, the reputation of this product was so great that even Eichmann, after a visit to Treblinka, "that frightful place," believed that he could recall the gas being used there.[87]

147

In December 1942 the extermination operation was not yet completed. In February 1943, Himmler himself came as far as Lublin. But he was not shown Bełżec, where the exterminations had stopped since December 1942 and where, since that date, the burning of corpses and destruction of the camp had begun.[88] The Jewish prisoners who had survived were led in April 1943 to Sobibór, where they were killed. In the spring and summer of 1943, the convoys arrived only irregularly at Treblinka and Sobibór.[89] The existence of the two camps could no longer be justified, other than by the necessity of keeping a safety valve in case of an overflow from Auschwitz.

On August 2, 1943, a revolt broke out at Treblinka.[90] The same thing happened at Sobibór on October 14 of the same year.[91] These uprisings hastened the dissolution of the two camps, organized by Globocnik, starting in August 1943.[92]

After the killings of the last Jewish laborers, Globocnik announced to Himmler that he had completed Operation Reinhard on October 19, 1943, and that he had dissolved all the camps.[93] After August 1943 he was named regional chief of the SS and the Adriatic police.

Auschwitz and Zyklon B

(L. Levi)

In the history of Nazi exterminations, Auschwitz occupies a place apart, in every sense of the term. It was the largest camp; prussic acid was first used there for the mass slaughter of human beings; and the camp is the source of many erroneous speculations, deliberate or not. Auschwitz was simultaneously a concentration camp, a labor camp, and an extermination camp. In November 1943, after successive transformations, the camp was divided into three parts:

- *Auschwitz I*, the main, original concentration camp
- *Auschwitz II*, Birkenau, a labor camp and extermination camp
- *Auschwitz III*, Monowitz and many other labor camps, created in October 1942 near the Buna factory of I. G. Farben, built at Dwory in April 1943[94]

In May 1940, Auschwitz, called in Polish Oświęcim, was planned on the grounds and in the buildings of an old artillery barracks. It comprised twenty permanent buildings and barracks and could hold 10,000 persons. In Summer 1941 the SS began extending the main camp. Eight extra one-story buildings were constructed, as well as several barracks and administrative buildings, so that the capacity was enlarged to 30,000 persons. In the course of this phase of transformation, a crematory oven was installed that could burn a maximum of 340 corpses every twenty-four hours. For practical reasons, it was built beside an old munitions dugout of sixty-five square meters, which served for storing the dead bodies.[95] This crematorium, designed to deal with the new capacity of the camp, received a daily "ration" of dead that needed to be burned: those who succumbed to hunger, illness, and exhaustion, and those who had been executed. From May 1940 to January 1942, 20,500 prisoners died at Auschwitz, almost 1,000 per month.[96] Put into working order in August 1941, the crematorium signaled a new purpose for Auschwitz. Originally, the camp was intended to receive "prisoners held in security detention for nonserious offenses, likely to be reformed." The camp's purpose would later change to receiving prisoners of a second category, "those with serious charges against them but still potentially able to be reformed and rehabilitated."[97]

Prussic acid, or Zyklon B, used in the camp as a disinfectant or insecticide, was first utilized to kill camp inmates in September 1941. According to Rudolf Höss, the first camp commandant, it was his adjunct officer, SS Captain Fritzsch, who performed the experiment on some Soviet commissars. After September the process was repeated on Russian prisoners of war. Block 11, then the mortuary depot of the main camp, "the morgue," was arranged for gassings. In the concrete and clay roof of the depot, otherwise airtight, several holes were pierced. Zyklon B flowed through these holes in the form of little pellets. Then the corpses were burned in the crematorium.[98]

───

On the occasion of his first visit to Auschwitz in May 1941, Himmler gave the order to construct a camp for prisoners of war outside the main camp. The chosen site, Birkenau, called Brzezinka in Polish, was located about two kilometers from the main camp, and was to be capable of holding 100,000 persons. Construction began in October 1941. In March 1942, Auschwitz I's Russian prisoners of war were transferred there. Other enlargement projects planned in August 1942 were designed to double Birkenau's capacity, but though the work went on until the end of 1943, the additions were never completed.[99]

In January and February 1942, after the arrival of the Jews from the eastern part of Upper Silesia, Rudolf Höss looked for other places to install new gas chambers. He found them in two farms in Birkenau, which were duly prepared in a manner to receive first "Bunker I," with two gas chambers, and then "Bunker II," with four of them. The latter could accommodate 1,200 persons.[100] On July 17 and 18, 1942, Himmler attended one of the first mass asphyxiations achieved in "Bunker II" in order to follow the operation in detail.[101]

At the beginning, Birkenau was to be a prisoner-of-war camp, receiving prisoners of the same "category" as the main camp. However, starting in May 1942, it became a "mixed" camp, that is, of labor, concentration, and extermination. Most of the deportees, as soon as they arrived, were led directly to the gas chambers without any entrance procedure. In July 1942, "selections" began on the train arrival platforms between Auschwitz I and Auschwitz II. Persons who seemed in good health were put to work at Birkenau or Monowitz. The others were quickly led to the gas chambers. At regular intervals, selections were also made of the occupants of the labor camps.

From then on, Auschwitz's problem was no longer the insufficient output of the installations of death: hydrocyanic acid killed at the expected rate. In the gas chambers the victims, pressed one against another, always radiated the heat necessary to reach the point (25.7° C) at which the acid was transformed into gas. The victims located closest to the gas entry vents died fairly quickly. The others died after five minutes at most. Twenty-five more minutes were counted, and then the doors were opened and the corpses' gold teeth were removed. Unlike the procedure in Operation Reinhard, here women's hair was cut only after they were dead. The corpses were then carried to the ovens on cars or flat wagons.[102] The real problem was the accumulation of bodies; the planned graves were scarcely big enough. In the summer of 1942 the stench became unbearable. The danger of underground water becoming contaminated was clear. After Himmler's visit in July 1942, two decisions were made: to dig up and burn the bodies, and to begin to build crematory ovens connected to the gas chambers. In July the SS Central Office for Construction at Auschwitz opened negotiations with certain subsidiary businesses.[103] In August 1942 the project to enlarge Birkenau planned two buildings with a crematory oven in each, and construction began in October 1942. Each oven could burn 1,440 corpses in twenty-four hours. The gas chambers and the rooms where the victims undressed were located underground. The Zyklon B entered through openings in the ceiling and was removed by mechanical means. These installations could kill up to 2,500 persons at a time. At almost the same time, construction was begun on two other crematoria (with smaller gas chambers) that could each burn 768 corpses every twenty-four hours. These four crematory ovens were put to work between March 22 and June 25, 1943. The four gas chambers could hold 1,500, 800, 600, and 150 persons. If the number of persons that could be killed was thus limitless, the crematoria could only burn about 8,000 persons at the most, working at their maximum rate for a limited time.[104] So corpses were burned in trenches outside the crematoria. In August 1944, Auschwitz attained its optimum "output." In one day 24,000 Hungarian Jews were killed.[105]

The last convoys of Jews arrived on November 3 and November 26, 1944. Himmler gave the order to destroy the crematoria.

To sum up, the facilities included:

At *Auschwitz I:*

- An experimental gas chamber used on September 3, 1941, called "Block 11."
- A gas chamber installed in the camp crematorium called "the Morgue" and used until October 1942.

At *Auschwitz II, Birkenau:*

- Two gas chambers in "Bunker I" that functioned from January 1942 and were subsequently demolished.
- Four gas chambers in "Bunker II" that functioned from June 1942 and which, with interruptions, were kept in service until the autumn of 1944. Destroyed in 1945 by the SS, their ruins still exist.
- Finally, the four installations put into service in the spring of 1943, called "crematoria," and numbered I through IV or II through V accordingly. Crematorium IV was destroyed by a revolt by the forced laborers on October 7, 1944. Crematoria II and III were demolished at the end of 1944 and the beginning of 1945. Crematorium V, which functioned until the end to burn the dead, was itself destroyed on January 26, 1945.[106]

In 1942 and 1943 more than 19,500 kilograms of Zyklon B were sent to Auschwitz, and during the first four months of 1944 more than 3,000 kilograms were sent.[107] These amounts permitted the SS to gas between 1 million and 1.2 million human beings.[108]

Majdanek and the Other Camps

Lublin-Majdanek resembled Auschwitz in many ways. It was at the same time a concentration camp and an extermination camp, although far less important than Auschwitz. To this day, it has received the least research from historians.

151

Majdanek was constructed on the orders of Himmler, who visited Lublin on July 21, 1941, and ordered Globocnik to make every arrangement for building a concentration camp.[109] The preparations were time-consuming. Only in March 1942 was the head of Operation Reinhard, SS Captain Hans Höfle, able to announce that the camp was being constructed.[110] In April 1942 the Main Economic-Administrative Office of the SS mentioned Lublin-Majdanek as being one of the concentration camps, even though it was not yet functioning.[111] As Höfle indicated, Majdanek was planned as a labor camp for Jews, who were inscribed in a register and could be assigned to various jobs.

The camp was put into operation during the summer of 1942. It contained two gas chambers in a wooden barracks. In the spring of 1943 the camp was equipped with other gas chambers, built of concrete and provided with metal doors with rubber hinges.[112] The first gas chambers had a capacity of 300 persons. These were hardly superior to the chambers at Bełżec. Those built later were of differing sizes. One was capable of holding 300 persons, while the smallest ones held 150 persons each.[113] A large crematory oven completed the killing installations.[114] Lublin-Majdanek was not, truly speaking, an extermination camp, in that its primary role was to furnish laborers rather than to kill human beings.

As an officially recognized concentration camp, it obeyed the Main Economic-Administrative Office in Berlin. Odilo Globocnik also clearly considered Majdanek a sort of concentration camp for carrying out his own orders, working in various ways to collaborate with the extermination camps of Operation Reinhard.[115] Were the passengers in the convoys that arrived at Majdanek quickly and surely consigned to death? This is extremely doubtful. It seems that as soon as the convoys arrived, the rule was to make regular selections, separating the Jews who could work from the women and children, the old and ill, who would be gassed then and there.[116] Immediate extermination was also the fate reserved for Russian prisoners of war and Polish partisans.[117]

A partial enigma remains concerning the methods used at Majdanek to gas the victims. According to the eyewitness accounts of certain survivors, the first massacres, beginning in September 1942, were done with bottled carbon monoxide. Then, starting in 1943, Zyklon B was used.[118] According to the Düsseldorf tribunal, the two processes were used alternately, which is doubtlessly incorrect.[119] The bottles certainly came from unused reserves of the T4 euthanasia operation. Globocnik must have called upon specialists from this operation, including Christian Wirth. At this time, bottled gas was replaced by exhaust gas. Once the reserves were gone, Globocnik had to use Zyklon B, whose use was already established.

The number of victims varies according to the authorities.[120] According to the testimony of a Polish resistance fighter, from July 1943 up to 6,000 Jews from the Lublin district were brought to Majdanek and a large number were immediately gassed.[121] During this period, Majdanek functioned as an extermination camp, with a total capacity of 25,000 prisoners. In October 1943, Majdanek stopped functioning, at the same time as Operation Reinhard, which indicates that the camp was directly linked to the latter. On November 3, 1943, as part of an operation called "Harvest Festival," the SS shot 40,000 Jewish prisoners, of whom 15,000 were from the camp itself, the rest from work camps.[122] After this massacre the gas chambers stopped being used.[123] In July 1944 the Red Army reached Majdanek, which was the first extermination camp of the Third Reich to be liberated. The SS left Lublin in such haste that they did not have time to completely destroy all the dugouts where the gas chambers and crematory ovens were located.[124]

It is established that there were gas chambers in several camps situated in German territory: at Mauthausen, after the autumn of 1941; at Sachsenhausen, where installations of this type existed from mid-March 1942; in the women's camp of Ravensbrück, which was equipped in January 1945 with a wooden barracks used to gas prisoners; at Stutthof after June 1944; at Neuengamme after September 1942; and at Dachau after the summer of 1942. The documentation we have is insufficient regarding the dates when installations were built and the times during which they functioned. The Natzweiler-Struthof (Alsace) camp occupies a separate position, as only once were deportees gassed there in a place provided for this. The eighty deportees were gassed because Professor August Hirt of the University of Strasbourg (then called the University of the Reich) believed that, because of their anatomical construction, the prisoners would provide an interesting collection of skeletons. This episode has been retold numerous times to demonstrate the repugnant aspect of Nazi "scientific" research and was examined at the Nuremberg Trials of Nazi doctors.[125]

In addition, thousands of mental patients and invalids were sent to concentration camps, notably Auschwitz, to be gassed in the euthanasia institutes of the Reich, as part of the "14 f 13" Operation.[126]

That said, even if it is an inarguable fact that there were gassings in the territories of the German Reich, notably with Zyklon B, it would be totally absurd to compare these killings with the massive exterminations of the "Final Solution." They were not recorded as a collective institutional murder like the latter. The gassings on the territory of the Reich, except for those involving euthanasia, functioned for only a little while, in installations annexed to already existing crematoria. They only served to eliminate detainees with the maximum of discretion. In this sense all comparisons between the two activities remain quite unjustified.[127]

The locations of the extermination processes have assumed aspects difficult to define and situate in time, apart from their abominable character and the difficulty of postwar generations to conceive of and accept them. Hence, the disagreements among historians on their evolution. Some existed in the capacity of crematory ovens such as Auschwitz, as well as the historic fact of Lublin-Majdanek. Study of the Chełmno, Bełżec, Sobibór, and Treblinka camps is made more difficult because of their own important transformations. These uncertainties are both habitual and traditional in building an historic reality. This is especially true when dealing with a subject so charged with emotion. Yet these same uncertainties have served as pretexts for casting doubt and indeed for denying the reality of massive exterminations.[128] The so-called "scientific" approach consists of contradicting a number of sworn documents. This is nothing more than a stubborn refusal to accept evidence, the revival of a hidebound attitude formed by a single ideology, namely anti-Semitism. This approach can be summed up as follows: "There can not exist what must not exist."

9

The Statistic

RAUL HILBERG

On November 26, 1945, an SS major in the Security Service, Dr. Wilhelm Höttl, signed an affidavit in which he described a conversation he had had with Adolf Eichmann in Budapest at the end of August 1944. On that occasion, according to Höttl, Eichmann had told him that 6 million Jews had been killed, 4 million of them in camps and 2 million in other ways, particularly in the course of shootings during the campaign against the USSR.[1] The International Military Tribunal, in its judgment of September 3, 1946, repeated the figure of 6 million, attributing it to Eichmann, without mention of Höttl.[2]

Eichmann may well have indicated 6 million,[3] but one of his own subordinates, SS Captain Dieter Wisliceny, recalled that at a meeting at the end of the war Eichmann had remarked that he would laughingly jump into his grave for the death of 5 million Jews.[4] When Eichmann was placed on trial in Jerusalem, the question could be put to him directly. His answer centered on 5 million victims.[5]

Of course, Eichmann, who served in the Reich Main Security Office (RSHA), was in possession of numerous reports with statistics which could be categorized and added.[6] Jewish organizations also made calculations, but in a totally different manner. Their principal method was the subtraction of postwar figures (including voluntary enlistments) from those of the prewar census or estimates. According to one unpublished compilation, presented in June 1945 by the Institute of Jewish Affairs, in New York, the number of victims fell somewhere between 5,659,600 and 5,673,100, of which 1,250,000 were within the USSR frontiers of August 1939. To obtain this last figure, it was assumed that 2,100,000 Jews lived in that part of Soviet territory which the Germans were to occupy, that the Soviet authorities had evacuated half of these citizens from the region (though a lesser percentage of the rural population), and that there remained 30,000 survivors. One year later, Jacob Leszczynski of the World Jewish Congress suggested a global figure of 5,978,000, of which 1,500,000 were Soviet Jews living within the August 1939 frontiers.

To this day, the majority of published estimates have hovered between five and six million. Beyond that, their methods of calculation remained much the same. The numbers had been extrapolated from information, sometimes fragmentary, coming from the German military, their related agencies, and various Jewish sources; they were also taken from the comparisons established between prewar and postwar statistics. One must bear in mind, however, that the raw data are self-explanatory, and that to interpret them often requires the compilation of voluminous material which itself must be submitted to analysis. Assumptions may therefore be piled on assumptions, and the margins of error may be wider than they seem. To state the matter simply, exactness is impossible.

Adding

Any assessment based on additions must reflect the origins and meanings of the numbers found in wartime documents. The most important characteristic of the large majority of these figures is that they stem from an actual count of the victims. There was a reason for this phenomenon. The head count was the basis of bureaucratic accountability; numbers were essential to orderliness. By and large, the figures can be grouped into three broad categories: (1) deaths as the result of privation, principally hunger and disease in ghettos, (2) shootings, and (3) deportations to death camps. The division is natural, because it corresponds to a jurisdictional segmentation in the bureaucratic apparatus. One component handled ghettoization, another shootings, a third transport, and each made records of its sphere of activity.

156

The statistics of privation were kept by Jewish councils and reported to German supervisory organs that utilized the figures to decrease rations and space. There are tabulations indicating mortality in the Jewish communities of the Reich, Austria, and the Protectorate of Bohemia-Moravia.[9] Detailed enumerations exist also for the ghettos of Warsaw and Łódź,[10] but the data are sparse for other localities. Hence, privation is hard to measure. Among the major causes of death, it is the smallest category, but in the realm of conjecture, it is the largest.

Statistics for shootings were produced by SS and Police units, especially the so-called Einsatzgruppen of the RSHA. At times, these formations seemed to justify their actions and even their existence with numbers. The attention to detail is revealed in a field report by Einsatzkommando 3 of Einsatzgruppe A, which lists "executions" at seventy-one localities in Lithuania, Latvia, and White Russia, complete with a breakdown of Jewish men, women, and children, as well as of non-Jewish victims such as Communists and mental patients, shot in the course of each operation.[11]

Einsatzgruppe situation reports were consolidated daily in the Reich Main Security Office for distribution to privileged recipients. These long documents contain many statistics, but they are not nearly as detailed as the numbers which fill six pages in the progress report prepared by Einsatzkommando 3 in the field. Some of the cumulative figures in the daily consolidations are not provided with the time span that they cover, and sometimes they do not disclose whether credit is being taken for the entire result of a joint operation undertaken with some other formation. Whenever the shootings of another organization, such as the Order Police deployed by a Higher SS and Police leader, are acknowledged, the numbers are at best approximate. For example, Einsatzgruppe C mentioned 10,000 Jews killed in Dnepropetrovsk by units of the Higher SS and Police Command South, whereas the army (perhaps with more complete information) noted 15,000.[12] Aside from such variations, there are some major gaps in the picture. The reports of shootings in 1942 and 1943 are less complete than those of 1941, and small-scale killings by army or SS units in the rear areas behind the Russian front, or by civil agencies, are generally underreported.

The third set of statistics, dealing with deportations, is numerically the largest category. Again, there was occasion for meticulous counting. In western countries, the Reich, and Slovakia, transports were planned with lists.[13] In Belgium, France, and Italy, the rosters of names, made up in transit camps, have largely survived intact.[14] For Yugoslav Macedonia and Greek Thrace, which were under Bulgarian domination, and also for Hungary, there is more than one set of statistics. The differences between these multiple reports are slight.[15] In Poland the railway administration sometimes admonished its personnel to report the number of deportees by train, so that the Security Police could be billed accordingly.[16]

Occasionally, the documentation indicates not only the place of deportation, but also the point of arrival. The routes of some of the transports are discernible in reports of the railroads or guards of the Order Police.[17] Stops in the ghettos of Łódź or Theresienstadt were recorded.[18] Deported Jews shot in Minsk, Riga, or Kaunas (Kovno) were mentioned in the context of local killing operations.[19] The death camp of Treblinka was identified in one report as the destination of 310,322 Warsaw Jews.[20] It should be noted, however, that there was no systematic counting of arrivals by camp administrations. The deportees in the pure killing centers of Treblinka, Bełżec, and Sobibór were hastily unloaded, undressed, and shoved into the gas chambers. Even in Auschwitz and Lublin, which were more elaborate camps operated by the SS's Main Economic-Administrative Office (WVHA), only those Jews were registered who were to be kept alive for a while. Not counted were the multitudes who were gassed immediately.

The keystone among all of these German records is a recapitulation by the statistician of the SS, Dr. Richard Korherr, about the "final solution of the European Jewish question." The sixteen-page document, dated March 23, 1943, summarizes the situation as of December 31, 1942. A six-page supplement, confined to deportation statistics, deals with the first three months of 1943.[21]

Much about the Korherr report, including its origin and purpose, remains obscure. From the fact that the end of the lethal year 1942 was chosen as a bench mark, one might surmise that it was intended as a progress report. But more was involved than a summation. By the end of 1942, Reichsführer-SS Himmler was under attack from Albert Speer, minister for armaments and war production, and General Friedrich Fromm, the chief of the reserve army, who were increasingly concerned with the preservation of manpower. The "Final Solution" was threatening a reservoir of Jewish labor, and concentration camps were swallowing potential German soldiers. Speer and Fromm, evidently in collusion, approached Hitler himself to challenge the adequacy and veracity of roundup and arrest statistics offered by the Reich Main Security Office.[22]

The implication of the complaint, that the SS was refusing to disclose the extent of its inroads on human resources, presented Himmler with an odd dilemma. How could he present the full range of his achievements to Adolf Hitler, yet couch them in appropriate terms for "camouflage" (*Tarnung*)? For this task he needed his professional statistician, Korherr, a man whose credentials could not be impugned. On January 18, 1943, Himmler instructed Korherr to compile the report,[23] but then demanded deletions of references to "special treatment" (*Sonderbehandlung*) in the draft and ordered substitute phraseology that would tell a casual reader the number of Jews who had been "dragged through" (*durchgeschleusst*) unnamed camps.[24]

Not surprisingly, most of Korherr's statistics came from the Reich Main Security Office. In his postwar statements he was vague about meetings and discussions,[25] but Eichmann distinctly recalled a "sullen" statistician in search of an overall view. There were talks, says Eichmann, about camps and "naturally" about how many Jews SS and Police Leader Globocnik had put to death (*ums Leben gebracht hatte*) in the General Government of Poland and how many Jews the chiefs of the Einsatzgruppen had killed under their own jurisdiction (*in eigener Zuständigkeit getötet hatten*).[26]

Although Korherr consulted also with the SS Economic-Administrative Main Office about registered Jewish inmates in Auschwitz, Lublin, and other regular concentration camps, and with a Jewish functionary about data pertaining to the German Jews, he did not, according to his testimony, probe elsewhere. To be sure, it would have been difficult, if not unthinkable, to approach the Foreign Office or the railroads, let alone foreign governments involved with deportations. In fact, the Korherr report has no references to Hungarian Jewish labor companies, Romanian shootings, or Croatian camps. Far less credible, however, is Korherr's assertion that he did not even understand the figures in his report or that he did not even realize that the Einsatzgruppen killed people. Throughout the postwar years, Korherr, as a potential witness in West German court proceedings, was a frightened man and ignorance was his banner.

No final summary was prepared in 1944 or 1945, although statistics of new deportations were assembled in Eichmann's office.[27] During the last six months of the war, at a time when foot marches began and shifts of inmates took place from one camp to another, the Nazi system broke down, and with it the counting.

Subtracting

If the principal problem in the course of adding numbers is their incompleteness, the difficulty in the subtraction of postwar counts or estimates from prewar data is the need for adjustments. The first of these corrections must be made for changes in the boundaries, from those of 1938 to those of 1946, notably in the case of Poland and the USSR. The second involves causal factors. Thus, in the interval between the last prewar and the earliest postwar determinations of the Jewish population in any given country or region, there were deficits not only due to the Holocaust but also because of war, migrations, or changes in birth and death rates. The task of calculating these components is magnified if— to cite the Soviet Union—the two relevant census figures are dated 1939 and 1959. It may be equally difficult to draw conceptional lines between normal deaths and the Holocaust or between the war and the Holocaust.

The question of who was a Holocaust victim arises for deaths from privation, particularly if someone succumbed to conditions short of complete ghettoization, or died while in hiding or after flight. The Reich, for example, had a Jewish community after 1939 in which the average age was high, and even in Poland there were people old enough or ill enough to have had short life expectancies. Still, the Holocaust toll cannot be discounted for deaths that would have occurred in any case. Real hardships, not hypothetical normalcy, faced the Jews of Germany and Poland after the outbreak of war, and normal deaths from that moment must therefore be presumed to have become fewer and fewer.

Quite different, however, is the attribution of cause to victims who died after flight or escape. In this case the key is the motivation of the refugee. Possibly a million Jews were on the move after Germany invaded the USSR on June 22, 1941. Inasmuch as even larger numbers of non-Jewish inhabitants fled—or were evacuated—only to suffer higher than normal death rates in the interior of the Soviet Union, one would have to know how many Jews left their homes because they feared a specifically Jewish fate under German rule. Theoretically, the question is not unanswerable. If a third of the Slavic residents and two-thirds of the Jewish population in a given city had fled or been moved, the difference would at least have to be analyzed. Some, though by no means all, of the dead among the refugees were Holocaust victims. Practically, however, such conclusions are not easily written in numbers.

One figure, in the tens of thousands, which would not be revealed in a subtraction, is that of the Christians who died in the Holocaust because they were considered Jews by the perpetrators. Under Reich law, a Christian with three or four Jewish grandparents was defined as a Jew. A Christian with only two Jewish grandparents, but with a Jewish marital partner, was also classified as a Jew. Similar definitions were written into decrees by other Axis states, including Slovakia, Croatia, Hungary, and Italy. Many of these baptized Jews were in fact exempted by reason of a mixed marriage, but many others were drawn into the vortex of destruction. In the Warsaw ghetto, Christians were not altogether rare.[28]

Recapitulation

In every computation there are question marks. For some countries, including above all Poland and the USSR, one may at least seek some clarification by juxtaposing the results obtained from an addition with the findings from a subtraction. To be sure, such a cross-check entails yet another complication. The Germans and their allies referred in their reports to geographic areas that have no counterparts on the maps of 1938 or 1946. Major examples are the Protectorate of Bohemia-Moravia, the General Government in Poland, the Generalbezirk of White Russia, the Reichskommissariat Ukraine, and the Romanian-administered zone of Transnistria between the Dniester and the Bug rivers. Slovakia and Croatia were creations *de novo*, and the military territories of Serbia and Salonica had novel configurations as well. The conversion of figures, reported for such entities, into numbers that are appropriate for recognizable countries with familiar frontiers is a formidable undertaking.

However elaborate or cumbersome these computations may be, their purposes are simple. The primary goal is a single number that in a quintessential manner expresses the Holocaust as a whole. The total may, however, be broken down in several ways. One may be by year, another by cause, a third by country. A country list, which is most commonly attempted in recapitulations of the dead, is appended here. Korherr's report is at least partial evidence for most countries. In the case of Norway, the Netherlands, Belgium, or France, the complete additions have been made to a point where they cannot be much improved upon. For three countries some specific comment is necessary. One is Romania, which on its own brought about the deaths of a large percentage of its Jews. The other two are Poland and the USSR, which together account for more than two-thirds of all the dead by any reckoning.

161

Romania In 1940 Romania lost territory to Hungary, Bulgaria, and the USSR. The Jews of the northern Transylvanian region, incorporated into Hungary, were engulfed in the deportations of 1944. In the Dobruja, annexed by Bulgaria, there were fewer than a thousand Jews, who survived. The Jews of Northern Bukovina and Bessarabia were under Soviet rule, but in 1941, German and Romanian armies reconquered these provinces, and in the course of the invasion, Einsatzgruppe D and Romanian gendarmerie shot about 10,000.[29]

Romanian authorities then decided to push the Bukovinian and Bessarabian Jews, along with those of the Dorohoi district, across the Dniester into Romanian-occupied Transnistria. There are only partial or rounded figures of the mass deaths in the internment camps in which the Jews were concentrated before the crossings, but this toll is about 25,000.[30] The first Jewish columns across the river were shoved back by the Germans, as thousands of Jews lay dead in the mud.[31] Thereafter, about 124,000 Jews were incarcerated in Transnistrian ghettos, where epidemics and hunger raged unchecked.[32] By September 1, 1943, the Romanian count of the surviving deportees was 50,741.[33] "Transnistria" may therefore be translated into a destruction process in which close to 110,000 Romanian Jews lost their lives.

Romanian Jews suffered more than Transnistria. There were pogroms in Jassy and Bucharest and there was a ghetto in Cernăuti (Czernowitz). Inside Greater Hungary, Transylvanian Jews were drafted into Hungarian labor companies and, in 1944, deported en masse to Auschwitz.[34] The addition for Romania, with its 1939 borders, consequently approaches 270,000.

Poland On the map of Nazi Europe, Poland did not exist. To reconstruct it with prewar frontiers from German administrative regions, one must examine (1) the incorporated territories (including Upper Silesia, Łódź, areas attached to East Prussia, and Białystok), (2) the socalled General Government comprising five districts named Crakow, Warsaw, Radom, Lublin, and Galicia, and (3) northeastern regions that became part of the Reichskommissariat Ostland (Vilna and Polish White Russia) and part of the Reichskommissariat Ukraine (Volhynia). Each of these three sectors presents its problems.

For the incorporated territories and the General Government, the most complete statistic may be found in Korherr's report. In the following two equations all the numbers are taken from his tables. The figures in the first three columns represent estimates or counts. The two figures in the last column are, as he states, derivative.

	Estimated number of Jews before German takeover		Remaining population on December 31, 1942		Count of "evacuations"		Excess of deaths and emigration over births
Incorporated territories	790,000	−	{233,210	+	222,117}	=	334,673
General Government	2,000,000	−	{297,914	+	1,274,166}	=	427,920

All of these numbers need interpretation. The starting populations, despite the rounding to 790,000 for the incorporated territories and to 2,000,000 for the General Government, are remarkably similar to figures that would be obtained from a straight projection of 1931 Polish census data.[35] The 297,914 Jews stated as remaining in the General Government on December 31, 1942, include a figure of 161,514 given to him for Galicia, and estimates for the four other districts, among them Warsaw listed with 50,000. Such inferences as may be drawn from known materials indicate that the Galician number (probably not up to date) is too high and that Warsaw's total is too low. The "evacuation" counts of 222,117 and 1,274,166, respectively, undoubtedly incorporate some non-Polish Jews temporarily quartered in ghettos. Thus, there were 19,953 Jews from the Old Reich, Vienna, Prague, and Luxembourg, in the Łódź ghetto,[36] and other thousands from the Reich and Slovakia in the General Government.

Korherr provides enough statistics for the following breakdown of the "evacuation" figures:

FROM THE INCORPORATED TERRITORIES [Total: 222,117]

From the Warthegau (Łódź and environs)
"dragged through" the camps of the Warthegau
(meaning Chełmno) — 145,301

From the Białystok district (meaning
deportations to Auschwitz and Treblinka) — 46,591

From Upper Silesia and regions
attached to East Prussia (meaning
deportations to Auschwitz) — 30,225

FROM THE GENERAL GOVERNMENT   1,274,166
    "Dragged through" the General Government
    camps (meaning that about 90 percent
    were sent to SS and Police Leader
    Globocnik's camps at Bełżec, Sobibór,
    and Treblinka, and that of the remainder
    a few were shipped to Lublin-Majdanek and
    quite a few were shot, particularly in Galicia

Supplementing these totals are partial data for 1943 and 1944. The Łódź ghetto, which according to Korherr still had 87,180 inhabitants at the end of 1942, was wiped out in August 1944, when, as noted in the files of the Statistical Office of Łódź, 73,563 people were deported. Warsaw, with about 70,000 remaining Jews, was the scene of a ghetto battle in the course of which all but a few thousand were either killed on the spot or transported to Lublin and Treblinka.[37] In Galicia, SS and Police Leader Fritz Katzmann reported on June 30, 1943, that 21,156 Jews were left.[38] Other documents about other localities tell a similar story.

Korherr had no count for "emigration" and "excess mortality," and he could not separate the two concepts when he calculated their combined totals as 334,673 for the incorporated territories and 427,920 for the General Government. Compared with the starting populations, these figures are clearly disproportionate. Their ratio is not, as one might have expected, 2:5, but more nearly 4:5. The principal explanation for this apparent discrepancy may be found in flights and expulsions *from* the incorporated territories *to* the General Government at the beginning of the German occupation. There is no close estimate for these movements, but the shift is almost certainly in the 50,000-to-100,000 range.[39] The addition of 334,673 and 427,920, which totals 762,593, may therefore be taken as an indication of a real deficit for the two regions as a whole, but not as the unqualified measure of deaths from privation. About 150,000 to 200,000 Jews fled from this area, particularly to the interior of the Soviet Union. Their number, which is the "emigration" in Korherr's heading, must be subtracted.[40]

The third major region of Poland, about which Korherr provides no details, had a starting population of about 550,000 Jews. It was divided into several administrative compartments, listed here with the number of Jewish inhabitants crudely projected from 1931 census data:

REICHSKOMMISSARIAT OSTLAND
    Generalbezirk Lithuania
        Vilna region   over 100,000

Generalbezirk White Russia	
Hauptkommissariat Minsk	
Wilejka-Głebokie region	up to 20,000
Hauptkommissariat Baranovichi	over 100,000
REICHSKOMMISSARIAT UKRAINE	
Generalbezirk Volhynia-Podolia	
Volhynia and most of Polesie	about 330,000

It is likely that about a third of the Jewish population of the Vilna region, but relatively few residents of the other districts, fled to the interior of the USSR. In Vilna, Einsatzkommando 9 of Einsatzgruppe B killed thousands of Jews during the summer of 1941.[41] Einsatzkommando 3 of Einsatzgruppe A then took over the region and shot 34,622 Jews as of November 25, 1941. By that time, according to the Commando, only about 15,000 Jews remained in the Vilna ghetto. The retention of these people was a concession to war production.[42] Two years later an armament-economy office reported that all of the 12,332 Jewish workers still employed in the ghetto during 1943 had been withdrawn.[43]

The Wilejka area was subjected to shootings in March, 1942,[44] and on July 31, 1942, Generalkommissar Kube of White Russia reported renewed killings. Kube also noted a precipitous action by the German army in neighboring Głebokie and environs resulting in the deaths of 10,000 Jews.[45]

The Baranovichi Hauptkommissariat was inundated with shootings during 1941 and 1942. By August 8, 1942, a total of 95,000 Jews were reported killed, and 6,000 were presumed to be in hiding.[46] In the fall of 1942 an expedition of the SS and Police leader in White Russia reduced the population of escaped Jews in the western part of the Hauptkommissariat by killing 2,958.[47]

Volhynia was traversed in 1941 by Einsatzgruppe C and a detachment of Security Police from the General Government.[48] In November 1941, units of the Higher SS and Police Command South carried out a massacre of about 15,000 Jews in the town of Rovno.[49] A massive wave of killings began in the summer of 1942. On December 20, 1942, Himmler reported to Hitler the following numbers of Jews "executed in the Ukraine, South Russia, and the Białystok district:[50]

August 1942	31,246
September 1942	165,282
October 1942	95,735
November 1942	70,948
	363,211

165

There is little doubt that the large majority of these victims had lived in the Volhynian portion of the Generalbezirk Volhynia-Podolia. The sweep was conducted without regard to the production of carts and textiles in the factories. In ghetto after ghetto, laborers and their families were wiped out overnight.[51] The Volhynian Jews were annihilated.[52]

Polish Jewry as a whole lost more than 500,000 people in the ghettos, well over 600,000 in shootings, and over 1,800,000 in camps. Some who sought sanctuary in the Soviet Union, but who died there of privation, were victims as well. Given the nature of this calculation, one should of course regard it as a tentative approximation. The thrust of the addition, however, may be compared with the result of a simple subtraction:[53]

Official Polish estimate of Jewish population as of August 1939		3,351,000
Reported registration of survivors on Polish soil in 1945	55,000	
Repatriations from USSR	185,000	
Displaced persons in Germany, Austria, Italy, Romania, Czechoslovakia, and elsewhere in 1946	over 100,000	
Polish Jews in military forces, 1945	about 15,000	
Emigrants to Palestine and other areas, 1939–44	over 15,000	
Survivors in Polish areas annexed by USSR	several thousand	
Refugees remaining in prewar territory of USSR	several thousand	
Victims of Soviet deportations	several thousand	
War casualties	several thousand	

Although accuracy is difficult to achieve even in postwar counts, these numbers are small enough to suggest that the survivors, and the dead from non-Holocaust causes, could not have been more than about 400,000.[54] Thus, the overall picture is that of a toll approaching 3 million. Albert Speer, who pondered the losses of Polish Jewry when he wrote his last book, did not think that the figure was less than that.[55]

The USSR   In 1939 and 1940 the Soviet Union annexed the Baltic states, eastern Poland, and parts of Romania. When the Germans

attacked the USSR in June 1941, they pushed through these buffer regions into the old Soviet domains. The German reports about the occupied USSR did not feature the Soviet frontier of August 1939, and some
plenary statistics of Jewish dead cover areas on both sides of this vanished
line. To focus on the old territory of the USSR, one must therefore refer
to a great many detailed figures pertaining to specific locations. Herewith
is a basic compilation for the old Soviet Union:

GERMAN AREA
   Einsatzgruppe Operations
      Einsatzgruppe A:
         February 1, 1942: 218,050 Jews.
         Ultimate toll much higher.
         Operated in Baltic region, north Russia,
         Minsk, Baranovichi.
         Soviet portion: low tens of thousands
      Einsatzgruppe B:
         September 1, 1942: 126,195 people.
         Ultimate toll not much higher.
         Operated mainly in military area of Army Group
         Center. Jews only; Soviet portion: about 100,000
      Einsatzgruppe C:
         Sonderkommando 4a, to November 30, 1941: 59,018 persons.
         Einsatzkommando 5, to December 7, 1941: 36,147 persons.
         Ultimate toll of entire Einsatzgruppe probably
         over 120,000.
         Operated mainly in Ukraine. Jews only;
         Soviet portion: over 100,000
      Einsatzgruppe D:
         April 8, 1942: 91,678 persons.
         Ultimate toll about 100,000. Operated
         mainly in southern Ukraine, Crimea,
         and Caucasus. Jews only;
         Soviet portion: under 90,000
      HIGHER SS AND POLICE COMMANDS
         Killings of Soviet Jews in 1941
         at Kamenets-Podolsk, Berdichev, Dnepropetrovsk,
         and other localities   about 50,000
         Killings in 1942 and 1943 within
         old Soviet portion of White Russia: several thousand
         Old Soviet portion of 363,211 Jews
            killed in 1942 in Białystok district,
            Ukraine, and south Russia: high tens of thousands

Smaller-scale killings by German army, local authorities, and in prisoner-of-war camps:	low tens of thousands
Deaths in ghettos and of fleeing Jews:	tens of thousands

ROMANIA AREA (TRANSNISTRIA)

Shootings of Soviet Jews in Odessa-Dalnic, the Golta prefecture, and the Berezovka area:	about 150,000
Deaths of Soviet Jews in Transnistrian ghettos:	tens of thousands

TOTAL is probably more than 700,000

The Einsatzgruppen reported cumulative figures from time to time. The latest available dates are cited here,[56] but there are fragmentary data for subsequent killings, and sometimes there are indications that shootings were going to take place. For example, Einsatzgruppe C reported on February 4, 1942, its extensive preparations for the shooting of the Jews in Kharkov,[57] and Einsatzgruppe D, which in the summer of 1942 moved through Rostov to the Piatigorsk-Yessentuki-Kislovodsk region of the Caucasus, left behind a proclamation, dated September 7, 1942, ordering the Jews of Kislovodsk to assemble.[58] Korherr's report contains a single reference to the "evacuation" of 633,300 Jews in the "Russian areas, including the former Baltic countries, from the beginning of the Eastern campaign." The figure, according to the report, was furnished by the Reich Main Security Office, and in a postwar interrogation, Korherr called it a "house number" in the jargon of the German statisticians for seeming exactness devoid of known meaning.[59] There is little question, however, that the RSHA meant to convey an overall toll of the Einsatzgruppen, and that a distant observer, working with available documents, might calculate a similar result.[60]

Korherr specifically states in the concluding paragraphs of his report that he had recorded the "deaths of the Soviet Russian Jews in the eastern occupied territories" only in part. He did not have the statistics for the killings organized by the Higher SS and Police leaders, who reported to Himmler directly, and he did not attempt to estimate the ghetto dead.[61]

The Romanian data can only be rounded. For the Odessa massacre, probably the largest of the war, a German intelligence officer in contact with a Romanian informant heard the figure 59,000, but postwar Romanian estimates are somewhat lower.[62] For the Romanian killings in the Golta prefecture, the total established in postwar trials is close to

70,000,[63] and for the killings in the Berezovka region, which were carried out by an ethnic German Commando organized by the Volksdeutsche Mittelstelle (an SS office), there is documentary indication of 28,000 dead.[64] The deaths of Soviet Jews from starvation and disease can be assessed only on the basis of reports indicating the numbers of Romanian expellees and indigenous persons living in the same Transnistrian ghettos.[65] The heavy death rate of the Romanian Jews is known, and that of the Soviet Jews could not have been much lighter.

Given the importance of a total figure for the Soviet Union, one should attempt to derive it also from Soviet census data. The starting point for this subtraction is the census of 1939 and that of 1959:

Jewish population, January 1939	3,020,171
Jewish population, January 1959	2,267,814
Difference:	752,357

The 2,267,814 counted in 1959 include at least 100,000 survivors of territories that had not been part of the Soviet Union in 1939; hence, the deficit, adjusted for the old boundaries of the USSR, is more than 850,000.[66]

The next major question is the impact of births and normal deaths between the two census dates. For this analysis some clues are furnished by the census of 1970, which reveals a count of only 2,150,707. The shrinkage of 117,107 from 1959 to 1970 is attributable only in very small part to emigration. The decline occurred because deaths exceeded births.[67] The 1970 census contains data also for age cohorts in the Jewish population:[68]

0–10	6.9%
11–15	4.3% } 8.2%
16–19	3.9%
20–29	10.9%
30–39	15.1%
40–49	16.0%
50–59	16.3%
60 and over	26.4%

Translated into raw numbers, the balance of deaths and births is approximately the following:

Deaths per year, 1959–70	about 24,000
Births per year, 1959–70	about 13,500

| Births per year, 1954–59 | about 18,500 |
| Births per year, 1950–53 | about 21,000 |

This configuration indicates that during the nine years preceding the 1959 census there must have been a small population loss, even if deaths were somewhat fewer than 24,000 per annum. For the 1940s the picture is more complicated, because the age group 20–29, which made up 10.9 percent of the 1970 census count, should be augmented with the 30-year-olds (born in 1939) and all those born during the 1939–43 period who were killed in the Holocaust. Births per year during the period 1939–50 may have been in the vicinity of 28,000, but in a similar way the corresponding average of normal annual deaths would have had to reflect not only the possible low points after the war but also the higher totals in the larger population of January 1939, to June 1941. By and large then, the overall gain, if any, for the two decades between the census counts could not have been more than some tens of thousands.

The adjusted deficit is therefore still 850,000 to 900,000, and from this number one must deduct at least five categories of victims that are not attributable to the Holocaust: (1) Jewish Red Army soldiers killed in battle; (2) Jewish prisoners of war who died in captivity unrecognized as Jews; (3) Jewish dead in Soviet corrective labor camps during the period 1939–59; (4) civilian Jewish dead in the battle zone, particularly in the besieged cities of Leningrad and Odessa; and (5) deaths caused by privation among Jews who had fled or who had been evacuated for reasons other than fear of German anti-Jewish acts. Numbers can be affixed to these upheavals only with difficulty. There are no reliable statistics of overall Soviet losses in most of these categories, let alone the appropriate Jewish share of each. Nevertheless, one might make an assessment on the basis of available data, using medium assumptions to avoid results that are impossibly low or impossibly high. Such a calculation of non-Holocaust Jewish victims might yield a figure in the range of 100,000 to 200,000.[69] Subtracting this number from the deficit of 850,000 to 900,000 allows the tentative conclusion that the Holocaust brought death to 650,000 to 800,000. This is the magnitude that emerges from the additions as well.

The following is a breakdown by country, with the borders of 1937. Converts are included in the toll, and refugees are counted with the countries from which they were deported.

| Poland | up to | 3,000,000 |
| USSR | over | 700,000 |

Romania		270,000
Czechoslovakia		260,000
Hungary	over	180,000
Lithuania	up to	130,000
Germany		120,000
The Netherlands	over	100,000
France		75,000
Latvia		70,000
Yugoslavia		60,000
Greece		60,000
Austria	over	50,000
Belgium		25,000
Italy (including Rhodes)		9,000
Norway	under	1,000
Luxembourg	under	1,000
TOTAL	(approx.)	5,100,000

171

10

The Nazis and the Jews in Occupied Western Europe, 1940–1944

MICHAEL R. MARRUS *and*
ROBERT O. PAXTON

Nazi policy toward the Jews of occupied western Europe evolved in three phases, determined by far-flung strategic concerns of the Third Reich.[1] In the first, from the outbreak of war in the west in April 1940 until the autumn of 1941, all was provisional: Nazi leaders looked forward to a "final solution of the Jewish question in Europe," but that final solution was to await the cessation of hostilities and an ultimate peace settlement. No one defined the Final Solution with precision, but all signs pointed toward some vast and as yet unspecified project of mass emigration. When the war was over, the Jews would leave Europe and the question would be resolved. Until that time the various German occupation authorities would pursue anti-Jewish objectives by controlling the movements and organizations of Jews, confiscating their property, enumerating them, and sometimes concentrating them in certain regions. Throughout this phase, the circumstances of Jews varied importantly according to various occupation arrangements worked out by Germany following the spectacular blitzkrieg of 1940.

In the second phase, from the autumn of 1941 until the summer of 1942, Hitler drew implications from a gradually faltering campaign in Russia: the war was to last longer than he had planned, and the increasingly desperate struggle against the Bolsheviks prompted a revision of the previous timetable and general approach to the Jewish problem. Now Nazi leaders were told to prepare for the Final Solution itself, which could not be postponed. The Jewish question had to be solved quickly, *before* the end of the war. Nazi Jewish experts soon adopted the new rhythm, and began urgent preparations. Henceforth, mass resettlement was taken to be impractical, and Jewish emigration was indeed forbidden. By the end of 1941, in a dramatic reversal of policy, Jews were no longer permitted to leave German-controlled Europe. With the exception of Norway and Denmark, where the numbers of Jews were unimportant, the Jews were subjected to a concerted series of new harassments, beginning with segregation by means of a yellow star. More Jews were interned in camps, made ready for deportation to the east.

The third phase began in the summer of 1942, and continued to the end of the war in the west. Following a conference of experts in Berlin in June 1942, deportation trains to Auschwitz began to roll from the west, and the facilities for mass murder in that camp began to function. Jews were first systematically deported from France, Belgium, and Holland in the summer of 1942. Norwegian Jews left at the end of the year. Some Italian Jews followed, sent from areas controlled by the Germans after the surrender of the Italian forces to the Allies in September 1943. Only the Jews of Denmark, against whom the Nazis did not move until the latter part of 1943, entirely escaped deportation to the east and murder in the Polish camps. Roundups and deportations continued to the very end of the war, and the death factory of Auschwitz, to which most deportees were sent, continued its work. In the end, between 220,000 and 230,000 west European Jews perished, close to 40 percent of those alive in 1939.

The toll varied significantly from country to country, ranging from the Netherlands, where about 75 percent of the Jews were lost, to Denmark, where virtually the entire Jewish community was saved.[2] What governed the scale of killing was, for the most part, the degree to which the Nazis were willing and able to apply themselves to their task. But the occupied people themselves could affect the outcome, as we shall see. Generally, the Nazis were well on the way to accomplishing their goal in the west by mid-1944, and had the war continued for a few more years the remainder of the Jewish population would, in all likelihood, have been destroyed. Railway timetables set the pace for the massacre, and few trains left without their quota of about a thousand Jews. The Danish case stands out, for in that country the government, administration, and public opinion obstructed the German plan. In Italy too Hitler met with frustration, until the fortunes of war brought down the fascist structure and the Nazis took over. Elsewhere, collaborationist regimes and civil servants did much to clear the way for deportations. In what follows we attempt to sort out what happened, assessing the forces at work in individual countries.

The First Phase: Provisional Measures, 1940–1941

The war in the west began with the German attack upon Denmark and Norway on April 9, 1940, a campaign which widened a month later, with an undeclared war against the Netherlands, Belgium, and Luxembourg. Nazi success was spectacular. Within hours the Danish government surrendered, practically without firing a shot. By the end of April, the Wehrmacht eliminated Norwegian resistance. The Dutch surrendered on May 15, by which time German troops had broken through Belgium, traversed the supposedly impregnable French defenses of the Maginot Line, and at several points crossed the Meuse River. On June 22, French representatives signed an armistice at Compiègne. For west Europeans, it seemed at the time, the war was over.

Hitler's planning for a settlement in the west seems to have been extremely vague or nonexistent. On a global scale, as he explained many years before in *Mein Kampf,* the great objective for the German Reich was the conquest of "living space" in the east. National Socialists, he said, "stop the endless German movement to the south and west, and turn our gaze toward the land in the east."[3] The purpose of the campaign of 1940 had been to assure a steady flow of raw materials from Scandinavia, to forestall British attacks from the sea and from the north, and also to secure Germany's western flank by eliminating the military strength of her old enemy, France. Eventually, the decisive battle would be fought against the Soviets, temporarily aligned with Nazi Germany. By the end of 1940, when the Luftwaffe failed to clear the way for an invasion of England, the strategic energies of the Reich turned toward Russia. Hitler issued the secret order to prepare for "Barbarossa," the attack upon the Soviet Union which would be launched on June 22, 1941.

In view of this priority, the determination of German occupation structures in the newly conquered western territories flowed pragmatically, with a view to an ultimate resolution when the main objective of the Reich had been won. For the moment, ideological and military

174

considerations competed for attention; various branches of the Nazi hierarchy tried to impose their visions of things, hoping to influence long-range settlement. Hitler resolved the issue, establishing a variety of administrations. Economy was the rule, for the great strategic vocation of the Hitlerian regime lay elsewhere. Not much was incorporated into the Reich—Luxembourg, and Alsace and Lorraine. Not many German troops, police, or bureaucrats were available for the control of the conquered countries—fewer than 3,000 civilians for occupied France in August 1941, for example, and just over 3,000 for the Netherlands.[4] Everywhere in the west the Nazis preferred to see indigenous civil servants and police remain at their posts and carry on with their jobs, except of course for a few deemed unreliable who would be weeded out.

Hitler considered the peoples of Norway and Denmark to be racially akin to the Germans, and he appears to have envisioned their ultimate independence, albeit under the shadow of an all-powerful Third Reich. In both countries German civilians represented the interests of the victorious power. Denmark posed few problems. The Danish government and monarch remained in place and were permitted a substantial degree of autonomy, supervised by a diplomatic official, the long-time German ambassador to Copenhagen, Cecil von Renthe-Fink. Norway, which had offered a brief but stout resistance, was controlled by a civil governor or *Reichskommisar*, the former gauleiter of Essen and *Oberpräsident* of the Rhine province, Josef Terboven. Indicative of the lack of German planning, however, both the army, the Foreign Office, and even Alfred Rosenberg's Foreign Political Office of the Nazi Party attempted to impose their own models for control of the Norwegian state. After several months of intrigue and conflict among the various German agencies, internal affairs in the country were turned over to a Norwegian government effectively dominated by Rosenberg's protégé, Vidkun Quisling, a Norwegian politician and leader of a party of the extreme right. Ultimate control, however, remained in the hands of the Germans, unlike the situation in Denmark.

In Holland and Belgium, despite the racial affinity which was held to exist among the German, Dutch, and Flemish peoples, there were concerns which did not exist in the north. The area was of great military sensitivity, because of the imminent possibility of an attack upon Britain. Following the determined resistance to the Wehrmacht in the Low Countries, both the Dutch government and royal family and the Belgian government fled to England. In both countries local matters were left to the top civil servants, but the arrangements for Nazi control differed substantially. Holland became a "protectorate" (*Schutzstaat*) presided over by a *Reichskommissar* responsible directly to the führer, the one-time Viennese lawyer Arthur Seyss-Inquart, previously a deputy of Hans Frank in the General Government of Poland. Belgium, closer to the likely war zone and with a mixed population including French-speaking Walloons, came under direct German military control, which extended to the departments of the Nord and Pas-de-Calais in northeastern France. Authority there went to the Wehrmacht commander General Alexander von Falkenhausen and his administrative chief Brigadier General Eggert Reeder.

France was unique, for in that country the Germans established both a military occupation and permitted an autonomous government with a wide degree of independence. A demarcation line separated the northern three-fifths of France, the richest and strategically most important part of the country, where the military governor, General Otto von Stülpnagel, had principal authority, as the Militärbefehlshaber in Frankreich (MBF). But the French government, now established in the sleepy provincial resort town of Vichy, was theoretically responsible for the whole of France, even the occupied zone, so long as its decisions did not contradict those of the Germans.

Nowhere in the west were these diverse and hastily improvised arrangements supposed to be permanent. Nazi theorists had not suggested important German designs upon Scandinavia, and racial considerations there projected that local people would eventually prove reliable neighbors without much geopolitical manipulation from Berlin. The Dutch and the Flemish, also considered Nordics, could be expected to rise to preferred status in the new Germanic order, possibly to be incorporated into the Reich itself. With the Latins, however, it was difficult to articulate clear racial guidelines in view of the Nazi alliance with Italy and an entente with Spain. Clearly the French, a despised and hereditary enemy, were a corrupt and degenerate people, who could never again be permitted to threaten the Reich. But the means by which they were to be tamed, and the territorial adjustments best suited to do this, were left for the future. Faced with the perplexing issues of peacemaking, made even more murky by racialist nonsense, Hitler preferred to concentrate upon other problems, specifically the renewal of the war in the east.

Policy regarding the Jews in the occupied west flowed from these considerations. At issue were some half a million Jews, who had come under German domination after the victories of 1940.[5] Plans for these Jews, together with the final settlement in the west, could wait. The

176

Nazis had other Jews on their minds. The great field for the implementation of racial policy in the first flood of Nazi success was eastern Europe, in Poland, where for the first time nazism found itself face-to-face with millions of Slavs, in Nazi eyes among the lowest of racial groups, and Jews, the great enemy of Germandom and the Nazi Reich. Here, not in the west, Germany would undertake great movements of population, carve out zones for colonization by Aryan people, and begin the elimination of Jews from European life. Here the SS, and not the Wehrmacht, the Nazi Party, or the Foreign Office, would be given preponderant authority to effect these changes. Here there was to be no peace treaty, as eventually in the west, but rather a progressive building of new living space for the Reich.

This is not to say that there was no long-range goal for west European Jews. Hitler considered them at least as destructive as other Jews, but they constituted less of an immediate obstacle to Nazi goals. In the Hitlerian vision eastern and western Jews were fundamentally the same. Jews were a tremendously powerful parasitic force, eating away at the foundations of state and society, utterly lacking in allegiance to any nation, spreading corruption, demoralization, and degeneration. Their ultimate goal was to subdue the world. Western Jews had assumed the language and culture of the societies in which they lived, but this only helped them mask their unshakable and biologically conditioned program:

> When he speaks French [the Jew] thinks Jewish, and while he turns out German verses, in his life he only expresses the nature of his nationality. As long as the Jew has not become the master of other peoples, he must speak their languages whether he likes it or not, but as soon as they become his slaves, they would all have to learn a universal language . . . so that by this additional means the Jews could more easily dominate them.[6]

Hitler's goal, expressed on many occasions, was to rid European society of this plague, by whatever means necessary.

In practical terms, Nazi policy for western Jews involved emigration. This was the declared objective of the Reich from the mid-1930s, coordinated by a central office for that purpose directed by Reinhard Heydrich, head of Himmler's vast security apparatus—the Reich Main Security Office (Reichsicherheitshauptamt, RSHA). Whether through encouraging Jews to leave for Palestine, expelling Jews across German frontiers to other countries, or hounding them out of the confines of the Reich, the objective was that they should depart, leaving their property behind. Nazi leaders even hoped that through forced emigration of Jews, anti-Semitism would spread to other western countries, which would come to recognize the correctness of the German approach. By the outbreak of war, according to contemporary estimates, some 329,000 Jews had emigrated from the Greater German Reich—215,000 from pre-1938 Germany itself, 97,000 from what had been Austria, and 17,000 from Czechoslovakia.[7] More would certainly have left had visas been available for other nations, especially America; more would continue to leave, however, despite enormous difficulties, even after war had begun. For Nazi policy continued to favor Jewish emigration even after September 1939.

Considering the new difficulties which war conditions posed for refugees, with limited shipping space and with new barriers to immigration, the Nazi hierarchy set its priorities: Jews from the Reich itself should be the first to go, then Jews from occupied Europe, who should take precedence over Jews from unoccupied areas. On more than one occasion, notably with the dumping of 6,500 hapless Jews from Baden and the Palatinate upon an unwilling Vichy France in October 1940, the Germans sent Jews out of their own hands, deporting them from occupied or incorporated territory.[8] Throughout 1940 the Nazis viewed unoccupied France as a dumping ground for German Jews. In the German Foreign Office Martin Luther later explained that until mid-1941 the Reich had promoted Jewish departures by all possible means. The Foreign Office cooperated with Adolf Eichmann of the RSHA, the man in charge of Jewish emigration, to help clear the bureaucratic path for Jews traveling overland to the Far East.[9] One year after the defeat of the west European countries, when shipping space was extremely limited, Heydrich even halted Jewish emigration from Belgium and occupied France in order to hasten Jewish exits from the Reich.[10]

Since there were few countries willing to receive Jews, Nazi officials speculated on colonization schemes. In the autumn of 1939, immediately after the German defeat of Poland, Heydrich approved a plan to force Jews into a temporary reservation south of the Polish city of Radom, near the Nisko River. The idea seems to have been eventually to push the Jews farther east, deep into the Soviet Union, a long-range objective which would require either the diplomatic agreement of the Russians (a most unlikely prospect), or their military defeat.[11] In July 1940, following the victory in the west and after consultations with the Reich Ministry of the Interior as well as with party agencies, an expert on Jewish affairs in the Foreign Office, Franz Rademacher, revived another idea— to send the Jews to the French colony of Madagascar. Final details could only await a peace settlement. The Foreign Office, Rademacher explained, would play a key role in solving the Jewish problem by building into a peace treaty all necessary arrangements for the Madagascar settlement with the defeated states.[12] Among other considerations France would have to transfer the island to Germany as a mandate, so that it could be used for this purpose. Simultaneously with the Foreign Office, Heydrich's RSHA was preparing its own version of the Madagascar Plan, which typically assigned the SS a predominant role. But both versions depended upon an ultimate peace agreement.[13]

Until these schemes could mature, until the various German agencies could be assigned their respective roles by the führer, and until hostilities ended, no final decisions could be made. But the general directions seemed plain. Carl Theo Zeitschel, for example, the "Jewish expert" in the German embassy in Paris, referred vaguely in January 1941 to Hitler's postwar version of "a colonial action . . . in a territory which remains to be determined."[14] Werner Best, of the military occupation authority in France, explained in April of that year that "the Germans must progressively rid all the European countries of Judaism," and invited the French to consider "preliminary measures" for the future deportations.[15]

These "preliminary measures" provided the substance of German policy during the first year of occupation in the west. Notably, however, the Germans moved slowly and hesitantly, anxious not to disturb local sensibilities and unable to invest men or resources in preparing an as yet ill-defined operation. Indeed, high-level Nazi strategists were concerned to restrain some of their more zealous representatives in the defeated states. Otto Abetz, the newly appointed German ambassador in Paris, made urgent proposals for a series of anti-Semitic measures: refusal to readmit to the occupied zone Jews who had fled south; the registration of Jews in the occupied zone; marking of Jewish enterprises with a special placard; the appointment of trustees over Jewish enterprises whose owners had fled.[16] In Berlin, Göring's and Himmler's staffs pored over these relatively modest suggestions for weeks, and finally issued a cautious reply: there was no objection to the proposed measures, but they should be carried out by French services as Abetz had recommended, and it was "indispensable" that the German police should watch the French closely. Should any of these moves backfire, the French and not the Germans

179

would bear the odium of failure. The first German ordinance explicitly concerned with Jews in France thus did not appear until September 27, almost two months after the occupation began.

Elsewhere, it was the same—caution and delay. The first such ordinance in the Netherlands—forbidding the employment of Jews in the Dutch civil service—was announced on September 30, but this was understood not to be retroactive.[17] The first in Belgium—prohibiting the ritual slaughter of animals—came only on October 23.[18] In Denmark, where there were only about 8,000 Jews, the Germans did not even attempt seriously to pressure the local government, which objected in principle to anti-Jewish measures.

The only west European countries where there appeared a determined and energetic anti-Jewish drive from the very beginning were Vichy France and Norway, where collaborationist governments forged ahead on their own, eager to set their national stamp upon a new political and ideological order. But the situation in the two countries was very different. As part of its widely acclaimed Révolution Nationale, capitalizing on a popular disposition to seek scapegoats for a humiliating defeat, Vichy France energetically issued a series of new laws which defined Jews, excluded them from the army and the civil service, interned many of them, and set the stage for their elimination from economic life.[19] In Norway the Quisling-dominated government—Nazi-imposed and extremely unpopular—punished the tiny Jewish community of under 2,000 by various measures: removal of Jews from the state bureaucracy and from university and high-school teaching, removal of books by Jewish authors from the library of Oslo University, and so on.[20] Unlike the situation in Vichy France, these were not the actions of an independent government, acting with widespread popular support. Yet in both countries the Germans were able to let someone else take the public initiative in anti-Jewish policy.

Eventually, the Germans achieved some rough similarity in these "preliminary measures" in all west European states under their control, with the exception of Denmark. Eichmann's representatives were dispatched from the RSHA to the three countries with the largest Jewish populations to help direct anti-Jewish moves and to be ready to implement the great Jewish evacuation to come—SS officers Theodor Dannecker to Paris, Kurt Asche to Brussels, and Wilhelm Zöpf to The Hague. Significantly, however, the measures in various countries were not closely coordinated with each other, and there was constant care in introducing them to address local conditions and to work with indigenous agencies.

By the end of 1941 the Jews of France, Belgium and Holland had been defined and counted—the essential preconditions for the prospective deportations. Important Jewish property had been taken away in a process referred to as Aryanization. In France, where the Vichy government was eager to take a hand in this spoliation, partly in order to forestall a transfer of Jewish wealth from France to the Reich, the Germans do not seem to have taken much for themselves; in both zones of the country the complex and time-consuming task of Aryanization fell largely to a French agency, the Commissariat Général aux Questions Juives, set up by Vichy in March 1941 to coordinate anti-Jewish measures throughout the country. At its head was an anti-German militant French nationalist, the anti-Semitic war veterans' leader Xavier Vallat.[21] In Belgium and Holland, on the other hand, where no indigenous political leadership existed to assume responsibility, agents of the German government, banks, and business swarmed through the occupied territories, robbing the Jews even more quickly than did French officials in France. Two-thirds of all Jewish property in the Netherlands, according to one estimate, went directly into German hands.[22]

In all three countries the Nazis saw to the establishment of a local council of Jews, exercising some of the functions of the *Judenräte* of eastern Europe—taking charge of the dwindling assets of the Jewish community, providing for the increasing number of Jewish indigents, serving the Germans in levying special taxes and other burdens upon Jews, and standing ready to assist the authorities in their ultimate anti-Jewish plans. First to be established, in February 1941, was the Dutch Joodse Raad, set up by German order in the wake of the anti-Nazi disturbances in Amsterdam earlier that month. The Belgian Association des Juifs de Belgique and the French Union Générale des Israélites de France both dated from November of that year, the latter decreed by the Vichy regime, again in order to forestall the Germans' acting on their own.

The Second Phase: Toward the Final Solution, 1941–1942

The clearest indication of a new direction in Nazi policy toward the Jews in the west was the ending of Jewish emigration throughout all

Europe in the Germans' grasp. On October 23, 1941, Gestapo chief Heinrich Müller, Eichmann's superior at the RSHA, passed along an order from Himmler: apart from a few exceptions, no more Jews were to emigrate from Germany or anywhere in occupied Europe.[23] Previously, as we have seen, the Nazis took the opposite line, favoring a Jewish exodus from both central and western Europe so long as the Jews' property was left behind. In the spring of 1941 the Nazi leadership may even have wanted to accelerate departures. In May, for example, Göring ordered Jewish emigration from Bohemia and Moravia speeded up.[24] By autumn, however, Nazi Jewish policy had assumed an entirely new orientation, and a far more drastic solution was envisaged for Jews wherever they were to be found. Final preparations for the solution of the Jewish question had begun.

Occupation officers knew about a change. As early as July 1, 1941, Eichmann's delegate in France, Theodor Dannecker, had heard about an order from Hitler to Heydrich "to prepare the solution of the Jewish question in Europe." Even for unoccupied France, the solution was due, "if not today, then in the immediate future."[25] Zeitschel, at the German embassy in Paris, told his superior Otto Abetz in August that the Madagascar Plan, while a good idea, was impractical; it would be better to deport all the Jews to the newly conquered territory in the east.[26] Elmar Michel, head of the economic section of the Militärbefehlshaber in Frankreich, was informed in December that, following a recent speech by Hitler, the Jewish question was acquiring a new political significance, whereas previously the focus had been on eliminating the Jews from economic life.[27]

Behind these hints of change lay a chilling new definition of the "Final Solution," which emerged during the early part of the Nazi campaign in Russia: henceforth, a small group of officials began to consider the physical destruction of all European Jews. It is impossible to determine precisely when Hitler decided on this new approach, but it is virtually certain that he set the new course himself.[28] Killing came easily to the Nazis, and a murderous intention may well have slumbered in their anti-Semitic ideology from the beginning. What roused it now to European-wide proportions was the war in the Soviet Union. With this campaign the possibilities for emigration finally appeared unrealistic. Indeed, as the German advance slowed and Soviet resistance hardened, the Reich faced the unwelcome prospect of absorbing millions more unwanted and unexpellable Jews. Moreover, the Russian campaign transformed the character of the Nazi conflict, in which all moral restraint was abandoned. In the Hitlerian worldview Russia always represented an especially dark and demonic force—an implacable rival, the home alike of bolshevism and the Jews, confused in one insane vision. Faced with such a foe, Hitler declared, everything was permitted. War with Russia was not to be an ordinary conflict; describing it as a clash of civilizations against inferior peoples, the führer gave the Germans license to commit the most savage atrocities, to destroy and lay waste.[29]

New vistas opened in the east for the most grandiose schemes, including the long-postponed "final solution of the Jewish question." Orders to murder Jews and Communist Party leaders in the occupied east were prepared in the spring of 1941. Throughout the second half of that year, as the fighting raged, they were carried out by the Einsatzgruppen, special action squads following the advances of the Wehrmacht. At first the victims were shot. Then, in the autumn, as that proved inefficient, the Nazis experimented with gas, employing specially constructed motorized vans using carbon monoxide. Within four months some 300,000 Jews perished by such hurried and sometimes chaotic means. Before the end of the summer it became evident that victory over the Soviets would not be achieved in six weeks as originally hoped. Killing developed a momentum of its own. Simultaneously, the administrative wheels began to turn in the direction of something wider and more organized: Göring wrote to Heydrich on July 31, commissioning him "to carry out all necessary preparations with regard to the organizational and financial matters for bringing about a final solution to the Jewish question in the German sphere of influence in Europe."[30]

Experiments in murder continued. Methods were refined, and practical experience accumulated. Improvisation diminished as the Germans began to centralize and coordinate their murderous operations. At the very end of 1941, secret killings using gas took place at Chełmno, north of Łódź, in reconquered East Prussia, and at Birkenau, part of the vast Auschwitz complex in Upper Silesia, former Polish territory now incorporated into the Reich. In the months which followed, Bełżec, Sobibór, Majdanek, and Treblinka joined the list. Once in place, the death factories needed people to kill; European-wide coordination was now essential, and the entire continent had to disgorge its Jews.

To achieve this Heydrich convoked a meeting of interested officials from the SS and from various Reich ministries in the Berlin suburb of Wannsee on January 20, 1942. Heydrich reviewed previous anti-Jewish efforts, which had centered upon the emigration of Jews from Reich territory—"the only possible provisional solution." In view of the problems associated with this approach, he explained, Himmler had forbidden more emigration, considering also dangerous wartime conditions and "in view of possibilities in the east." Following Hitler's authorization (*Genehmigung*), it was said, Jews were now to be evacuated to the eastern territories as a further possible solution. Heydrich went on to explain what would happen next—a grisly prospect of huge labor columns, the "natural decline" of the majority, and some undefined special treatment for the tenacious hard core of Jewry which had survived this process of natural selection. Something new was afoot, evident despite the fact that the minutes (kept by Eichmann) fell silent on details. Even now, it was indicated, practical experience was being accumulated which would be of major significance in "the final solution of the Jewish question."[31]

Western Europe received considerable attention during this meeting, and if one can believe the minutes, it was even to be given top priority in the deportations after the Reich itself and the Protectorate of Bohemia and Moravia: Europe was "to be combed from west to east." Foreign Office representative Martin Luther recommended postponement of deportation from the "Nordic states," where there were few Jews and where he envisioned difficulties, but saw no such problems for the west. No timetable was proposed, but the tenor of the meeting demonstrated that a period of drift was finished.

East and west posed very different problems. In the former, where Jewry was concentrated, the Nazis were unchallenged and did not foresee difficulties for some time. There was a rich indigenous current of anti-Semitism, which the Nazi invasion had done nothing to arrest.

But in the west, as occupation officials scurried to prepare the deportations, considerable care and diplomacy were necessary. Norway, Denmark, the Netherlands, Belgium, France, and Italy all had strong traditions of liberalism and independence, each setting its own particular obstacles in the way of the drastic measures now planned. Here there was local opinion to consider, bureaucracies to manage, and sensitive relationships among various German agencies which required attention. The relatively small numbers of Jews in the west only made matters worse, for the Jews tended to be well integrated in the societies in which they lived, and the idea of Jewry posing a mortal threat was sometimes difficult to sustain—especially in Scandinavia, where the Jewish population was minuscule. Apart from Italy, an ally and hence for years able to pursue its own path, France had the only authentic government with which the Germans had to deal. However, France had by far the largest western concentration of Jews—about 350,000 in 1941—and the majority of these lived in the southern zone, out of the Nazis' reach until the German armies moved across the demarcation line in November 1942. More than ever, caution was essential in the west, despite the fact that the goal was now clear.

Although Berlin had signaled the necessity for a coordinated effort, this was not immediately achieved, and Nazis on the spot still exercised local initiative. On his own, the headstrong twenty-eight-year-old Theodor Dannecker stepped out ahead of his colleagues in Brussels and The Hague, urging an exemplary deportation from France in order to nudge the French government into a more aggressive posture. Meeting with Eichmann in March, he secured permission to dispatch a few deportation trains east even before regular schedules from the west had been worked out.[32] One transport left later that month, sending the first groups of west European Jews to Auschwitz. Hans Rauter, the top SS man in the Netherlands, moved boldly in another direction—to concentrate Dutch Jews prior to deportation. During the second half of 1941 Jewish identity papers in the Netherlands were stamped with the letter J, those holding such documents were partially excluded from public life, cleared from the provinces, and, early in 1942, forced into three ghetto districts of Amsterdam.[33]

Recognizing the need for common action in the west, Nazi officials in Berlin hoped to bring their colleagues in France, Belgium, and Holland together to impose upon all Jews in those countries a distinguishing sign—the yellow star.[34] Marking Jews in this way had proven useful in the east, where since 1939 a white armband had been mandatory for Jews in the General Government and stars had to be sewn on the front and back of outer garments in the parts of Poland incorporated into the Reich. In Germany itself, a yellow star was ordered in September 1941. Eichmann's representatives in Paris, Brussels, and The Hague were summoned to meet together in March 1942, and hope was expressed that authorities would publish the star ordinance in all three countries simultaneously, in a matter of weeks. But the star decree demonstrated how difficult it was to synchronize persecution in countries with different occupation structures and where public opinion did not support anti-Jewish moves of this kind. Unwilling to stir up local opposition, the military authorities in Belgium, notably Brigadier General Reeder, opposed the idea, and refused to accept a low-level SS decision to proceed with its imposition. On the other hand, SS representatives in the Netherlands, after having failed to attend a planning meeting in mid-March, went ahead without further consultation and issued their star decree in April.

Delays occurred in France, as some of the Nazis there attempted, in vain, to persuade Vichy to take responsibility for the decree, or at least to see to its application in the unoccupied zone. Diplomatic questions also had to be answered, for it turned out that there were in France large numbers of Jews from countries which were allied with Germany, or neutral, or other belligerents. In the end, only the star decrees for Belgium and France appeared together, early in June.

With the marking of the Jews, planning could proceed for the deportations themselves. On June 11, Eichmann assembled his representatives from France, Belgium, and Holland, together with the "Jewish expert" in the Foreign Office, Franz Rademacher, to consider technical arrangements. Discussions continued to the end of the month. In the first round of shipments, Dannecker agreed to come up with 100,000 Jews from France, equally divided between the two zones. SS officials in Holland would send 40,000, and those in Belgium 10,000.[35] Logistical problems loomed large in all these conversations. The war in Russia proved a tremendous drain upon railway resources, and General Otto Kohl of the Railway Transport Division reported in mid-June that preparations for a spring offensive required a sudden redirection to the Reich of rolling stock which would otherwise have been earmarked for deporting Jews.[36] Railway schedules were extremely rigid, and dictated the eventual pace of the Final Solution in the west. Everything depended on careful planning, and close cooperation among the respective occupation authorities.

To assure the smooth functioning of the Final Solution, it was essential to clear away any obstacles which lay in the path of the SS, to which full operational responsibility had been assigned. In this regard the military chiefs in Belgium had long given cause for concern. As we have seen, Brigadier General Reeder dragged his feet on the matter of the yellow star, and had to be overruled by superior officers, possibly Himmler himself.[37] Although an honorary SS commander, like many high Nazi officials, Reeder was a military administrator of the old school, keen on the Prussian bureaucratic style, which found the rounding up and murder of large numbers of civilians extremely uncongenial. Reeder's staff officer, Franz Thedieck, was a right-wing Catholic and anti-Nazi who scandalized SS purists by attending church in full uniform. For men such as these the Final Solution was a vexatious scheme of the SS and an unwarranted challenge to the German military. They disliked the needless expenditure of effort involved in the project, were reluctant to stir up opposition locally, and some may even have found the deportations distasteful from

186

a humanitarian point of view. Fortunately for Reeder, the two successive Gestapo leaders in Belgium, Karl Canaris and Ernst Ehlers, were closer to the viewpoint of the military than to that of the RSHA in the struggle among German agencies for power in Belgium, and they did not force a confrontation with him over the issue. The practical effect of such opposition, supported by the anti-Nazi Wehrmacht commander General Alexander von Falkenhausen, was in the long run probably slight, in view of the priority given to the Jewish question in Berlin. But it certainly made planning awkward during the second phase, and led to subsequent difficulties, as we shall see.[38]

Himmler managed to circumvent the possibility of such trouble in France, where the relatively large number of Jews and the existence of a French government would have made military opposition disastrous. There had been more than a hint of conflict in the latter part of 1941, notably in October when the local SS, together with a splinter group of French extreme rightists, bombed several Paris synagogues (including that of the rue Copernic, where another bomb exploded exactly thirty-nine years later). This outraged the Militärbefehlshaber, General Otto von Stülpnagel, and although he immediately asserted his preeminence in matters relating to the maintenance of order, he failed in his effort to remove SS Major Helmut Knochen, who commanded the Gestapo in France.[39] In preparation for the Final Solution, Himmler eliminated the capacity of Stülpnagel's military command to direct Jewish matters. In April 1942 he managed to remove from the Militärbefehlshaber control over police matters and in the following month dispatched to Paris as his personal emissary a top SS general, Higher SS and Police Leader Karl Albrecht Obert. To signal the SS victory Heydrich himself inaugurated the new police boss in a ceremony at the Hôtel Ritz. Oberg now entered directly into negotiations with the French police and helped organize the operations to come. Circumvented in this as well as other spheres, Otto von Stülpnagel left his post in July, to be replaced by his cousin, Karl Heinrich von Stülpnagel. Werner Best, head of the military administration civil staff in France, who had also been considered too soft by the RSHA, similarly found himself eased out of his job.[40]

Fewer problems arose for the SS in the Netherlands. It will be recalled that occupation authority there had been turned over to a *Reichskommissar*, Arthur Seyss-Inquart, who was directly responsible to Hitler. Seyss was a loyal Nazi and a unswerving anti-Semite, who took his honorary SS rank seriously and was not looking for trouble. Unlike his military colleagues in France and Belgium, Seyss did not quarrel importantly with the local SS representative and fellow Austrian, Hans Rauter. The *Reichskommissar* did not pretend to direct police matters. The Wehrmacht chief in Holland was General of the Air Force Friedrich Christian Christiansen, son of a Protestant pastor, whose principal administrative experience before the war was in aviation schools. A rather weak personality, Christiansen also labored under the disability of being the protégé of Göring, which did not count for much after the abysmal failure of the Luftwaffe in the Battle of Britain. Christiansen's job was akin to a garrison commander, and he was hardly in a position to interfere with high-level policy.[41]

Freed from a good deal of military interference, the SS could indulge its inclinations to hound and harass the doomed Jews of the west. In the spring and early summer of 1942, Himmler's agents in France, Belgium, and Holland issued scores of regulations dealing with Jews—excluding them from public places, confiscating their possessions, controlling their every movement. The SS may also have prompted the move by Quisling's government in Norway to register all Jews in June. Thousands were interned, sent to work camps, or otherwise held ready for deportation. The three Jewish councils in the west received ever more humiliating and ominous instructions which they were forced to execute, draining their energies and beginning to undermine their credibility among increasingly bewildered and frightened Jewish communities.

Everywhere in the west Nazi leaders worried about what would happen when deportations eventually turned to local Jews—those who were long-standing citizens of the countries in which they lived. Occupation authorities were all aware that civil servants and police in western states often distinguished between well-assimilated, fully integrated Jews, and outsiders. German officials frequently reported, as did Werner von Bargen, the Foreign Office man in Brussels, that because of this distinction the locals showed that they had no real "understanding" of the Jewish question.[42] To relieve the injured sensibilities of many bureaucrats, the Germans issued a sweeping decree in November 1941 denationalizing every Reich Jew living abroad. This automatically made most Jewish refugees stateless, putting them in the lowest possible category of administered persons—a perception and a legal reality which had evolved throughout Europe since the early 1930s.[43] Continuing to address this problem, Nazi experts and SS officers now enticed local authorities with the attractive proposition: stateless Jews would go first. Bargaining and discussions along these lines continued with indigenous police and civil servants throughout the spring and summer, before the trains started to roll. At the same time, the Foreign Office pondered the endless complications arising with Jews holding passports from countries allied with the Reich.

But following the Wannsee meeting, everyone in authority knew that these were temporary difficulties, soon to be resolved. Before long, all the Jews would go. Eichmann himself went to Paris on June 30 to oversee preparations, and apparently stressed this point.[44] Time was short. Franz Rademacher called for a new assistant at the Jewish Desk in the Foreign Office in March 1942, because of the press of work: "The stronger the German victory looms, the greater and more urgent becomes the task of the Referat, because the Jewish question must be solved in the course of the war, for only so can it be solved without worldwide outcry."[45]

The Third Phase: The Final Solution, 1942–1944

The Final Solution was launched in the west in the summer of 1942, at a high point in the history of Hitler's continental empire. But one should not assume from the outstanding fact of German hegemony from the Atlantic to the outskirts of Moscow and Stalingrad that the Nazis had unlimited power everywhere in Europe. On the contrary, German forces were stretched thin, and nowhere more so than in western Europe. There were enormous new demands upon German manpower. After the blitzkrieg stalled in Russia at the end of 1941, Hitler ordered a transformation of the wartime economy of the Reich, building for a longer war which would require a vastly greater production of arms and equipment. Together with increasing calls for men by the armed forces, this meant a growing reliance upon foreign workers in Germany. By the end of 1941 there were close to 4 million of these, eventually to reach more than 7 million by mid-1944—20 percent of the German work force—when 7 million more were working in their own countries for the German war effort. Despite this heavy reliance on foreign labor, there were few Nazi police and troops available in the west to handle the deportations of Jews. Without the extensive cooperation of indigenous police forces and other officials, the Germans were therefore incapable of realizing their plans for the murder of west European Jews.

Help came easily to the Nazis during the early stages of deportation. Participation by the Belgian police was extremely limited, but both the French and the Dutch police rounded up Jews, held them in camps, and saw the convoys off to the east. Frequently, the mere presence of the local gendarmerie helped lull the Jews who were taken away; certainly, their participation reduced apprehensions among the surrounding population by making the arrests seem as normal as possible. In addition to the police, who were the most directly involved, there were countless others—prefects and their subordinates, judicial officials, mayors, railwaymen, concierges—who had a part to play. The French government at Vichy authorized their involvement, and indeed welcomed a situation in which French and not German personnel exercised authority in the country. In Belgium and Holland the captive administrations, with each ministry headed by a secretary-general, carried on in a similar fashion, although municipal officials in Brussels took a clear stand against persecution after the yellow star was imposed in June. In all west European states there were local, homegrown fascists to join domestic or German police from the beginning in rounding up Jews—Jacques Doriot's Parti Populaire Français in France, Rexist and Flemish bands in Belgium, Anton Mussert's National Socialist movement in the Netherlands, and Quisling's Nasjonal Samling in Norway.

Such collaboration, especially that of ordinary officials who were not particularly sympathetic to nazism, reflected in part the momentum generated by two years of working with the Germans. During these two years officials had acquired the habits of a new chain of command, sometimes involving unpleasant tasks. Many could not conceive deporting Jews in any other context. Collaboration also reflected the disposition on the part of local authorities to view refugees harshly, particularly Jewish refugees. Since the Germans encouraged the rounding up of foreign Jews at the start, many bureaucrats lent a hand to what might simply be considered a long-standing national effort to rid their countries of unwanted outsiders. The proportion of foreign Jews was by far the highest in Belgium, where only 6.5 percent of the over 57,000 Jews enumerated by the Gestapo had Belgian citizenship.[46] About half of the 350,000 Jews in France were noncitizens, as were 19 percent of Denmark's 8,000 Jews, and almost 16 percent of Holland's 140,000. In this regard, French authorities outdid any in Europe except the Bulgarians and possibly the Slovaks, by actually volunteering to hand over such unwanted Jews from unoccupied territory.[47]

Collaboration was never complete, and in France, Belgium, and the Netherlands various officials showed signs of reluctance by the beginning of 1943. Only in Norway did this not pose a serious problem. There were almost twice as many German police in that country (3,300) than there were Jews, and so even when some of Quisling's men turned unreliable for the deportations, it was possible to send more than a quarter of the Jews from the port of Bergen to Auschwitz by the end of 1942.[48] Proportionately, deportations went furthest in Belgium during the first three months of convoys, when close to 30 percent of the Jews were taken from that country. Yet many Jews fled successfully from Belgium into France or Switzerland, found hiding places provided by non-Jews, or procured false identity papers with which they could evade capture. Already in December 1942 Martin Luther was pressing for the inclusion of Belgian citizens, a sign that all was not quite going in Belgium as he had hoped.[49] Thanks to the intervention of von Falkenhausen, responding to local appeals, Belgian citizens were not deported for about a year. In September 1943, when the first and only mass roundup of Jews of Belgian nationality occurred, there was once again a loud protest, and General Reeder ordered their release from the assembly camp of Malines.[50] Once native French Jews were included in the shipments, the police in France proved less and less reliable; much the same was true in the Netherlands. Of course, the Germans were able to continue their work despite these problems with local authorities. Yet the job required more German effort than at the beginning, and the momentum of the first months of the Final Solution in the west could not be sustained.

The Germans encountered a very serious obstacle in 1943 owing to the position of the Italian government. Anti-Semitism had never struck deep roots among the Italian people, or even the Fascist Party, which had considerable Jewish support and membership during the 1920s and early 1930s. Mussolini himself did not particularly like Jews, but shared the indifference of most of his countrymen to a "problem" which did not exist in their society. In 1938, to bring Italy into ideological tune with the Reich, Mussolini opportunistically adopted a racist posture, and issued laws against the 50,000 Italian Jews. But persecution was mild in comparison with the Hitlerian version, involved many exceptions, and did not have the enthusiastic support of the Italian population.[51] When in November 1942, in response to the Allied landings in North Africa, the Germans swept south across the demarcation line in France, the Italians moved west to the Rhône River and occupied eight French departments. To the Nazis it was bad enough that the duce had seemed unwilling to contribute his Jews to the contingents deported from western Europe since the summer of 1942; by the beginning of 1943 it became apparent that the Italians were also shielding French Jews as well. The Italian troops shared much of the anti-German sentiment of the increasingly war-weary Italian population, and in this climate the idea of a racialist crusade on behalf of Aryan civilization seemed even more alien and absurd than before. Italian occupation officers not only refused to turn Jews over to Vichy or the Germans, they also blocked the application of French anti-Semitic legislation. As with their occupation policy for Croatia and part of Greece, the Italians held firm, and by one means or another resisted every effort to bring them into line. Ribbentrop failed to convince Mussolini to change his policy when he visited Rome in March 1943, and the SS ground their teeth over the obstruction they encountered. The Italian zone of France became a haven for some 50,000 Jews, protected by *carabinieri* against both the Germans and the French police.[52]

Unfortunately, this protection was not to last. It continued after the fall of Mussolini in July 1943, but could not survive the surrender of Italy to the Allies early in the autumn. The Italians evacuated their zone of France suddenly when the armistice was announced prematurely on September 8, too quickly to implement an evacuation scheme which had been negotiated by an Italian Jew, Angelo Donati. As the Italians left, the Germans moved in, and the Jews were caught. Very few escaped, and most were sent to Auschwitz in a matter of days.

Only now did the deportation of Italian Jews begin. Despite Hitler's restoration of an Italian fascist regime, the phantom Republic of Salo, the renewed persecution and the deportation of Jews from the parts of Italy outside Allied hands was entirely a German operation. Himmler pressed for the application of the Final Solution, and neither the severe difficulties associated with the worsening war situation in the peninsula nor the widespread opposition to the deportations among Italians, and even some Germans on the spot, prevented the dispatch of more than 8,000 Jews to the east.[53]

As in Italy, the Germans knew that the Final Solution could be extended to Denmark only through their own efforts. Anti-Semitism had flared briefly in Denmark in the wake of surrender, as elsewhere in western Europe, but the Danish political leadership, continuing in place from before the war, remained adamantly opposed to all manifestations of anti-Jewish feeling. Danish Nazis were hopelessly divided among themselves, and politically incompetent. Nazism and anti-Semitism remained unpopular. For three years the Danes collaborated economically with the Reich, in exchange for which the Germans did not interfere in internal Danish affairs. When the German representative in Copenhagen, the traditionalist Cecil von Renthe-Fink, was replaced by the former police and military administrator Werner Best in November 1942, the latter searched imaginatively for some means to move against the Jews without unduly disturbing relations with a cooperative Danish government. No real opportunities appeared, however. Even the ambitious Martin Luther at the Foreign Office, never one to neglect an opportunity for pressing forward with Jewish persecution, felt unable to recommend a change in policy.[54]

Until the summer of 1943, therefore, the Germans left the Danes alone with their Jews. The Jewish issue suddenly came to a head, however, with the general crisis in Danish-German relations that arose in August 1943. As political and social conditions worsened dramatically throughout the country, due largely to Danish protests against mounting German exactions, the occupation imposed a state of emergency. The government of Erik Scavenius resigned, leaving internal control of Denmark in the hands of its civil service. Taking advantage of the upheaval, Ministerialdirigent Werner Best triggered the persecution of local Jews, with the object of deporting them by sea, from Copenhagen.[55]

This operation failed utterly, as is well known, and in the end the Nazis were able to lay their hands on only 475 of the close to 8,000 Jews in Denmark. During the first week of October 1943, within a matter of days, thousands of Danes organized a rescue expedition unprecedented in the history of the Final Solution, which transferred nearly the entire community of Jews across the Sund to Sweden in small boats. In part the impotence of the Germans flowed from internal divisions among the occupation authorities. Best failed to obtain the cooperation of the Wehrmacht in Denmark because of his rivalry with its commander, General Hermann von Hannecken, who opposed the deportations, and he failed also to win full authority to seize control of the Danish civil service because he was so distrusted in Berlin, particularly by Himmler, who seems for the moment to have had other priorities in mind than the deportation of a small number of Danish Jews.[56] But most importantly, Best failed to get the support of the Danish administration and public opinion, without which the deportation could not succeed.

The source of this failure has often been pondered by those concerned with drawing some moral lesson from the terrible events we have been considering. The most important study of the rescue, by the Israeli historian Leni Yahil, discusses several explanations, but judges the decisive factor to have been "the special character and moral stature of the Danish people and their love of democracy and freedom."[57] Hannah Arendt saw in the Danish response an exemplary demonstration of the efficacy of nonviolent resistance to tyranny. The Nazis, she wrote in *Eichmann in Jerusalem*, changed their entire posture when faced with open native opposition. "They had met resistance based on principle, and their 'toughness' had melted like butter in the sun."[58] While not wishing to depreciate the significance and moral import of the rescue or strategies of nonviolence, it is well to remember that the community of Jews in that country was small, that the haven of Sweden was close (between five and fifteen miles across open water), that the Swedes were willing to accept all the Jews, and that the persecutions occurred in a country already seething with opposition to nazism. These conditions greatly facilitated the rescue operation, which would, indeed, have been impossible without them.

It is also worth considering how the timing of the Nazi attempt to implement the Final Solution in Denmark differed so sharply from the other cases in western Europe we have been discussing. The attack upon the Danish Jews coincided with a sharp reversal of occupation policy which, after three years of encouraging a model protectorate, suddenly subjected the entire state to humiliating subservience and oppression. The contrast is obvious with other west European countries, where deportations of Jews followed two years of habituation to anti-Jewish laws and policies, introduced at a time of national prostration and soul-searching following an overwhelming military collapse. Defenders of Jews everywhere in Europe claimed that the Jewish fate was part of the general fate of people conquered by nazism. Unfortunately, it was not always easy to demonstrate how this was so, when the Jews were so sharply singled out. But in Denmark, as Yahil suggests, the victimization of Jews coincided exactly with a sudden political assault upon the entire Danish people.[59]

Notably, all this happened when the Reich was in retreat, following the German defeats at El Alamein, Stalingrad, and Kursk, and the Allied landings in Italy. By the autumn of 1943, as the British and American air offensive against the Reich reached spectacular proportions, Hitler no longer seemed invincible—a sharp contrast with the beginning of the occupation in 1940, or the launching of the Final Solution in the summer of 1942. The implication is clear: because of the delay in preparing deportations in Denmark, it was easier for Danes to perceive the attack on Jews as an attack upon themselves and hence to rally to their defense; it was also morally easier to challenge the power of the Reich, which by late 1943 showed signs of its eventual collapse.

Proper timing was obviously crucial to the success of opposition to

Nazi Jewish policy. On one rare occasion in western Europe public pro-test came too soon—the Dutch workers' strike of February 1941, in sol-idarity with persecuted Jews. This was the first massive, open opposition anywhere in occupied Europe to Nazi anti-Semitism. The strike was crushed by overwhelming force, and to an important degree the coura-geous Dutch opposition continued for years to be demoralized by the brutally effective display of German power so early in the occupation. And the strike had no effect whatever on the substance of Nazi anti-Jewish activity in Holland, except perhaps to worsen the plight of native Jews. This resistance therefore seems to have come prematurely; on the other hand, resistance more often came too late to help at all. By the latter part of 1943 the unpopularity of the deportations of Jews caused problems for the Nazis in France, Belgium, and the Netherlands, pre-cisely at the moment when protests against the conscription of the indig-enous labor force to work in the Reich made local police less reliable. But by that time it was not possible to do more than slow the deportation machinery, and even then the rescue of Jews does not seem to have ranked high for resistance strategists in selecting targets. In any event, by late 1943 the great majority of Jewish deportees were already dead.

Assessment: The Holocaust in Western Europe

The Final Solution did not succeed in western Europe because the war ended too soon and the Nazis did not have time to complete their task. Nevertheless, the scale of destruction was staggering—some 40 per-cent of west European Jews killed. With 105,000 deported, or 75 percent of its Jews, the Netherlands suffered the greatest losses, both in absolute and relative terms. Belgium came next, with the murder of over 24,000, more than 40 percent of its Jewish population of late May 1940. Norway lost about the same proportion—760 Jews. In France 20 percent of the Jews—about 75,000—were murdered. Italy lost about 8,000, or 16 per-cent.[60]

What accounts for these variations? Let it be clear at the outset that these figures do not reflect any absolute measure of Nazi capability, but rather the results of a program interrupted prematurely by the military reverses suffered by the Reich in the latter part of 1944. For the Nazis' will to destroy the Jews weakened only at the end of that year, among certain top leaders, in the face of impending defeat. So what we are really considering is the relative pace of deportations from west European countries.

We hope that enough has been said to caution against relying on any single factor to explain this. A recent effort by a sociologist to isolate, quantify, and assess the significance of variables which would account for the incidence of genocide in European countries failed notably to produce a clear answer because the work ignored the evolution of German strategy and certain basic problems associated with comparison.[61] None of these variables makes sense outside of the particular experiences of individual states. The availability of a haven to which Jews could flee, for example, was unquestionably crucial in the rescue of Danish Jews, but did not prevent the proportionately high level of destruction in Norway, despite the existence of a thousand miles of frontier with Sweden. Concentration of Jews in one place clearly could be dangerous, as in the cases of Amsterdam and also Oslo, where the Jews could easily be identified and rounded up. But concentration in the port of Copenhagen, only a few miles from freedom, helped save the Danish Jews. Without it, the rescue could not have succeeded. Sheer numbers could be important. Clearly, the Nazis felt that Denmark, with a mere 8,000 Jews, could wait for the implementation of the Final Solution, whereas France, with the largest Jewish population in the west, received a high priority. But in France, owing to the circumstances of the military defeat in 1940 and the peculiar armistice arrangement with the Germans, the Jews remained scattered across a large and, relatively speaking, sparsely settled country. In view of the thin screen of German troops and police available for the job, it is not surprising that the proportion of deported Jews from France was relatively low, despite the valuable aid given the Germans by the Vichy government.

Generalizations break apart on the stubborn particularity of each of our countries. Nowhere is this more obvious than in considering the dominant religious traditions in western European states. Catholic Italy and Protestant Denmark provide the two outstanding cases of consistent popular resistance to the persecution of the Jews. Lutheran theologians made the earliest and most forceful denunciation of anti-Semitism in Denmark, which was decidedly not the case among their coreligionists in Germany. The notable lack of public protest against Jewish deportations from the Vatican, about which there has been so much discussion, does not seem to have affected the deep antipathy toward anti-Semitism among the Italian population, including the Catholic clergy. In the Netherlands, the Catholics and the Protestant Dutch Reformed Church were about equally divided in their numbers of adherents. When they were about to issue a joint public denunciation of the deportations in the summer of 1942, the Germans threatened reprisals unless they desisted. The Synod of the Dutch Reformed Church complied, but the Catholics did not, immediately resulting in the inclusion of Catholic Jews in shipments to the gas chambers.[62] There has been anguished discussion about this episode ever since it occurred, but it seems unlikely that one can draw from it any useful generalization about how the behavior of particular denominations might have influenced the Final Solution.

Each case was different. It makes little sense to attempt to deduce laws about victimization from an examination of so few cases, in which the degree of particularity was so high. Our conclusion is more modest. It seems plain that German policy, and also the ability of the Nazis to apply their power, were decisive in determining how far the destruction process went by the time of liberation. Nazi policy in the first phase, when the European war was going well for the Germans, was governed by pragmatic considerations. During this period some groundwork was laid for a final solution, the outlines of which remained unclear and the timing obscure. Because conditions for occupation differed, and because of the lack of urgency, the degree to which the Jews were isolated from the surrounding population differed considerably, and remained incomplete. Then, in response to the changed war situation in the east, policy changed: the Final Solution was defined, and declared a compelling necessity. The second phase involved adjustment to these new circumstances, by sometimes feverish planning and preparations. In the third phase, from the summer of 1942, the plans were implemented. For a time all went according to projection. But by 1943 serious military setbacks suffered elsewhere by the Reich took their toll: the Germans were unable to supply sufficient men and railway transport to keep up the pace of the first deportations and to finish the job quickly. Geography, administrative difficulties, conflicts among German agencies, Jewish resistance, and the actions of some west Europeans all helped to slow the process of deportation at various points. But only the outcome of the military conflict itself could have a decisive effect upon the Final Solution.

Only the defeat of the Reich brought the trains to a halt. This is especially clear when one observes how long the shipments of Jews continued. The last regular deportation from Drancy, outside of Paris, left France for Auschwitz on July 31, 1944, almost two months after the Allied landings in Normandy; two more smaller convoys followed from France, the last departing on August 17, only a week before the first tanks of General Leclerc arrived to liberate Paris. The last convoy from Belgium left Malines for Auschwitz on July 31, with 554 Jews. The last convoy from Holland went to Auschwitz on September 3, with over 1,000 Jews. Deportations from northern Italy continued the longest of all, due to the tenacious and successful German resistance against the Allies: trains went to Auschwitz until October 24, when the death factory in Poland had only days left to function, and on December 14 to Ravensbrück and Flossenbürg; a final convoy of Jews went from Trieste to Bergen-Belsen on February 24, 1945.[63]

11

The Reaction to the Nazi Anti-Jewish Policy in East-Central Europe and in the Balkans

BELA VAGO

The Nazi onslaught in east-central Europe and in the Balkans was far from being frontal and uniform in time and intensity. The timetable of the German expansion, unforeseen crises and events in the area, abrupt and surprising changes in the relations between the Great Powers, and military developments from 1939 to 1941 were all factors which transformed post-1938 east-central Europe into a political kaleidoscope of conquered and annexed territories, satellite and independent states, where Nazi influence, especially regarding the Jewish problem, varied from area to area. In addition, cultural, political, and religious traditions greatly influenced the local reaction of both the population and the ruling circles to the Nazi practice of handling the Jewish question.

Besides chronological dissimilarities we have to register the ups and downs of the intensity and efficacy of German pressure upon the conduct of Jewish policy in the east European countries. Thus, for example, Antonescu's regime in Romania showed much more independence in Jewish matters in the second half of the war than earlier, and the Jewish policy of the Kállay government in Hungary, from the second half of 1942 until its fall in March 1944, reflected the successful attempts to elude the Nazi dictate in the deportation of the Jews. In Romania as in Hungary there is an easily discernible link between the endeavor to loosen the dependence on Germany with a view to the future, and the handling of the Jewish question.

We also have to keep in mind that in those countries which preserved their formal independence, a distinction should be made between official Jewish policy and the attitude of the local population; in the case of the other territories (Poland, Bohemia-Moravia after March 1939, the Serbian entity after May 1941, Greece after its occupation) we shall be limited to the study of the local population, or at best to complementing this study with the Jewish policy of the local underground leaderships. Thus, our scrutiny, as dictated by the complexity of reality, should follow the course of the impact of Nazi Germany on the Jewish policy of the respective governments and on the attitudes of the local population in the satellite countries, and the effect of the Nazi propaganda and practice on the attitudes of the population in the conquered territories.

It would be commonplace to underscore the well-known fact that nowhere in the area did anti-Semitism begin with the inclusion of the respective countries in the Nazi sphere of influence. Nor can there be any doubt that in none of the surveyed countries which preserved their real or fictitious independence was the fate of the Jews determined solely by Nazi Germany. The apologetic pretension voiced by all present Communist regimes in the area—that the Holocaust was due exclusively to Nazi Germany—is a simplistic rationalization, contradicting historic truth, but it is in accordance with the thesis of "good people, bad leaders" in capitalist societies, and it also conforms to the fictitious image of the toiling masses resisting both the German Nazis and the local collaborators.

Economic, social, cultural, religious, and, of course, political factors produced a variety of attitudes in the area. It should also be made clear that there was never an automatic and complete identity between the official policy and the attitude of the different strata of society, or, of course, the legal or illegal opposition. Nevertheless, we shall seek generalizations, albeit with strong reservations, and we shall keep in mind the limitations of any research touching public opinion, popular reaction in dictatorial regimes, and the wide margins of error inherent to this kind of scrutiny.

Before the Holocaust

In some of the surveyed countries anti-Semitism was endemic and virulent in the 1920s, in others it flared up only in the late 1930s, undoubtedly ignited by Nazi propaganda and by the initial successes of Nazi Germany, but nowhere were the elements and manifestations of the autochthonous anti-Semitism missing in the interwar period and during the war. The virulent anti-Jewish mood characterized only Hungary, Romania, and Poland. Czechoslovakia, Yugoslavia, Bulgaria, and Greece knew only anti-Semitic undercurrents, and the Jewish problem never came into the focus of public interest; in Slovakia and Croatia, the two by-products of the disappearance of Czechoslovakia and Yugoslavia, popular and official anti-Semitism came to the forefront only after the creation of these puppet states.

Hungary   When World War II broke out, the Hungarian political scene was dominated by two types of anti-Semitic forces acting along parallel lines: on the upper level, the ruling circles, adopting Pál Teleki's and also Béla Imredy's moderate, not yet Nazi-type anti-Semitism, while below, a petty-bourgeois and plebeian extreme anti-Semitism, mainly represented by Ferenc Szálasi's Arrow Cross. The radical anti-Semitism of the local Nazi movements made deep incursions in the popular strata in the late 1930s and during the war, and the competition between the two anti-Semitic camps paved the way for the undisguised Nazi interference after 1939. However, in spite of the differences in the degree of the extremism of anti-Semitism, it was on this platform that a national consensus evolved during the war years.

The Nazi slogans about the "Jewish-Bolshevik plutocracy" worked among those destitute petty-bourgeois and semiproletarian, or even proletarian, elements who believed in the Nazi redistribution of wealth resulting from the nationalization of Jewish property. But then, what was the motivation behind anti-Jewish radicalization of the upper-class elements? Count Pál Teleki could serve as a reliable witness on behalf of the social ruling elite. In 1939 he wrote that the flaring up of anti-Semitism in a country "where anti-Semitism was age-old as a feeling" was a natural phenomenon. He accepted that some outside (Nazi) influence had been at work, but only *some*, because in his opinion Hungarian anti-Semitism was not a copy of German anti-Semitism and "it will . . . never grow to such cruelty." However, the Jews represented a "catastrophic danger," in his view, because Jewish ideas and morality intoxicated the middle classes and the aristocracy, and unless an immediate and radical change could be effected in eliminating Jewish influence, it would cost the life of the Hungarian people.

While the Jewish question was one of the central issues of interwar Hungary, after the partial fulfillment of the territorial aspirations it became *the* problem which preoccupied political life and public opinion. Its centrality in the country's daily life conditioned the soil for the Holocaust long before the first massacres and the fateful events of 1944. The forced-labor system humiliated and degraded tens of thousands of young Jews; the forced "Aryanizations" deprived many Jews of their property; tens of thousands lost their jobs; the state administration became completely "*judenrein*"; yet Jews still maintained their seats in Parliament, and a tolerant section of the Hungarian population and even liberal elements in government circles still left enough loopholes to enable the pursuit of a tolerable life-style for a second-rate category of citizens, harassed and humiliated, but spared from concentration camps and ghettos, from pogroms and from deportation. The vociferous extremist propaganda of the local Nazis and the German interference in the Jewish problem was counteracted by the governments, which resisted any German and local pressure beyond the second Jewish law, refusing the adoption of extreme Nazi practices.

Many Jews whose Hungarian citizenship was not acknowledged fell victim to the witch-hunt by the police organ in charge of the foreigners, but thousands of refugees from Nazi-occupied Europe were able to find asylum in Hungary. From the outbreak of war until the summer months of 1941, German pressure had not yet become decisive; the local National Socialist parties were not yet in command and public opinion was not yet clamoring for a radical solution of the Jewish problem, meaning segregation, deportation, or physical liquidation.

Romania   Romania, the second state after Hungary to enact anti-Jewish laws, but second only to Germany in establishing an authentic anti-Semitic regime in Europe (by the end of 1937), embarked on an essentially different course in handling the Jewish question and in tackling Nazi interference. Unlike the Hungarian authoritarian regime which amalgamated semifeudal elements with parliamentary democracy, the Romanian patterns followed the example of the Western democracies; the pre-1938 governments were eager to preserve the image of a genuinely democratic society, and some of the outstanding representatives of the establishment took drastic steps to curtail not only left extremism, but the radical, anti-Semitic right as well.

Romanian Jewry suffered heavy blows from Cuzist and Legionary terror; occasionally synagogues and Jewish institutions were vandalized, armed attacks claimed victims, thousands were beaten up, the universities were progressively made "*judenrein*" by the extremist students, while a vast network of anti-Semitic periodical publications were poisoning public opinion. Yet until December 1937 no laws had been enacted which explicitly discriminated against Jews, and their normal life had not yet been imperiled by the authorities. While legalistic chicaneries embittered their daily life, they were not exposed to major threats from any pre-1938 government. Nazi pressure was on the increase in the mid-1930s and manifestations of popular anti-Semitism were ubiquitous, but Romania's traditional links with the Western Powers, its territorial interests, and the pro-British and mainly Francophile mood which still prevailed among the upper strata precluded a Nazi-type takeover.

After the fall of the incompetent anti-Semitic cabinet of Octavian Goga, which during its forty-four days (December 30, 1937, to February 10, 1938) plunged Romania into chaos and unleashed a Nazi-type anti-Semitic terror, King Carol inaugurated his personal dictatorship. The Nazi interference was curtailed, and the most extreme anti-Jewish decrees were abolished. However, the anti-Jewish line followed its course.

The royal dictatorship also rationalized that a policy of restrained anti-Semitism was advisable as a weapon against the extremists. King Carol's government thought that an official, "moderate" anti-Semitism could serve as a lightning conductor both toward Nazi Germany and the internal right extremists. But as the revisionist threat became acute and German political and economic pressure mounted, Romania's rulers realized that their western orientation would be impractical. In the first half of 1940 a *volte-face* was worked out in Bucharest, and it was precisely the Jewish question over which the king and his advisers sought to curry favor with Germany and to make his regime acceptable to the domestic extremist opposition. The slogan "taking the wind out of the Nazis' sails" proved to be of no use to King Carol, and was fatal from a Jewish point of view. The royal dictatorship's anti-Jewish policy (from July to August 1940 a Nuremberg-type legislation was passed) not only preceded the Holocaust of Romanian Jewry, but paved the way for it as well. King Carol's regime did not survive the dismemberment of Greater Romania (July–September 1940), and in the beginning of September, General (later Marshal) Ion Antonescu seized power, together with the Iron Guard.

In the short period between September 1940 and the end of January 1941, a ferocious terror swept the whole country, mainly affecting the Jews. It was at this point that Nazi Germany could at last dictate its anti-Jewish policy to Romania, albeit against a drastically diminished Jewish community (with the loss of Northern Transylvania, Bessarabia, and

Northern Bukovina, Romanian Jewry dwindled from 760,000 to about 350,000 persons). The impending major catastrophe was avoided by the collapse of the Antonescu–Iron Guard partnership; by the end of January 1941, the Iron Guard staged an armed rebellion against Antonescu, aimed at the monopoly of power. Antonescu, backed by the army, and ultimately by Hitler too, crushed the rebellion; the Iron Guard again stepped down, but not before indulging in the most brutal anti-Jewish massacres. Romanian Jewry was given a respite, since Antonescu's military dictatorship, interested in restoring order and discipline and normalizing economic life, put an end to the anti-Jewish excesses, excluding violence from its envisaged "de-Jewification" project.

After five months of relative security, the Holocaust of Romanian Jewry, at least of those in Bessarabia and Northern Bukovina, was precipitated by Romania's joining Hitler's anti-Soviet war.

Poland The assumption that the new Polish state, born with the active help of the Entente Powers and in the atmosphere dominated by Wilson's principles, would be democratic and tolerant toward its huge bloc of national minorities proved to be unfounded. Illusions were nurtured among the more than 3 million Jews that the preponderance of the socialist and bourgeois democratic forces in the first administration was a guarantee of safety and freedom for the whole population, the Jewish minority included. However, the age-old anti-Semitic tradition, the rise of an exuberant extreme nationalism, serious economic troubles, and a fierce struggle for power between the ruling forces, linked to Piłsudski's name, and the main opposition party, the National Democrats, thwarted these expectations. The Jewish question became one of the central issues which preoccupied Polish political life, and official policy underwent a transformation from veiled to overt anti-Semitism.

The fatal crisis which developed after March 1939 and foreshadowed the showdown between Germany and Poland could have eased the tension between the majority and the Jews, threatened by the common enemy. However, even during these tense months there were no signs of relaxation in the anti-Semitic course. At the very end of the interwar era Polish authorities were still active in elaborating unrealistic plans for the mass emigration of the Jews, and the anti-Jewish edge of the regime was not changed in the least.

In interwar Poland there were no influential political forces or liberal intellectual circles to oppose the anti-Jewish drive; interwar Polish society was basically permeated with anti-Semitic feelings, a fact which must

204

be considered in the scrutiny of the reaction to the Holocaust in occupied Poland.

Czechoslovakia   When assessing the relations between the Jews and the host peoples in interwar Czechoslovakia (with 356,800 Jewish citizens out of a total of 14,730,000 in 1930), one is bound to take into consideration the blatant differences between Bohemia-Moravia (with a Jewish population of 200,000) and Slovakia, and also Carpatho-Ruthenia.

In the Czech parts of the only genuine interwar democracy of the area, there was no Jewish problem, nor was popular anti-Semitism virulent in the two other main components of the republic (Slovakia and Carpatho–Ruthenia). Tomaš Masaryk's liberal and tolerant spirit permeated Czech society, and except for some small, insignificant extreme rightist and fascist groups, political life was free of anti-Semitic manifestations. The Munich agreements and their disastrous consequences prompted an anti-Jewish upsurge, which bore out the viability of latent prejudices. The opportunistic right-wing Agrarians, now in command of the frustrated and demoralized masses, favored a rapprochement with Germany, in Jewish policy as well. Prime Minister Rudolf Beran, along with his fellow politicians and statesmen, voiced extreme nationalist and anti-Semitic slogans advocating the reestablishment of "national purity" and the reign of the "Christian spirit" in the reshaped and reoriented country. Nazi propaganda, rejected by the masses in the past, made significant inroads in almost every social stratum, with the possible exception of the intelligentsia. Nevertheless, the Beran administration refrained from going to extremes in handling the Jewish problem. The two anti-Jewish laws enforced by Beran (in January and February 1939) only affected those Jews whose Czech citizenship was not in order and the refugees (mainly from Germany and Austria), but did not question the status of the majority of the Jews in the Czech lands.

The liquidation of Czechoslovakia in March 1939 constituted a radical turning point in the situation of the Jewish population (in post-Munich Czechoslovakia the number of Jews decreased to 251,000, a bare 2.5 percent of the total population). Any scrutiny of this problem after the establishment of the Protectorate of Bohemia-Moravia should be restricted to the attitude of the local population, since the Prague Czech authorities were merely puppets of the occupiers.

Conditions in Slovakia differed from those in Bohemia-Moravia. In the midst of the backward, rural majority of the Slovaks, anti-Semitism

205

was endemic. The weak Slovak nationalist intelligentsia was, in its majority, anti-Czech, anti-Magyar, and anti-Semitic; they saw in the Jews not only a foreign middle class, but also the bearers of Hungarian assimilatory tendencies before 1918, which were alien to the Slovak people and its culture. The anti-Semitic Catholic People's Party of Andrej Hlinka, the most influential Slovak party on the eve of Munich, actually reflected the mood of the majority of the population.

In the short span between the Munich agreements and the creation of the independent Slovak state (March 14–15, 1939), the Slovak leaders displayed more eagerness in their anti-Jewish drive than their Czech counterparts. Authoritative voices in Bratislava demanded that Slovakia be "swept clean" of the Jews, and that the Aryanization of the country be the order of the day. As early as the beginning of November 1938, the government of Monsignor Josef Tiso announced anti-Jewish measures, and in the spark-laden atmosphere before the disintegration of the First Republic, anti-Semitic gangs committed acts of terror against the Jewish population. German influence on local anti-Semitism was stronger in Slovakia than in the Czech lands, and after Munich the incendiary Nazi propaganda was focused on Bratislava rather than on Prague.

When Tiso took over in mid-March 1939 as the virtual head of an alleged independent state, the time was ripe for the smooth implementation of a Nazi-type anti-Semitic policy.

The three Balkan countries of Bulgaria, Yugoslavia, and Greece (Albanian statistics registered only a few hundred Jews) shared a common denominator from the point of view of our study: their political life was free of the burden of a Jewish problem. The reasons for this were the relatively small number of Jews in the Balkan Peninsula and their inconspicuous role in the economy, as well as in the political and cultural life of the three countries.

Bulgaria　The small Jewish community in Bulgaria (about 50,000 in 1939 out of a total of over 6 million), was well integrated into Bulgarian society—albeit less assimilated than Hungarian Jewry—and it did not have to face major anti-Semitic parties, let alone anti-Jewish legislation before 1939. The policy of the various governments, led by the authoritarian King Boris in the 1930s, reflected the feelings of the great majority of the Bulgarians, who displayed tolerance and even empathy for the Jews and worked out the conditions of a natural coexistence with this small, uninfluential minority.

The Nazi drive in southeastern Europe and the strengthening of the revisionist trend in Bulgarian foreign policy inevitably resulted in a detrimental change in the official policy toward the Jews. The first anti-Jewish decree was published in the very first days of the outbreak of the war, in September 1939, demanding the expulsion of Jews bearing foreign passports.

In spite of the fact that public opinion and many members of the Sobranje opposed the anti-Jewish policy of the government of Bogdan Filov (in office from February 1940), the pro-Nazi shift pursued its course, and in 1940 anti-Semitism became perceptible in the state-controlled mass media. In July 1940 an anti-Jewish draft law for the "Defense of the Nation" was published in Sofia. The law, passed by the Sobranje in December 1940, was much milder than those in effect in Romania, Hungary, and Slovakia at that time. More important than the actual harm done to the Jews (a *numerus clausus* in the professions, confiscations of part of their property, their exclusion from public posts, and a special tax levied on the whole Jewish community) was the public reaction to it. Large sections of the population opposed the legislation, and some of the most influential public bodies protested against it. Such an uproar against Nazi-inspired anti-Jewish legislation had no precedent in the area and was not to occur anywhere else during the Holocaust.

When the military operations turned the Balkans into an operational zone and Bulgaria joined Hitler's war in April 1941 as an active participant in the liquidation of Yugoslavia, the Jewish problem inevitably came to the forefront.

Yugoslavia   The small Jewish community in Yugoslavia (in 1931 less than 70,000 out of a total of almost 14 million) did not constitute a "Jewish problem," even after the outbreak of the war. As in the other Balkan countries, the Jews were not prominent in the economy, and were even less so in the cultural and intellectual life of Yugoslavia. Although they were not entirely acculturated, their integration into the multinational state was complete, and there was no discriminatory legislation during the interwar period which might have provoked complaints from the Jewish leadership.

In spite of the almost permanent tension caused by the struggle between Croatian and Serbian nationalism, in which religious prejudices were strong, the Jewish community enjoyed an attitude of tolerance from every national group and religious community. However, it should be mentioned that there was a slight difference between the attitude of the local population in the eastern and southern parts of the country and that in the territories that had been under Austro-Hungarian rule before World War I. Thus, Slovenia and Croatia were more prone to anti-Jewish discrimination than the tolerant populations in the territories formerly under Turkish rule, or in independent prewar Serbia.

Although Nazi propaganda did have some influence on Yugoslavia, and the mass media was not entirely free of anti-Jewish overtones, no drastic anti-Jewish shift menaced Yugoslav Jewry, not even during the last months of Prince Paul's regency when Yugoslavia actually joined the Axis Powers (in March 1941).

The tragedy of Yugoslav Jewry began with the liquidation of the state by Germany and Italy in April 1941. While the anti-Jewish acts were carried out in the former Serbian territories mainly by the Germans, in the Croatian puppet state most of the crimes were committed by the Ustasha authorities and by the local Nazi sympathizers.

Greece   The turbulent interwar years in Greece were free of the Jewish problem: the 77,000-strong Jewish community (in a total population of 6.2 million in 1926), was well integrated in Greek society and economic life, although as elsewhere in the Balkans, its role was not prominent in the political, cultural, and economic domains.

General Ioannis Metaxas's Crown-sponsored dictatorship, inaugurated in 1936, favored the strengthening of ultrarightist movements; extreme nationalism became part and parcel of the somewhat nebulous fascist-type ideology of the dictatorship, and Metaxas himself flirted with the Axis. However, his pragmatism and a sound realpolitik, practiced in turn by every ruler in interwar Greece, pleaded for western orientation and for a foreign policy based on Great Britain's friendship and help. The lack of an endemic anti-Semitism and foreign policy considerations blocked the way to Nazi activity of any consequence. When the German war machine crushed the Greek state in the spring of 1941 and the fate of Greek Jewry seemed to be sealed, the Nazi occupiers had no anti-Semitic mass organizations or anti-Semitic quislings to rely on in carrying out their plans.

Even though the Nazi drive in interwar east-central and southeastern Europe was systematic and efficient, becoming overt and aggressive after

1936, its influence on local anti-Semitism, and the pro-Nazi reaction of the local authorities and population, are usually overrated. There is no question that the Germans took advantage of almost every foreign connection, the summit meetings included, to induce their east European partners to embark on an anti-Jewish course. There is a wealth of documents bearing out the exploitation of economic negotiations for the same purpose. However, it would be a mistake to explain any shift in the Jewish policy of the east European governments as resulting from Nazi pressure, the more so since some of the countries in the area actually resisted and adroitly circumvented the implementation of some undertakings under Nazi pressure and blackmail. Nazi activity in those countries with an anti-Jewish tradition (e.g., Poland and Romania) had a stimulating effect on the attitude of the population and gave impetus to the radicalization of the local propaganda, but it was not the determining factor of the local policy toward the Jews. Concerning the reaction of the local population to the Nazi policies, public opinion was favorable toward them, for example in Hungary, and in the late thirties also in Slovakia, mainly because of foreign-policy or national considerations, and not because of the Jewish problem per se. In Romania public opinion remained prowestern, and even the pro-Axis political forces, among them the Iron Guard, were anxious to emphasize the autochthonous character of their anti-Semitism rather than admitting the prevalence of German Nazi influence.

As a matter of fact, between the outbreak of World War II and the end of June 1941, German pressure did not lead to major and disastrous changes in the fate of the east European Jews—with the exception of those in German-occupied parts of Poland. The radical change in Nazi influence and in the local reaction to Nazi policies was a consequence of the outbreak of the war against the Soviet Union, and a result of the German occupation of part of eastern Europe. Direct German interference and the rise to power of anti-Semitic parties created a propitious soil not only for the segregation and later the extermination of the Jews, but also for the cooperation of the local population—or part of it—in the anti-Jewish crimes.

The Holocaust

Poland   One of the neglected topics in the historiography of the Holocaust in eastern Europe is the reaction of the local population, of the mass organizations, of the churches, and of other civilian factors to the Nazi policy of persecution and extermination. The inaccessibility of relevant sources in most east European countries and the slanted, unilateral documentation published by the Communist historians do not facilitate the task of the unbiased researcher. Surprisingly enough, the one country about which scholarly research into this topic is rather scarce is Poland, the country which had the greatest concentration of Jews in Europe and was the scene of the liquidation of the majority of European Jewry.

Since Poland was the only country in eastern Europe in which the Nazis did not manage to set up, or had no intention to establish, an administration run by local leaders, and since the attitude of the Polish government-in-exile in London is less relevant to our topic than the deeds of the Poles in occupied Poland, we shall emphasize the reaction of the *oppressed* Polish population to Nazi practices. Any scrutiny of the Polish reaction to the Nazi Holocaust should revolve around one basic question—namely, to what extent did the Polish people, the Polish underground organizations, and the Polish political and military organizations in the free world offer assistance to the Jews.

The deep-rooted popular anti-Semitism and the omnipresence of anti-Jewish feelings in the ranks of every type of resistance organization (mainly in the Armia Krajowa, and even more so in the National Armed Forces—the NSZ) created a negative image of the average Pole, viewed through the angle of his attitude toward the Holocaust. The Nazi conquerors encountered mostly hatred among the Poles toward their Jewish cocitizens. The collaboration between Nazis and the local population was less significant than elsewhere in occupied Europe, Serbia not excluded, and the Nazis were not assisted even by those who fared quite well during the occupation. The only area where they could count on the passive, or even active, support of the Poles was in the anti-Jewish drive.

Although the huge majority of Poles were passive onlookers, many of them aided and abetted the Germans in the spoliations and the casting out of the Jews before the start of the large-scale massacres.[1] When thousands of Jews tried to go into hiding, often with the help of Polish friends, other Poles thwarted the rescue attempts by denouncing them and delivering them to the Nazis.[2]

A debasing manifestation of endemic Polish anti-Semitism was the betrayal of some Jewish POWs by their fellow prisoners in German military camps, and the general discrimination against Jewish POWs not only by the German authorities but by the Poles themselves. In many cases Polish prisoners, incited by the Germans, deprived the Jewish inmates of their personal belongings; cases of physical maltreatment were reported, anti-Semitism being the sole motive of the Polish inmates.[3]

There are on record many cases of collaboration between Nazis and Poles in actions which led to the killing of Jews,[4] but on the other hand information is meager in connection with acts of sabotage (for example, against the transports to the extermination camps). There is also no evidence of actions by the armed underground to obstruct the Nazi mechanism of extermination, the railway lines included.

Polish underground sources supply us with evidence about cases of the murder of Jews committed by Poles, even by Armia Krajowa and National Armed Forces fighters, crimes motivated solely by anti-Semitism.[5] While there is, of course, no proof of anti-Jewish crimes committed jointly by Nazis and resistance fighters, the records of the underground organizations, those of the extreme left included, bear out an inimical attitude toward the hunted Jews which precluded initiatives to include Jews in the ranks of armed resistance or to organize joint operations between Polish and Jewish armed units.[6] Nor was the purchase of arms by the Jewish resistance in any way facilitated by any Polish underground organization (although we must not overlook the fact that the Poles themselves had great difficulties in acquiring arms and ammunition).

On the civilian scene there were no initiatives undertaken by Polish intellectuals to assist the Jews—while, at the same time, one should keep in mind the decimation and the oppression of the Polish intelligentsia itself by the Nazis. The powerful Polish Catholic Church, albeit itself under heavy pressure from the Nazis, did not strive to influence its followers to adopt a humanitarian stand concerning the plight of their Jewish cocitizens.[7]

Contemporary Jewish historians deplore the lack of activity on behalf of the Jews both on the part of the Polish government-in-exile and of the Armia Krajowa. One can accept the prevailing view of these historians that the Delegatura (the board of the "delegates" of the government-in-exile operating in Poland) did little to help the Jews, and even less to provide the material means for organizing the Jewish armed resistance.[8] While the "Delegatura" is blamed for its passivity concerning the Jewish problem, some of the historians have leveled grave accusations against the Armia Krajowa, which refused to cooperate with the Jewish underground and did not fight anti-Semitism in its ranks.[9] Obviously, these accusations are much more severe in the case of the extremist NSZ, which did not refrain from murderous acts against the Jews.[10]

Anti-Semitic manifestations were frequent in the ranks of the Anders army and in other Polish military units fighting on the Allies' side,[11] and severe criticism is voiced by some historians against a kind of conspiracy of silence of the government-in-exile, which amounted to the concealing of information about the Nazi process of extermination.[12] Recurrent recriminations in the work of Jewish historians emphasize the lack of vital assistance by the Polish population and resistance movements during the Warsaw ghetto uprising.[13]

However, there is a credit side to the balance sheet which is not to be totally disregarded. Many Poles sacrificed their lives by hiding or helping Jews in various other ways. Some sources of information reveal that a number of underground members were executed by their righteous resistance commanders for anti-Jewish crimes.[14] Armia Krajowa sources provided valuable data about the fate of the Jews in the ghettos and in the extermination camps—albeit at a late phase of the war—and the Polish government-in-exile tried to exploit this information in 1944 for the benefit of the persecuted Jews.[15]

One of the outstanding organizations, not only in Poland but in the whole of occupied Europe, established in the name of assisting and rescuing the Jews, was the Polish "Żegota."[16] The Provisional Committee for the Aid of Jews, transformed later into the Council for the Aid of the Jews (Żegota), was established between September and December 1942 and functioned until the days of the liberation of Poland. Its members were Poles of various political affiliations, or simply apolitical persons drawn to Żegota by humanitarian motivation.

The scope and the achievements of the activities of Żegota constitute even today the object of disputes between Polish historians—mainly those publishing in Poland, and thus representing the regime's views—and Jewish historians. The former tend to present grossly exaggerated claims of the involvement of hundreds of thousands or even millions of Poles in assisting the Jews, while the Jewish historians encounter difficulties in finding reliable documentation and testimonies to bear out the organization's large-scale help and rescue activity. One of the competent Jewish historians estimated that a bare 4,000 Jews enjoyed the organization's help,[17] but a leading Jewish activist of the Żegota contended that this number amounted to at least 20,000.[18] In any case, the mostly anonymous Poles who joined Żegota—conservative Catholics, socialists,

Communists, and politically uncommitted persons—took upon themselves the greatest risk in rescuing and helping the Jews.

Nevertheless, the balance sheet of the attitude of the great majority of the Polish people is far from favorable from the humanitarian point of view. A considerable percentage of the Polish population accorded the Nazi crimes in Poland tacit approval, and many even seemed to feel that the destruction of their country produced at least one positive by-product—namely, the elimination of the Jews.

In view of the enormous suffering of the Polish people at the hands of the Germans, one wonders why a sense of solidarity did not prevail among the Poles and the Jews. The explanation should be sought in the all-pervasive Polish anti-Semitism, which was exploited by the Nazis.[19] Further research might add more information about different sides of the story, but it is unlikely that any new documentary evidence could invalidate our conclusions about the essentially anti-Jewish attitude of the Polish masses during the period of the destruction of Polish Jewry.

Slovakia   When the participants at the Wannsee Conference pondered the readiness of the local populations and of the authorities to cooperate with them in carrying out the "Final Solution," they concluded that "in Slovakia and Croatia the matter is no longer too difficult, as the most essential, central problems in this respect have already been brought to a solution there."[20] Their assessment was right, for there were indeed similarities between wartime Slovakia and Croatia, although a few differences should not be overlooked.

Both so-called independent states resulted from the destruction of their former multinational frameworks, and in both countries ultra-nationalist, fascist-type, fanatical, retrograde *and* Catholic forces took over with Nazi help. Both the anti-Czech Slovak fascists and the anti-Serb Croatian Ustashi were eager to curry favor with the Nazis regarding the Jewish problem, and at the time of the Wannsee Conference the respective regimes were ready and public opinion was ripe for the most drastic anti-Jewish steps.

Although the links between the ruling forces and the Catholic Church were more evident in Slovakia than in Croatia, and although the Croatian leadership was more homogeneous than the Slovakian, a blatant common denominator between the two countries was the fact that among the Nazi satellites "Slovakia and Croatia were the most thorough in introducing anti-Jewish measures, thus creating the prerequisites

213

for deportations."[21] From the beginning the Germans considered the Slovak population as basically anti-Semitic,[22] despite their mistrust in the anti-Jewish feelings of certain elements of Slovak society.[23]

The Aryanization of Jewish enterprises started in the second half of 1939. Jewish property became the free prey of the regime and of the masses (the peasants included), and the middle class was overjoyed to rid itself of its Jewish competitors. The Central Office for Economy set up in September 1940 became the main vehicle for the spoliation of Slovak Jewry, and during 1939–40 a Nazi-type press sprang up inciting people against the Jews, in *Stürmer* style. Unlike in Hungary and Romania where anti-Semitic press agitation preceded the Nazi onslaught, the anti-Semitic slant characterized the Slovak mass media only after the puppet state was set up. The state-controlled press agitation was complemented by the anti-Semitic campaign of the influential Catholic press.[24]

The economic phase of the anti-Jewish attack was qualitatively altered to a typical Nazi stage with the enacting of the Nuremberg-type racialist "Jewish Codex" in September 1941. Forced labor, the wearing of the yellow badge, and other humiliating measures preceded the concentration and finally the deportation of the great majority of the Jews. The racial legislation was so severe that both Catholic and Protestant clergymen protested against its purely racist paragraphs, which contradicted their attitude toward the converted Jews.[25]

The regime, which boasted that it represented but a Slovak variant of National Socialism, assumed the initiative for the deportations. While German encouragement and open guidance were not missing, it was Prime Minister Voytech Tuka who raised for the first time the necessity to deport the Jews.[26] In spite of the all-pervading Nazi propaganda, Berlin preferred—for tactical reasons—to leave the initiative for the anti-Jewish persecution and for the deportation to the Slovak government.[27] Thus, after a long period of harassment (the setting up of labor camps, partial evacuation), the deportations started in March 1942. Catapulted by German intervention, but formally as a result of Slovak initiative, 57,000 Jews out of 89,000 (in December 1940) were deported by October 1942. The process of deportation was smooth and was carried out by the local authorities with minimal German interference. The Bratislava parliament, convened *after* the start of the deportations (in June 1942) to sanctify the act, fully endorsed the government's measures. Although voices of protest could be heard even before the truth about the fate of the deportees had become known in wider circles, the regime enjoyed the support of the bulk of the population, mainly for economic reasons.

214

Various factors induced the government to halt the deportations in October 1942. At the time, Slovakia had become the center for the gathering of information about deportees to the Polish extermination camps, and the Bratislava Jewish leadership provided ample information to the Zionist delegates operating in Geneva and Istanbul,[28] and also to the Zionist activists in Budapest.[29] The horrors about the fate of the deportees as well as the crimes committed on Slovak soil produced the first change of heart among wider circles in the midst of the population; leading Catholic clergymen and, above all, Protestant (Lutheran) pastors at last raised their voices against the official anti-Jewish policy.[30] Moreover, even some moderate elements in the government and in the higher echelons of the administration queried the desirability of the deportations, and some of them secretly took a few positive steps in an attempt to rescue the remnants of Slovak Jewry.[31]

Hans Ludin, the German minister in Bratislava, informed the Foreign Office as early as the end of June 1942 that "the deportation of the Jews is becoming unpopular in large circles of the Slovak population."[32] The majority of the masses, which earlier had supported the regime's anti-Jewish policy, had second thoughts after being confronted with information and even facts about the fate of the Jews. Doubts tormented many Slovaks, mainly during 1943 and 1944, over whether their collaboration with the Nazis would turn out to have been a fatal error. The Germans discerned such feelings mainly among intellectuals and Catholic priests.[33] In March 1943 the Catholic Church condemned the anti-Jewish persecutions in a pastoral letter[34] which, although watered down after heated debates between the bishops, the authorities, and the lower clergy, still had a moderating impact on the official policy. The moderate, so-called Catholic wing of the governmental leadership, which would have preferred to ascribe the deportations to German pressures, began to dissociate itself from the extermination of the Jews, motivated perhaps by more resolute Vatican interventions.[35]

At the end of August 1944 the outbreak of the National Uprising, in which hundreds of Jews participated, brought to a tragic end the standstill in the status of some 20,000 Jews, living in suspense and awaiting the day of their liberation. After the German army crushed the uprising, the hour of the delayed second phase of the deportation struck. This time the Germans did not need the formal initiative of the local leaders, although the Hlinka Guard extremists, who took over the occupied *Gau*-like state, impatiently demanded the eviction of the Jews and zealously assisted the SS in carrying out the deportation. Father Tiso

215

reassured the Germans that the remnants of the Jews on Slovak soil must be deported without any humanitarian considerations.[36] From October 1944 to March 1945, the Germans and the Slovak collaborators managed to deport about 13,500 Jews. When the whole area was liberated, only 4,000 to 5,000 Jews were living in Slovakia, most of them in hiding, or submerged with false identity, or some of them still lingering in forced-labor units.

As in any other satellite country, there is no way to assess the percentage of the population which actively collaborated in the spoliation and later in the elimination of the Jews. During the first four years after Munich, the Tiso regime could count on the mass support of the population. Second thoughts among the masses arose only from 1942 onward, but until the very end of the war, the Hlinka Guardists, the hard-liners of the Catholic People's Party, the gendarmerie, and the security services remained faithful to Nazi Germany, and they had to bear the responsibility for the extermination of Slovak Jewry. Tiso himself, who apparently moderated his policy from 1942 on, could not and did not retract his initial views about the Christian duty to expel the Jews, and to rid the nation of this "pest."[37]

There are controversies as to whether the tragedy of Slovak Jewry was due solely to the Slovak pro-Nazis or whether they acted under the unbearable weight of Nazi pressure. We are inclined to believe that the Tiso regime not only collaborated with the Nazis but also initiated some of the anti-Jewish measures and carried out the first deportations, although in the later phase of the war the authorities merely assisted the SS, while the bulk of the population probably turned anti-German and dissociated itself from the radical anti-Jewish steps. With all the exceptions and the *volte-face* which occurred in October 1944, Slovak society and political life stands, beside the Croatian parallel, as a typical example of a subservient, retrograde satellite that endorsed, acclaimed, sometimes initiated, and always shared the anti-Jewish Nazi crimes.

Croatia The essential difference between Croatia and Slovakia lies in the fact that while on the territory of the Slovak state only a small number of Jews perished at the hands of local Nazis, the Croatian Ustashi murdered the greater part of Croatian Jewry in concentration camps and elsewhere on Croatian territory.

The anti-Jewish zeal of the Ustasha regime was in contradiction to the secondary place allotted by Ustasha doctrine to the Jewish problem. In spite of his lack of interest and, as a matter of fact, lack of an organized

216

anti-Jewish camp, events in Croatia testified to a wild explosion of hatred against the small Jewish minority, concomitant with a savage anti-Serbian wave of violence. The Ustashi did not wait for orders or instructions from the Nazis. The German occupiers were ubiquitous, their example was seen as obligatory to follow, but the initiative for the first outbursts of violence, for example the pogrom in Sarajevo on April 16, 1941—one day after the Germans entered the city—was carried out by Croatian fascists. Sarajevo, a historic center of Balkan Sephardic Jewry, witnessed a new wave of massacres at the end of June 1944. At the beginning of September 1941, the concentration of the survivors began, most of them being sent to the Kriscice camp and finally to the infamous death camp in Jasenovac.[38] The Croatian Catholic clergy, faithfully supporting the Ustasha regime, became divided on the Jewish question. In connection with Sarajevo, it should be mentioned that its archbishop, Monsignor Saric, had a leading role in fomenting anti-Jewish feelings in this part of the country.[39]

Almost immediately after the creation of the puppet state, new Nazi-inspired anti-Jewish legislation enabled the systematic extermination or deportation of the Jewish population. As to the racial law adopted on April 14, 1941, Monsignor Stepinac, the cardinal primate of Croatia, himself an adept of the Ustasha movement, deplored that not even in Germany were the racial laws applied with such rigor and speed as in his country.[40]

The anti-Jewish crimes committed by Croatian extremists should be seen as part of the anti-Serbian, antidemocratic, and anti-Communist hysteria which claimed the lives of hundreds of thousands of civilians, putting the Ustasha regime and Croatia itself on top of the list of Nazi-type criminals in World War II. Outside historical Croatia, for example in Croatian-occupied Bosnia and Herzegovina, the great majority of the Jews were exterminated by the Ustashi (from November 1941 until August 1942).[41] Everywhere in the new state the Ustashi succeeded to find nonuniformed criminals ready to help them in perpetrating their crimes, which unlike in Slovakia, Hungary, or Romania, included atrocities, such as the burning alive of children, the axing to death or decapitation of victims, and similar bestialities.[42] Among the top criminals quite a number of Franciscans made headlines, and at least one of them, the friar Filipovic-Majstrovic, ranks with the most ferocious mass murderers.

Those Jews who survived the atrocities in Croatia itself—in Zagreb the lives of about 1,000 Jews were spared until May 1943—were deported to Auschwitz. In May 1943 about 4,200 Jews were turned over to the

Germans by the Croatian authorities. However, in certain parts of the country where Croatian sovereignty was more than doubtful, for example in the province of Strem, a kind of Nazi-Ustasha condominium was established which enabled the extermination of the whole Jewish population—by the Nazis, local ethnic Germans, and the Ustashi—without any specific instructions from Zagreb.

Even in the case of Croatia we are advised to abstain from generalizations. After 1942 a growing number of Croatians joined the antifascist partisans, and others tried to moderate the anti-Serbian and anti-Jewish extremists of the Ustashi. Even among supporters of the regime, for example in the case of the collaborationist Cardinal Stepinac, protests were voiced against anti-Serbian and anti-Jewish atrocities.[43] On the other hand, it would be an error to ascribe all the crimes to the Ustashi alone, since they undoubtedly enjoyed the support of the Croatian masses, at least at the beginning of the short history of this satellite state, and the regime had no reason for concern regarding any substantial opposition among the population. Ante Pavelić's regime got even the blessing of such established and moderate Croatian statesmen as Macek, the influential leader of the Croatian Peasant Party. The moderating influence of the pro-Pavelić Stepinac, and on the other hand, the collaborationist record of Macek, the respectable statesman of interwar Yugoslavia, only emphasizes the complexity of the problem in the turbulent and stormy Croatia of the Ustashi.

The loss of Croatian Jewry is estimated at 80 percent; part of the survivors were hidden by Croatian friends, others reached the Italian occupied territories,[44] and a considerable number of Jews survived the war fighting in the ranks of the partisans. The militancy and fanaticism of the Ustashi, as well as their cruelty, matched only by the SS and similar Nazi criminal formations, raise the difficult question of distinguishing local initiatives and independent actions from German directives or dictates. Regardless of the answers, the Croatian chapter of the Holocaust and of the crimes committed against other ethnic groups remains one of the most deplorable in the history of World War II.

The Protectorate of Bohemia–Moravia   The parallel between Slovakia and Croatia should be extended to Bohemia-Moravia and Serbia, although the dissimilarities in this case prevail over the similarities. In both areas the effective rule was in German hands. The local authorities lacked any independence, and in both territories the bulk of the population opposed, passively or even actively, the Nazi occupation. Collaboration was minimal in both cases and there were only peripheral manifestations of anti-Jewish feelings; local support for Nazi anti-Semitic persecutions was negligible. However, regarding two aspects of the Jewish tragedy, the dissimilarities are obvious: the bulk of Serbian Jewry was liquidated on the country's territory, while the armed resistance, which saved many Jewish lives, was considerable in Serbia, unlike in the Czech territories.

The first anti-Jewish laws, mainly of an economic character, were passed in the Czech parts of the Second Czechoslovak Republic in January and February 1939. After the creation of the Protectorate of Bohemia-Moravia, one should ascribe any anti-Jewish step to direct or indirect German interference. However, local fascist elements and a noisy anti-Semitic minority staged anti-Jewish demonstrations, brutalized Jews, and demanded a Nazi-type process of Aryanization and de-Jewification. Moreover, certain categories in the professions and, above all, merchants took advantage of the elimination of the Jews from various sectors of economic and professional life.[45] When the Nazis passed their *own* anti-Jewish laws—in June 1939—protests from leading Czech personalities, for example Archbishop Kaspar of Prague, and other expressions of solidarity with the persecuted Jews testified to the resistance of a part of Czech society to the Nazi's anti-Jewish drive. It should be emphasized that from the beginning the attitude of the Czech population toward the Jews, and specifically toward the Nazi policy of systematic de-Jewification of the Protectorate, was ambiguous.

The anti-Nazi resistance, which was taking shape slowly, and, above all, the socialist and Communist members of the underground, displayed great courage and goodwill in helping and rescuing Jews.[46] When the deportations began, many Czechs had the courage to strongly condemn the persecutions. On the other hand, many cases of denunciation were registered, and "moderate" anti-Jewish slogans were voiced.[47] The deportation of the Jews, reducing their number from about 90,000 in October 1939 to about 8,700 by mid-1943, was solely the result of German initiatives and was carried out by the German authorities, while the Czech gendarmerie and other local forces fulfilled only an auxiliary role. Only the Germans bear responsibility for the atrocities committed against the Jews on Czech soil, and not even the small groups of collaborators were involved in the crimes in the Protectorate. On the other hand, the Jews were offered only minimal assistance from the population and the members of the resistance. While the number of those rescued was insignificant—a mere 400 to 500 Jews surviving with false identity papers or in hiding[48]—quite a few managed to evade deportation (without any help).

Dissonant overtones could be heard long before the end of the war raising doubts about the desirability of the return of the Jews after the victory over the Nazis. Many Czechs feared an outburst of anti-Semitic feeling in the event of a massive return of the deported Jews, and few denied the fact that latent anti-Semitism had been kindled and radicalized by the Nazi occupiers.

The Czechoslovak government in London and its civilian and military representatives in different parts of the world were sympathetic toward the persecuted Jews. The government had an important role in publicizing information about Nazi atrocities and in influencing the subjugated Czech population against the anti-Jewish Nazi deeds;[49] a considerable number of Jews returned in uniform in the ranks of the Czechoslovak forces, and quite a number emerged in May 1945 from the fighting under ground.[50] But the records are rather skimpy concerning the Czech population's part in trying to help and rescue Jews.

Serbia   When the first Nuremberg-type anti-Jewish law was published in Belgrade, in May 1941, it was a purely German matter. The puppet government of General Milan Nedić, formed by the end of August 1941, was not entrusted with the tasks of carrying out the concentration or the extermination of the Jews, but was called upon to assist the German authorities in performing these assignments. The concentration of the Jews who had survived the first waves of massacres committed by the Germans immediately after the occupation of the country began in the summer of 1941, and was carried out mainly in September—that is, in the days when the Nedić administration was only taking shape. Nevertheless, the Nazi officials in charge of the Jewish problem in Serbian territories reported that "no resistance of any sort is to be expected on the part of the Serbian government and population, all the less so since partial measures thus far have proved to be very effective."[51] The "very effective measures" meant the liquidation of Jewish hostages and the killing of some 2,000 Jewish men out of a group of 8,000 Jews singled out for deportation in September–October 1941.[52] At about the same time, some of the Jews of Banat were murdered and others deported; the Germans were assisted by local ethnic Germans (Volksdeutsche). The Jewish Commissariat of the so-called government assisted the Nazis, providing them with a kind of mercenary personnel recruited from the riffraff.

Rescue activities were hindered by the fact that the Germans threatened to punish all those who sheltered Jews with the death penalty. However, the end of 1941 also saw the flare-up of both the Chetnik and the Tito struggles, which enabled some of the younger Jews to join the armed resistance. Thousands of Jews joined the partisans, and, strangely enough, even Draža Mihajlović's nationalist Chetnik troops accepted some Jewish fighters.

Excepting those who joined the armed resistance or went underground, no Jews were left in Serbia after August 1942, some of them having been murdered by the Germans and the Volksdeutsche, with little Serbian help in these crimes. About 5,000 Jews were murdered in Mitrovica, and in other death camps, or shot in the Sava, the Drava, and the Danube, and thousands were killed in gas vans in Northern Serbia;[53] others were deported. In August 1942 Serbia was proclaimed "*judenfrei*" before any other European country.

It would be an impossible task to assess the number of collaborators guilty of assisting the Germans in their anti-Jewish drive. There were certainly thousands of collaborators who, in the service of Nedić, or enrolled in the Ljotić-gangs, perpetrated crimes against the Jews. However, the huge majority of the population kept at a distance from the Nazi crimes. Tito's partisans welcomed the Jews, and although there are some testimonies about unfriendliness and reticence toward the Jews even among the partisans,[54] many Jews fought bravely in their ranks and quite a number are remembered as heroes of the Yugoslav resistance.[55] The Jews have never questioned the positive role of the great majority of the population in the Serbian entity, or of the Serbians in the other occupied territories of Yugoslavia (in Bačka, for example) in opposing the Nazi policy toward the Jews.

Out of a total of approximately 70,000 Jews in prewar Yugoslavia (and about 5,000 Jewish refugees in Yugoslavia), nearly 60,000 perished during the Holocaust. But unlike in most other satellite or occupied countries, the Germans could not count on the collaboration of the Serbian population at large. This response was determined by the fierce anti-German nationalist struggle, and also by the absence of anti-Semitic mass movements in pre-1941 Yugoslavia.

Greece   Little research has been done on the fate of Greek Jewry during the Holocaust, and even less attention has been paid to the attitude of the Greek population toward the Jews. When independent Greece disappeared from the map and the country was partitioned into two occupied zones, one German and one Italian (parts of Thrace and Macedonia were occupied by the Bulgarians), nearly 60,000 Jews out of a total of 70,000 had the misfortune to find themselves under German rule.

Collaborators were plentiful in German-occupied Greece, and the occupiers succeeded in setting up a quisling-type government by the end of April 1941. Anti-Semitic agitators assumed a dominant position in the German-controlled press in Athens, and minor right-extremist groups, such as the ESPO, a dummy student organization, staged anti-Jewish riots.[56] The Germans boasted, without much justification, that the "judicious," and therefore pro-German, Greeks pressured the Nazis to take anti-Jewish measures. The Tsolacoglu government—in office until November 1942—indeed enacted some racial laws, but their efficacy and even their Greek origin is questioned,[57] and there is no doubt that every anti-Jewish step, even those taken by the Greek authorities, should be seen as dictated by the German authorities.

When the German-initiated spoliation of the Jews began, there was no shortage of Greek collaborators to assist the Germans in the management of Jewish property. Among those who were maintained by the occupiers in command of the police and other auxiliary forces, some were well-known pro-Nazi figures like the director of police in Athens.[58]

During the first year of the occupation, when the conditions of the Jewish population had not yet become critical, not even in the German-occupied zone, Greek public opinion did not manifest itself against the still moderate anti-Jewish decrees and instructions. The American ambassador in Athens had every reason to state that "without our [American] intervention . . . I doubt if anyone will help the Jews."[59]

In the summer of 1942 forced labor disrupted the life of the Jewish community in Salonika, and soon preparations were under way to deport the Jews to Auschwitz and other extermination camps. In spite of the impending danger and the increasing Nazi pressure, both on the Greek authorities and on the Italians, in 1942 Prime Minister George Tsolacoglu still had the courage to deny the existence of a Jewish problem in Greece, and his successor, the likewise collaborationist J. D. Rhallis, still displayed independence in Jewish matters.[60] It is significant that until the middle of 1942 there was still a Jewish member of the Athens Municipal Council. Regarding the absence of a strong protest movement against the anti-Jewish measures prior to the deportations, one should keep in mind the ordeal of the Greeks themselves in a country where famine claimed 300,000 victims in the winter of 1941–42; in these conditions one could hardly expect dramatic manifestations in favor of the Jews. However, when the Jews in the German-occupied parts of the country were deported in the spring of 1943, impressive protests were registered. Leading intellectuals and clergymen, led by Archbishop Genadios, repeatedly raised their voices against the deportations.[61] In spite of the fact that the Germans enjoyed the support of some collaborators, the crime of deporting the Jews weighs solely on the Germans. The masses were basically anti-German, the Jewish problem did not preoccupy them, and many were successful in attempts to rescue Jews. During 1943 and 1944 the growing armed forces of the partisans, and even some units of the Royalist resistance, were joined by quite a number of young Jews.

A huge majority of Greek Jews—84 percent—perished in the extermination camps. The collaboration of the local elements in the "de-Jewification" of the country was minimal, and if the contribution of the population to the rescue of the Jews was likewise only minimal, this fact should be ascribed to the prevailing objective conditions rather than to the passivity and indifference of the Greek people.

Bulgaria Bulgaria is remembered as the only satellite country which successfully resisted Nazi pressures to deport its Jews. It is also often mentioned that the Bulgarians were exceptional—not only did they not deliver their Jews to Germany, neither did they commit atrocities against the Jews on Bulgarian territory. While these assertions correspond to reality, the Bulgarian "exception" nevertheless cannot be compared to Denmark, or even to Finland, in spite of some common features between it and the latter country.

As a result of German pressure, and also of the opportunistic policy of Prime Minister Filov, supported by anti-Semitic elements, the Bulgarian government enacted the "Law for the Protection of the Nation" (November 1940). The 1940 law was seen by the Germans as the first step in the process of integrating Bulgaria into the anti-Jewish "New Europe." The legislation was welcomed by quite a number of Bulgarian public figures and it was hailed by the small pro-Nazi groups. However, it turned out that the government found itself in the cross fire of opposing pressures: while the Nazis encouraged the government to radicalize its measures, public opinion exerted moderating pressure on Filov's cabinet.

As in Romania, a commissariat for Jewish problems was set up under

223

German authority, and the Ministry for Internal Affairs was eager to execute the German instructions. Even though the November 1940 law went into effect only in the summer months of 1941, in April 1941, after Bulgaria joined the Axis Powers in dismembering Yugoslavia and occupying Greece, Bulgarian Jewry faced the real danger of Nazi-type persecution and later of deportation.[62]

Public opinion and the outcry of some politicians and of many leading intellectuals caused great concern in Germany. In November 1941 the Bulgarians "encountered difficulties in carrying out the laws directed against the Jews,"[63] and although reference was made only to the expulsion of foreign Jews, it was no longer a secret that Filov's hands were tied by a wave of protests from various sectors of public and political life. Without precedent in a satellite country, members of the Sobranje signed protest manifestos and memoranda against the anti-Jewish policy of the government,[64] and prominent intellectuals and the highest representatives of the Orthodox Church openly expressed their sympathy for Bulgarian Jewry, condemning the anti-Jewish measures. Among those who joined this chorus were even some known rightist, extreme nationalist personalities.

During the autumn of 1942, Germany energetically intervened in Sofia in order to carry out the "Final Solution" of Bulgarian Jewry. The Germans were encouraged by the fact that during 1941 and 1942 further anti-Jewish laws and decrees prepared the soil for a radical solution. However, already in November 1942—at about the same time that it became evident that Antonescu was resolutely resisting similar German demands in Romania—the Nazis realized that the procrastinating maneuvers of the Bulgarian government were actually sabotaging the deportation plans.[65] There is no evidence of a strong Jewish lobby in Sofia, so the opposition to the deportation from various sections of Bulgarian public life is even more remarkable. Yielding to public pressure, even the minister of internal affairs and other influential members of the cabinet eased the anti-Jewish measures and ultimately opposed the deportation.[66] The imposition of the yellow star aroused a reaction of sympathy among the masses matched only by the Danish example. Although the attitude of King Boris was at no time unequivocal, it seemed that any resistance to the German demands was supported by him.[67]

Since the Germans realized that the plan to deport Bulgarian Jewry was not feasible, an alternative and preliminary solution was worked out between the Nazis and the Filov cabinet: the deportation of the Jews from the annexed territories (the idea may have been borrowed from the

224

Romanian example, namely the liquidation of the Jews in reannexed Bessarabia and Northern Bukovina, while Antonescu spared the lives of the country's "own" Jews). On February 22, 1943, the Germans and the Bulgarians signed a plan for the deportation of the Jews from Vardar (Yugoslav) Macedonia and from Aegean Macedonia. The number of Jews deported to the extermination camps is estimated at 11,400; almost all of them perished.[68]

The Bulgarian consent to the deportation of the Jews from Macedonia reveals the logic which guided Marshal Antonescu, and to a certain extent Horthy, too: "You can take the foreign Jews, we are glad to get rid of them, but we do not agree to the deportation of *our* Jews." Yet even sacrificing the "foreign" Jews caused an uproar which was without precedent in other satellite countries in similar situations.

Since the number of deportees from Macedonia fell short of the figure mentioned in the German-Bulgarian agreement (20,000), leaving the over 50,000 Bulgarian Jews unaffected, the Germans pushed toward the elimination of Bulgarian Jewry by the end of May 1943. However, at that time, the altered military map, Romania's and Hungary's examples, and the public condemnation of the Macedonian deportations, as well as the strong opposition to any radical plans against Bulgarian Jewry by a growing circle of public figures, institutions, and associations, definitely foiled the Nazi plans.[69] One of the outstanding acts of Bulgarian public figures meant to prevent the deportations was a protest signed by forty-three members of the Sobranje.[70] When the Bulgarian government decided to expel most of the Jews from Sofia and from other urban centers and to concentrate them in a few camps, sending many thousands to forced labor, a new wave of protests exerted pressure upon the government and forced Filov and the king to reject the Nazi demands for a radical solution—in other words, the deportation (April through June 1943).[71] Although thousands of Jews were indeed gathered and driven to forced labor, the Nazis had to realize that the "specific Bulgarian mentality," the indifference, or even the sympathy, toward the "diligent" Jewish man-in-the-street, constituted a serious impediment to the implementation of the German liquidation plans.[72] The Germans reached the conclusion that there was no room for more resolute German pressure upon Bulgaria without risking a major confrontation with the government, and especially with public opinion.[73] In May and June the Nazi authorities were still trying to convince the Bulgarians of the necessity of the radical solution in spite of "the inactivity of the police and the complete indifference of the majority of the Bulgarian people."[74] But when the autumn months of 1943 brought about contrary steps—the relaxation of the anti-Jewish measures by the Bulgarian authorities—the Nazis relinquished their insistence, presumably arguing that the pursuit of their intense pressure for the "Final Solution" might be counterproductive, and not worth risking confrontation with the Bulgarian authorities and provoking the open enmity of the population. The death of King Boris in August 1943 and the formation of the Bozhilov government in September 1943 did not affect the official attitude toward the Jewish population, although in the first half of 1944 new concentration camps were set up.[75]

Two days after the Romanian *volte-face* on August 25, 1944, the Bagrianov government, formed in June 1944, and still undecided whether to follow Romania's example, took an unprecedented step in the Nazi orbit: it abolished all anti-Jewish laws. The possibility of deportation at the last minute was unrealistic since Germany was not in a position to carry out preventive action, as in Hungary in March 1944, or to retaliate, as in October 1944 in Budapest.

The credit for the rescue of Bulgarian Jewry has been claimed by different political groups, and the historiographical dispute in this matter is still animated.[76] When analyzing the Bulgarian response to Nazi policy, one should refrain from idealizing conditions from November 1940 until September 1944. Bulgarian Jewry was actually displaced, and conditions in the concentration and labor camps were far from idyllic. Many supporters of the Filov regime and the majority in the Sobranje acclaimed the anti-Jewish measures, and the small fascist groups and leading extremists would even have welcomed the deportation of the Jews. However, the majority of the population was not really a "silent majority" but, through many courageous leading public figures, actively opposed any German demand for a radical solution. The Communist regime in today's Bulgaria claims for itself—that is, for the Communist Party—a monopoly over the Bulgarian "miracle."[77] Although the Communist underground and resistance undeniably fulfilled an important role in rescuing, hiding, and helping many Jews, perhaps even in influencing public opinion, it has to share the merit with many non-Communist, or even anti-Communist factions. Ultimately, it was the Bulgarian people as a whole, their lack of hatred and their tolerant mentality, that exerted the decisive influence over the Bulgarian governments and also over Nazi policy in their country. The Bulgarian example underscores our contention that the Nazi determination to annihilate the Jews in the satellite

226

countries was decisively influenced by the readiness or the refusal of the local population to cooperate with the Nazis.

Hungary and Romania   Due to the drastic zigzags in the fate of the Jews in these two countries, because of their numerical preponderance in comparison with other countries in the area (some 1.5 million Jews lived in the two countries at the end of June 1941), and also because of the relative independence of these two satellites from Germany, the destiny of these Jewish communities has been and still is in the center of interest of historical research and even of public debates.

The attitude of the local regimes and that of the population toward the Jews during the Holocaust was far from a logical consequence of the prewar readiness of the host peoples to accept the Jews as their own; it was not a natural outcome of the gravity of the Jewish problem and of the anti-Semitic character of the prevailing regimes. A great variety of specific local factors generated unpredictable developments in the relations between Jews and non-Jews and in the regimes' policy toward the Nazi demands or dictates.

The two Hungarian governments of the early war years—the Teleki and the Bárdossy cabinets—cautiously followed Germany in their anti-Jewish drive. Pál Teleki's government was guilty of enacting the second Jewish law and of introducing the slave system of forced-labor service, and it took the fatal step of joining Nazi Germany. László Bárdossy took over after Teleki enacted the third, Nuremberg-type Jewish law (in August 1941), and had to share the responsibility for two major crimes: the deportation of the "alien" Jews to Kamenets-Podolsk, where about 16,000 out of 18,000 were massacred, and the Délvidek massacres (in Hungarian-occupied Northern Yugoslavia), where in January 1942 the Hungarian army and gendarmerie murdered more than 3,300 persons (2,600 Serbians and some 700 Jews).

It should be made clear that the Kamenets-Podolsk massacres were carried out mainly by the Germans, while in Délvidek the crimes were ordered by the local Hungarian commanders, presumably without the formal approval of the government. From the point of view of this survey, it is worth mentioning that while the Kamenets-Podolsk massacres went almost unnoticed, the Délvidek massacres aroused an angry reaction in various political and public circles, and led—during Miklós Kállay's pre-miership—to the indictment of the main criminals.[78]

When the moderate Kállay took over in March 1942, public opinion was still enthusiastically pro-Nazi, and the overwhelming majority of the masses seemed intoxicated by Nazi and local anti-Semitic propaganda, applauding every step in the segregation and then total elimination of the Jews from every sphere of national life. However, the last residue of Horthy-type democracy had not been discarded as yet, and both Horthy and Kállay were determined to oppose the total Nazi subjugation of Hungary. Accordingly, when the Germans started their pressure for the Final Solution and suggested the deportation of Hungarian Jewry, Kállay, with Horthy's consent, resisted these pressures. Kállay invoked some rather surprising reasons for doing so—namely, the opposition of the Hungarian people, specifically the peasants[79]—to radical solutions such as deportation; at the same time, he had to cope with the radical right, which supported the Nazi demands, condemned the official lukewarm anti-Semitism, and denied his assumptions about the lack of support of the masses for the implementation of the "de-Jewification" of Hungary.

In the summer and autumn of 1942, when Antonescu resisted heavy German pressure for deportations from Romania, the Nazis were eager to induce the Hungarians to deport at least 100,000 Jews as the first phase of the solution of Hungary's Jewish problem. Thorough research of all available information convinces the researcher that the reasonable real-politik of Kállay, fully endorsed by Horthy, enabled the Hungarians to resist the Germans plans and those of the local extremists. Kállay had in mind first and foremost Hungary's independence and its future rather than humanitarian considerations or sympathetic public opinion, which in fact was nonexistent, or at best was weak and negligible. In spite of the fact that Germany was at the peak of its military successes, influential conservative circles in Budapest, supported by small anti-German nationalist groups, started sending out peace feelers toward the Western Powers, and opposed the liquidation of the Jews, which, they realized, could only deepen the abyss of the Nazi alliance.

The Kállay era (from March 1942 until March 1944) was burdened by inner contradictions. On the one hand, the gendarmerie and other armed forces had a free hand in treating the Jews as hostile and outlawed elements; the anti-Semitic press and the extreme right organizations went berserk in spite of, or precisely because of, the changes on the military map; the increasing interference of Germany poisoned the atmosphere and created a psychological gap between Hungarians and the

228

Jews, disrupting the long-standing coexistence that had survived even the White Terror; and tens of thousands of young Jews perished on the eastern front not as victims of the war, but at the hands of sadistic Hungarian officers and soldiers.[80] On the other hand, Kállay's government tried to build up secret contacts with the Allies, systematically disengaged the army from Hitler's war, and resolutely refused to deport the bulk of the Jewish population, or to set up ghettos, or to enforce the wearing of the yellow badge (except for those enrolled in the forced-labor units). And then the hour of the Hungarian episode of the Holocaust struck when the Jews themselves were quite confident about their rescue and the moderate minority hoped to be able to extricate the country from the war. In order to prevent Hungary from a *volte-face*, and also invoking Kállay's reluctance to solve the Jewish problem, the Germans occupied Hungary on March 19, 1944, and at last started to segregate, to concentrate, and to deport the Jews.

The most surprising aspect of the German occupation was the smooth and almost instant transition to the new pro-Nazi rule. From a Jewish point of view, this fact meant the lack of any opposition, let alone resistance, to the ghettoization and the deportation. On the contrary: the gendarmerie and other security organs—headed by the extremely anti-Semitic under secretaries of state for the interior—carried out the whole complex operations, supervised and directed by a handful of SS men. The overwhelming majority of the population approved, or at best passively witnessed, the events. Many were overjoyed by the "de-Jewification," tens of thousands of written denunciations flooded the authorities against Jews who had gone into hiding, or against Hungarians who helped the victims, but not one single protest was registered and no appeals were sent to Horthy or to the government.[81] The ghettoization and deportation of some 600,000 Jews, carried out with the utmost brutality, was the crime of the Hungarian authorities, aided and abetted by the population at large.

The turning point in the deportation occurred only in June-July 1944, at a time when, except for Budapest, Hungary had been made *"judenrein."* Horthy halted the deportation of the Jews from Budapest after the invasion of Normandy, after the breakthrough on the southeastern front, and after the energetic warnings of the Western leaders and the intervention of some neutral powers and the Vatican. Only then were the first protests of a few representatives of the Catholic and Protestant churches heard. Not before July 1944 did some junior members of the establishment start to contemplate the rescue of the remains of Hungarian Jewry.[82] August 1944 was the first month when Horthy managed to regroup his followers and to operate the amateurishly constructed machinery for the extrication of Hungary from the war. In the meantime, a weak Hungarian resistance movement appeared on the scene, cooperating with the small but efficient Zionist underground, which provided tens of thousands with false identity cards and other documents.

Horthy's belated *volte-face* was proclaimed on October 15, 1944, but barely had the proclamation been read on the radio than the Germans took over—for the second time—and Szálasi's Arrow Cross was installed in Budapest. The Arrow Cross's reign of terror decimated the Jewish population of Budapest, perpetrating atrocities unparalleled in any other satellite country except Croatia. While the most significant transports of Jews from Budapest were organized by the Germans themselves, they could not have carried out these late deportations without the active help of the Arrow Cross *and* the civilian population.

While hundreds of Hungarians risked their liberty and even their lives by helping Jews—even peasants tried to assist ghetto inmates and members of forced labor battalions—the great majority of the Hungarian people remained at best passive, or actively supported the ghettoization, the deportation, and indirectly the extermination of the Jews. The Szálasi regime continued to stay on Hitler's side until the führer's last hour. There is a consensus among historians, including those in Communist Hungary, that the Hungarian people, or at least the huge majority, cooperated with the Nazis in the deportation, that many Hungarians committed criminal acts on Hungarian soil itself, or on the eastern front, and that the pace and the extent of the tragedy of Hungarian Jewry was due, to a large extent, to the zeal of the Hungarian collaborators.

The Romanian "National-Legionnaire" regime instigated pogroms against the dwindled Jewish population (which in January 1941 numbered about 442,000). In spite of systematic Nazi propaganda and subversion, the anti-Jewish drive in the last months of 1940 was not set off by the Germans. The German presence was ubiquitous in Romania after September 1940, but all legislation and any anti-Semitic action was the outcome of Romanian initiative.

The failure of the Iron Guard rebellion in January 1941 and the installation of Antonescu's military dictatorship temporarily averted the danger which had been threatening the Jews. But after Antonescu joined the anti-Soviet war, the mass murders were resumed and the deportation of the Jews from Bessarabia and Northern Bukovina began.[83] The massacres in Jassy and the bestialities committed in connection with the so-called "death train" were among the most shocking anti-Jewish crimes of the Holocaust.[84] In July and August 1941 it looked as though Romanian Jewry would share the fate of Polish Jewry or of those in the occupied parts of the Soviet Union. In the newly created province of Transnistria, ghettos and extermination camps were improvised in which tens of thousands were murdered in the second half of 1941. Bucharest was flooded with German military, SS, and SD personnel, as were the eastern territories under Romanian military rule. An SS officer was dispatched to Bucharest to take charge of the Jewish problem, and in the summer and autumn months of 1942 detailed German plans were elaborated for the deportation of Romanian Jewry, which was to start in Southern Transylvania. But the unforeseen and singular resistance of the Antonescu regime foiled the German deportation plans. The stubborn and independent-minded dictator, fully supported by the ruling military and civilian personalities, embarked on a cautious path of dealing with the Jewish problem, resisting Nazi pressure for deportation and annihilation. While Antonescu and his aides rejected the German deportation plans, they favored emigration, in conformity with the Nazi "de-Jewification" policy.

Romania's war, on Hitler's side, was not popular (mainly after the recuperation of Bessarabia and Northern Bukovina), and opposition to Antonescu's Nazi alliance was strengthened during 1942. Although a *Stürmer*-type press staged fierce anti-Jewish campaigns, and the Germans invested much energy in fostering extreme anti-Semitism, no pogroms occurred in Romania during 1942. On the eastern front, excesses similar to those committed in the second half of 1941 were no longer tolerated by the High Command. Unlike the situation in Hungary, and in even greater contrast to that in Slovakia and Croatia, influential circles in Romanian political, cultural, and religious life backed Antonescu's government in resisting German demands. These circles included the leaders of the two banned "historical parties"—the National Peasant Party and the National Liberal Party—leading clergymen of the Orthodox Church and the Greek Catholic Church, and the royal court.[85] Undoubtedly, public opinion encouraged the rejection of the German plans; the same factor probably accounted for the milder treatment of the deportees in Transnistria during 1943 and 1944.

German pressure was again applied in the beginning of 1943, and at this time the change in the military constellation brought new elements to the Jewish policy as well. Marshal Antonescu's deputy, Mihai Antonescu, sent out peace feelers to the Allies, and the revitalized opposition—still underground—intensified its efforts to prepare the *volte-face* and remained in permanent contact with the Western Powers. In the meantime, the administration maintained working relations with the traditional Jewish leaders—disregarding the official leadership installed by the authorities jointly with the Nazis[86]—and fostered emigration to Palestine, defying German reproof. In the second half of 1943 and the first half of 1944, it became clear that the administration considered any radical anti-Jewish measure unwise and counterproductive, while the opposition made a point of contributing to the foiling of extreme anti-Jewish steps.

The significance of the Jewish factor in any plan concerning Romania's future gained momentum in the months preceding the August coup d'état. In the spring and summer of 1944 the Romanian authorities tacitly condoned the influx of refugees from Nazi-occupied Hungary, so that thousands of Jews were rescued in this way. In the first half of 1944 the War Refugee Board and different Jewish organizations operating in Romania under Zionist leadership were able to arrange the retransfer of thousands of deportees, among them children, from Transnistria, and facilitated the emigration of a part of these people to Palestine. The local Zionist leaders adroitly exploited the Nazi myth of "omnipotent Jewish world power" and benefited from the cooperation of the mollified Mihai Antonescu at a time when the danger of massacres by the retreating German forces appeared imminent.

After March 1944 it became obvious that the Antonescu regime was expecting to capitalize on the fact that unlike in Hungary, where the bulk of the Jews perished during the last phase of the war, in Romania proper (although not in the reannexed provinces of Bessarabia and Northern Bukovina) the huge majority of the Jews had survived.

Romanian policy toward the Jews, and thus the attitude toward the Nazi extermination policy, had its ups and downs, oscillating between deportation and massacres committed by the Romanians together with the Germans, or on their own, and large-scale rescue gestures. The Romanian attitude to the Jewish problem was intrinsically linked to the degree of its dependence on Germany. While the majority of Jews in Northern Bukovina were deported and killed, and Bessarabian Jewry was virtually wiped out, only a small number of Jews were deported from Romania proper, and those who perished in Transnistria or farther east numbered less than 10,000. But to this figure should be added the more than 10,000 victims of the Jassy pogrom and of the "death train" in

Moldavia. The Romanians were less indoctrinated with Nazi anti-Semitism than, for example, the Hungarians, and were more tolerant toward their national minorities (perhaps excepting their feelings toward the Hungarian minority) than was the dominant group in most east European countries. The relations between the Jews and the host people (Romanian) were less poisoned than were such relations in Hungary, Slovakia, or Poland. The humanitarian motivation in the relations with the Jews was strong in Romania, and many leading personalities had the courage to dissociate themselves from Nazi anti-Semitism. Likewise, the number of pro-Allied and anti-German figures in the ranks of the political elite was higher than in any other satellite country. Antonescu's unusual policy toward the Jews saved the lives of the greater part of Jewry in the so-called Old Kingdom and in Southern Transylvania. A proud bid for independence and strong internal pressure, both from the oppositional forces and public opinion, coupled with a strong anti-German popular mood, induced Antonescu to resist the German pressure for deportation and annihilation, and to restrain the local extremist minority. A cool realpolitik, traditional pragmatism, a great deal of opportunism and even widespread corruption, and also genuine humanitarian feelings deeply rooted in the Romanian nation, mainly in the peasantry, accounted for the survival of hundreds of thousands of Jews in Romania.

Because of the greatly divergent conditions of the German presence and occupation in eastern Europe, the dissimilarities in the relations between Germany and its various satellites, and also the prewar attitude toward the Jews, both official and the popular, response to the Nazi policy was multifarious. Any generalization that attempts to explain the east European reactions through laws or that views the responses in the different countries as cases of a general rule would entail the risk of simplification and misrepresentation. However, the outlining of some patterns of response seems to be justified.

The responses to the Nazi-engineered Holocaust cannot be separated from their interwar roots. Deeply ingrained anti-Semitism facilitated the German task of inducing the local authorities and the population to cooperate in the persecution and ultimately in the destruction of the Jews (e.g., in Slovakia and Hungary). Conversely, the absence of this factor foiled, or at least made it more difficult to implement, the German plans (e.g., in Bulgaria). Traditional anti-Semitism or its absence influenced even the armed resistance movements (e.g., in Poland, or in Yugoslavia, respectively).

In every country a mood of *"mitmachen"*—to join the Nazis—partially accounts for the catastrophe, but this political vogue was greatly influenced by the strength of prewar Nazi-type movements. Thus, the Nazis could count on strong Hungarian National Socialist mass organizations, while in the Protectorate of Bohemia-Moravia the absence of such prewar mass movements deprived the Germans of an organized, massive collaboration.

In at least three countries the bid for national independence exerted a favorable impact on the attitude toward the Nazis' Jewish policy: in Hungary, Romania, and Bulgaria the handling of the Jewish problem seismographically registered the degree of their dependence on Nazi Germany. In those countries where national sovereignty was not completely extirpated, a great deal of realpolitik, pragmatism, and opportunism determined the ups and downs in the collaboration with Germany, also in dealing with the Jews. The negative attitude toward Nazi Jewish policy was less motivated by humanitarian reasons and more by national considerations—at least in Romania and in pre–October 1944 Hungary. The endeavor to preserve a margin of freedom of action against Germany, and concern for their nation's future after the war, dictated the resistance to German pressures for the annihilation of the Jews in Romania and Hungary (in Bulgaria the humanitarian motives were not less important than the opportunistic reasons). This policy, partly successful, actually saved the lives of a fraction of the Jews in Hungary, and of the majority of the Jews in Bulgaria and in Romania.

While Nazi Germany planned and ignited the Holocaust, it could not have succeeded without the collaboration of its allies. The dimensions of the Holocaust were determined not exclusively by the Germans: collaboration in eastern Europe encouraged the Nazis, with disastrous consequences, while resistance, regardless of its motives, attenuated Nazi pressure and reduced the dimensions of the Jewish tragedy.

12

Jewish Resistance and Passivity in the Face of the Holocaust

YEHUDA BAUER

Nazi policy toward the Jews was not guided primarily by economic, political, or military considerations, but by a pseudoreligious ideology. Based on concepts derived from Christian Jew-hatred, Jews were seen as a satanic influence in history. Translated into secularist, anti-Christian, pseudoscientific concepts, Jews were defined as parasites, as an antirace corrupting and destroying healthy, "natural" races. Nazi racism's main differentiation was between Aryans and non-Aryans, and the only non-Aryans that had to be radically opposed were the Jews. In this sense anti-Semitism was not a logical outcome of Nazi racism; rather, racism made possible the pseudoscientific rationalization of Nazi anti-Semitism. Nazi internal and external policy was conducted with two aims in mind: one was the "positive" aim of establishing the rule of the Germanic peoples, with Germany as their core, over Europe and the world; but that aim could not be achieved unless the satanic parasitic element ruling the world in fact, namely the Jews, was first removed. The uniqueness of the Holocaust lies in its motivation—in the fact that for the Nazi regime the removal of the Jews was a sine qua non of the survival of mankind, a matter of global, if not cosmic, importance, and not an ordinary political matter. Nazi policies toward the Jews were never a tactical issue, though political tactics would dictate timing and some particular measures.

These policies were part of the central core of nazism, to be sidetracked by other considerations only temporarily.

At the same time, nazism developed two types of approaches to the final disposal of the Jews—that of extrusion, emigration, and sale against ransom, and that of murder. These attempts at solutions were pursued sometimes consecutively in time, and sometimes parallel in time. Both were based on the assumption that the Jews were not human beings, but only looked like humans; they were evil creatures whose tribe had introduced into humanity notions such as conscience, humanism, pacifism, socialism, and democracy, to corrupt mankind. They could either be chased out to purify the Germanic core of regenerated healthy, strong humanity and corrupt Germany's enemies who accepted them in the process, or be killed—or both in succession. Jews under the Nazi regime were therefore quite unlike all others perceived as enemies by the Nazis: the others, with the possible exception of the Gypsies, could escape if they changed their views, their attitudes, or their life-styles, or submitted unquestioningly to Nazi rule. Jews were punished because they were born with at least three Jewish grandparents and after 1941 all of these persons were to be punished by death for having been thus born.

Jewish reaction to Nazi policies was radically influenced by the lack of comprehension of the Nazi policies. Rational arguments and rational reasons were sought to explain policies that were essentially based on the practical application of a myth. It was therefore only after the mass murder of the Jews had already gone a long way that the Jews realized the fact of the total Nazi design of murder. Paradoxically, the Nazis themselves had no systematic extermination plans before 1941; until that time, extrusion by emigration or forced deportation abroad was the prevalent policy. Mass murder was inherent in Nazi ideology, but did not emerge into consciousness or practical policies until a situation arose in 1940–41 when extrusion could no longer serve as a practical means to make the Jews disappear, to use Himmler's phrase.[1] If the Nazis were not aware, until 1941, of their intent to murder the Jews, it is difficult retroactively to ask of their victims to be so aware.

The Jews were, of course, an absolutely powerless minority in Europe. They numbered about 500,000 in Germany, 300,000 in France, 200,000 in the Netherlands and Belgium combined, and even in Poland they were a minority of 3.3 million, or 10 percent of the population. Including the USSR, there were about 8 million Jews among a European population of 500 million, scattered, without a government, without cohesion or identity of purpose. Contrary to legend, they were economically powerless: a few captains of industry and banking apart, Jews were a largely middle-class and lower-middle-class group, very visible because of their traditional middle-class position, and very vulnerable because of it. Their propensity for intellectual pursuit tended to make them prominent in the intellectual and professional life in Europe, thus strengthening both their visibility and their vulnerability.

A great deal has been researched and written about resistance in Europe under the Nazis. However, the term "resistance" as far as Jewish resistance is concerned has been used in a sense different from that used for the resistance of other people in the German occupation in Europe. Henri Michel, the doyen of resistance historians, wrote that to "accept defeat while still capable of fighting is to lose one's self-respect; self-respect dictates that one should not yield to the blandishments of collaboration."[2] Clearly, the Nazis did not use any blandishments of collaboration on the Jews, and therefore Michel's definition cannot be applicable to the Jewish case. I would define Jewish resistance during the Holocaust to be any group action consciously taken in opposition to known or surmised laws, actions, or intentions directed against the Jews by the Germans and their supporters. Obviously, in order to accept such a definition we have to subject it to the test of known facts.

It is much easier to check such a definition against the record of armed resistance than it is to do so regarding nonarmed resistance. I shall therefore start with Jewish armed resistance, although we shall see as we go along that that is by no means the only or the main form of Jewish resistance to the Nazis.

For reasons already stated it was difficult for Jews to collaborate consciously with the Germans. There was only one clear case of collaboration in the sense of identification with German war aims and a desire to help the Nazi regime to win the war. This occurred with a group known as the Thirteen (*Dos Dreizentel*) led by Avraham Gancwajch, in Warsaw. Gancwajch was convinced that the Nazis were going to win the war, and therefore he thought that the only way to assure the survival of the Jewish people would be to persuade the Nazis to accept them, on however lowly a level, within the Nazi scheme of things.[3] If collaboration was impossible, so was armed resistance for most Jews during the Holocaust. A basic requirement for armed resistance was the support of the surrounding population and the existence of the possibility of acquiring arms. Jews locked in ghettos generally had no way to procure arms. The surrounding population in eastern Europe was largely indifferent, a fairly large minority was actively hostile to the Jews, and only a small minority

237

was actively friendly to them.[4] Non-Jewish underground movements wanted to keep their own arms, and had no intention of handing them over to the hated Jews.[5] To buy arms was extremely difficult, and to obtain arms by force from the Germans was a dream rather than a real possibility. The pervasiveness of Nazi terror and the stringency of security measures taken by the Nazis to guard the ghetto entrances insured that a minimum of arms could be smuggled into the ghetto from outside.

In Poland the Jews had no access to the arms buried by the collapsing Polish army in 1939, such as the access enjoyed by the budding Polish underground in 1940 and 1941. There had been very few Jewish officers in the Polish army, even fewer holding high rank, and the secret of the buried arms was kept by those who had hidden them. The official Polish government underground, the Armia Krajowa, did not buy arms from deserting German soldiers either. No partisan detachments of any importance were established before 1943, and in any case Jews were not only not accepted in AK ranks but a number of AK detachments were actively engaged in hunting down and murdering Jews.[6] The Communist underground in Poland, later known as the Armia Ludowa, was founded as late as the spring of 1942. It was very weak, had few arms, and about half of its partisan forces were in fact Jewish detachments in the forests, mainly in the Lublin area. By the time the AL grew stronger, in 1943, the Jews were by and large no longer alive, but survivors did join the AL. Its weapons were bought or stolen from peasants; in most cases the weapons came originally from the Soviet Union, which dropped them by parachute.[7] The AK had a policy of not fighting the Nazis unless they had to. As late as November 10, 1942, the AK Command issued an order that "the time of our uprising has not yet come." It added that "the occupant is exterminating the Jews" and warned Poles not to be drawn into "premature" action against the Germans.[8] Orders were issued in 1943 by the AK to kill Jewish "bandits," who were supposedly robbing and otherwise endangering the Polish population.[9]

It is true to say, nevertheless, that without the help of that minority of the Polish population that was willing to support the Jews, at tremendous risk to themselves, Jewish resistance would have been much less than it actually was.[10] In October 1942, after the destruction of most of the Warsaw ghetto in the preceding summer, a group of liberals, mainly Catholics and Social Democrats, established a group called Żegota, in which Jews and non-Jews cooperated in helping escapees to the non-Jewish side of Warsaw under the general aegis of the AK and its political

238

supervisory organization, the so-called Delegatura, which owed its allegiance to the Polish government-in-exile in London.[11]

From another point of view, the question of timing was an essential
problem. In very few cases did organization for armed resistance begin
before the main so-called *Aktion,* or *Akcja,* as the Nazi extermination
enterprise was known. Clearly, a population forming a minority in a
country where it did not enjoy support from the surrounding population,
without arms, without government or any central bodies, would not
think of armed resistance unless it was obvious that the only other alternative was certain death. Jewish armed resistance, therefore, depended
very largely on the perceived threat of extermination. The conviction
that, contrary to all rational argumentations, the Nazis would devote
material human resources and rolling stock in the midst of a war to destroy a population that might have worked for them dawned slowly. By
the time the nuclei of Jewish armed resistance developed in eastern Europe, most of the Jewish populations there had either already been destroyed or were in the process of radical decimation. The radical despair
engendered by this situation, the loss of families, the destruction of the
internal workings of a whole community, did not make the decision to
take up arms any easier. In fact, in eastern Europe, it was largely a matter
of generational differences that prompted the establishment of underground movements. Young people could more easily perceive the threat
to their existence and be rid of illusions still held by their elders. Ideological youth movements were more likely to reach the conclusion that
armed resistance was the only possible response to a regime which they
viewed as the embodiment of evil, in accordance with prewar ideology.
This was true especially of left-wing Zionist movements, of Jewish Communists, of youth associated with the socialist anti-Zionist Jewish party,
called the Bund, and to a certain extent also with right-wing Jewish
Zionist nationalists of the Betar movement. These groups had compact
organizational setups and leadership groups which had not cooperated
with the Jewish councils set up by the Nazis to rule over the Jewish communities.[12] It was they, therefore, that in most cases originated the
armed resistance to the Nazis in eastern Europe.

In Warsaw an alliance of Jewish Communists and left-wing Zionists
had established an antifascist bloc as early as March 1942. But these
groups had no arms, and the Communist underground in Warsaw had
none to smuggle to them either. In April and May of 1942 the Nazis,
apparently following denunciations, effectively paralyzed the Communist

239

underground in the Warsaw ghetto, and the antifascist bloc ceased to operate.[13] By July 1942, the Zionist groups, who had no previous paramilitary, military, or indeed underground experience, were at a loss as to how to obtain arms for the budding Jewish underground. On July 22, 1942, the great deportation from Warsaw began, and on July 28 the Jewish Fighters' Organization was founded by the Zionist youth movements. During the following weeks, ending September 12, the vast majority of Warsaw's Jewish population was sent to be killed in the Treblinka death camp.[14] At the beginning of the deportation, the armed Jewish underground's arms cache consisted of one pistol. It was hardly surprising that the ghetto inhabitants did not heed the underground posters calling upon them to resist the Germans with their bare hands. Attempts by the underground to smuggle people out into the forests failed almost completely, as group after group of people were caught by the Nazis in trains and on roads leaving Warsaw. It was only by tremendous effort that in August 1942 the underground Zionist groups managed to obtain a few pistols, some hand-grenades, and some dynamite. Early in September, however, a young man who had been caught by the Nazis and tortured until he told his captors what he knew, led the Gestapo to a shop in the ghetto where one of the main leaders of the underground, Joseph Kaplan, was working. In order to protect the few arms that had been collected, a girl took the arms in a sack under a vegetable basket from the hidcout in Kaplan's workplace to a new hiding place. On the way, she was apprehended by a Nazi patrol and the arms were lost. Another leader of the underground then emerged from a house and, accosted by Nazi policemen, tried to attack them with a knife. He was killed instantly.[15] On one day then the few arms which had been collected and two of the main leaders of the Zionist youth groups were lost. When, therefore, on September 12 the roundup ended, and between 35,000 and 65,000 Jews were left in the remnant of the ghetto, the assembled surviving members of the Zionist youth movements were on the point of deciding to commit mass suicide by attacking the Germans in broad daylight on the street, with no arms. In a long and painful discussion, the remaining leaders convinced the youth to give up this idea and to start the process of organizing an armed underground from scratch.[16] The result was the first armed action of the Jewish underground in Warsaw, in January 1942, and later of course the April 19 outbreak of the great Warsaw ghetto rebellion. By that time the underground had assembled one, possibly two, machine-guns, 14 rifles, possibly 500 handguns and a large number of homemade hand grenades. Of these no more than one machine-gun and

240

50 pistols had been supplied to the Jews by the AK. By way of comparison, the AK in 1941 claimed to possess 566 heavy machine-guns, 1,097
light machine-guns, 31,391 rifles, and 5 million rounds of ammunition.[17]
The Jewish underground in Warsaw, led by a young Jewish youth leader,
Mordechai Anielewicz, of the left-wing Zionist movement, Ha'Shomer
Ha'Tzair, fought the German armed forces, which were supported by
tanks and heavy guns, for more than six weeks. A second armed group
of young Jews, the Jewish Military Organization, had in the meantime
been established by the Betar movement, probably in October 1942. It
had contacts with two small Polish groups loosely attached to the AK,
and it supplied the one or two machine-guns mentioned above to the
united movement, when the JMO and the JFO joined forces under Anielewicz in April. Even after the defeat of the rebellion, which the Nazis
achieved mainly by setting fire to each building in the ghetto and forcing
the Jews out of it, as well as by the introduction of poison gas into the
underground bunkers (the only case of the use of poison gas in armed
action during World War II), the remnants of the fighters and the other
ghetto inhabitants continued to appear in the ruins of the Warsaw ghetto
to fight the Germans as late as September, possibly October, 1943.[18]

It is true that only 750 people at most were members of the Jewish
underground in the Warsaw ghetto. However, this was not a fight of a
few hundred youngsters against the Nazis; it was rather the fight of tens
of thousands of unarmed people, who hid rather than hand themselves
over to the Nazis, and who were looking for arms but did not have them.
Among these were 750 who had some kind of arms at their disposal and
were more than willing to use them. The Warsaw ghetto was the first
armed urban uprising in Europe under the Nazis, but it was by no means
the only ghetto armed resistance during the Holocaust. In central Poland—the so-called General Government—there were three armed rebellions, four attempted rebellions, and seventeen places where armed
resistance groups existed and from where they left for the forests. In
eastern Poland, which had been occupied by the Soviet Union in September 1939, armed resistance was even more widespread because of the
forests, which did not abound in central Poland. There is evidence of
armed underground groups in ninety-one ghettos in the western Belorus-
sian area alone, and in sixty-one of these ghettos there were actual organized underground movements. In a few of these places, such as in
Tuczyn, Łachwa, and Mir, there were armed rebellions or attempts at
armed rebellions, whereas in other places action usually took the form of
escaping into the surrounding forests. Sometimes, as in Nieswiez, there

241

was a combination of the two, because armed rebellion was followed by an escape into the forests. In central Poland we know of thirty Jewish partisan detachments, most of them connected with the AL, and a further twenty-one detachments in which Jews formed over 30 percent of the members. The total number of Jewish fighters in central Poland during World War II, including the ghetto rebellions, was about 5,000, of whom 4,000 were killed in the fighting. In eastern Poland and the western USSR, especially in the area of Belorussia and Volhynia, there were probably around 15,000 partisans out of the 47,000 who managed to escape in the forests. Most of these, of course, did not survive to the end of the war.[19]

There were only four ghettos in Lithuania after the first mass-murder campaign there by the Nazis in 1941, and in three out of these four, namely in Vilna, Kovno, and Oszmiana, there were armed underground groups. In Vilna, which was the seat of the first Jewish underground organization, called the FPO, the attempt to call upon the ghetto inhabitants to rebel against the Nazis failed. Contrary to the situation in Warsaw, in Vilna the Jewish fighters found themselves isolated and opposed by the ghetto population. Therefore, after a short armed engagement in September 1943, the Jewish fighters left the ghetto through underground sewers and escaped into the forests of eastern Lithuania, to fight the Nazis from there.[20] From the very beginning the Kovno underground had no intention of fighting in the ghetto itself and organized a gradual mass escape of hundreds of people into two areas in Lithuania, where they joined existing partisan detachments or founded their own detachments.[21]

A major rebellion occurred in Białystok, which was neither a part of central Poland nor of occupied Russia. It was, in fact, part of East Prussia under the Nazis. A rebellion there, in August 1943, was led by the same kind of combination of forces as existed in the ghettos already mentioned—namely, under the leadership of left-wing Zionists, a coalition of youth groups of various ideological convictions.[22]

In the original Soviet area, somewhat similar forms of resistance developed. In the ghetto of Minsk, the fourth-largest ghetto in Europe, with over 80,000 inhabitants, an armed resistance group led by Jewish Communists, joined and aided by the Jewish council of the ghetto, organized a mass escape into the surrounding forests, thereby enabling 6,000 to 8,000 Jews to try their luck in joining the partisans.[23] Most of them did not make it—whether for lack of arms or for other reasons—but those who did joined Soviet partisan detachments, which already

242

contained a number of Jews. We have no real knowledge of the participation of Jewish fighters escaping from ghettos in the Russian areas occupied by the Nazis, their number or the weight of their participation in
the Soviet detachments. We do know that there were large numbers of
them, but because of the Soviet policy of neither permitting research in
Soviet archives nor presenting information regarding the breakup of the
partisan detachments or their exact histories, it is, at this stage, impossible to give an estimate regarding the Soviet area proper.

In eastern Europe we are talking of Jews who, by and large, acted
within Jewish environments, such as ghettos or Jewish detachments, or
joined mixed Soviet or Polish left-wing partisan detachments as Jews. In
other words, they were set apart quite clearly from the rest of the population, whether they acted separately or within general units. There were
few exceptions and these usually concerned either people who were hiding their Jewish identity or individuals who saw themselves as Communists, internationalists, and saw their Jewishness as nothing but an
accident of birth. These were relatively few in number. Detailed analyses
of these individuals would probably show that even in that situation,
their Jewishness was more than accidental in the way they behaved, both
before and during the war, and in their motivation for fighting the Nazis.
In the case of the rebellion in camps, this, of course, applies even more.
In the camps the only rebellions which took place against Nazi rule were
engineered and executed by Jews. This applies to the two rebellions in
the death camps of Sobibór and Treblinka, in the summer and autumn
of 1943, as well as to the chaotic fight of the Sonderkommando in the
gas chambers of Auschwitz in October 1944.[24] There was no ideological
motivation there, nor was the organization based on any prewar political
groupings. It was simply a matter of people who knew that there death
was approaching and who decided to rebel against the Nazis, whether
motivated by a vague hope of escape or simply to sell their lives as dearly
as possible. At Treblinka and Sobibór rather large numbers of people
managed to break out, but many of them were caught afterward and only
a few dozen of them survived. In the case of Auschwitz no survivor of
the actual rebellion is known to us. Other rebellions, some of them unarmed, took place at Kruszyna, Krychow, and Lublin prisoner-of-war
camp, the Kopernik camp at Minsk-Mazowiecki, at Sachsenhausen, and
perhaps elsewhere.[25] Non-Jewish underground organizations in concentration and death camps, such as at Auschwitz and Buchenwald, did not
act against the Nazis for a number of reasons, and in Auschwitz a promise
by the general underground to support the Jewish rebels was not kept.

243

When we summarize the motivations of Jewish resistance fighters in eastern Europe, we find that hopes for survival were a factor in eastern Poland and in some of the camps. Elsewhere, it was more a matter of selling one's life at the highest possible price, and also the desire to defend what was regarded as the honor of the Jewish people in those circumstances. Overwhelming everywhere, however, was the desire for revenge, and this motivated the Jewish fighters in most of the cases.

In western Europe the situation was different in that most Jews fighting the Nazis with arms in hand were members of general underground movements rather than Jewish ones. There were some exceptions to this rule, as in France, for instance. There a small group, calling itself the Armée Juive, existed in the south of France and was rather active not only in armed resistance proper but also in large-scale escape movements of Jews to Spain. However, insofar as one talks about Communist underground movements, many Jews in France, for instance, were members of the MOI, which was a front organization of the party for people of foreign nationality who were living in France. There were Poles and Romanians, Greeks and Armenians, and others, but a fairly large proportion of the leadership and the membership of the organizations were Jews. Jewish units were established where the prevailing language was Yiddish, and these groups participated from the very beginning in armed activities against the German occupant. The first armed actions in Paris were carried out by groups of the MOI and, as far as I know, the first French resister to the Nazis killed in the course of armed action or its aftermath was Szmul Tyszelman.[26] One could, of course, argue that there was a certain contradiction between the internationalist and territorial ideology of the Communist Party, which was opposed to ethnically defined units, and the existence of just such units in France, among them rather prominently the Jewish ones. The claim made at the time and later by participants and others, that these Jews participated in the armed resistance not as Jews but as Communists or Frenchmen, looks rather like a rationalization and not the psychological truth. The number of Jewish participants in the French underground, both Communist and non-Communist, was very high, though I do not possess any accurate figures. From a formal point of view it is undoubtedly true that the Jews did not fight, by and large, in Jewish units and that they participated in the underground as individuals, as loyal French citizens or as members of a particular ideological direction. In this of course there is a great difference between the situations in western and eastern Europe. Jewish participation in armed action against the Nazis can be documented on a

244

fairly large scale in Italy, where indeed the Jews did not participate as Jews but as members of the Italian underground, and in Yugoslavia, where approximately 6,000 Jews out of a population of 75,000 (most of whom were murdered by the Nazis) participated in the partisan detachments of Tito.[27] Jewish participation in armed fighting by Bulgarian and Greek partisans is also documented, though not sufficiently to give exact figures or ratios of participation. Jews formed a very important segment of the participants in the Slovak national uprising in August 1944, and there was even a specific Jewish unit which participated in a battle near the town then called Batovo (now renamed Partizanske).[28] After the rebellion was put down by the Nazis, in October 1944, probably up to 2,000 Jews carried on within the partisan detachments, mostly commanded by Soviet partisans who fought on in the Tatra Mountains until liberation.

We are confronted by the paradox that while all the conditions in Europe, especially in eastern Europe, militated against the mass participation of Jews in armed action against the Nazis, we nevertheless find precisely such large-scale participation. The question therefore arises as to why and how the Jews participated in such high ratios, and occasionally even in large absolute numbers, in armed underground operations and in guerrilla fighting against the Germans. Jews, of course, were more threatened than others, and once they realized that that was the situation, there was greater incentive for them, in comparison with others, to participate in armed action. The relatively strong cohesion of the Jewish family was originally one of the reasons that young Jewish men and women found it extremely difficult to join underground organizations, thereby abandoning their parents or siblings to murder by the Nazis. However, as the destruction of the Jewish populations proceeded apace, some young people found themselves without their families, who had been deported to their deaths. Thus, released from all family responsibility, or, in other cases, prompted by the fierce desire to cut themselves loose from their families, these youngsters were able to act against the Nazis in radical fashion, whether in ghettos or in partisan units.

In the Soviet Union, the partisan units came into existence as a large-scale phenomenon rather late. In 1941 and 1942 there were but the beginnings of such units in the forests, especially of Belorussia and Russia proper. Large-scale partisan activities occurred only from the winter of 1942–43 on. By that time, of course, Jewish ghettos no longer existed (except for the one at Minsk, which was finally liquidated in October 1943), and the number of Jewish labor camps was also diminishing rapidly. As a matter of hypothetical guesswork, which of course is hardly in line with historical research, one might argue that had partisan units in the Soviet Union come into existence earlier than they did, larger numbers of Jews would have joined them. As it was, however, they came too late to provide a solution for many Jews who had thus far survived. Also, anti-Semitism was rampant in many of these Soviet units, especially at the beginning, before the Soviet High Command managed to make its weight felt among these groups that had arisen in various ways and under different conditions from one place to the other. With all these obstacles in mind, it is again a surprise to note the phenomenon of relatively large numbers and ratios of Jewish participants in partisan fights. The explanation seems to be that, for those who survived the first mass-murder actions and the later systematic destruction of the community remnants, which in fact means for a fairly large number of mostly young people, there was literally no other way of survival but escape into the forests and the attempt to either hide or fight, or both.

Armed Jewish resistance, therefore, was much wider and much more intensive than the first historians recording the facts of antinazism generally, and the Holocaust specifically, thought. We find ourselves asking questions opposite in character to those that we asked originally: we no longer ask "Why did the Jews not resist," but the opposite question, "Why did so many resist by force of arms?" In this area, much further research is needed to answer questions, especially for the territory of the pre-1939 Soviet Union. As we now turn to unarmed resistance, we in fact must move chronologically back from armed resistance, which obviously was the last stage and in many places was preceded by other forms of resistance to the Nazi occupiers. Again, one must remember that until the summer of 1942 Jews in central Poland were generally unaware of the murderous intent of the Nazi regime. In eastern Poland, the Baltic countries, and the pre-1939 Soviet regions, realization of these intentions came only with the actual murder, so that no time was left to prepare for any kind of reaction. The Germans made every attempt to prevent effective communications between different Jewish centers, so that these centers, mostly ghettos, were isolated from each other and from other concentrations of Jews in other countries. Information or knowledge gained in eastern Poland or the Baltic countries took a long time to penetrate into central and western Poland, and an even longer time to penetrate a consciousness which refused to accept the information thus received. The preceding era, namely the one between the conquest of the different countries and the beginning of what the Nazis termed the

"Final Solution," is the period in which unarmed resistance took place. The areas covered by such resistance were hinted at in my definition of resistance at the beginning of this paper. Unaware that Nazi policies had developed from persecution to mass murder, Jewish communities, including both leaders and the general population, thought in terms of outlasting a regime of oppression, brutalization, mass starvation, and epidemics. There was never a doubt in the minds of all but a tiny minority that Germany would lose the war and that the only problem they had to solve was how to act in such a way as to ensure that the majority of the Jewish population would survive to the end of the war.

The problem of unarmed resistance has to be examined both regionally, because different conditions obtained in different parts of Europe, or in other words "horizontally," and also vertically, in order to observe the reactions of the Jewish leaderships, the so-called *Judenräte*, on the one hand, and of the general Jewish population on the other hand. Brutal Nazi police actions in Poland, as well as laws and regulations issued by the leaders of the General Government there, would have caused the destruction of the Jewish community and most probably the quick demise of the Jewish population had all these laws and orders been obeyed by the Jews. To give just one example, had the Jews lived on the official rations that the Germans allowed them, they would have simply died quickly in vast numbers. The official caloric value of the rations allotted to the Jews in Warsaw was 220.[29] Social or economic intercourse with the surrounding population was forbidden, as was education (until September 1941 in Warsaw) and religious life. By 1942 the worst of the typhoid and typhus epidemics had been overcome, the mass deaths that had occurred in 1940 and 1941 had receded to a considerable extent, education, though illegal, was widespread, a religious life had been reactivated, and social aid by half-legal or illegal groups and organizations was alleviating at least some of the prevalent misery.

The attitudes and policies of the *Judenräte* varied greatly in that period. Some of the *Judenräte* were absolutely helpless in the face of the mounting problems, whereas others were seeking more or less ingenious ways of circumventing Nazi orders and regulations. Most of them occupied a position in between, yielding to the Germans on the one hand, and trying to save as many as they could from German policies on the other. A good example of this is the *Judenrat* in Białystok led by Ephraim Barash, which tried to save the Jewish population by making the ghetto economically useful to the Germans. Of course, this rational policy did not take into account the irrational basis of Nazi attitudes toward the

Jews. Yet for quite a long time the policy actually achieved some measure of success. Except for Łódź and Będzin, Białystok was the last ghetto in the former Polish area to survive and was not destroyed until August 1943. On the face of it, all the activities of the Białystok *Judenrat* were within the framework of Nazi regulations. The *Judenrat* even went so far as to try to refuse acceptance into the ghetto of refugees from other places, so as not to arouse the wrath of the Nazi authorities. Yet at the same time, Barash also maintained close ties with the underground organizations in the ghetto, providing them with illegal papers, receiving reports on illegal operations, and providing them with food and other necessities to enable them to carry on their work.[30] But the main burden of unarmed resistance was shouldered by organizations that in general did not participate in the *Judenrat* system but were independent of it, partly or wholly. The main organization in this area was the JDC (American Jewish Joint Distribution Committee), a social agency, which had a Warsaw bureau and had given the directors of that bureau, *nolens volens*, a more or less free hand in their operations after the outbreak of the war. The JDC received part of its funds legally, but a very considerable proportion of the monies it used were recruited in a strictly illegal way. It fought starvation and epidemics by a series of measures which, insufficient as they were to save the lives of tens of thousands of victims, were yet important not only in saving the lives of many others but also in providing the Jews in Poland with hope and a trust in their own group, that they would not be left to die helplessly. In Warsaw the JDC not only financed a whole illegal educational system and provided the wherewithal for intensive cultural activity, consciously directed against the perceived Nazi intent to demoralize the Jewish population, but also organized so-called house committees. In these house committees people organized themselves, by living quarters, to provide each other with much needed material and moral support, including the education of children.[31] We find basically the same kind of structure of Jewish reaction in other countries of Europe. The *Judenräte* were bound, after all, by German regulations, and while they tried on the whole to help the Jewish population materially as much as they could, they were, when all is said and done, subject to German control. On the other hand, unofficial organizations, sometimes legal, sometimes illegal, were able to provide the Jewish populations with the needed leadership and direction to contravene Nazi intentions. Thus, in France, the UGIF, the official *Judenrat*, provided children's homes, social aid, and other services. But it was the half-legal OSE, an agency for looking after children, which proved to be a mainstay of operations, attempting to hide people, or to smuggle them across the borders to neutral Switzerland or Spain.[32] In western, northern, and southern Europe, where there were populations that were not, on the whole, unfriendly to the Jews, hiding and flight were clearly unarmed reactions to German intent and foiled Nazi murder plans.

On the level of popular reaction, one should perhaps mention the tremendous effort by the Jewish population, especially in eastern Europe, to smuggle food into closed ghetto areas. This was often done by children, and the most famous stories are concerned with those children. But one must also mention the adult smugglers, people who were, before the war, usually counted among the criminal or semicriminal elements in Jewish society, whose activities during the war helped to maintain large parts of the ghetto populations. In some places, such as in Kovno, the ghetto police, itself a part of the Jewish armed underground, aided in smuggling food into closed areas. Diarists such as Haim A. Kaplan of Warsaw recorded in their notebooks that the reactions of the general Jewish population was one of determination not to succumb to a perceived Nazi intention to kill them off by starvation, humiliation, and disease. One should conclude from this description that the morale of the population was maintained at a consistently high level. Far from it. There were areas, towns, countries, and periods where the opposite was the case. Many of the *Judenrat* organizations were perforce subject to corruption introduced by the Nazi system. Corruption then spread from these centers into the general population. This in itself is hardly surprising, but what is perhaps surprising is the fact that there were cells of resistance to this process and, on the whole, corruption and degeneration were met by increasingly stiff opposition.

Armed resistance, where it could and did take place, was itself proof that unarmed organization and opposition to the Nazis had preceded it. Armed resistance could hardly have developed without a base in unarmed reaction before its rise.

Let me conclude with one concrete example, which concerns the ghetto of Częstochowa, where unarmed resistance to the Nazis was ended by a tragic armed rebellion. In Częstochowa the ghetto wasn't sealed off until April 1941. Starvation and epidemics on the scale of Warsaw never occurred in Częstochowa, partly perhaps because of the lateness in establishing the ghetto, partly also because the Jews were employed there in arms factories and other economic enterprises that proved to be useful to the German war machine. A meek and submissive *Judenrat* was opposed by a workers' council, which forced the *Judenrat* at various times into

249

granting greater rations of bread obtained by various means, and also into carrying out a series of social measures helpful to refugees from other places and to the local population as well. These achievements were the result, in part, of strike actions, unheard of anywhere else in Poland. Youth groups—Zionist, Communist, and Bundist—were part and parcel of this rebellious intermediary body. From these groups an underground organization developed, originally active in propaganda and adult education and later concentrating on preparations for armed resistance. In June 1943 the Nazis discovered the underground organization and managed to surprise its commander, who was guarding the main arms cache. Most of the members of the organization were apprehended and the rebellion failed. However, groups of members of the organization staged armed actions against the Germans after the failure of the main attempt at rebellion, and two groups managed to escape from the ghetto and attempted, one successfully and one unsuccessfully, to maintain themselves in forested areas until the end of the war. In this case, as in so many others, armed action was prepared by educational activity, economic and social aid, and other forms of social organization, which stood in stark contradiction to Nazi intentions.

The picture that we obtain from all I have tried to depict in this brief outline may well be different from the accepted picture in general histories of World War II. There is no doubt that the Jews were victims, but they were not passive victims. They were destroyed by the overwhelming power of Nazi Germany, which had conquered most of Europe, crushing in a very short time mighty armies and great countries. There was absolutely no way in which the Jews could have physically resisted their fate. Even in western Europe, with populations relatively friendly to the Jews, there was a high percentage of victimization. But the percentage was higher in eastern Europe, where the populations were generally indifferent or hostile. The small Jewish minority was in a hopeless situation, and one could well have understood the spread of complete and total despair and demoralization. The extent of armed and unarmed resistance to the Nazis is perhaps evidence of a culture that refused to die. That, however, is quite a different statement from one that would argue that the Jewish culture of Europe did not, in fact, die. The Nazis succeeded to a great extent. The unarmed and armed resistance of the Jews proved to be futile, because the forces aligned against it were too powerful to be opposed by these means. When all is said and done, Jewish resistance of all kinds to the Nazis is but a small footnote to what happened to all of Europe generally, and to the Jewish population in particular. For Jews it is a very important footnote, because it indicates possible ways of rebuild-ing and regenerating the Jewish people. For non-Jews it should be equally important or even more so. What happened to the Jews might well hap-pen to others. What are the means, if any, to oppose ideologically moti-vated tyranny? More importantly, what may be the means of avoiding a situation where such a tyranny can operate? Those are some of the ques-tions that a study of Jewish resistance may well arouse.

13

The Jewish Councils
An Overview

RANDOLPH L. BRAHAM

Postwar Attitudes Toward the Jewish Councils

Perhaps no other topic in the history of the Holocaust has elicited more agonizing questions and given rise to more heated debates than the role played by the Jewish councils[1] in German-dominated Europe during World War II. The dominant viewpoints on this issue have varied with the passage of time.

During the immediate postwar period a condemnatory attitude was most discernible. Many of the survivors as well as a considerable proportion of the governmental and political figures in liberated Europe were inclined to identify the leaders of the Jewish councils and of their auxiliary enforcement organs as collaborators and to call for their indictment and punishment as war criminals. In response to these pressures, in several countries a number of council leaders were indeed arrested, tried, and convicted.[2]

In more recent years the pendulum of historical evaluation appears, with a few notable exceptions, to have swung in the opposite direction. Some well-known historians and philosophers, including Hannah Arendt, have continued to embrace the condemnatory position, deploring the "role of the Jewish leaders in the destruction of their own people."[3]

Many contemporary students of the Holocaust, however, portray the Jewish councils in a more lenient and understanding fashion, emphasizing the mitigating factors for their behavior. These students focus on the lack of alternatives available to council members and the predicaments with which they were confronted in the context of the extraordinary conditions created by an enemy bent on the physical destruction of an entire people. In this context council members are viewed as faithful representatives of the Jewish communities, dedicated to protecting the constituents' fundamental interests by whatever means they had at their disposal.

In this article I shall endeavor to offer as balanced an evaluation as possible of the intrinsically thankless and unenviable role of the Jewish councils during the war in the context of the conditions in which they had to operate. In pursuit of this objective the following observations are advanced *ab ovo:*

- Concurrently with their invasion of the Soviet Union in the summer of 1941, the leaders of the Third Reich resolved to replace their original plans, which would have "solved" the Jewish question by resettling the Jews of Europe, with a diabolical, ideologically conceived scheme to exterminate the Jews during the course of the war.
- In pursuit of this "Final Solution" (*Endlösung*), conceived after the spring of 1941 as a central mission of the war, it was the Nazis and their accomplices who determined the time, place, and scale of the various anti-Jewish operations (*Aktionen*) in terms of their priorities and interests and particular local conditions.
- The local conditions varied with the prevailing attitude of the particular governments and Christian populations. Such attitudes ranged from full collaboration in many parts of eastern Europe to reluctant cooperation, or resistance, in some parts of western Europe.
- The ultimate fate of the Jews was not determined by the attitudes and actions of the Jewish councils, for their members, like the Jewish people as a whole, were basically helpless and defenseless. The determining factor in the destruction of the Jews was neither the composition nor the specific actions of the Jewish councils, but the conditions and reality under which they had to operate. The fate of the Jews was the same in Warsaw, where Adam Czerniaków committed suicide rather than cooperate in the impending deportations, as it was in Łódź, where Chaim Rumkowski had believed in the possibility of "salvation through cooperation and labor," or

253

in Białystok and Minsk, where Ephraim Barash and Ilya Moshkin respectively supported and embraced resistance. Their fate was also the same in Slovakia, where the Jewish leaders sought to buy off the SS representatives in pursuit of the so-called "Europa Plan," as it was in Hungary (excepting Budapest), where the council leaders employed time-tested techniques designed to win the desperate "race with time."

The Councils and the Final Solution

While the Jewish councils were conceived to play an important role as an accessory instrumentality in the Nazis' bureaucratic machinery of destruction, they were not essential for that purpose. Indeed, the Nazis adapted the tactics of the Final Solution to the particular circumstances in the various countries under their domination. The specifics were often dictated by the degree of urgency to solve the Jewish question in a particular area as well as by the readiness of the local authorities to cooperate in the implementation of the Nazis' sinister plans. In the areas where the Nazis exercised exclusive jurisdiction, or enjoyed the wholehearted cooperation of the local authorities, neither the existence nor the conduct of the Jewish councils could have made any difference in the outcome of the Nazis' Final Solution drive.

Thus, in many parts of the Soviet Union occupied by Germany, including the formerly free Baltic states, much of the Final Solution program was carried out directly by the Germans through their specially trained Einsatzgruppen, which were usually assisted by readily available local volunteers (Lithuanians, Ukrainians, and others). Even in the few localities in this area where diminishing numbers of "working" Jews were allowed for a while at least to survive and form ghettos with duly established Jewish councils, it was the SS that carried out directly many of the anti-Jewish measures. In Vilna, for example, following the completion of the first wave of exterminations in July and August 1941, the 46,000 surviving Jews were driven into the local ghettos by the Germans themselves. In Minsk, too, the great *Aktionen* of November 7 and November 20, 1941, in which approximately 20,000 Jews were massacred, were carried out with the SS completely bypassing the Jewish council.[4] In Serbia, also, the Germans, relying primarily on the Wehrmacht rather than on the Einsatzgruppen, massacred the Jews in a series of reprisals during the fall of 1941 and spring of 1942 without involving the local

254

Jewish leaderships.[5] The Germans occasionally acted directly even in matters that were usually in the purview of the Jewish councils. Thus, in Brussels, where both the local authorities and the Jewish council refused to engage in the distribution of the distinctive yellow badge, the German Military Administration assumed this task.[6]

The Germans also bypassed the Jewish councils in the ghettoization-concentration-deportation drives wherever they could safely rely on the local governmental authorities to carry out the "dirty work," preferring to act merely as advisers and supervisors in the implementation of the Final Solution program. They did this not so much to safeguard the psychological integrity of the relatively few Germans who were assigned to the program (for these were ideologically indoctrinated and fully committed to the idea that the Jews had to be exterminated as bacilli to assure the survival of the Aryan races) but to spare their matériel and manpower for other purposes. This was especially true in countries they fully dominated. Thus, in Lithuania the Jews living in the smaller localities were rounded up on orders transmitted directly by the local authorities without involving the Germans or the Jewish Councils.[7] This was also true in German-occupied Hungary, a country which remained only nominally sovereign after March 19, 1944. In all the communities of the country except Budapest, the Jews were rounded up and deported within a short period of time exclusively by the Hungarian gendarmerie and the local law-enforcement agencies.

In some countries the Jewish councils or communal leaderships were not only uninvolved in the ghettoization and deportation, let alone the destruction process, but actually enjoyed a degree of maneuverability that enabled them to frustrate to a considerable extent the intent of the Germans. This was the case in Italy[8] and the smaller Axis-allied states (including Hungary up to March 1944) as well as those conquered countries in which the Nazis failed to set up a totally submissive quisling government. In all of these states the Germans could not act unilaterally and so endeavored to bring about the solution of the Jewish question through the cooperation of the local governments whose consent they needed. Clearly, the attitude and actions of the Jewish leaders reflected the position of the local governments. The more the latter manifested their independence and asserted their sovereignty vis-à-vis the Germans, the greater were the opportunities for the Jewish leaders not only to maneuver in pursuit of rescue operations, but also to refuse their cooperation in the anti-Jewish drives.

By far the most dramatic case is that of Finland. Although Hitler

255

complained about the "subversive activity" of Finland's small Jewish community,[9] and in 1942 Himmler actually urged the Finnish government to solve the Jewish problem, the Finns stubbornly resisted this intervention in their internal affairs. Although the Finnish authorities reportedly handed over to the Germans a number of refugees and several "Jewish criminals and Communists,"[10] they were insistent on protecting their small indigenous Jewish community. The Germans apparently abstained from exerting further pressure on Finland in this respect. However, this was due not so much to "Hitler's great esteem for the Finns" as emphasized by Hannah Arendt, but primarily to the führer's belief that it would be unwise to jeopardize his relations with a fiercely independent Finland, one of his staunchest allies in the anti-Soviet war, in order to eliminate a few thousand Jews. In Romania, a country noted for its anti-Semitic policies, the ultrarightist regime of General Ion Antonescu refused to go along with the Nazis' Final Solution program and the Jews of Romania proper, i.e., those of Muntenia (Walachia), Moldavia, and Southern Transylvania survived the war almost intact.[11] They were not even placed in ghettos and wore no yellow badges. As part of its defiance, the Romanian government did not permit German control over the Jewish council, the Bucharest office of which directed a network of local organizations.

The same situation also applied to Vichy France, where the regime exercised considerable autonomy and the Germans depended to a large extent upon the local bureaucracy and law-enforcement organs not only for the administration of this conquered country but also for the "solution of the Jewish question."[12] In this country the Jewish council, the Union Générale des Israélites de France (UGIF), was in a position to escape many of the agonizing tasks that its counterparts had to fulfill in other parts of Europe. Established in November 1941, the UGIF was legally defined as an autonomous civilian public institution and placed under the tutelage of the General Commissariat on Jewish Questions (Commissariat Générale aux Questions Juives), which had been set up under French jurisdiction earlier in the year. The relatively independent posture of France was reflected in the policies of the commissariat during the tenure of Xavier Vallat (March 1941 to May 1942), the Vichy appointee, and to a lesser extent of Darquier de Pellepoix, the Germans' choice, in the sense that both well-known anti-Semites took into consideration Marshal Pétain's differentiation between indigenous and foreign Jews, albeit with varying degrees of enthusiasm or adherence. This posture was reflected by the permission given the General Consistory of the

Jews of France (Consistoire Générale des Israélites de France), the traditional Jewish organization under the leadership of Jacques Helbronner, to continue its operations—to the great dismay of the Germans.[13] (In their drive for an effective implementation of the Final Solution, the Germans normally insisted on the existence of only one central Jewish organization in a country or a larger isolated area.) Although the UGIF, operating in northern, occupied France, was compelled to deal with the German Security Police in matters affecting the lives of the Jews, including those interned at Drancy, it was able because of the conditions prevailing in the country to refuse participation in the arrest, expulsion, and deportation process. Neither did it provide lists or assistance to the drives launched for the apprehension of Jews in hiding. As in Romania, the UGIF did not operate within the framework of ghettos and could dispense with the use of special Jewish police forces. It served "primarily" as a relief and welfare organization.[14]

The correlation between the effectiveness of the Jewish leaders and the manifestation of independence by their state is also proven by the cases of Bulgaria and Hungary, both Axis-allied countries. In Bulgaria, only about 11,300 "alien" Jews were deported from the Bulgarian-occupied territories of Macedonia and Thrace in March 1943. Almost all of the 50,000-member Jewish community of Old Bulgaria survived the war.[15]

That the Germans refrained from imposing their will in Jewish matters when they encountered determined opposition is proven poignantly by the case of Hungary—twice. Despite ever increasing German pressure, the Hungarians refused to engage in any radical solution of the Jewish question. And while, as in Bulgaria, the Hungarians also deported close to 18,000 "alien" Jews to near Kamenets-Podolsk (where most of them were slaughtered in August 1941),[16] they protected the close to 800,000 "Hungarian" Jews—by far the largest surviving Jewish community of Europe—until the German occupation of the country on March 19, 1944. The currently available evidence shows that even after this date the Germans would have refrained from embarking on the Final Solution program had the new quisling government, and especially its experts on Jewish affairs who acted in close collaboration with the Eichmann Sonderkommando, not shown such great enthusiasm for the program. The second demonstration of this point came on July 7, 1944, when Miklós Horthy, the regent of Hungary, decided to halt the deportations. The Germans and their Hungarian accomplices had no alternative but to abide by his decision and refrain from the deportation of the

Jews of Budapest. But by that time the Hungarian countryside was already *judenrein.*

The active though involuntary involvement of the Jewish councils in the Nazis' sinister designs against the Jews was a phenomenon restricted almost exclusively to the Third Reich and the countries annexed or occupied by it. This was particularly true in eastern Europe, whose Jewry— the cradle and reservoir of modern Jewry—was the special target of the Nazis' fury. But here too the behavior of the Jewish councils varied, because of a number of factors, making generalizations impossible. Even in these areas the extent to which the Jewish leaders cooperated depended less on their religious, factional, or political-ideological affiliation than on local conditions;[17] in particular, it depended on how exclusively the Jewish question was the province of the Germans, the eagerness with which the quisling authorities served the interests of the Germans, and the extent to which the local Christian church leaders and populations reflected compassion, hostility, or indifference toward the Jews. This is abundantly proven by the case of Greece, where great variations can be noted between the treatment of the Jews in Salonika and in Athens. In the former city, which contained 56,000 of the 77,000 Jews of Greece, the Germans were empowered to exercise absolute control over the Jewish question. Here Rabbi C. Koretz, the head of the *kehillah,* was turned, against his will, into an important tool of the Germans. Presumably unaware of the ultimate scope of the deportations, he was, like many of his counterparts in Nazi-dominated Europe, ensnared in an endless web of deceptions. According to recent accounts, Rabbi Koretz attempted to persuade the Germans not to remove the Jews, and when his efforts failed, he contacted the Greek authorities, including Prime Minister I. D. Rhallis, but to no avail. He paid with his life for his audacity. The picture was completely different in Athens, where Rabbi Eliyahu Barzilai, supported by the top city officials, refused to cooperate with Dieter Wisliceny. The SS leader came to Athens on September 20, 1943, to continue the deportation program, but found a Jewish community that could count on significant protection from the local Greek authorities. The pleas of Rabbi Barzilai were sympathetically received by Damaskinos, the metropolitan, and Krisurdaov, the police chief in the Eighth District of Athens. Even the prime minister was more considerate in "the case of the ancient Jewish community of Athens, whose members (were) considered to be true Greek citizens."[18]

The role played by Rabbi Koretz was duplicated and indeed far exceeded by that played by his counterparts in many communities in

Nazi-occupied Europe, especially Poland and Lithuania. In these communities, the councils were nearly exclusively under the control of the Nazis, in an almost totally hostile environment, acting as helpless pawns. They were naturally eager to save themselves and their loved ones, but they also wanted to help the ever shrinking communities to the limit of their constantly diminishing opportunities. Their actions and attitudes reflected the extraordinary conditions created by the Germans and their accomplices who alone—to repeat—determined the time, place, and scale of the liquidations in accordance with an diabolical, ideologically conceived plan.

Having demonstrated the close correlation between the attitudes and actions of the Jewish leaders in the various countries of Nazi-dominated Europe with the degree of independence or autonomy manifested by their governments, one may proceed to an examination of (a) the guidelines relating to the establishment and the functions of the councils; (b) the variations in their creation; (c) the structure of the councils and the characteristics of their leaders and members, including their awareness of the Final Solution; (d) the functions they performed voluntarily and involuntarily; and (e) the attitudes manifested toward them during the war.

Guidelines

Beginning with the establishment of the Reichsvereinigung der Juden in Deutschland (succeeding the Reichvertretung) on July 4, 1939, and ending with the legalization of the Association of the Jews of Hungary on April 19, 1944, the Jewish councils operating in Nazi-dominated Europe were set up on the initiative of the Germans. This was as true in independent Romania and in Vichy France, where the national legislatures enacted the necessary laws, as it was in Poland, where the German occupants issued them. While the Jewish councils varied to some extent from country to country and to a lesser degree within the few countries in which the internal administration of Jewish affairs was not nationally centralized (e.g., Poland), in general their composition and activities conformed to the basic guidelines outlined by Reinhard Heydrich, the head of the Reich Main Security Office, on September 21, 1939.[19]

Heydrich identified the functions of the councils as ephemeral, a means for the achievement of "the ultimate goal (which requires a prolonged period of time)."[20] Although the ultimate goal was not yet fully

259

crystallized—at the time, the Nazis were still toying with the idea of possibly concentrating the Jews of Europe in a "Jewish reservation" in the eastern part of the continent or of resettling them somewhere else, possibly in Africa—the plan for centralizing the local administration for the solution of the Jewish question by utilizing the Jewish councils was firmly established. This idea was clearly identified in the decree on the Jewish councils, which was issued on November 28, 1939, by Hans Frank, the governor-general for the Occupied Polish Territories. Article 5 of this decree stipulated not only that the Jewish council leaders had to take orders from the German authorities and were responsible for "the conscientious execution of these orders to their full extent," but also that all the Jews had to obey the instructions issued by the Jewish council regarding the execution of the German orders.[21]

The central idea was to place the councils within the wheels of the Nazi bureaucratic machinery, serving as the primary contact between the authorities and the individual Jewish communities. This objective compelled the Nazis to reject any attempts by the Jews to continue to operate their many local and national institutions on an autonomous or federal basis and actually to dissolve most of them and place those they considered temporarily useful under the jurisdiction of the councils. The councils emerged both as one of the major links of communication between the authorities and the Jewish communities in carrying out orders, and as the representatives through which the particular communities could express their needs. In fulfilling their often contradictory tasks, they wielded considerable power over the day-to-day affairs of the communities they led. This was especially true in the ghettos that survived a relatively longer period of time. In many of these the councils were empowered not only to regulate all aspects of their internal economies but also to preside over matters of life and death. This power was, of course, highly circumscribed; the councils never enjoyed any independent decision-making power over the ultimate fate of their communities. Their jurisdiction and longevity were determined by the Germans and their accomplices.

The power of the councils was derived from and was propped up by the authorities, who always insisted that their orders be carried out promptly and fully. These orders ranged from the surrender of property to the preparation of lists and the selection and transfer of Jews for "special treatment." In fulfilling these tasks the councils inevitably became transformed into instrumentalities serving the interests of their mortal enemies, and were turned against their will into accessories to the very crimes they were trying to deter. But while they unwillingly and unwittingly cooperated—there were virtually no cases of outright voluntary collaboration—they exerted considerable effort toward easing the suffering of their fellow Jews and to gain time in the hope of liberation following a quick Allied victory. Unfortunately, their wishful thinking about the imminence of the Third Reich's collapse was constantly overtaken by the speed and effectiveness with which the Nazis carried out their Final Solution program.

Types of Councils and Their Origins

The councils varied considerably in terms of their origin, longevity, jurisdiction, and composition. Some of the councils, especially in the smaller communities, were ephemeral, lasting only a few days or weeks. Following the transfer of the Jews into the larger ghettos or areas of concentration, these councils were disbanded and their members shared the fate of the rest of their community, as, for example, in practically all the provincial Jewish communities of Hungary in 1944. Others, both local and national, lasted for several years. One such example was the Joodse Raad of Holland and the councils in the larger ghettos of Poland. The Jewish council of Łódź, which holds the record, lasted from shortly after the German conquest of Poland in September 1939 to the liquidation of the ghetto in August 1944. In the course of their long existence, many of the councils underwent radical changes in terms of their structure, composition, and function.

Some of the councils were national in jurisdiction. This was the case, for example, in France, Holland, the Reich, and Romania. There, the councils operated outside the context of formal ghettos, although each of these countries had a number of internment or labor camps for Jews. The Jewish council of Budapest was both local and national, acting not only on behalf of the Jews of the capital but also—until the Hungarian countryside became *judenrein* on July 9, 1944—as the major vehicle of communication between the authorities and the many local ghetto leaderships all over the country. In Latvia, Lithuania, Poland, Transnistria, and the occupied areas of the USSR, the councils functioned almost exclusively within the framework of the local ghettos. The only exception was the Council of Sosnowiec, which served as a regional council for eastern Upper Silesia, having under its jurisdiction the local councils in the area. At both levels, and in all the affected countries, the councils operated in virtual isolation from each other except for official censored communications and occasional underground contacts through special messengers. Deprived of every means of genuine contact, the councils usually acted "independently" of each other in response to the orders and directives of their particular German or collaborating national authorities.

Although the councils were everywhere founded on German initiative, there were great variations in their establishment and composition. In some places, including Vilna and Minsk, the council leaders were appointed directly by the Germans. In several places, including Kovno, the council leaders had to be persuaded by the old-time civil and spiritual leaders of the Jewish community to accept the position, which they feared and loathed. Although many of these enjoyed the confidence of the particular community's leaders, they were not traditional representatives of the *kehillahs*. This was true in practically all the Jewish communities that had previously been under Soviet domination. In these areas the Jewish organizations and institutions had been disbanded in accordance with Soviet policies regarding nationalities, as a result of which the traditional communal lay and spiritual leaders were either imprisoned or exiled. Consequently, the leaders of the Jewish councils in most of these communities were either "foreign" Jews, that is, persons with no roots in the particular communities, or had not previously been active in communal Jewish affairs. Nevertheless, they normally tried to further the best interests of the communities into which historical events had thrown them. There were, of course, exceptions, as in the case of Minsk, and in Romania, France, Belgium, and Hungary.[22]

These modes of appointment, however, were the exception. By far the most prevalent manner in which a council was established was through self-organization by the traditional leaders following an order by the German or quisling authorities. In most places the Jewish councils were composed of the long-established, trusted lay and spiritual leaders of the particular communities. Many of these councils were, in fact, coalitions of the various local religious, political, and Zionist leaderships banded together to share the burdens and responsibilities that were thrust upon them. In this respect they were indeed authentic organs of communal leadership whom the Jewish masses trusted and looked upon for guidance and assistance. This image of the councils, like the discretion they had in local matters, was totally in accord with the Nazis' diabolical plan. In contrast to German policies toward the defeated nations, and especially the Slavic ones, whose planned permanent enslavement in the envisioned thousand-year Third Reich required the immediate physical elimination of their elites[23]—a practice followed by all ideologically oriented conquerors—the Nazis' Final Solution program called for the elimination of the Jewish leaders only at the end. Their plan required that the authentic Jewish leaders be turned into accomplices by ensnaring them in an endless web of deceptions that would induce them, *inter alia*, to help lull the Jewish masses into submission and occasionally even to participate in the physical processes of destruction. In a way, the Jewish councils served the interests of the Nazis even by their charitable and humanitarian activities, since to the extent that they provided the wherewithal of survival to their ever shrinking communities they relieved the burden from the Germans.[24] Indeed, this was in accord with the Nazis' strategy, which envisioned not only the imposition of these impossible burdens upon the councils, but also the channeling of the Jewish masses' anger and bitterness over the inadequacy of these services against their own leaders rather than against the Germans. This was clearly revealed by Heinz Auerswald, the Nazi commissar of the Warsaw ghetto, in his November 24, 1941, letter addressed to Berlin: "When there is suffering (in the ghetto), the Jews' wrath is directed primarily against the Jewish authorities, and not against the German supervisory authorities."[25]

The legitimacy of the Jewish councils certainly, though obviously unintentionally, aided the Nazi authorities by making their job easier. But important as this element was, it was not a determining factor in the Final Solution program even in the case of those councils (for example that of Budapest) which were fully aware of Nazi designs.

What options did the councils have? To burden the Nazis by failing to provide, however inadequately, the Jews with food and housing in the ghettos? To resign? To commit suicide? Many of the council leaders remained in their positions from a sense of duty and devotion to the community. It would have been relatively easy, in some cases at least, for them to follow the example of other Jews with money and connections and to escape. Most of them concluded that by staying instead of escaping or resigning they could mitigate and perhaps avert the losses by continuing to provide experienced leadership. If they had resigned en masse, there is no doubt that the Nazis and their accomplices could easily have found another or yet a third set of Jewish leaders to serve in the council: they would have found this just as easy a task after a mass suicide by all the members of a council as after their liquidation.

Could the Jewish councils have refused to carry out the orders of the

263

Nazis? Yes, and in many cases they did. It was possible, to some extent, especially in the countries that retained and exercised a considerable degree of independence. There were also many cases of active defiance on the part of the council leaders, but then the Nazis and their accomplices carried out the tasks themselves and frequently much more cruelly. On the other hand, it is quite possible that, in some countries at least, the replacement of the traditional and trusted leaders of a community by a collective of unknown figures universally perceived as quislings might have awakened the masses to the realities of the fate awaiting them and induced them not to cooperate or possibly even to resist. In a way, the Jewish council leaders were in a no-win situation. It was part of the Nazis' plan that they too were to be eliminated immediately after the completion of their assigned tasks. But had they refused to serve in the council and by some miracle survived the war while tens and hundreds of thousands of their fellow Jews were massacred, they certainly would have been condemned by the survivors for having represented their community only while prestige and honor were the reward, and for having abandoned it in its darkest hour.

The Structure and the Leadership of the Councils

The internal structure of the councils frequently determined the efficiency with which they performed their tasks vis-à-vis the authorities and their communities. However, the structure was no more important than their membership or any other characteristic in determining the ultimate fate of the Jews. Whatever the differences in their characteristics, the councils usually acted and reacted similarly when they were confronted with similar conditions. The leadership and internal administration patterns tended to reflect the prewar modes of operation, adapted of course to the requirements imposed upon them. The councils usually operated within the existing institutional structure in their communities. Many of them, especially the national ones and those operating in larger ghettos, had numerous departments offering a variety of social-welfare, medical, educational, cultural, and religious services that were traditionally delivered by the *kehillahs*. Because of the isolation of the ghettos, the Jewish councils had to assume additional functions that were normally the responsibility of the local state administrations. The councils were compelled to deal with such state-related functions as housing, utilities, the acquisition and distribution of food, transportation, and mail. They had special departments or sections dealing with administration, finance, housing, and economic and technical services. In the larger ghettos they even had well-organized though unarmed Jewish police units. The staff of most of these departments enjoyed a modicum of well-being and security, which was, of course, only ephemeral. Many councils were merely opportunistic, trying to safeguard their own and their families' interests; many others, however, were genuinely committed to serving the best interests of their communities with the constantly diminishing resources at their disposal. While the extent to which a ghetto "flourished" depended upon the resourcefulness and talents of the Jews, the duration of its existence was always determined by the Germans and their accomplices.[26]

While a ghetto or community was allowed to exist, the Germans did not particularly object to the varied communal activities of the Jews, in as much as these too essentially served German interests. Since the destruction of the communities followed a predetermined timetable— which the Jewish leaders were obviously neither aware of nor able to influence—until the time came for a particular ghetto to be destroyed, the Germans were perfectly content not to have to provide even a minimal level of those social services the Jews themselves were providing. At the same time, it suited the Germans to foster Jewish illusions about eventual survival by permitting such normal activities as theatergoing and attendance at concerts; in their view, the busier a ghetto was, the less preoccupied its population was bound to be with the impending disaster.

In many ghettos, especially in eastern Europe, the Jewish police played a particularly important role. In almost all of the eastern communities the Jewish police was established on German orders and was frequently infiltrated by informers and Nazi agents who often intimidated and occasionally dominated the council as well as the police leadership. Subordinated to the Jewish councils, the Jewish police were responsible not only for maintaining law and order but in several places also for carrying out some measures involved in the Final Solution program.[27]

Although many of the prewar Jewish communities of eastern Europe, especially those of Poland, were organized on a democratic basis, with leaderships periodically elected in communal assemblies, the Jewish councils were generally organized and led in an autocratic manner. They were naturally neither elected by nor responsible to their particular "constituencies." Some of the councils were dominated by their dictatorial chairmen. This system was favored by the Germans not only because it

265

was in accord with their own leadership principles, but also because it proved for them more effective than the collective or democratic system. In many ghettos the council members tried to act as a collective body. In still others the most influential members of the council acted as a clique. The close cooperation between the top leaders of many of the councils was usually based as much on their mutual trust and on long-standing personal friendship as on their collective mistrust of some other members of the councils. The secrecy of their deliberations and actions often chagrined their colleagues, who not only mistrusted their judgment but also resented having to bear collective responsibility for decisions they had no part in making.

During the period of relative normality, that is, before the launching of the Final Solution program, the councils often held formal meetings, and their deliberations and decisions were neatly recorded, albeit in cautious and discreet language.[28] During most of their life spans, however, the councils met on an emergency basis in a desperate attempt to cope with the ever more frequent and harsh challenges confronting them. The dictates of constantly arising emergencies, which required the speedy decisions that larger deliberate bodies would have made more difficult, if not impossible, compelled most councils to become ever more autocratic.

The quality of the Jewish council leaders and members varied. While many of the well-to-do and the influential Jewish leaders with good connections fled their countries—this was especially the case in Germany in the 1930s and elsewhere in east-central Europe shortly before and after the outbreak of World War II—the consequent decline in the quality of the Jewish elites was not fatal.[29] In many a community the Jewish leadership consisted of highly motivated, dynamic lay and religious leaders who were imbued with a deep sense of Jewish consciousness. They reached their positions in the community by virtue of their wealth, class, generosity, learning, profession, prestige, and, not infrequently, family tradition. Because of their prominence in the communities, they were usually routinely renominated and reelected. In many communities in western and central Europe, the Jewish leaders were primarily patriotic, anti-Zionist and assimilationist. In these parts of Europe, the Jewish leaders were highly committed to the values and principles underlying their particular state and social systems. They usually belonged to the upper middle class, and some, especially in Hungary, to the lower aristocracy. Reflecting their class background, they were basically conservative, and tended to identify with the political and socioeconomic views

266

and national aspirations of their Christian counterparts. In many parts of eastern Europe and the Balkans, they were primarily Orthodox and traditionalist. In countries like Poland and Romania, where the Jewish communities were politically mobilized to a remarkable degree, Jewish leaders were also active in the political arena, playing important roles in the Jewish parties and in the various Zionist movements at both regional and national levels. In the former Soviet-held territories, as was pointed out earlier, Jewish elites were all but nonexistent. But whatever their background, quality, and peacetime effectiveness, the ability of the Jewish leaders all over Europe to protect their communities during the Nazi era depended on factors over which they had no control. The primary factor, to repeat, was the extent to which the Germans and their accomplices exercised exclusive jurisdiction over Jewish affairs in a particular country.

Jewish leaders of the communities not yet engulfed by the Final Solution process lived and operated under the psychologically understandable illusion that their particular community might somehow survive the catastrophe that was befalling other Jewish communities. This was as true of the leaders of the national Jewish communities that were still relatively intact as of many local communities within countries where the Final Solution was already in progress. This psychological defense mechanism, a retreat from reality, was based partly on their inability to perceive the possibility—and indeed very few logically thinking people could conceive of it at the time—that a systematic, assembly-line mass murder could be perpetrated in supposedly enlightened twentieth-century Europe. In many places the Jewish leaders were misled by the belief that the Nazi measures affected only the "foreign" Jews and that the fully assimilated indigenous ones had little if anything to fear. In some countries this idea was quite well founded. For example, in Bulgaria only the "alien" Jews of Macedonia and Thrace were affected; Romania deported to Transnistria primarily the "alien" Jews of Bessarabia and Northern Bukovina; the French were eager to be rid of their "foreign" Jews;[30] in Belgium the deportees consisted almost exclusively of stateless Jews of Czech, German, Polish, and Russian origin;[31] in Hungary the close to 18,000 Jews who were deported to near Kamenets-Podolsk in the summer of 1941 were identified as "alien"; and finally even in Holland the drive was at first directed only against the German and other "alien" Jews. This was one of the factors that induced the Joodse Raad to cooperate more readily with the Germans in order to assure the better protection of the Dutch Jews. The Dutch council remained for a long time under the mistaken impression that the anti-Jewish drive was directed exclusively against the "foreign Jews"—a faulty assumption that resulted, in Hannah Arendt's words, in "a catastrophe unparalleled in any Western country."[32] The Dutch Jewish leaders at the time did not know—any more than the leaders of most other European Jewish communities knew—that this was only a tactical aspect of the Nazis' strategy to liquidate *all* Jews.

Declarations by the Allies (including that of December 17, 1942, which for the first time defined the extermination of the Jews as a crime), like the broadcasts by the BBC and other official and underground anti-Nazi radio stations, were not taken at face value during the first years of the war, either by the Jewish leaders or by the representatives of the oppressed nations. The broadcasts were in fact well substantiated, for the mass executions perpetrated by the Einsatzgruppen in the former Soviet-held territories during the second half of 1941 and the deportation-extermination process launched early in 1942 could no longer be entirely hidden despite Nazi attempts to conceal them. Early in 1942, information on these activities was beginning to reach the Allies and the governments-in-exile with increasing frequency and in ever greater detail. However, broadcasts about the extermination of the Jews were quite infrequent and lacked specific details.

Only gradually did the awareness of the Nazis' designs enter the consciousness of the Jewish leaders. The timing and extent of the awakening differed in various parts of Europe, depending upon the leaders' degree of isolation and their relative status. Thus, although the measures enacted by the Germans almost immediately after the occupation of Poland were quite draconic, very few, if any, of the Jewish leaders, let alone the masses, thought or indeed could think that these were merely the first steps of a diabolical plan which would eventually lead to the physical destruction of all the Jews. Nothing in the history of the Jewish people—not even the harshest measures of the past, the expulsions and the pogroms—could have prepared them for this ideologically conceived objective that excluded even the traditional avenue of escape: conversion.

When the mass executions began in Lithuania and the other German-occupied Soviet territories, Jewish leaders at first thought they were facing isolated incidents directed primarily against persons whom the Nazis considered "useless" and "unemployable" and that the Jewish communities, though greatly diminished and totally impoverished, would nevertheless survive the war. As the nature of the periodic *Aktionen* became known to the ghetto dwellers at large, the survivors of these operations were increasingly aware of the dangers and did everything in their power to render themselves "useful." Unaware of the Nazis' goals, they viewed the local exterminations as "the incarnation of unrestrained hatred and disregard for human lives." As Yisrael Gutman correctly observed, they viewed the extermination campaign "more as an unwillingness to distribute food and other vital necessities to a population which the Germans considered to be inferior and inefficient."[33] Unlike the leaders of the free world—both Jewish and non-Jewish—they were not aware of the Nazis' plan relating to the Final Solution.[34] By the time those Jewish council leaders who eventually did realize the diabolical character of the Nazis' actions came to their senses, they were already trapped, together with their shrinking communities.

Voluntary and Involuntary Actions of the Councils

The Jewish councils were confronted from the beginning by an impossible dilemma: how to reconcile their responsibilities to the communities they voluntarily served with the involuntary activities the Germans imposed upon them. As successors to the traditional *kehillah* leaderships, whose tasks they were eager to continue to fulfill, they were entrusted by the Nazis with functions they were not accustomed or prepared to handle. The conflict and the contradictions between the German orders and Jewish communal interests became increasingly irreconcilable. Powerless and helpless, the councils were very quickly transformed into unwilling and unwitting instrumentalities of the Germans while still trying to serve the interests of their communities with their constantly diminishing resources and options. But, as emphasized earlier, even these latter activities indirectly served the interests of the Nazis. Once trapped in the Nazi web, they had no alternative but to cooperate. Among other things, they were compelled to cooperate in the compilation of lists that were used in the ghettoization and deportation process; they prepared inventories of personal and communal properties that were subsequently confiscated; they raised funds for the financing of many aspects of the Final Solution program, including the purchase and distribution of the yellow badges, the erection of ghetto walls, and the support of work and concentration camps; they lulled the masses into submission; and they participated in the apprehension of Jews for deportation.

The council leaders carried out the tasks imposed upon them with various degrees of reluctance and effectiveness.[35] In several cases, they also worked with the underground resistance movement. Many of them paid with their lives for their heroic actions. Most council leaders were involved in a desperate struggle to save not only themselves and their families, but also as many others from their ever shrinking communities as possible.

Some councils, including those already aware of the Nazis' intent to annihilate the Jews, thought they could save at least the working remnant of their communities by making themselves "indispensable" to the Germans. Their rescue-through-labor strategy was based upon the supposition that some of the German organs of power, especially the Wehrmacht, were interested in preserving Jewish manpower for their own needs. They were convinced that the Germans could neither do without the skills of many of the Jews nor train non-Jews to replace them quickly enough.[36] While this approach managed to postpone but not to prevent the ultimate destruction of all of the ghettos (none lasted to the end of the war), it caused considerable tension between the Jewish councils and the various groups of "skilled" and "unskilled" Jews in the ghettos. The periodic *Aktionen* of the SS, timed according to schedules with well-defined priorities, at first primarily affected the unskilled—the elderly, the very young, the ill, and the unemployed. When the councils tried to protect some in these vulnerable categories of Jews by classifying them as "skilled" or "employed," the truly skilled workers often virtually rebelled, fearing that their own lives and the lives of their families were being endangered.[37] Little did the skilled workers in possession of special certificates know that they were destined merely to live a little longer. They could not possibly be aware of the Himmler order that once non-Jewish replacements were found they too were to be expeditiously eliminated "in accordance with the wishes of the Führer."[38]

It was this same posture engendered by their helplessness that induced many council leaders to cooperate with the Germans even in the selection or apprehension of Jews for deportation and certain extermination. In some places (e.g., Budapest) the Jewish councils were used only as intermediaries for the preparation and distribution of summonses for the Jews specified on lists prepared by the SS and their accomplices. In others, they were compelled to participate in the roundup. In still others, they were ordered to select a certain number of Jews for surrender to the SS by a specific date. In all these cases, the Jewish leaders used almost the same rationalizations to justify their actions. Their assumption was that by obeying and carrying out the Germans' order themselves they could mitigate the suffering of the victims and save at least part, if not the majority, of the ghetto population, whereas disobeying, let alone resisting, would not only aggravate the immediate situation of the Jews but also inevitably lead to their total destruction. The choice, as many of them conceive it, was basically one between total extermination and partial survival.[39]

The actions and reactions of the Jewish council members reflected both the different realities of the respective communities and their perception of these realities. The Jewish leaders' perceptions of the policies and objectives of the Nazis were distorted and to some extent influenced by the personal favors the SS extended to them and their families. This was a standard SS approach in all the countries under Nazi rule, not only toward Jewish leaders but also toward Christian local officials, as a way to acquire their confidence and cooperation.[40] In the case of the Jewish leaders, these favors consisted primarily of exemption for them and their immediate families from anti-Jewish measures. The benefits were normally short-lived; at the close of Final Solution measures in a particular area, the leaders would normally also be picked up and subjected to the same treatment as the rest.

Wartime Attitudes Toward the Councils

No empirical data are available on the attitudes toward the councils of the Jewish masses within or outside the ghettos. The documentary materials that are available, including the minutes of the council meetings, the diaries, and postwar memoirs and personal narratives, reveal a complex picture which precludes generalizations. In most of the ghettos, the Jewish councils were perceived—at the beginning at least—not so much as instrumentalities created by the Germans primarily to serve their own interests, but as institutions run by Jewish leaders eager and willing to help their communities. In many places the ghettos were at first perceived as enclaves of safety, where the Jews, led by their own community leaders and protected by their own militia, would be shielded from the wanton attacks of the Nazis and their local accomplices. The idea of Jewish autonomy was in fact exploited by the Nazis, who deceived the Jews by taking advantage of their predilection for self-government. The case of Theresienstadt illustrates the extent to which the Jews were unaware of the Nazis' sinister designs. The first "settlers" of this camp were idealistic Zionists who thought of setting up a *hachshara*, a training and vocational education center for the Jews of Bohemia and Moravia, in order to retrain them to become pioneers for Palestine.

However, with the passage of time, the deepening frustration and anger of the ghetto dwellers, caused by the ever increasing hunger, disease, and executions, was increasingly directed against the councils—to the great satisfaction of the Germans. The perceived and real inequities of the measures enacted by the councils became the subject of vocal criticism and occasionally of outright defiance. The intensity of the opposition and its manifestations varied. Occasionally, much of the opposition came from within the council itself. Sometimes this was due to intrigues; at other times it was on matters of principle. Opposition from outside the council was most frequently articulated by the representatives of the Zionist groups and political parties operating underground. In many places the councils were also under pressure from various gangs and cliques, which occasionally relied on the influence of the Nazis to pursue their selfish interests. In still others, opposition to the council came from the ghetto population. For example, during the first year of the war, there were mass street demonstrations in the ghettos of Częstochowa, Łódź, and Lublin, among others. Individuals in many ghettos showed their opposition by refusing to heed the orders of the councils pertaining to the payment of taxes and fees and the fulfillment of labor obligations. As a matter of fact, the taxation policy, the housing program, and the labor plans of many of the councils were indeed quite unfair. Through bribery and other means the rich and those with connections could, before the deportations at least, escape the brunt of many anti-Jewish measures, placing a commensurately greater burden upon the poor and unprotected. Emanuel Ringelblum, the noted chronicler of the Warsaw ghetto, in his diary entry of January 1942 bitterly remarked that the council's work was "an evil perpetrated against the poor that cries to the very heaven."[41] During the early phase of the war, the underground leaders did not openly challenge the councils. In most places they agreed in principle with the positions taken by the councils in the attempt to assure the continued existence of the ghettos, even after the first *Aktionen* were launched in the former Soviet-held territories. In the context of the conditions at the time, they recognized that revolt within the ghettos was not a means of rescue but a road to certain, though honorable, death. This option was almost universally recognized as reasonable, for during this period the majority of the ghetto populations were still alive and there was no inkling of the impending general disaster. However, when the patterns of the Nazis' design became discernible to the underground leaders, they adopted a more militant and antagonistic posture toward the councils. They began to subject the council leaders to increasingly severe criticism both within and outside the ghettos. In Warsaw and in many other ghettos in eastern Europe, the Jewish resistance organizations, composed primarily of Zionist-oriented young men and women, were increasingly appalled by the involvement of the Jewish leaders and the Jewish police in the deportation process and openly challenged the councils, offering themselves as alternatives to the leadership. They frequently expressed their opposition by arresting and executing persons they identified as collaborators.[42] In other instances the underground interfered with the work of the councils or issued stern warnings to them. In Brussels, for example, a detachment of the *Partisans Armés* (Armed Partisans) under the command of Charles Rochmann occupied the council's building on July 25, 1942, destroyed most of its files, and warned the Jewish leaders about their nefarious activities.[43] Similar warnings were issued by the underground to the Hungarian Jewish leaders.[44]

While in retrospect the underground obviously had a more accurate perception of the Germans' intentions and was more sensitive to the plight of the masses, in the context of the Nazi era it is somewhat unfair to compare their activities with those of the Jewish councils. The council leaders were openly identified as established leaders—whether designated, elected, or self-appointed—and had the dual responsibility of carrying out the tasks imposed by a relentless enemy and of fulfilling their obligations, however meagerly, to a constantly dwindling community; the resistance leaders, on the other hand, obviously had no such explicit responsibilities and enjoyed a modicum of security by virtue of their cover of anonymity.[45]

The conflict between the councils and the resistance movements was not evident all the time, and in many places it did not even exist. For one thing, in many communities there were no resistance movements (Jewish or non-Jewish) at all. In many others the councils covertly cooperated with the underground leaders in rescue operations and even in the preparation of battle plans in anticipation of the liberating Allied armies. In still others, albeit in only a limited number of smaller Jewish communities, including Łachwa, Tuczyn, and Zdzieciol in Poland, the Jewish councils were in fact in the forefront of the resistance.[46] The paths and techniques adopted both by the councils and by the underground groups varied. Ultimately, neither provided a means of rescue for the masses—something that was beyond their power—in the face of a totalitarian enemy who was strong enough to defeat temporarily most of the well-equipped armies of Europe and who was single-mindedly devoted to the achievement of its ideologically defined high-priority goal: the extermination of an entire people. The activities of the Jewish councils, including their unwilling and unwitting cooperation with the Nazis, reflected primarily the helplessness and defenselessness of the Jewish people. The record of the councils varied from country to country for reasons beyond their control. Some of them were more successful in serving their communities than others. But whatever their mistakes and whatever the level of their cooperation and collaboration, one must never forget that the ultimate responsibility for the Holocaust must be borne almost exclusively by the Germans and their accomplices all over Europe.

14

Theological Interpretations of the Holocaust
A Balance

AMOS FUNKENSTEIN

The Meaning of Meaning

That the extermination of the Jews in Europe ought to arrest the attention of theologians seems obvious. That it has actually done so, especially in the last decade, and continues to do so, is a fact. But what we *mean* when we ask about the theological "meaning" of the Holocaust is far from obvious. For some it means the meaning *of* the catastrophe in inherited theological terms: an attempt to salvage a theodicy from the rubble left by the eruption of evil as an apparently autonomous force. For others it means the meaning of the catastrophe *for* theology: either in a polemical vein, when they address the failure or even complicity of rival theologies; or critically, when they question the legitimacy of their own theological heritage in the shadow of the systematic destruction of human life and dignity. I shall call these trends, in turn, the direct, the polemical, and the critical-reflexive modes of theologizing about the Holocaust. And I shall argue that the first is offensive, the second hypocritical, and the third not radical enough even in its most radical manifestations.

The Holocaust as Punishment and Signal

One of the few who dare to state that the Holocaust is perfectly comprehensible in traditional theological terms shall serve as our starting point. From the extreme case we may learn something about seemingly more reasonable attempts in the same direction.

Shortly after the foundation of the state of Israel, there appeared a book with the typical rabbinical title *And It Pleased Moses (Vayo'el Moshe)*.[1] Its author, R. Yoel Taitlbaum, was the leader of an ultra-Orthodox, anti-Zionist, cohesive movement whose branch in Israel is known as the "Guardians of the City" (Neture Karta). It summarizes all traditions in support of passive messianism—I shall explain the term immediately—and concludes that the Holocaust was an inevitable consequence of, and punishment for, a formidable sin: the transgression of the divine warning not to seek redemption by one's own hands, through human initiative. His argument is as follows:

"Because of our sins we have been exiled from our land." The dispersion and oppression of the Jewish nation in the diaspora has a punitive-cathartic function, and only God can call an end to the punishment. Those who wish to "precipitate the end" and force God's hand through human action are, whether or not they know it, rebels. Three times the Song of Songs repeats an oathlike formula: "I put you under oath, the daughters of Jerusalem, in the name of the deer and the gazelles of the field, not to hasten nor to precipitate love until it desires." An old exegetical tradition justified the inclusion of such eminently secular love songs in the canon of sacred scriptures on the grounds that it ought to be read *only* allegorically, as a dialogue between God and the spirit of Israel (or, in other quarters, the *ecclesia*). The three oaths, we are taught in the tractate Ketubot of the Babylonian Talmud, have a particular allegoresis.[2] The threefold repetition of the formula refers to three oaths imposed on Israel and on the nations of the world after the destruction of the temple. Israel was held by oath not to rebel against the nations among which it is held as a "prisoner of war," and not to try and "hasten the end." In return, the nations of the world were held by the third oath not to oppress Israel *too* much.

From these premises Taitlbaum draws an outrageous conclusion. Because, in the course of the Zionist movement, an ever growing number of Jews broke the oath and took their fate into their own hands—they wished to turn, in Herzl's words, "from a political object into a political subject"—the nations of the world, in turn, likewise felt themselves free of the oath not to oppress Israel too much, and oppress they did. Why did they? Taitlbaum assumes, as a matter of course, that "Esau always hates Jacob," inherently and incessantly. The Holocaust is the inevitable consequence of the Jewish spontaneous drive toward sovereignty or even autonomy. It is not even the last catastrophe: The perpetration of the sin continued with the foundation of the state of Israel. A catastrophe is imminent, after which only a few, the "remnants of Israel," will survive to witness the true redemption. Indeed, Taitlbaum's whole argument is embedded in the apocalyptical premise that the true redemption, through divine miracle, is very close at hand. The times preceding it are, in the traditional imagery, times of extreme wars and tribulations, times replete with false hopes and false Messiahs.

In a curious way Taitlbaum shares the belief that the messianic days are at the threshold with his Orthodox adversaries, the "Bloc of the Faithful" (Gush Emunim).[3] They too assume that hatred against Jews is inherent in the nations of the world because the choice of God fell upon Israel, or, in the more secular version of U. Z. Greenberg, because Israel is "the race of Abraham, which had started on its way to become master."[4] They regard the Holocaust and the subsequent formation of the state of Israel and its wars as a divine signal for an active preparation in "the dawn of our redemption." Since our time is the time of the messianic war, and redemption has already started, it is incumbent upon Jews to conquer and hold to the promised borders of their holy land, to shape it into a *civitas dei*. For Taitlbaum the Holocaust came because Jews were too active; for the Gush Emunim, because Jews were too passive; for both it is a portent of the Messiah.

Two distinct traditions of Jewish messianism clash here in their exaggerated forms: the passive-utopian messianic tradition as opposed to active-realistic messianism. The former has been by far the predominant tradition, an antidote of the rabbinical establishment against dangerous messianic eruptions; the latter, although a minority tradition, has had a continuous career and some notable authorities on its side: Maimonides, Jacob Berab, Zvi Kalisher. Maimonides, to whom world history is a continuous history of the monotheization of the world guided by God's "List der Vernunft"—i.e., "Miracles of the category of the possible"—saw also in the messianic days a period within history without change in cosmic or human nature.[5] He believed that there were some ways to precipitate them through human initiative, as by the reconstruction of the old court system in the land of Israel. Jacob Berab, who tried to implement this plan through the attempt to renew the pristine ordination, was rebuked by the Jerusalemite head of the court, who insisted that the messianic days can come only as a package deal: no element of them can be taken out of its miraculous context to be implemented now.[6] Kalisher, in the nineteenth century, devoted his life to encouraging settlement in Israel or even the renewal of some sacrifices in the present for the very same reasons. Note that this "active messianism" is not a precursor of Zionism. On the contrary: Zionism started with an antimessianic claim, a desire for sovereignty irrespective of messianic expectations. Both Taitlbaum and the Gush Emunim represent pre-Zionistic mentalities. Both are, in different ways, fossils of the past, albeit poisonous fossils.

The ideology of passive messianism, to which Taitlbaum is an heir, should not be confused with the myth of the physical passivity of diaspora Jewry. Why did Jews not offer resistance in the face of their extermination? Raul Hilberg, in the introduction to his monumental book,[7] refers to the alleged two thousand years of mental conditioning in appeasement. Passivity, he believes, was an intrinsic mental feature of diaspora Jewry. This is a myth as widespread as it is dangerous; dangerous it is because it suggests an artificial gap between the passive diaspora mentality and the active, healthy mentality of the new species of Jew in Israel. Neither in antiquity nor in the Middle Ages did Jews abstain from physical resistance in the face of persecution, whenever feasible. They resisted during the Crusaders' pogroms, the Chmielnicki pogroms, and modern pogroms. Resistance during the Nazi occupation was no less than among most other occupied populations. At best, one could ask why German Jews were not more active in the resistance movement until 1939, or why there was more cooperation than necessary later. But if there was passivity, it was not a heritage of diaspora mentality but rather of modern vintage. To the modern European Jew, who identified himself with the state he lived in, resistance against his state seemed outside the universe of discourse; nor could he conceive of a state acting against the *raison d'état.* The preemancipation Jew, by contrast, always saw himself as an alien, as a "prisoner of war," and was always on the alert. The legal principle, "the law of the kingdom is valid law," which was quoted by some reformers of the nineteenth century to prove the priority of state law even in Jewish terms, originally meant the opposite. It pertained to property only and delineated a *Widerstandsrecht:* only if a ruler acts in accord with the law of the land is one obliged to obey him.[8] The ideology of passive messianism is the only true nucleus of the myth of passivity: it served to emphasize the lack of acute political aspiration. In a way, then, the political emancipation and acculturation of Jews in Europe opened

278

the way for two extreme, new possibilities: total passivity and total self-assertion. In the language of Sartre, the postemancipation Jew may be said to live in a constant "situation" of "*être-vu*":[9] he shunned it by identifying with the aggressor, or defined it by becoming Zionist.

At best, passive messianism was an ideology, not a legally binding position. It was prevalent once, but is obsolete today even among the Orthodox. Why then dignify Taitlbaum's insult to common sense and decency with a detailed discussion? Because in theology, as in the law, much can be learned from extreme-limit cases. An overt absurdity is better than a covert one. Jewish theologians who are less extreme than either Taitlbaum or the Gush Emunim, such as E. Fackenheim or E. Berkovits,[10] admit that they can see no theological rationale to the Holocaust. The Holocaust is incomprehensible, they say, and defies all theodicies. But they do find a theological meaning in the survival: the survival of each man or the survival of the nation and the rebirth of the state. In both they find a confirmation of the divine presence and a promise to preserve Israel.

Even these diluted versions of a theodicy are offensive. Having survived while others—close family and friends—have not is a terrible burden to many survivors. Haunted by excruciating memories, many of them refused to talk or reminisce in the years following internment; some of them do so only now, fearing that true memories will be lost within their generation. It may well be that the state of Israel too owes its establishment in part to the Holocaust; but this also is a terrible burden, not a sign of chosenness or divine grace. Similar perceptions may have moved George Steiner in his recent book, tasteless as it may otherwise be.[11] There is only one instance of theologizing in Primo Levi's account of his survival in Auschwitz. It reads:

> Now everyone is busy scraping the bottom of his bowl with his spoon so as not to waste the last drops of the soup; a confused, metallic clatter, signifying the end of the day. Silence slowly prevails and then, from my bunk on the top row, I see and hear old Kuhn praying aloud, with his beret on his head, swaying backwards and forwards violently. Kuhn is thanking God because he has not been chosen.
>
> Kuhn is out of his senses. Does he not see Beppo the Greek in the bunk next to him, Beppo who is twenty years old and is going to the gas chamber the day after tomorrow and knows it and lies there looking fixedly at the light without saying anything and without even thinking any more? Can Kuhn fail to realize that the next time it will be his turn? Does Kuhn not understand that what has happened today is an

abomination, which no propitiatory prayer, no pardon, no expiation
by the guilty, which nothing at all in the power of man can ever clean
again?

If I was God, I would spit at Kuhn's prayer.[12]

Anti-Judaism and Anti-Semitism

Recent history may or may not have a theological meaning, but it
certainly carries a meaning for theology—more concretely, for Christianity. Jewish and Christian theologies devote considerable energies to accusing, expiating, or reformulating past and present Christian attitudes
toward Jews and Judaism. How deeply is Christianity implicated in the
formation of the preconditions for the genocide of Jews? Is Christianity
at all capable of changing its anti-Judaic attitudes without risking its very
foundations?

No sincere historical interpretation doubts that the anti-Jewish postures of Christianity were the single most important factor in the continuity of anti-Jewish sentiments since antiquity, that at least the silence
of the churches while Jews were deprived of their legal rights, then
chased and exterminated, was in part made possible by the previous theological alienation. This is a silence in contrast to the firm and effective
stand of the German clergy against euthanasia. If, however, it could be
shown that the antagonism between church and synagogue were not part
of original Christianity, then—so we hear from some theologians—it
could also be severed successfully from the main body of Christian doctrines.

This is a fallacious argument, logically as well as historically. It is
logically fallacious because, hard as it may try, Christianity cannot return
to the conditions of the *primitiva ecclesia:* an apocalyptic Jewish sect
withdrawn from the world. The very program of *"reformatio"* is inacces-
sible. At best, one could arbitrarily choose some elements of original
Christianity and declare them to be essential, while inevitably discarding
others; but then one need not exclude the further history of Christianity
either and distinguish sharply between *"Christentum und Kultur"* (Over-
beck). The very same arguments which have already constituted the crisis of Protestant theology for a hundred years apply also in regard to its
treatment of Judaism.

But we ought nonetheless to separate the various ingredients and
driving forces in Christian anti-Jewish doctrines. It is true that the anti-

280

Jewish ideology of the Church was not contingent upon social, political, or economic conditions only. But neither was it a product of hatred only. The Jews have always been, and remain, a *mysterium tremendum et fascinosum* to the Christian Church. The preoccupation with the phenomenon of Judaism and of continuous Jewish existence belongs to the very essence and self-definition of Christianity as a historical religion. But, contrary to common opinion, I hasten to add that the ambivalence of fascination and rejection is equally characteristic of the Jewish attitude toward Christianity—more than toward any other religion, including Islam. We shall also see that some of the Christian attitudes were religious-theological in nature, while others were not even that when given a theological guise. The latter distinction may clarify the present theological situation. The historical progress of Christian attitudes toward Jews and Judaism seems to me as follows.

The Pagan Attitude[13]   Christian anti-Judaism appears in a much sharper light when compared to its antecedents. Christianity did not inherit the anti-Jewish arguments of pagan antiquity: those were political and ethnic in origin, born in part out of the aggressive Hasmonaean policies against the Greek population of the land of Israel and in part out of competition over privileges in Egypt. Under the Roman Empire, Jewish insurrection and the menace of the missionary impact of Judaism combined to perpetuate anti-Jewish propaganda and attitudes.[14]

Christianity may have, since the second century, inherited some of the pagan anti-Jewish sentiments; it could, however, make no use of pagan anti-Jewish propaganda. Christians, for example, never denied the title Jews once had to the land of Israel up to the time of the rise of Christianity, when the choice of God shifted from "Israel according to the flesh" to the "true Israel" (*verus Israel*), "Israel in the spirit," i.e., the "Church from among the nations" (*ecclesia ex gentibus*). The keener minds among the pagan polemicists employed a typical technique: they manipulated an inverted reading of biblical passages so as to construct their own version of Jewish origins—they constructed a counterhistory, just as Jews were later to do to Christianity in the *Sefer Toledot Yeshu*. The Bible itself aided pagan polemicists in their anti-Jewish diatribes. Does not the Bible admit that the Canaanites were driven out by force?[15] And more: does not the Bible itself concede that the people of Israel lived as outcasts in seclusion in the Egyptian province of Goshen; that Moses grew up as an Egyptian; that a riffraff (*assafsuf*), a mixed multitude (*erev-rav*), went out of Egypt? Indeed, for the Hebrews were not a ven-

erable old nation nor is their constitution authentic and worth preserving. Rather, they started out as an Egyptian leper colony, secluded and
despised, until they called to their aid the Semitic tribes of the Hyksos
and established a reign of terror for over a century (this inverts the story
of Joseph's rise to power). Expelled by Iachmes I, the Hyksos, together
with the outcasts, left Egypt, led by a renegade Egyptian priest named
Osarsiph (Moses). He gave them a constitution which was, in all respects, a plagiarized, inverted mirror image of Egyptian mores. Or, as
Tacitus was later to say: "Moses . . . introduced new laws contrary to
those of the rest of mankind. Whatever is sacred to us, is profane to
them; and what they concede, we regard as sacrilege."[16] They conquered
Canaan by force and established a commonwealth worthy of outcasts—
secluded and disguised by a sense of election—calculated to perpetuate
their rebellious spirit and their hatred of the human race (*misanthropia;
odium humani generis*).

And ingenious propaganda it was. Indeed, Manetho's description of
the way in which outcasts preserve their sense of value by constructing a
counterideology in which their discrimination is interpreted as a sign of
special election, is strongly reminiscent of what modern sociologists of
knowledge describe as the formation of a "counteridentity."[17]

This tradition of pagan anti-Jewish propaganda is notable for what it
lacks as much as for what it contains. It would be futile to look for a
religious polemic against monotheism, since most of the pagan intelligentsia was, in a manner of speaking, likewise "monotheistic." From
Xenophanes through Aristotle to Plotinus, Greek philosophy developed
an ever more deanthropomorphized and rarefied image of God, a natural
religion (*theologia naturalis*).[18] Already Xenophanes advanced the most
dominant critical argument in the history of the critique of religion until
Feuerbach and Freud: that man makes his gods in his own image, that is,
transfers, or projects, his (and his society's) vices and virtues upon the
transcendent. The educated Greco-Roman intellectual believed, by and
large, that beyond the "political cult" (*theologia politica*), religion is one
of a variety of cults.

Augustine puts similar words into the mouth of Porphyrius;[19] and
even our Sages let a pagan philosopher conversing with Rabbi Akiva say,
"We both know in our heart that there is no reality in idolatry."[20] In
other words, church fathers and *tana'im* alike were aware that theirs was
not the only monotheistic creed among polytheistic ones. The clash between Judeo-Christian and pagan theologies was not over the number of
gods but over the nature of the one God. To the Greek mind God was

282

the embodiment of the principle of cosmic harmony, passive and self-contained: the idea of God as a moral personality active in history, an all-powerful busybody, was repulsive. That God abandoned the care of the cosmos in order to concentrate on the affairs of a small, dirty nation in the provinces seems to Celsus "a frog-and-rainworm perspective."[21]

Nonetheless, monotheism was one of the most attractive features of Judaism to the pagan mind; was not Judaism a true philosophical religion, worshiping a philosophical principle rather than anthropomorphic images? The very first reaction of educated Greeks to the encounter with Judaism was one of admiration.[22] No pagan polemicist could attack the monotheistic idea as such. But he could venture to show that there is nothing original or authentic in Jews of Judaism, nothing venerable and worth preserving in their laws and customs. The missionary successes of Judaism and later of Christianity proved how hopelessly unpersuasive this pagan propaganda was.

The Christian Attitude Christianity, we have said, had no use for the body of pagan anti-Jewish propaganda. But Christian-Jewish antagonism reaches back to the time when Christianity was still a Jewish apocalyptic sect. With other sectarian movements—for example, the Dead Sea Scrolls sect—Christians shared a hatred for the normative Jewish establishment. Already the sectarians of Qumran defined themselves as a "holy community" (*adat kodesh*) and the establishment as a "false city" (*ir shav*)—*civitas dei* against *civitas terranea*. They alone were remnants of Israel; they alone possessed the key for the eschatological "decoding" (*pesher*) of Scriptures; they were, in short, an avant-garde of the new, magnificent cosmic order in the midst of the old and corrupt one. At times, they imply that only they, "the eternal stock," will be saved at the imminent end of days. And they subsume the existing establishment under the category of "children of darkness" and are admonished "to love all children of light each according to his lot and to hate all children of darkness each according to his guilt in the vengeance of God."[23] Like them in many respects, the early Christians saw themselves as *verus Israel* and the rest of the Jews as condemned. Belief in Christ, as earlier the belief in the "Righteous Teacher" (*moreh zedek*),[24] became the true sign of salvation. Like them, early Christianity developed a hatred of the establishment of "Pharisees and Sadducees."

Soon early Christianity was to compete with the Jewish establishment in their missionary efforts—first among the God-fearing people (*yire'ei shamayim* [Hebrew] or *hoi sebomenoi* [Greek]), the large groups of adorers of Judaism on the fringe of many diaspora communities, and later among real pagans. Mutual antagonism was reinforced by the competition over proselytes. It was also reinforced by the inner conflicts in Christianity between Gentile and Jewish Christians. It was further sealed by the abstention of Christians from the second revolt (132–135 C.E.) against Rome, a revolt which, unlike the first, seems to have been unanimous. But after the second revolt against Rome and the Hadrianic persecutions that followed, Judaism lost its missionary impetus; eventually, Christianity became the dominant imperial religion—"the kingdom became heretical";[25] and the once strong Judeo-Christian elements in the Church disappeared.

What purpose could Christian anti-Jewish doctrines have served thereafter? Why did no generation pass without leaving various anti-Jewish tracts? What is the logic behind such an enormous body of literature which is as unsavory as it is repetitious? For it ceased to be a record of living polemics and became, more and more, a stereotypic enumeration of veiled hints in the Old Testament for the veracity of the New Testament.

The function of anti-Jewish propaganda was not external—to convert Jews—but internal. Precisely because the Church failed to convert the Jews, their very existence became a theological paradox of the first order. Not so for Islam: unlike the Church, Islam does not view its raison d'être as the individual conversion of each and every infidel. True, the world must be made "safe for Islam" through political hegemony; but under Muslim rule, the people possessing a genuine (monotheistic) revelation like Jews and Christians—the legal term is "people of the book" (ahl al kitāb)—may retain their religious-political autonomy as a protected, second-class minority (dhimmis).[26] By contrast, the Christian Church proves its veracity through worldwide mission: it is an ecclesia militans. Yet the conversion of the Jews, who were originally the chosen people and still held to the Old Testament in its original language, was impossible either by persuasion or force.

"Israel according to the flesh" (Israel secundum carnem), they were called: Christianity and Judaism alike shared the fiction that the Jews were literally the descendants of Abraham; they differed only in the assessment of the value of such ethnic continuity. Secundum carnem also refers to the mentality of the Jews: they understand their Scriptures and laws "literally" rather than with a sublimated understanding (spiritualis intellegentia); they are, therefore, "blind" to the various veiled hints in the Old Testament as to the veracity of the New Testament; they are a

284

living anachronism—"These Jews refused to change with the times"[27]—
a fossil. They failed to understand that Judaism (circumcision) was "good
for its time" only[28] and had to be superseded by a new dispensation for
which it paved the way (Hugh of St. Victor). In short, Jews are a stubborn lot.

But then again, was not their very stubbornness also admirable? Augustine thought so,[29] and wished for Christians of his day to have some
of it in the face of persecution and temptation. More than that, Jews
and Judaism continued to fascinate Christians by virtue of their antiquity—that very antiquity which in theory was denigrated. Throughout its career, the Church feared Judaizers (*Judaizantes*) in its midst.
After all, the very claim of the Church to be a *new* dispensation introduced a shift of values both in the classical world and among the
converted Germanic tribes of the Middle Ages. "New" was to both mentalities a suspicious attribute: only the old was a mark of quality and
authenticity. The classical political term for a dangerous revolutionary
was *homo rerum novarum cupidus;* in the legal consciousness of the early
Middle Ages, only old law (*altes Recht*) was good law (*gutes Recht*),[30] and
Pope Gregory VII shocked his imperial adversaries when he claimed his
right to establish new laws (*novas leges condere*).[31] An inherent tension
was thus introduced into the European mentality between the veneration
of the old and the glorification of the new. The antiquity and very existence of Jews and Judaism was used by Christians in their antipagan
propaganda—to prove the authenticity of the Bible. That Judaism was
the authentic monotheistic religion because it was the oldest had also
been a Jewish argument—witness Judah Halevi's *Kuzari;* and the few
cases of medieval conversions of Judaism we know of were prompted by
such sentiments.

Eventually, the church fathers developed a doctrine to justify the
continued existence of the Jews as part of the economy of salvation,[32]
and a praxis of anti-Jewish legislation to go with it. The Jews fulfill a
threefold function. Their physical existence proves the authenticity of
their Scriptures against pagan contentions; they guarantee the preservation of the authentic revelation and must continue to do so. Moreover,
their very humiliation in dispersion is an everlasting proof (*testimonium
aeternum*) of the Christian claim that, with the coming of Christ, "the
scepter has ceased from Judah" and God's choice was transferred from
"Israel in the flesh" to "Israel in the spirit." The present status of the
synagogue as a "slave" to the Church testifies to the superiority of the
latter. And finally: the Jews have an eschatological function. At the end

of days their remnants will convert to Christianity en masse and perhaps even save Christianity from the Antichrist. Such was the explanation of Jewish existence—and of the relative tolerance to be extended toward them. It rested on the firm assumption that the Jews did not change; that they adhered now as before to the letter of the Bible. Perhaps even their clothes had not changed. To Anskar, we hear from his biographer, Christ appeared "tall of stature, clothed as a Jew, beautiful in appearance."[33]

New Patterns of the Twelfth Century   The Jews then were to be tolerated by the Church on the condition that they play the double role of slave and fossil. They refused to conform to either. In fact, they were a privileged minority and developed distinctly aristocratic tastes. Legally and mentally, they were all too close to the ruling powers-that-be, "pertaining to the royal palace." A Jewish boy in Germany could daydream about becoming a knight even in the twelfth century. Much later, Schlomo ibn Verga, reflecting on the Spanish Expulsion of 1492, identified the drive to reach the pinnacles of society and to boast about it as a major cause of the catastrophe. Throughout the Middle Ages, Jews were seen and saw themselves, as "prisoners of war" on alien soil, but they hardly acted like it. Nor did they agree to remain a fossil. Instead, they developed an impressive, adaptable system of laws and institutions and created a vast body of interpretive and speculative literature. The discrepancy between image and reality, and the ever present reserves of popular hostility toward strangers, and Jews in particular, served as possible sources of tension.

The turning point in the history of Christian anti-Jewish doctrines came at a crucial moment of Jewish life in Europe, during the twelfth century. Several factors contributed to the deterioration of the status of Jews then: the growing independence and power of the Church, the Crusades, the growth of popular religious movements, and the fact that, since the Spanish *reconquista*, the majority of Jews in Europe lived in Christian countries. Anti-Jewish doctrines changed now in quantity and in quality. Not only did they increase; they changed patterns. The new patterns created then were to last to the eighteenth century. Alongside the other categories of stereotypes, new kinds of propaganda are clearly recognizable.

Sometimes the new image could be fitted to older stereotypes. The image of Jews as economic exploiters, "usurers," was born out of new circumstances; in antiquity, Josephus only repeats a commonplace when he regrets the Jewish lack of commercial skills compared to Greeks and

286

Phoenicians. Once born, the new stereotype comfortably adapted to old theological ones. "Israel in the flesh" is always oriented toward worldly rewards, even when keeping the precepts, and all the more so in the secular domain. Sometimes new stereotypes collided with the old or replaced them. The latter process, which led to the alienation and demonization of the Jewish image in the later Middle Ages, deserves further scrutiny.

An altogether new stereotype of this kind was the stereotype of menace and secrecy; it operated, from now on, on all levels, from the theological to the popular. Beginning with the twelfth century, more and more clergymen became acquainted with Jewish doctrines and with the massive body of postbiblical literature. Some of them turned to Hebraic studies for exegetical advice;[34] others employed it in a new brand of anti-Jewish argument. The Talmud in particular served them as evidence that the Jews were not the simple preservers of the Bible they seemed earlier, that the Jews adhered now to another, new law (*nova lex*), which superseded the biblical laws which Jews were supposed to adhere to "according to the letter." Was not such a new law a heresy even in terms of Judaism proper—as understood by the Church? Was not the tolerance extended toward them based upon the premise that they did not change—and if they did and looked for a new law, then should they not look only toward the true law? Instead of both the Bible and the *lex caritatis,* they seem to have created a new law of their own making. And they adhered to it secretly, so as still to appear as the carriers of the Old Testament.

The first tract in this vein was written in the middle of the twelfth century by Peter the Venerable, abbot of Cluny. This professional peacemaker promised to "unveil" the Jewish secrets: that they had ceased to adhere to the divine law and in fact adhered to a diabolical, man-made, legislation.[35] Bits and pieces of the Talmud, taken out of context, serve him to prove that, far from being a mere literal interpretation, the Talmud itself admits that even God must bow before the decisions of earthly courts, that God himself is bound by Talmudic law. No longer is Judaism seen as an anachronistic, perhaps even ridiculous, but at any rate understandable, religion: its image turns into one of secret, diabolical traditions. Such were also the accusations which led to the trial and burning of the Talmud in Paris (1240).[36]

This dehumanization and demonization of the Jewish image was not confined to a few polemical tracts only. It characterizes first and foremost the popular sermons and the popular imagination.[37] The twelfth century saw the first appearance of the blood libel. Thomas of Monmouth's narrative of the alleged case contains a reference to a converted Jew who revealed to him stipulations in "the old Scriptures of the Jews" according to which Jews are obliged to shed Christian blood at least once a year if indeed they wish to be redeemed. For this purpose a secret rabbinical synod convenes periodically from all over Europe to determine which community is in turn to commit ritual murder.[38] A clear line leads from here to the images invoked in the infamous *Protocols of the Elders of Zion.*[39]

The twelfth century thus revived—if unintentionally—elements of pagan anti-Christian and anti-Jewish propaganda: accusations of secrecy and secretive mores and beliefs generated by the Jewish "misanthropy" (the *odium humani generis* of Tacitus). The Jewish "secrets" (*arcanae*) are directed against the healthy social texture of their environment. Christianity was at first unable to use such arguments: they were also directed against Christians and Christians claimed a share in the Jewish "secrets." In the later Middle Ages, beginning in the twelfth century, Jews once again became mysterious, incomprehensible, and dangerous. The popular demonic image of Jews, including the blood libel, never became the official theological stand of the Church; the Church never actually denied or confirmed those biases and, when convenient, it used them. Nor did the attack on the Talmud continue in the way it had started. How could the Church, always apprehensive of heretics who wish to turn to the "Scriptures alone" and eliminate the authoritative tradition of the Church, ask Jews to adhere to the Scriptures "without a gloss"? Not that the Church could not justify such lack of consequence, but some figures of thought become taboo in any age. The attack on the Talmud continued on other grounds—for example, that it contained blasphemies which should at least be eradicated.

Now the renewed acquaintance of Christian theologians with Jewish writings generated not only repulsion or awareness of polemical opportunities. It also heightened the fascination with Jews which we have already mentioned: fascination with Jewish exegesis (the *veritas hebraica*) and an even more intense fascination with the Kabbalah later on.[40] The Kabbalah is, in a particular way, an example of the dialectics of repulsion and attraction on both sides. It manifests the Jewish fascination with emanatory—even trinitarian—speculations, and early Kabbalists were promptly accused of Christianizing tendencies. The Kabbalist endowed hitherto heretical readings of the Bible with deep mystery—for example, the reading of "God" in Genesis 1:1 as the direct (grammatical) object, rather than subject, of the verse. To the Humanists and Renaissance

288

Platonists it seemed as if an old, secret, pre-Jewish and pre-Christian tradition of the most profound truths was unveiled through the Kabbalah. The "secrecy" and "secret traditions" of the Jews thus implied not only pejorative connotations, connotations such as those captured in the word "cabal" in several European languages. To some they seemed to be of inestimable value and attraction.

Secrecy, secret traditions, and secretive plotting may be ready attributes for minorities in every society. In the later Christian medieval context such popular fears may also have been a mode in which society externalized internal fears and guilt feelings. The Church, the major bulk of serious theologians, may not have generated such images, but at times they succumbed to them. So much so that in later medieval Spain even converted Jews would not avoid suspicion. The massive influx of *conversos* into Spanish society in the fourteenth and fifteenth centuries, far from being perceived even by the Church as the fulfillment of an urgent dream, awoke in it fears of heterodoxy and secret Jewish relapse. An unprecedented social and legal effort to lay bare the secret elements of society poisoned the texture of Spanish life for two centuries and more, turning it into a society obsessed with suspicion, the first state in modern European history to be governed by racial policies. In the name of purity of blood, *marranos* were removed from public office or social position. In these and similar processes, which started in the twelfth century, I do not see religious antagonism but rather antagonisms under the guise of religious differences.

Toward a Non-Christian Attitude Luther's venomous attacks notwithstanding, why did the obsession with Jews and Judaism abate within the Protestant horizon?[41] For one thing, relatively few Jews remained in Protestant parts of Europe; most of them were expelled from western Europe during the later Middle Ages. But the absence of Jews in itself had never impeded anti-Jewish propaganda earlier: it served internal functions. Another reason for the growing indifference towards Jew may be drawn from Protestant theology itself.

The Catholic Church viewed Jews and Judaism—*mutatis mutandis*—as a living example of a life *sola scriptura*, of the sorry fate of those who adhered to the letter of the Scriptures only; it wished to show how necessary the mediation of the Church was, of which authority Augustine once said that unless compelled by it, he would not even believe the Sacred Scriptures. On the other hand, the Church feared, not without cause, possible impacts of this very example. Ambivalence was built into the Christian attitude toward Jews from the outset.

Protestantism could—but did not always successfully—overcome this ambivalence. Protestant theologies oscillated and still oscillated between two poles. Depending on the characteristics they lent to the primitive Church, they either wished to revive biblical mores and institutions—hence the swelling of literature on the "Jewish Republic"—or to separate the New Testament more emphatically from the Old; either way, their attitude toward Jews and Judaism was much less burdened because it was less immediate. There was no *auctoritas sanctae ecclesiae* which the Jewish existence threatened to undermine or promised to confirm. In a few instances, as the late H. H. Ben-Sasson has shown,[42] some sectarian minorities even developed a sense of identification with the Jewish lot *in partibus infidelium*. In other instances, they blamed Judaism and Catholicism alike for obscuring the word of God—and the latter foe was, of course, the more formidable one.

Rationalists of the seventeenth and eighteenth centuries inherited from the Protestant attitude this basic indifference, for better or for worse. Whether a fossil or not, Judaism ceased to be a prime object of altercation.[43] At best, the lot of Jews was employed to exemplify Christian—that is, religious—intolerance. At worst, Judaism was called upon to exemplify religious ethnocentric particularism. At times, attacks on Judaism just served as a guise for attacking Christianity. In all cases, historical-cultural curiosity prevailed over theological discomfort, as we see in Schudt's *"Jüdische Merkwürdigkeiten."*[44]

How much then is the rise of modern anti-Semitism rooted in the Christian tradition?

Anti-Semitic propaganda, whether extreme or moderate, has one outstanding feature.[45] Its target is not so much the traditional, Orthodox Jew who is recognizable as such. The anti-Semite fights first and foremost what he believes to be the Jew in disguise: the emancipated, assimilated Jew who is about to disrupt the healthy texture of the new nation he pretends to belong to. Whether assimilated or not, the Jew is—and remains—an alien, a dangerous, disintegrating force. Being Jewish is a *character indelebilis*, unchangeable by baptism or other external signs of changed identity. Therefore, the first political aim of the anti-Semite is to undo the original sin of nineteenth-century Europe: to revoke legal emancipation granted to Jews and, by discrimination, make them recognizable again. Moderate anti-Semitic ideologues may concede that Jews are subjectively sincere in their wish to assimilate, but in fact are incapable of doing so; more extreme anti-Semites will insist that the outward signs of Jewish identification with the surrounding society and assimilation to it are a dangerous pretext, if not even an (international) Jewish plot to take power; the most extreme anti-Semites will call not only for the annulment of emancipation, but for expulsion and genocide.

Such, in rough outline, is the phenomenology of anti-Semitic utterances. They presuppose emancipation and are directed against it, which makes them a new phenomenon altogether in Jewish history. Needless to say, the anti-Semitic aversion is again only another side of fascination. The anti-Semite appeals to the segments of the population least adapted to the modern, industrialized, capitalistic, and mobile society. He is fascinated, rightly or wrongly, by what he conceives to be Jewish adaptability, and gives it a sinister interpretation. Yet whatever its driving forces,[46] anti-Semitism seems to be worlds apart from Christian anti-Jewish attitudes. Theoretically at least, a converted Jew was, in theological terms, a Christian in all respects. On the other hand, some Protestant trends, which called upon Christianity to sever totally its links to Judaism, even to the Old Testament, needed only a modicum of secularization to become even more anti-Semitic than any Catholic doctrine. From Adolf von Harnack's adoration of Marcion to Houston Stewart Chamberlain's proof that Jesus was an Aryan, the step is a small one to take. But these may be seen as exceptions; all in all, the *ecclesia militans* fights the visible Jew and Judaism; the anti-Semite fights the invisible Jew in society (and in himself).

Yet both theological anti-Judaism and ideological anti-Semitism draw from the same pool of popular biases accumulated over centuries; Christian theological postures, through their very continuity, provided a frame for popular biases. Some recent theologians, such as R. B. Ruether or G. G. Baum, have recognized this dependence. Moreover, from the twelfth century onward, Christian theological doctrines adjusted to popular biases and reflected them more and more: they enhanced the image of danger and secrecy beyond the demands of religious antagonism. Anti-Semitism may indeed be a secularized phenomenon, but here, as elsewhere, secularization does not follow religious attitudes as their pure counterpart. It grows within the framework of the religious mind and institutions long before it gains independence.

Theological Consequences   Such then are the contours of the development of anti-Jewish doctrines, stands, and images. It is, of course, not our task to reformulate or change theological doctrines. We may, however, draw attention to two possible fallacies in the interpretation of the historical diagnosis, the one resulting from an overemphasis, the other from an underestimation, of the power of history.

First, a theologian may argue: anti-Judaism is so inherent in Christianity as a historical continuum that nothing short of an absolutely new beginning will prevent it from becoming once again a depository of anti-Jewish sentiments. Anti-Judaism, we hear from R. B. Ruether, is "the left hand of Christology."[47] The self-criticism of Baum points at the "ideology of substitution" as the source of the heritage of "contempt."[48] E. Berkovits goes even further: only Christianity, in its emphasis on salvation through Christ alone, entails an antihumanistic ethics; Judaism is immune from such abuses.[49] *This is a hypocritical argument.* Jewish religion regards man no less as subservient to God than does Christianity. Judaism always endorsed a *bellum deo auctore,* war commanded by God (*milḥemet ḥova* as opposed to *milḥemet reshut*), while it took Christianity over a thousand years to find the right formula for sanctifying war as a holy mission. Up until the Crusades, even the justified killing of an enemy in a just war (*bellum justum*) required absolution. In the case of the Amalekites and the seven Kena'anitic nations, the biblical demand comes close to a call for genocide. The Edomites were converted by coercion; the Karaites persecuted; distinctions between Israel and "the nations of the world" are no less discriminatory than the principle *nulla salus extra ecclesiam.* Berkovits's claim that from the Jewish legal point of view even a non-Jew can obtain salvation is true only in the sense that it is also true from the Christian point of view—namely, conditionally. "All those who obey the seven laws of the sons of Noah," Maimonides teaches ex cathedra, "are amongst the pious of the nations" and may have a portion in the world to come. But he adds: "When is this the case? If they obey the commandments because these are the will of God. Should they obey them out of rational insight (*hechra hada'at*) only, they are not from the pious amongst the nations nor from amongst their sages." Maimonides goes even further and insists on the obligation to kill all true pagans who refuse to submit to the seven Noachidic precepts; they constitute his equivalent of the true Moslem *ahl el maut.*[50] And this obligation is not as theoretical as the obligation to exterminate the Amalekites and "the seven nations" who once inhabited Kena'an, nations now extinct in his view. Discrimination and degradation can and could be clothed in terms of both religions: to argue that only a Christian world could have led to a genocide is, to say the least, hypocritical.

Second, an underestimation of history can be just as detrimental, or at best result in arbitrary choices. Franklin Little sees the anti-Jewish postures beginning in Christianity only after Paul, with the strong influx of non-Jews.[51] But even if he is right—and our historical remarks suggest that he is not—it makes little difference whether Christianity started to define itself in contraposition to Judaism before or after Paul. The contraposition is part of its historical self-definition. It also matters little whether the origin of antagonism was pagan: so is much of the dogmatic-philosophical language of Christianity. But the contraposition—on which, it is worth remembering, orthodox Judaism insists no less than Christianity—need not be judged by its uncontrolled exaggerations. It need not be a malicious contraposition: my neighbor may well regard all music as cacophony, while for me it may be the very essence and meaning of life, yet I need not hate him for that. With some training I may even learn not to despise him. If our analysis of the course of anti-Judaic postures through history was correct, then the change came from extrareligious sources at the moment in which Judaism ceased to appear as merely an anachronistic, mistaken religious stand and instead came to be seen as a menacing, secretive plot. This evolution, though also a part of the actual history of the Church, can be separated in theory as well as in praxis, not because it came later, but because its source is not in religious images or doctrines at all.

There is one claim which divides Judaism from Christianity (or for that matter from Islam) *because* they share in that claim. At least in their *historical* manifestations, the so-called three monotheistic religions claim to possess the full, authentic, absolute revealed truths exclusively. Each of them may recognize the other monotheistic religions as incomplete, mistaken, or even falsified versions of true principles. The Jews, from the vantage point of Christianity, are fixated at an early stage of revelation. From the vantage point of Islam, both Christianity and Judaism are "people of the book" and need not be coerced to convert, as were pagans. From the vantage point of Judaism, Christianity and Islam seemed to be more or less monotheistic—"nations confined in the boundary of religion" (*umot hagedurot bedarche hadatot*)—though the first was founded by a heretic and the second, we hear from Maimonides, by a lunatic.[52] Yet the full truth resides only in one's own religion. It is this claim which distinguishes them from classical, Greco-Roman paganism, which was tolerant of other cults because *una est religio in varietate rituum*. A pagan intellectual usually despised what Varro called *theologia mythica*; he professed allegiance to the *theologia politica*, the gods of the body politic, and believed only in the *theologia naturalis*—the philosophical truth about all positive religions. Religious intolerance was conceived and introduced rather by the monotheistic religions, though in various degrees.

Can Christianity—or Judaism—abandon the claim for absolute truth without losing their identities altogether? I do not know; but I find suggestions made by some Christian theologians that Christianity should do so close to the conscious syncretism of later pagan antiquity. It is odd that Baum, who recommends the abandonment of the claim that *nulla salus extra ecclesiam*, at the same time blames the Holocaust on the influx of "pagan mentality" in twentieth-century Europe. A trace of hypocrisy can be detected in such fairly common theological prejudices. Whatever "paganism" may mean, in its historical manifestations it was certainly not less humane than Christianity—or Judaism.

"Paganism" often functions, explicitly and implicitly, as synonymous with "secularism." A good many theologians blame the horrors of our century on the loss of religiosity and the triumph of "secularization." This too proves that even the most sincere theologians did not advance their self-criticism far enough. The Holocaust was no more the consequence of irreligiosity than it was the consequence of religiosity. In fact, there are good reasons to suspect theology—Jewish, Christian, or Moslem—as one of the sources for the ideological relativization of merely human values. The very blame for absolute truth and the commitment to higher than human were paradigms for more secular ideologies. The *honor dei* which man is supposed to serve unconditionally could be, and was, transformed into an *honor patriae*. Christian and Jewish insistence on the primacy of God over man could be exchanged for other priorities, such as the working class, race, progress, or equivalent abstract objectifications. True, no religious attitude should be blamed for its misrepresentation or caricaturization. The fact that Hitler often chose to speak a language saturated with religious images ("*Vorsehung*"—providence—being the most common), is no proof that he was, consequently, a Christian: Hermann Rauschning's "*Gespräche mit Hitler*" and other documents are rather a proof, to the contrary, of his strong anti-Christian sentiments. But least of all may theologians blame areligiosity for ideologies and practices of "absolute dependence" on and subservience to abstract principles—a term which, we remember, Schleiermacher employed to *define* religion. We shall return to this point later.

Reading Jacques Basnages's *Histoire de la religion des Juifs depuis Jésus Christ jusqu'à présent* (Rotterdam 1707)—it was the very first endeavor of a Christian author to narrate the development of Jews and postbiblical Judaism in a coherent, nonpolemical vein—Heinrich Heine reacted with a poetic reflection, "To Edom" (1824). ("Edom" is a traditional Jewish metaphor for Rome and for Christianity.) The time was shortly after the *Hep–Hep* pogroms. It seems a fitting summary to this discussion.

TO EDOM	AN EDOM
A thousand years and more we suffer	Ein Jahrtausend schon und länger
Each other, for so long an age.	Dulden wir uns brüderlich;
You—you tolerate my breathing,	Du, du duldest das ich atme,
And I tolerate your rage	Das du rasest, dulde ich.
Only sometimes, in dark hours, When your curious mood just grows,	Manchmal nur, in dunkeln Zeiten Ward dir wunderlich zu Mut.
With my blood you seemed to color	Und die liebefrommen Tätzchen Färbtest du mit meinem Blut!
Your so neat and pious paws.	
Our friendship now grows stronger,	Jetzt wird unsre Freundschaft fester
And increases daily too.	Und noch täglich nimmt sie zu;
And I also begin raging,	Denn ich selbst begann zu rasen,
To become almost like you!	Und ich werde fast wie du!

[*Translation, A. F.*]

The Dialectical Theology of Meaninglessness

To the most courageous among recent theologians, the very meaninglessness of the Holocaust constitutes its theological meaning. To lose faith in the face of the Holocaust is itself, they say, a manner of faith, a positive religious act. When, in the eleventh century, Anselm of Canterbury advanced his ontological proof of God's existence, he also gave a new meaning to the Psalm's verse: "The fool [wicked] hath said in his heart: there is no God." Since God's existence is necessarily implied by his very concept, whoever thinks of God yet denies his existence cannot but be foolish (wicked). The modern theologians I have in mind—Rahner, Baum, Rubenstein, and others—turned Anselm on his head. "A person deeply troubled by the Holocaust and made unable to affirm God's presence is caught in an essentially religious question and hence already under the influence of God's grace. If a person were shallow, or wholly pragmatic, or egotistical, or only concerned about protecting his own interests, he would not be troubled at all. He is troubled because he is religious."[53] Even atheists, Vatican II reminds us, may be touched by grace.

The admission that God—or ethical theism—died in Auschwitz because Auschwitz defies all meaning calls, we are told, for a radical change of the most fundamental premises.

> What has emerged in our theological reflection based on Karl Rahner is a rather different religious imagination. Here God is not conceived of as a lord ruling history from above, but as the vitality at the core of people's lives making them ask the important questions and moving them toward their *authentic* existence. God is conceived here as the *ground* of human existence, as the summons operative in their lives, and as the *horizon* toward which they move. God is not so much lord of the universe as heart of the world. What is emphasized in this theology is what theologians call Divine immanence, which in ordinary [!] language means God's being *in-and-through the world*. . . . God's presence to people changes them, severs them from destructive trends, and moves them towards a more creative future. . . . But the in-and-throughness of God does not leave the world as it is; it judges the world and *summons* it to new life.[54]

Yet even here, where theologians are most courageous, false tunes are unavoidable. The key phrases underlined by us point unmistakably to a definite philosophical source. Exchange "God" for "being" (*Sein*); the rest of the vocabulary is Heidegger's. Seemingly without ethical judgments, Heidegger distinguishes two modes of human existence, the inauthentic and the authentic. So does the quoted passage. *Dasein*, "Being-there" or existence, is the only form in which the elusive *Sein*, "being" (in contrast to *Seiendes*, "entities") is concerned with itself: "[*Das Dasein ist ein Seiendes*], *dem es in seinem Sein um dieses Sein selbst geht.*"[55] Yet in its first and average occurrence it is alienated from itself, lost in the world (*In-der-welt-sein*) in such a manner that it uses things in the world (*Zuhanden-sein*) and is absorbed in it. With every man are inseparably others with whom he shares the concern (*Sorge*) with the mundane. *Dasein* is inauthentic in that state, it is "man"—everyone—characterized by *Seinvergessenheit*, disconcern with its true self-being. It flees fear (*Angst*) rather than facing it, facing its basic feature as *Geworfen-sein*, being "thrown into" (as well as "projected into": *geworfen*) the world. Only the authentic self, in contrast to the inauthentic "everyone" (*man*), and moved by fear and trembling (*Angst*), is capable of asking the question-of-being (*Daseinfrage*), the question to which there is *ipso facto* no answer because its answer is for that particular being to be no more. Here too the meaninglessness of the question constitutes its very meaning. Here too it is the characteristic of the authentic self which is not "lost in trivial concerns" to ask such questions to which there is no answer. Rather than the "chatter" (*Gerede*) of "everyone" (*man*), the authentic self lets Being which is in itself speak for itself through his very futile question of being.

Few who read Heidegger's *Sein und Zeit* failed to be caught by its spell. The fascination with Heidegger's thought is similar in many ways to the fascination with Spinoza's *Ethics*; both have a uniquely comforting power. In both, the ultimate meaning of everything that is resides in itself only. Spinoza's *Deus sive natura* reifies the logic of the Megarians to the utmost: only that which is, is possible; that which is not is impossible, even meaningless. Like Spinoza's God, Heidegger's being is always expressed through beings (*Seiende*), and is never capable of expressing "itself" immediately and without them; it illuminates without being seen, just as (if one may borrow a metaphor from Wittgenstein) a picture never points at itself. In contrast to Spinoza's substance, however, Heidegger insists on the necessary temporal structure of being. The acquiescence with the total immanence of the meaning of the world—including, for Heidegger, the temporality of being—means that there is no more to the life of a subject than itself; it cannot be endowed with a transcendent meaning or value; when it comes to its individual end, its meaning will be no more nor less than *that* and *what* it was. Annihilation does not deprive that which is from having meaning; it rather constitutes an integral part of that meaning.

This having been said, we turn back to the call for authenticity which some of the more courageous theological reflections on the Holocaust borrowed from Heidegger.

It is precisely at this point, namely with the distinction between authentic and inauthentic existence, that the ethical critique—a critique from the vantage point of ethics—must commence. Heidegger promises us that no moral judgment is implied in that distinction.[56] In an almost Hegelian manner, he even sees in the alienation of *Sein* in *Dasein* from itself through the flight into unauthentic existence a necessary stage for its return (*Kehre*) unto itself. Yet consider the further attributes of inauthenticity. Only the authentic self can be said to possess

297

conscience or even to be capable of "sinning." The anonymous "every-one" lives in a continuous degeneration and fall (*Verfall des Daseins*), a fall "into the world" (*in die Welt verfallen*). "Everyone" is, literally, inter-changeable with everyone else.

Without entering a sustained discussion about the nature of moral speech, let me assume that we ought to start with some "concrete abso-lutes" in an ethical discourse if we wish to navigate between relativization and empty, formal abstractions. Let me also assume that human life and human dignity are such absolutes—be it in a cognitive or axiomatic-thetic, descriptive or normative sense. They command our relentless re-spect; they are the "infinite right" of each subject. We may conceive of situations, such as the necessity of self-defense, in which we would be justified in violating them: it would be an evil act, even when justifiable.

Human life and the incommensurable value of each individual were assaulted in infinite ways in Nazi Europe. An ethical perspective of this sort cannot avoid being extremely narrow-minded, rigorously one-sided. It can make no concessions to higher gods and higher values, and it cannot permit any distinction between individuals based on higher val-ues. Life, the life of each individual, must be taken to be always mean-ingful in and of itself. The everyday reality of Heidegger's "everyone," the person who never attends to the question of being but is "lost unto the world," must be endowed from the one-sided vantage point of ethics with as much dignity and intrinsic value as the life of the searcher for funda-mental existential truths. The man who cultivates his garden and does all the things in the way he is supposed to cannot be called inauthentic except by his author. From an ethical point of view, *every life is authentic,* a value in and of itself, not interchangeable with any other human life, a mode *sui generis*. Once discrimination is permitted even in theory, its consequences are difficult to foretell. If the person of "everyone" is inter-changeable with everyone else, let alone if he is classified a nonperson—that is, without personality—then he is less valuable. And if less valuable, then perhaps also dispensable. Or again: is not crisis—say, war and destruction—beneficial in Heidegger's terms, because it "calls" man to his true self? Heidegger himself drew such conclusions after 1933.

But, you may object, the possible or even real abuses of a theory (even by its promoter) need not be held against it: in part, this has been my own argument. My critique, however, goes deeper than that. The very distinction between authentic and inauthentic existences, not only its possible career, is an intrinsic assault on the *dignitas hominis*, the integrity and worthiness of each concrete individual life, however lived. The latter attitude, with its difficulties and paradoxes, must constitute the absolute center of humanistic ethical theories, even at the cost of subscribing to a one-dimensional, flat philosophical anthropology. At best, Heidegger's distinction diverts from this focus; at the worst, it undermines it.

I do believe, however, that much of the force of Heidegger's insistence on the immanence of being, of which we spoke earlier, can be saved without redundant discriminations. An ethical monadology is conceivable in which the life of each is a unique and significant point of view of human possibilities for better and worse; each situation, individual and collective, is such that it is significant and something can be learned from it about man; and, should all human history have, finally, come to pass and leave behind no record, its meaning will be that and what it was, as replete with good and evil, the beautiful and the ugly, as it then will have been.

Mutatis mutandis, the flaws in the thought of Heidegger are also the flaws in those dialectical theologies which speak in Heidegger's idiom. Why is the person who "asks important questions," say, concerning God's presence in the face of massive evil, "more authentic" than the person who does not? And why are the questions of the *homo religiosus,* however broadly we define him, more important than the purely human questions asked by others about their experience in the concentration camps? Consider, for example, the most moving and reflective account written about the experience of Auschwitz, Primo Levi's *Se questo è un uomo* (published in English as *Survival in Auschwitz*). It asks many questions, but none of them theological. It refuses to see the concentration camp as meaningless: "We are in fact convinced that no human experience is without meaning or unworthy of analysis, and that fundamental values, even if they are not positive, can be deduced from this particular world which we are describing." Indeed, the religious-theological questions, were he to ask them, would distract from the power of Levi's reflections, which are centered around man, not around God.

As against the distinction between the begraced and those who lack grace, between authentic and inauthentic existences, the reality of the concentration camps taught Levi other distinctions, distinctions which are purely homocentric, such as the distinction between "the drowned and the saved."

We do not believe in the most obvious and facile deduction: that man is fundamentally brutal, egotistic and stupid in his conduct once every civilized institution is taken away, and that the *Häftling* is consequently nothing but a man without inhibitions. We believe, rather, that the only conclusion to be drawn is that in the face of driving necessity and physical disabilities many social habits and instincts are reduced to silence.

But another fact seems to us worthy of attention: there comes to light the existence of two particularly well-differentiated categories among men—the saved and the drowned. Other pairs of opposites (the good and the bad, the wise and the foolish, the cowards and the courageous, the unlucky and the fortunate) are considerably less distinct, they seem less essential, and above all they allow for more numerous and complex intermediary gradations.

This division is much less evident in ordinary life; for there it rarely happens that a man loses himself. A man is normally not alone, and in his rise or fall is tied to the destinies of his neighbours; so that it is exceptional for anyone to acquire unlimited power, or to fall by a succession of defeats into utter ruin. Moreover, everyone is normally in possession of such spiritual, physical and even financial resources that the probabilities of a shipwreck, of total inadequacy in the face of life, are relatively small. And one must take into account a definite cushioning effect exercised both by the law, and by the moral sense which constitutes a self-imposed law; for a country is considered the more civilized the more the wisdom and efficiency of its laws hinder a weak man from becoming too weak or a powerful one too powerful.

But in the *Lager* things are different: here the struggle to survive is without respite, because everyone is desperately and ferociously alone. If some *Null Achtzehn* vacillates, he will find no one to extend a helping hand; on the contrary, someone will knock him aside, because it is in no one's interest that there be one more "mussulman" dragging himself to work every day; and if someone, by a miracle of savage patience and cunning, finds a new method of avoiding the hardest work, a new art which yields him an ounce of bread, he will try to keep his method secret, and he will be esteemed and respected for this, and will derive from it an exclusive, personal benefit; he will become stronger and so will be feared, and who is feared is, ipso facto, a candidate for survival. . . .

They crowd my memory with their faceless presence, and if I could enclose all the evil of our time in one image, I would choose this image which is familiar to me: an emaciated man, with head dropped and shoulders curved, on whose face and in whose eyes not a trace of thought is to be seen.

If the drowned have no story, and single and broad is the path to perdition, the paths to salvation are many, difficult and improbable.[57]

Among the "saved" then are both the noble (such as his friend Alberto) and the ignoble, the cunning and the less cunning. Levi employs the theological idiom ironically: as if to say that being saved is not of a theological or other transcendental character; it is a most basic human property. Out of the experience of the concentration camp, Levi crystallized the building blocks of a true philosophical anthropology, more genuine and accurate than either Heidegger's or any recent theologian's. The power of his reflections, I repeat, lies in that they are centered around the concrete man, not around a chimera of the authentic self nor around God.

Indeed, religious questions may even be detrimental to ethical human concerns. They are detrimental, I believe, in the following sense. The assumption is made by even the most self-critical theologians that there exists a particular virtue in the commitment to values higher than human life and human integrity, that the person who lives his life *veluti pecora*, without asking existential-religious questions, lacks "grace." But the table may be turned as follows. A commitment to higher values above the sanctity of the individual not only distracts from the study of man, but can and did lead to abuses and crimes of much greater extent than selfish self-interest ever perpetrated. Concededly, this is not a *necessary* consequence of commitments to absolutes, but it has often enough been so. Now it matters little whether the higher values were transcendent or immanent, God, fatherland, race or the ideal society of the future. In the name of all of them crusades were fought, genocides committed, persons degraded. No major religion I know of was immune. Perhaps then dialectical theologians are not radical enough. Perhaps theology itself is one source of that very danger which they contemplate. William of Ockham, whose ethical theory recognizes very clearly the need for a concrete absolute if one wishes to navigate between the Scylla of relativization and the Charybdis of empty, formal abstractions, claimed it is wrong to say that God wants that which is good. Rather, it is good because God wanted it. The God of the Bible wanted, as it were, a genocide against the Amalekites, including women, children, and cattle. A more refined God of later centuries wanted heretics to be "compelled to enter" or be abolished. An even more refined God may demand the self-sacrifice of the believer so as to sanctify the name of God. A secular age translated such demands into world-immanent terms, among them race. *Tantum religio potuit suadere malorum.*

Again, I do not argue that religious commitments do, of necessity, lead to abuse. But neither should it be argued that because of lack of religiosity (so to say, as an "outburst of paganism") concentration and extermination camps became possible. I rather argue that the focus on the religious-theological implications of the Holocaust is intrinsically the wrong focus. The question of what it teaches us about God or any other higher norms and values is insignificant beside the question of what it teaches us about man, his limits, his possibilities, his cruelty, his creativity, and his nobility. In human terms the Holocaust was not meaningless. To say that it was seems as offensive as to say that it had a theological meaning, that is, a divine purpose.

For similar reasons we ought to object to the characterization of the Holocaust as "incomprehensible." It is one of the most prevalent predicates in the theological literature about the Holocaust—and not only in the theological literature. On the contrary: historians, psychologists, sociologists, and philosophers ought to make every effort to comprehend the catastrophe, and they ought to be guided by the reasonable expectation that they can comprehend it. The crime committed by the Nazis was of immense proportions: the horror and the suffering transgress our capacity of imagination, but it is possible to understand them rationally. Even if the perpetrators of the crime were madmen who lost all touch with reality, a reconstruction of their mentality and patterns of action would be possible. But they were not madmen, at least not in the clinical sense of the word: if madness entails loss of the sense of reality, then no society can be called mad, because reality is a social construct through and through. The prehistory of the genocide, its necessary conditions, can be illuminated more and more. The mental mechanisms by which Nazi ideology justified mass murder can be followed step-by-step. Germany stood fast in its illusion of apocalyptic "total war." The Jews, they were certain, are not only an inferior race on the order of Slavs and blacks, they are even more dangerous, because they are a universal, destructive parasite which (unlike other races) cleverly adapts to become almost indistinguishable from the host society in order to destroy the healthy texture of that society from within. Their extermination was spoken of in terms of hygienic medicine: Jews were labeled a dangerous bacteria. "*Entlausung*" (delousing) was the terrible realization of an ideological metaphor in the concentration camps. By degrading the inmates of the camps, by robbing them of their personalities, the victims were supposed to turn into that which the Nazi ideology claimed they had always been: subhuman. It was a mechanism which functioned to concretize, to visualize, the rationale for extermination. Nor is it true that the extermination of the Jews was carried out at the cost of the war effort, as Hilberg and others once believed. We cannot excuse ourselves from the obligation to understand the Nazi mentality if we want to condemn it, let alone if we want to prevent similar crimes from being committed again.

302

Theologians seem to emphasize the "incomprehensibility" of the Holocaust and the "madness" of those who caused it because they cannot find any theological meaning in it. Perhaps also it is because they hardly dare to say that if one were to believe in transcendent forces, the Holocaust would prove the autonomy of evil, an evil manifested not only or primarily by the number of its victims but by its sheer inexhaustible inventiveness, by the almost infinite number of methods found for systematic killing and degradation. If, however, we turn from God to man, the Holocaust is neither incomprehensible nor meaningless. It was neither bestial nor indeed pagan. It was, instead, an eminently human event in that it demonstrated those extremes which *only* man and his society are capable of doing or suffering. It pointed at a possibility, perhaps unknown before, of human existence, a possibility as human as the best instances of creativity and compassion.

15

Theses on Revisionism

PIERRE VIDAL-NAQUET

From One Revisionism to Another

I call "revisionism" here the doctrine that states that the genocide practiced by Nazi Germany against Jews and Gypsies did not happen, that it is a myth, a fable, a swindle.[1] I speak here of "revisionism" in the absolute sense of the term, but there also exist relative revisionisms, about which I will say a few words.

The word itself has a strange history that merits investigation. The first modern "revisionists" were the French partisans of the "revision" of Alfred Dreyfus's trial (1894). But the word very quickly returned to their adversaries.[2] This reversal must be considered symptomatic. Next, the word took on a sometimes positive, sometimes negative sense, always implying criticism of a dominant orthodoxy. Éduard Bernstein and his friends who confronted orthodox Marxism were revisionists. The term was transmitted to Maoists who thus termed their Soviet foes. In traditional Zionism, Vladimir Jabotinsky's disciples currently in power in Israel are also revisionists. And American historians who contest the official, traditionally accepted version of the origins of the Cold War are revisionists.

However, the revisionists of Hitler's genocide refer, with good reason,

304

to another American historical school, the one that may be represented by the name of H. E. Barnes (1889–1968).[3] Historian and sociologist, "radical" in the American sense of the term, at least at the beginning of his career, anti-imperialist and anticolonialist,[4] Barnes rebelled against the historical orthodoxy that attributed the responsibility for World War I to the Central Powers alone. If not absolute, this orthodoxy was nevertheless widespread in France, England, and America. The French "Yellow Book" of 1914 omitted the most embarrassing episodes, and sometimes indulged in pure sham, such as presenting the Russian general mobilization (July 30, 1914) as happening after the Austro-Hungarian mobilization (July 31). For the first time during the war, propaganda was operative in a massive way.[5] Historians from both camps joined the fray. In 1919 an American historian published a collection, paradoxically and significantly entitled *Volleys from a Non-Combatant*.[6] In the free world, orthodoxy was never imposed as it was and would be in the totalitarian countries. Yet it did not exist any less in free countries. The French historian Jules Isaac, author of well-known manuals for *lycée* students, wished to present to the Sorbonne in 1935 a thesis on Poincaré's ministry (January 1912 to January 1913). Isaac wanted to deal with the historiographic context of the era, and the problem of Poincaré's involvement in the origins of the war. The Sorbonne requested that "for seemliness," Poincaré's name not be included in the table of contents. Isaac refused to make this compromise and wrote to the head of the Faculty of Letters: "If 'for seemliness' the Faculty forbids me to use Poincaré's name in the title, then the Faculty might as well ask me, 'for seemliness,' not to mention Poincaré's role at all in the course of my work."[7]

What was true after World War I remained so after World War II. On December 22, 1950, President Harry Truman addressed the Congress of the American Historical Association. He asked them to help implement a federal historical program to fight communism.[8] He wanted to contrast truth with lies, but can truth be made so easily into something federal?

Unhappily, H. E. Barnes did not stop at destroying the orthodoxy on the Entente and their American ally. He inverted it. Barnes's book *The Genesis of the World War*[9] uncovers, or rather invents, a "French-Russian conspiracy that caused the War." He did not hesitate to "reveal," for example, that Jean Jaurès was assassinated "at the instigation of Iswolski and the Russian Secret Police."[10]

Jules Isaac could say, putting it mildly, that Barnes was "foolhardy and extremely capricious in applying historical method."[11]

Barnes's book still has a lesson for us. In addressing the French public the father of American revisionism invoked the Dreyfus Affair. He also cited the example of the Affair as he whitewashed Germany of any responsibility in the birth of world conflict. This is as absurd as the inverse thesis.[12] The Affair is thereby a reference point. As paradoxical as it may seem, the Affair remains just this for a number of revisionists of Hitler's genocide.[13]

The Dreyfus Affair is in fact a reference, but an unusual one. Hannah Arendt rightly saw the Affair as one of the first signs of the birth of modern totalitarianism.[14] *Mutatis mutandis,* the evidence of Dreyfus's guilt, in spite of proofs unfurled and stubbornly held, is for the core of anti-Dreyfusards a dogma as incontrovertible as the innocence of Hitler when accused of genocide to revisionists today. To declare Hitler innocent in the name of Dreyfusard values and with the narrowest nationalist obstinacy is a noteworthy modern refinement.

There are three instances that help us to understand the "good conscience" of the revisionists. First, the Dreyfus Affair. Second, the struggle against the nationalist versions of the history of World War I.[15] Third, the struggle against the "lies" of World War II and against the greatest of all "lies," Hitler's genocide, also known as "that twentieth-century swindle."[16] These are particularly the themes of "radical" or "leftist" revisionists, from Paul Rassinier to Jean-Gabriel Cohn-Bendit.[17] Rassinier's case is particularly remarkable. As a socialist and pacifist, he was nevertheless in the Resistance. Later, he was deported to a concentration camp. Rassinier is the true father of contemporary revisionism.

In a stubborn stance that we cannot wholly explain, Rassinier remains totally faithful to this absolute novelty, the concentration-camp world. He is also faithful to the lesson of 1914. He describes his camp experience in full detail. He works to conceptualize it and to thematize it. But this is not in order to convey the experience. Instead, he wants to suppress it, to cleanse it of anything that is more than mere repetitiveness. Rassinier does not magnify the SS out of fascination or some sort of masochism. He banalizes them for the goal of introducing the idea of "one war in another." He puts everything into compartments; the victims and executioners, the German soldiers and their adversaries; all are reckoned as the same "abject folly."[18] For a long while the only one to deny Hitler's genocide, Rassinier thought of himself in two ways. He was Romain Rolland in 1914, "above the brawl," and Bernard Lazare in 1896, the solitary fighter for truth and justice. Rassinier's example would influence H. E. Barnes and contribute to the transition between old and modern revisionism.[19] It is necessary to reconstruct these movements. We shall try to portray them precisely. Need we actually refute the "revisionist" theories, notably the most characteristic one, the negation of Hitler's genocide and of his privileged instrument, the gas chamber? It has sometimes seemed necessary to do so.[20] But such will certainly not be my intention in these pages. Ultimately, one does not refute a closed system. A total lie is not subject to refutation, because its conclusions were made before any proofs were found.[21] It was once necessary to prove that the *Protocols of the Elders of Zion* were forged. But as Hannah Arendt said, if so many people believed that the *Protocols* were authentic, "the historian's job is no longer (just) to uncover the imposture. Nor is his task to invent explanations which cloak the essential political and historical fact that a lie has been believed. This fact is more important than the circumstance (which is secondary, historically speaking) that it was a lie."[22]

On Myths of War and the Process of Truth

Propaganda, or, as it was called, "brainwashing," was present in both world wars. Hitler's great massacre is now put on the same level as the "children with their hands cut off" in 1914, simply another act of psychological warfare. This central theory of revisionism has the merit of reminding us of two basic givens in world conflicts. Allied propaganda made little use of the great massacre in its psychological warfare against Nazi Germany. Information about the genocide started to filter through very early, but when it did, it started to run into giant obstacles, not the least of which was the precedent of World War I. In one sense, we might say that the first "revisionists," among them Jews, were recruited during the war by Allied information agencies. Walter Laqueur's recent work has established this irrefutably.[23]

In the wave of information that issued from occupied territories, there was the true, the less true, and the false. The general sense of what was going on was never in doubt. On the modalities, there were often places to hesitate between one or another version. For example, dealing with Auschwitz, there were evasions at first. It was not until April 1944 that a firsthand description of the extermination process could be established. This was later verified as being remarkably exact. These "Protocols of Auschwitz" would be made public by the American War Refugee Board only in November 1944.[24] The deportation and massacre of Hungarian Jews, which started in May 1944, was an event announced day by day, so to speak, by the Allied and neutral presses.[25]

I spoke of true and false. This simple opposition does not really capture what went on. All forms of inexactitudes existed, from errors about the architectural forms to confusions about distances and numbers. Phantasms and myths existed too. But they did not exist in themselves like a creation *sui generis*, a "rumor" or swindle invented by a determined group such as New York's Zionists.[26] They existed as a shadow cast upon reality, like a prolongation of reality.[27] It should be added that even the most direct and authentic information needed to be decoded when it reached Allied information agencies. Writings in the coded languages of totalitarian systems often could not be plainly interpreted until after the end of the war.

Let us give an example of each of these two phenomena, starting with the later. The British secret services cracked the code used by the Germans in internal transmissions. The police documents that were revealed this way included some numerical data: the entry and departure of bodies for a certain number of camps, including Auschwitz, between the spring of 1942 and February 1943. One of the columns was marked "Departures by Every Means." This was interpreted as meaning death. But in these particular texts there is no mention of gassing.[28] This kind of document is perfectly familiar. An official Polish publication dated October 18, 1944, statistically establishes that at the Birkenau camp for women, "departures" that reduced the camp's size consisted of natural deaths, transport, and "special treatment," which can be decoded as meaning gassings.[29]

One of the main documents discussed in Walter Laqueur's book[30] is a telegram sent to London from Bern on August 10, 1942, by G. Riegner, secretary of the World Jewish Congress. That telegram, drafted on the basis of information communicated by a German industrialist, announces that those around the führer foresee collecting all Europe's Jews to "be at one blow exterminated." Prussic acid was among the means studied. The element of error and myth in this document is remarkable. The decision to carry out exterminations was made some months before. The use of prussic acid (Zyklon B), begun in September 1941 on Soviet prisoners of war, was current at Auschwitz after the beginning of 1942. The use of gas seems to be incompatible with an extermination done at one blow. This would presuppose an atomic weapon that did not yet exist. In Freudian terms, one might say that there was condensation and displacement of information here.

But condensation of what? In the same German scientific journal, Martin Broszat and Christopher Browning opposed each other in one of the most remarkable debates by historians of Hitler's extermination policy.[31]

Martin Broszat refuted a semirevisionist book by British historian David Irving that exonerated Hitler and blamed Himmler for the great massacre.[32] Mr. Broszat sees in the "Final Solution," which meant extermination, something partly improvised, that developed blow by blow, to a certain extent. To which Christopher Browning replied that we must take very seriously the information given by Hess and by Eichmann— the former speaking about Himmler, the latter about Heydrich[33]—that during the summer of 1941, Hitler decided to exterminate the Jews. Such an order, transmitted to such subordinates, was quickly put into action. By condensation, this response may have become the "one blow" of Riegner's telegram.

But Broszat's article specifies the vital role of a step-by-step development, following specific orders. Steps like the model ghetto of Thereisenstadt and the "family camp" at Auschwitz. Other steps were the formation of ghettos, with their differentiated social ranks. The privileged thought that their rank would permit them to escape a common fate that the rankings helped in fact to implement. These steps led to the extermination camps and the gas chambers. It was just this variety of steps that permitted the policy of extermination to unroll in full. Every moment of this process, each murderous step, serves as an argument against the revisionists. It is disingenuous to believe that because Jewish weddings were held at Majdanek, near Lublin, the camps must have been places of rejoicing.[34] On the contrary, such steps were temporary social events necessary for the smooth operation of butchery.

That at Several Locations . . .

Revisionism presents itself under multiple and various guises: tracts, "scholarly" books, banal propaganda efforts, mimeographed brochures, distinguished reviews, and videocassettes. Examining a collection of these documents on library shelves[35] one finds many translations of the same texts.[36] Reading the same scholarly references in obscure journals and books, one gets the feeling of a single vast international enterprise. An excessive conclusion, perhaps. Yet there inarguably exists in California a center for international revisionism which collects and distributes all this matter.[37] There is nothing surprising in that. It is simply the result of the global diffusion of information and of the dominant position of the United States in the world market.[38] In fact, the "information" is widely dispersed at very diverse levels, often by the same persons. There is the case of Dietlieb Felderer, born in Innsbruck in 1942. Now living in Sweden, Felderer is a Jehovah's Witness. Thus, Felderer belongs by conversion to a group that was persecuted but not exterminated, in Hitler's time.[39] Felderer is a contributor to the *Journal of Historical Review*, a periodical with scientific pretensions.[40] He also publishes, in Täby, Sweden, a suitably smudgy, mimeographed anti-Semitic periodical, *Jewish Information*.[41] He also publishes numerous tracts and tries to organize each summer "revisionist" trips to Poland. This new type of tourist is led through Auschwitz or to the remains of Treblinka and told that nothing very serious happened there. The trips are exciting adventures for the explorer of the unknown.

Revisionism finds itself at the crossroads of very diverse, sometimes contradictory ideologies. Among them are Nazi anti-Semitism, far-right anticommunism, anti-Zionism, German nationalism, diverse east European nationalisms, libertarian pacifism, and far-left Marxism. These doctrines occasionally appear in their pure state, but most of the time they are in various combinations. For example, a London publishing house produces, along with an English version of the *Protocols of the Elders of Zion*, a book entitled *The World Conquerors*. Here by a remarkable inversion it is explained that in World War II the true war criminals were the Jews.[42] This book is also violently anti-Communist, accusing all Hungarian Communists and even Spanish Communists of being Jews. Inversion is characteristic of this ideology. In *The Jew Süss* (1940) the Jews were the torturers.

Although traditional French anti-Semitism—Maurrassian—is happily pro-Israel, all revisionists are determined anti-Zionists. They slide from anti-Zionism to anti-Semitism, typically on the far left.[43] Others manage it vice versa. The absolute necessity of being anti-Zionist in revisionist discourse is easily explained. It is a question of anticipating the creation of the state of Israel. Today Israel is a state that sometimes employs means of violence and domination. By pretending that such an entity already existed in 1943, one can obscure the fact that Jewish communities in Europe were unarmed. Finally, one might even explain that nazism was a creation, doubtless phantasmagorical, of Zionism.[44]

That said, German nationalism perfectly combines with the defense of Arab interests.[45] There exists as well revisionism on the subject of

Palestine, with decided adversaries.[46] Even in Israel there are some Jewish revisionists, although very few, it seems.[47]

Generally, the themes of these works are greatly impoverished, particularly those inspired by German nazism, past or present.[48] One might say that all these books are programmed, that their pages follow one after the other without ever offering anything unexpected. The reader regularly meets the same facts: that the Jews declared war on Hitler's Germany in 1933, proven infallibly from quotes drawn from such and such obscure journal in the Midwest.[49] We learn that the losses the Jews might have incurred during the war, which anyway were moderate, were only due to the risks of partisan fighting. There were never any extermination camps. Deaths in the camps were almost exclusively due to typhus. I shall limit myself here to noting a point of method and answering a few errors.

A fundamental revisionist practice is to refuse to distinguish between words and reality. During World War II some Allied generals made ferocious declarations against the Germans. There were also acts, equally ferocious, that constitute war crimes in every sense of the term. But remarkably, revisionists would rather focus on wild texts than on events such as the bombing of Dresden, or dramatic evacuations of Germans from regions that became Polish or Czech. Such texts certainly reveal the elemental racism of war, but they never received the least bit of application in reality. Theodore Kaufman, personal adviser to Franklin Delano Roosevelt, published a pamphlet during the war entitled *Germany Must Perish*. The pamphlet, which predicted the sterilization of Germans, is placed by revisionists on the same level as speeches by Hitler and Himmler that had every likelihood of being carried out in full.[50]

Nadine Fresco has appropriately compared the revisionist method to a well-known joke that Freud discussed, the story of the caldron.[51] A borrows a copper caldron from B. When it is returned, B complains that the caldron has a big hole in it. A's defense: "First, I never borrowed B's caldron. Second, that caldron had a hole when I borrowed it. Third, I returned the caldron intact."

Such examples are multifarious. The "Wannsee Protocol" of January 20, 1942, shows a certain number of functionaries at work on the "Final Solution." This protocol is claimed or suggested to be untrustworthy because it is unsigned and because it reveals nothing dramatic.[52]

A new record is achieved with the *Secret Discourses* of Himmler, in which the theory and practice of collective murder are exposed with relatively little dissimulation.[53] But it is claimed that these texts, published under a title not given them by their author, are corrupted. Words are introduced that were not in the original, such as the verb "to kill" (*umbringen*). The original word was something else, "evacuate" perhaps, and the original meaning benign. The extermination of Judaism (*Ausrottung des Judentums*) is not the same as the extermination of the Jews.[54] Following Freud, we can continue the joke of the caldron. Why shouldn't A say: "I lent that caldron to B, not him to me, and it was intact!" An entire literature exists that tries to prove that the true murderers of Jews, and above all of Germans, were Jews: Jewish kapos, Jewish partisans, etc. Therefore collective murder, which did not exist, is amply justifiable and justified.[55]

Here we have the overweening revisionist norm. There is also overstatement by error. British historian David Irving guesses that the Final Solution was invented by Himmler and kept a secret from Hitler, in spite of a formal order from the German chancellor in November 1941 not to exterminate the Jews.[56]

On an Explosive Mixture

Let us return to the geography of revisionism and find out about its political and intellectual scope. Since I cannot be exhaustive here, the few hypotheses formulated will have to be both summary and provisory. There are, however, certain pointers to be indicated. Two countries dominate revisionist production: Germany and the United States. In the former, the books are extremely numerous, and they meet a certain success, if the number of editions some of them go through are any indication. However, they are narrowly tied to a single source, the far-right inheritors of nazism who dream of rehabilitating that movement.

Truly speaking, revisionism has made few or no converts among the far left. Certainly, small terrorist groups have slid from anti-Zionism to anti-Semitism pure and simple, with the help of the PLO, but without using revisionist argument.[57]

Ulrike Meinhof is often credited with the following formula: "Six million Jews were killed and tossed into the dung heap in Europe because they were monied Jews." Cited in this form, the text is an imbecilic error, attributing to this admittedly insane West German RAF militant anti-Semitic feelings she surely did not have. Meinhof simply wished to say that anticapitalist ideology was used by the Nazis in their fight against

312

the Jews.[58] But a steady shift in meaning has been at work over the past few years, and may even have accomplished its end.

In America revisionism is above all centered in a California group, W. A. Carto's Liberty Lobby, which has an old, solid tradition of being anti-Semitic, anti-Zionist, and antiblack. The Liberty Lobby also supports or tries to support the nationalism of German-Americans.[59] It does not seem that H. E. Barnes's best efforts toward accomplishing a libertarian world have had much success.[60] In the intellectual and academic world, a work like Arthur Butz's is almost entirely ignored.[61]

But on the contrary, in some countries, revisionism is not only a racist, anti-Semitic far-right movement; some far-left people are involved as well. In Sweden far-left sociologist Jan Myrdal intervened in defense of the Frenchman Robert Faurisson in support not only of the man, but also, in part, of his ideas.[62] In Australia, John Bennett, former secretary of the Victorian Council for Civil Liberties, acted similarly.[63] In Italy a small Marxist libertarian group supported Paul Rassinier.[64]

France's case seems to be the most interesting and the most complex. Curiously, no problem has attracted the international press to the subject of revisionism more than the Robert Faurisson case. Noam Chomsky wrote a text which was later used as a preface for one of Faurisson's books.[65] As a result of Faurisson's "theses," the world press, from Germany to America, has dug up and stated the revisionist point of view.[66] This is surprising, as both Germany and America have always had farther-ranging revisionists than Faurrison.

It is not that Faurisson offers a particularly impressive form of revision. His originality is that he sets the problem essentially on a technical level. Even in this aspect, he still owes much to Butz. Some of his most scandalous pronouncements are in reality simple adaptations and translations from the German original.[67]

Faurisson holds the rank of university professor in a large city, in a country where this title grants easier access to the media than elsewhere. Faurisson has a natural talent for shopworn scandal; attempts have been made to overwhelm him with lawsuits;[68] and his works have been presented by an honored anthropologist, Serge Thion,[69] all of which has played a role in his notoriety. Just as remarkably, in Britain, where freedom of the press was invented, revisionists do not have access to the large newspapers.[70] But in France certain liberal or libertarian newspapers (Le Monde, Libération) do include sketchy discussions of the matter, sometimes with the implication that the reader is invited to choose between two equally valid theses.[71] Like any other country, France has had a neo-

Nazi movement, led by Maurice Bardèche and his review, *Défense de l'Occident*. The New Right has recently renewed this movement. Revisionist themes appeared there very early on.[72]

Paul Rassinier (1906–67) was a Communist, later a socialist. He was deported to Buchenwald and then to Dora. Rassinier was always anticolonialist, but he was also a friend of Bardèche and a contributor to *Rivarol*. In Rassinier's case there was an alliance between the pacifist and libertarian left and a plainly Hitlerian far right.[73]

The junction between the two was formed by anti-Semitism, here again mixed with anti-Zionism. In the next generation the alliance was renewed by the publicity given to revisionist themes. Faurrison's theses in particular were spread by the Marxist groups the Vieille Taupe and other related groups (the Guerre Sociale, the Jeune Taupe, etc.).[74]

The political aims of these groups have been facilitated by decades of sacralization of the Jewish people by the belated remorse that seized the West after the great massacre was revealed. As a result, Israel has been protected by the West, even when it has acted arguably. What is the overall political aim here? The central purpose is perfectly clear: to break the antifascist consensus on the war that was formed by the news of the extermination of the Jews. The far-left approach is to downplay the importance of Nazi crimes and to play up instead the guilt of the West and the Communist world. Thereby, the blame will seem to be widely shared.[75]

So it is a matter of switching enemies. Is this all really new? Such ideologies had their true origins in France. At the end of the nineteenth century, the liberal consensus united farmers, workers, and bourgeois republicans in mutual hostility against the landed, "feudal" aristocracy. Édouard Drumont, the author of *Jewish France* (1886) was in the eyes of many socialists a great man and an important sociologist.[76] The author also proposed switching enemies: not the lord's castle, with its torture rooms, but the mysterious lair where the Jew amasses his wealth, using the blood of Christians. First, the official histories must be blamed. Drumont wrote in *Jewish France*, "the French school of history has more than once bypassed all this blindly, despite new methods of investigation that it pretends to have invented. It gawked at dungeons which, according to Viollet-le-Duc himself, were in fact latrines, and at crypts which were in fact cellars. But it did not enter the mysterious *sacrificarium*, the closet bloodier than Bluebeard's, where the child victims of semitic superstition lie, bloodless, their veins torn."[77]

Truly, a strange alliance . . .

314

On Other Nations and Israel

Greek cities erected costly monuments at Delphi and Olympus, expressing their rivalry in the cults of Apollo and Zeus. So the nations that were victims of Hitler, or at least some of them, have raised pavilions at Auschwitz recalling the misery that befell their nationals. Even the victims are competitive. Among these pavilions, oddly enough, is one called the Jewish pavilion. Not officially accepting any responsibility, the Polish government built it first and foremost to proclaim Poland's martyrdom.[78] A word is needed here about such "practices" among the east European countries—where the immense majority of murdered Jews came from—that make up "socialist" Europe today. It goes without saying that "revisionism" is absolutely banned there. But what about the history that is accepted? After a necessarily very brief inquiry, we can say a few words about the historiography of three socialist countries: the USSR, which controls the system and whose armies freed Auschwitz; the GDR, which inherited part of the territory and population of the Nazi state; and finally, Poland, on whose soil the majority of exterminations took place.[79]

To my knowledge no Soviet historiography exists on the genocide of the Jews. Some books and booklets of propaganda and reportage were published at the moment of victory.[80] The study of German concentration camps seems to have been completely rudimentary. The reasons for this deficiency are fairly evident. The only book in Russian on Auschwitz that I have been able to identify is translated from the Polish and published in Warsaw.[81]

The History of the Great Patriotic War, 1914–1945, by Boris Telpuchowski serves as typical post-Stalinist Soviet historiography. This book certainly mentions gas chambers and extermination as it was practiced at Auschwitz, Majdanek, and Treblinka, but the victims mentioned do not include Jews. Instead, 6 million murdered Polish citizens are mentioned. Two lines are devoted to the fact that on Soviet-occupied soil, the entire Jewish population was exterminated.[82] Jewish nationality exists in the Soviet Union, but it is in some ways a negative nationality. This situation is reflected in Soviet historiography.

The case of the GDR is rather different. In official ideology there is now an absolute break with the capitalist Nazi period. Anti-Semitism and exterminations are a heritage not to be accepted in any way, neither in paying indemnities to Israel nor in sending a government leader to kneel at the site of the Warsaw ghetto. On the contrary, East Berlin

315

believes that West Germany must assume the heritage of Hitler's Germany. For a long time it pretended to believe that West Germany alone was the continuation of the Nazi regime. East German studies on the extermination, studies whose existence is often denied,[83] focus less directly on gathering knowledge and historical thought than the need to complete or correct what West Germany has done or written, as a polemic against West Germany's leaders.[84]

Revisionists do not seem to have commented on this small but significant fact: since the end of the war Poland has sustained several political earthquakes. These have set off considerable emigrations of militant nationalists who generally hold no special tenderness toward either Jews or Communists. The latter were, according to revisionist ideology, among the great fabricators of the "lie" of extermination. Yet not one of these Poles has added grist to the revisionist mill.

In fact, the history of extermination camps rests heavily on works published in Poland. There are documents reproduced in the series by the Auschwitz Museum, works by the Polish Commission on War Crimes, and the volumes of the Warsaw Jewish Historical Institute.

It is self-evident that corrections need to be made in this literature. Its Polish nationalism is violently anti-Semitic in tradition. The problem is doubled by the frequent intervention of Communist censorship. Usually, publications attach more importance to anti-Polish repression, which was savage, than to the extermination of the Jews. And the murdered Jews are often naturalized postmortem as Poles—a naturalization that rarely corresponds with the facts during the period in question.[85]

One type of nationalism can discover another's faults rather easily. Polish historiography of the genocide and occupation is taken seriously by Israeli historiography. The Israelis discuss the Polish contributions, and eventually condemn them, continuing the great Jewish-Polish drama.[86]

There is certainly no one Israeli historiography. The Yad Vashem Studies are crossed with tensions, created by works brought in from abroad. Extremely violent confrontations resulted from the great syntheses of the Diaspora, by Gerald Reitlinger and Raul Hilberg, not to mention such fundamental thinking as Hannah Arendt's. Among the most delicate points are the questions of Jewish "passivity" and of Jewish collaboration, or, in other words, collaboration between the rope and the hanged man. Also disputed are the national character of Hitler's Jewish victims, and the unique aspects of the massacre. Finally, the "banality of evil" is debated, which Hannah Arendt opposed to the diabolization of Eichmann and his commandos.[87] These are some of the real problems raised by the writing of real history. Violent collisions are inevitable between a historiography that insists on a full study of specifics and one that tries to integrate the great massacre into the currents of world history, where it will not always readily go.[88] But insofar as Israel is concerned, can we control history? The Shoah overwhelms that approach, first by the dramatic role it played in the origins of the state. Second, there was what one must call the daily instrumentalization of the great massacre by Israel's political class.[89] From the first, the Jewish genocide ceased to be an historic reality lived in an existential manner. It became a banal instrument of political legitimization. The genocide was invoked to obtain such and such internal political adhesion, or to put pressure on the Diaspora so that it would unconditionally approve Israeli political developments. This is the paradox of an approach that makes of genocide at the same time a sacred moment in history and a profane argument, an occasion, if you will, for business and tourism.[90]

Need it be added that among the perverse effects of this instrumentalization of genocide, there is constant, knowingly maintained confusion between Nazi hatred and Arab hatred? No one knows what the years 1939–43 will inscribe in history's not always serene kingdom of medieval charts and Greek inscriptions. But the manipulation of these years for pragmatic ends removes their historic weight and makes them seem unreal. As a result, this manipulation brings to the madness and lies of revisionism its most useful and formidable collaborator.

History After Auschwitz

In conclusion we may try to state what tests revisionism presents to the historian. Theodor Wiesengrund Adorno, meditating after the war on the theme of "negative dialectics," asked in what measure it was possible to "think" after Auschwitz. What the Lisbon Earthquake was to Voltaire and the tomb of theodicy was for Leibniz, the genocide was to the generation who lived it, magnified a hundredfold. Adorno wrote: "With the administrative massacre of millions of persons, death acquired a new form in which to be feared. . . . Genocide is the absolute integration, prepared everywhere that men are leveled out and trained as if in the army, until, caught up in the idea of their complete inanity, they are literally exterminated. . . . Absolute negativity is predictable, it no longer astonishes anyone."[91]

317

Has the concept of absolute negativity a meaning for historians? Auschwitz has become a symbol, which it was not immediately after the war—a symbol of an enormous silence.[92] But even this symbol may be disputed. Auschwitz juxtaposed an extermination camp (Birkenau), a labor camp (Auschwitz I), and a factory camp for synthetic rubber (Auschwitz III–Monowitz). The place of absolute negativity would be Treblinka or Bełżec rather than Auschwitz. But one might always rate one crime as more absolute than another.[93] By definition, historians see things relatively. This is what makes the understanding of revisionist discourse so difficult. The word in itself contains nothing that shocks the historian. Out of instinct, he feels at home with this adjective. If it is demonstrated to the historian that no gas chambers existed at Dachau, that Anne Frank's *Diary*, though published in many languages, poses problems of authenticity, or that Crematorium I of Auschwitz was only built after the war by the Poles, he is prepared to listen.[94]

Events are not things, even if an irreducible opacity of the real exists. A historical discourse is a network of explications that can give way to "another explication"[95] if the latter is judged to take better account of the facts. For instance, a Marxist will try to reason in terms of capitalist rentability. He will ask himself if the pure destructiveness of the gas chambers fits easily into this interpretive system or not. Depending on the case, he will adapt the gas chambers to Marxism or suppress them in the name of the same doctrine.[96] However, the revisionist enterprise in essence does not seem to me to raise "another explication" by its researches. It reflects above all the absolute negativity that Adorno spoke of. It is precisely this that the historian has so much difficulty grasping. A gigantic effort is being made not only to create a fictitious world, but to erase an immense event from the records of history.

Along these lines, it must be admitted that two revisionist books, *The Hoax of the Twentieth Century* by Arthur Butz and *Der Auschwitz Mythos* by Wilhelm Stäglich, represent a rather remarkable achievement, the appearance of a historical narrative. Moreover, they seem to be critical inquiries with all the exterior traits that define the history book, except the one that precisely defines its value: the truth.

Naturally, one might search for precedents of revisionism in the history of ideological movements. Under the Restoration, did not R. P. Loriquet erase the Revolution and the Empire from the history he taught young people, for educational reasons? But that was merely "legitimate" deception, which we've known since Plato to be inseparable from education. This is an innocent game compared to modern revisionism.

Naturally, if I may speak here of the absolute, it is because we are on the level of pure discourse. We are not discussing the real. Revisionism is not new, but the revisionist crisis did not appear in the West until the massive diffusion of the television film *Holocaust.* That is, it appeared after the spectacularization of genocide, its transformation into pure language and into an object of mass consumption.[97] It seems to me that there is a point of departure here for thoughts that I hope will be continued by others.

NOTES

I / From Anti-Semitism to Extermination
A Historiographical Study of Nazi Policies Toward the Jews
and an Essay in Interpretation
SAUL FRIEDLÄNDER

1. Among the historiographical studies dealing with what is now commonly called the "Holocaust," let us mention, among others, Léon Poliakov, "Changing Views in Holocaust Research," *Yad Vashem Bulletin*, no. 20 (April 1967); Leni Yahil, "The Holocaust in Jewish Historiography," *Yad Vashem Studies*, vol. VII (1968); Philip Friedman, "The Study of the History of the Holocaust and Its Problems" (in Hebrew), in Israel Guttman and Livia Rothkirchen, eds., *Shoat Yehudei Europa* (Jerusalem, 1973); Shaul Esh, "Problems of the Study of the Holocaust" (in Hebrew), *Iyounim Beheker Hashoa Ve Yahadut Zmanenu* (Jerusalem, 1973); Yehuda Bauer, "Trends in Holocaust Research," *Yad Vashem Studies*, vol. XII (1977); Konrad Kwiet, "Zur historiographischen Behandlung der Judenverfolgung im Dritten Reich," *Militärgeschichtliche Mitteilungen*, vol. 27 (1980-81); Lucy S. Dawidowicz, *The Holocaust and the Historians* (Cambridge: Harvard University Press, 1981); Otto Dov Kulka, "Die Deutsche Geschichtsschreibung über den Nationalsozialismus und die 'Endlösung,'" *Historische Zeitschrift*, vol. 239 (1984).

2. Isaac Deutscher, *The Non-Jewish Jew and Other Essays* (London: Oxford University Press, 1968), p. 163.

3. Raymond Aron, "Existe-t-il un mystère Nazi?" *Commentaire*, no. 7 (1979), p. 349.

4. In using these three broad distinctions, we follow Wolfgang Sauer, "National Socialism: Totalitarianism or Fascism?" *American Historical Review*, December 1967, pp. 404 ff. See also Andreas Hillgruber, *Endlich genug über Nationalsozialismus und Zweiter Weltkrieg?* (Düsseldorf, 1982), pp. 24 ff.

5. This obviously applies to studies concentrating essentially on anti-Semitism or racial and *völkisch* thinking, such as Paul Massing, *Rehearsal for Destruction* (New York, 1949); Eva G. Reichmann, *Hostages of Civilisation* (London, 1950); Fritz Stern, *The Politics of Cultural Despair* (Berkeley, 1961); George L. Mosse, *The Crisis of German Ideology* (New York, 1964); Peter G.-J. Pulzer, *The Rise of Political Antisemitism in Germany and Austria* (New York, 1964); Léon L. Poliakov, *Histoire de l'Antisémitisme*, vol. III: *De Voltaire à Wagner* (Paris, 1968). On the other hand, some of the major postwar historical studies dealing with the German roots of nazism minimize or completely disregard the place of anti-Semitism within that past. Cf. chiefly Friedrich Meinecke, *Die deutsche Katastrophe* (Zürich, 1946); Gerhard Ritter, *Europa und die deutsche Frage* (Munich, 1948); Hans Rothfels, *The German Opposition to Hitler* (Chicago, 1962); Hans Kohn, *The Mind of Germany* (New York, 1960). On this issue, see Lucy S. Dawidowicz, *op cit.*, pp. 60–67; Konrad Kwiet, "Zur historiographischen Behandlung" *loc. cit.*, pp. 149 ff.

6. Cf. Zeev Sternhell, *La Droite révolutionnaire 1885–1914: les origines françaises du fascisme* (Paris, 1978); see also, by the same author, *Ni Droite ni Gauche: l'idéologie fasciste en France* (Paris, 1983) (Trans.: *Neither Right nor Left* [Berkeley, 1986].)

7. Richard S. Levy, *The Downfall of the Antisemitic Political Parties in Imperial Germany* (New Haven, 1975).

8. Egmont Zechlin, *Die Deutsche Politik und die Juden im Ersten Weltkrieg* (Göttingen, 1969); Saul Friedländer, "Die politischen Veränderungen der Kriegszeit und ihre Auswirkungen auf die Judenfrage," and Werner Jochman, "Die Ausbreitung des Antisemitismus," in Werner E. Mosse, ed., *Deutsches Judentum in Krieg und Revolution 1916–1923* (Tübingen, 1971). The contradictory aspects of German anti-Semitism during the first two decades of the century have been well presented in Donald Niewyk, *The Jews in Weimar Germany* (Baton Rouge, 1980), and in the first chapter of Sarah Gordon's *Hitler, Germans and the "Jewish Question"* (Princeton, 1984).

9. William Sheridan Allen, *The Nazi Seizure of Power: The Experience of a Single German Town 1930–1935* (London, 1966), see for instance p. 77.

10. In Lower Saxony, for instance. Cf. Jeremy Noakes, *The Nazi Party in Lower Saxony 1921–1933* (London, 1971).

11. This is also the conclusion reached in Richard F. Hamilton, *Who Voted for Hitler?* (Princeton, 1982), pp. 606–7.

12. See pp. 21–22.

13. Peter Merkl's analysis of the main ideological tenets of the SA and the SS in the 1920s (based on the personal file collected by Theodor Abel) shows that anti-Semitism ranks fourth in terms of importance, being of prime importance to 10.7% of the members only (14.9% within the rank and file of the party). Cf. Peter Merkl, *The Making of a Stormtrooper* (Princeton, 1980), p. 222.

14. It is sometimes difficult to distinguish between what may be the "general" characteristics of a social group and its "historical" German ones. In Raul Hilberg's *Destruction of the European Jews* (Chicago, 1961), the central role in the process of destruction is played by the bureaucratic machine, but is it bureaucracy as such, or German bureaucracy specifically, owing to the development of a particular national tradition?

15. However, it should be noted that the very concept of "fascism" is often criticized. Cf., among others, Gilbert Allardyce, "What Fascism Is Not: Thoughts on the Deflation of a Concept," *American Historical Review*, April 1979, pp. 367 ff.

16. See for instance recent studies on the various theories of fascism, such as Wolfgang Wipperman, *Faschismustheorien* (Darmstadt, 1980).

17. See for instance Stanley G. Payne, *Fascism: Comparison and Definition* (Madison, 1980).

18. Ernst Nolte, *Three Faces of Fascism* (London, 1956), p. 406.

19. Cf. Eberhard Jäckel, ed., *Hitler. Sämtliche Aufzeichnungen 1905–1924* (Stuttgart, 1980). The comparison was made possible thanks to the very detailed index of this volume. The centrality and predominance of Hitler's anti-Semitism within his ideological system and in his political agitation, during these early years, is confirmed by many other sources. For a general picture, see Helmut Auerbach, "Hitlers politische Lehrjahre und die Münchener Gesellschaft 1919–1923," *Vierteljahrshefte für Zeitgeschichte* (hereafter *VfZ*), 25 no. 1 (1977), pp. 15–16.

20. Adolf Hitler, *Table Talk* (quoted from Adolf Hitler, *Libres Propos sur la Guerre et la Paix*, vol. II [Paris, 1954], p. 347).

21. Hans Mommsen in *Totalitarismus und Faschismus. Eine wissenschaftliche Begriffskontroverse* (München, 1980), pp. 63–64.

22. Ibid., p. 24.

23. Hans Mommsen, "National-Socialism: Continuity and Change," in Walter Laqueur, ed., *Fascism: A Reader's Guide* (London, 1979), pp. 178–179. This is a transposition to the theory of fascism of the functionalist analysis of Nazi policies which we will examine at some length in the second part of this article.

24. Wolfgang Schieder in *Totalitarismus und Faschismus*, p. 58.

25. Karl Dietrich Bracher, "The Role of Hitler: Perspectives of Interpretation," in Laqueur, ed., *Fascism: A Reader's Guide*, pp. 201–2. For elements of the historiographical debate about the differences between Italian fascism and National Socialism, see Andreas Hillgruber, *Endlich*, pp. 40 ff.

26. On this issue, see for instance Lucy Dawidowicz, *The Holocaust and the Historians*, pp. 68 ff.; Erich Goldhagen, "Der Holocaust in der Sowjetischen Propaganda und Geschichtsschreibung," *VfZ* 28, no. 4 (1980), pp. 502 ff. and particularly p. 504.

27. Cf. Konrad Kwiet, "Historians of the German Democratic Republic on Antisemitism and Persecution," *Leo Baeck Institute Year Book*, vol. XXI (London, 1976), p. 174. Kurt Pätzold's work is something of an exception and his points are a mixture of Marxist orthodoxy and functionalism, allowing for various nuances. Cf., among others, his "Von der Vertreibung zum Genozid: Zu den Ursachen, Triebkräften und Bedingungen der antijüdischen Politik des faschistichen Deutschen Imperialismus," in Dietrich Eichholtz und Kurt Grossweiler, eds., *Faschismus—Forschung: Positionen, Probleme, Polemik* (East Berlin, 1980), pp. 180 ff. See also Kurt Pätzold, *Faschismus, Rassenwahn, Judenverfolgung: Eine Studie zur politischen Strategie und Taktik des faschistischen Imperialismus 1933–1945* (East Berlin, 1975).

28. The documents concerning the *unsuccessful* attempts of the Wehrmacht and even at some stage of the SS Wirtschafts- und Verwaltungshauptamt to retain Jewish skilled labor are numerous and well known. See for instance Enno Georg, *Die wirtschaftlichen Unternehmungen der SS* (Stuttgart, 1963), pp. 58, 61, 93–97. In each case the extermination orders from the RSHA or from Himmler himself prevailed.

29. Raul Hilberg, *The Destruction of the European Jews*, p. 645.

30. Cf. David Schoenbaum, *Hitler's Social Revolution: Class and Status in Nazi Germany 1933–1939* (New York, 1966).

31. Cf. pp. 21–22.

32. There are some variations to these classical Marxist approaches. Some historians, e.g., T. W. Mason, use, indirectly, the argument of the autonomy of the political sphere (and therefore of its actions and policies toward the Jews); others, e.g., Reinhard Kühnl, explain Nazi anti-Semitism by using a synthesis of Marxism and psychoanalysis, etc. For a good overview of some of these approaches, see Pierre Ayçoberry, *La Question Nazie: Les interprétations du National-Socialisme 1922–1975* (Paris, 1979), pp. 93 ff. and 233 ff.; Klaus Hildebrand, *Das Dritte Reich* (München, 1979), pp. 134 ff. More specifically for Mason's position, see T. W. Mason, "The Primacy of Politics: Politics and Economics in National-Socialist Germany," in S. E. Woolf, ed., *The Nature of Fascism*

(London, 1968) p. 192. For Kühnl's approach, see Reinhard Kühnl, "Probleme einer Theorie über den deutschen Faschismus," *Jahrbuch des Instituts für deutsche Geschichte*, vol. III (Tel Aviv, 1974), pp. 322 ff.

33. The very concept of totalitarianism and in particular its application to the Nazi system have been forcefully criticized since the early 1960s. See for instance Robert F. Koehl, "Feudal Aspects of National-Socialism," *American Political Science Review* LIV (December 1960), pp. 921 ff.; Wolfgang Sauer, *loc. cit.*, pp. 406–7.

34. The *arbitrary* choice of the enemy to be terrorized is supposed to be one of the fundamental characteristics of the totalitarian system. Cf. Carl Joachim Friedrich and Zbigniew Brzezinski, *Totalitarian Dictatorship and Autocracy* (Cambridge, Mass., 1956), p. 10.

35. This is the crux of Raul Hilberg's thesis in his *Destruction of the European Jews*.

36. Raul Hilberg, *op cit.*; Hannah Arendt, *Eichmann in Jerusalem: A Report on the Banality of Evil* (New York, 1963); H. G. Adler, *Der verwaltete Mensch: Studien zur Deportation der Juden aus Deutschland* (Tübingen, 1974); Christopher R. Browning, *The Final Solution and the German Foreign Office* (New York, 1978); Joseph Walk, *Das Sonderrecht für die Juden im NS-Staat: Eine Sammlung der geszetzlichen Massnahmen und Richtlinien—Inhalt und Bedeutung* (Heidelberg, 1981). Nearly 2,000 ordinances and decrees concerning the Jews were issued for the territory of the Reich alone. The last known decree, that of February 16, 1945, stipulates: "When it becomes impossible to transfer the files dealing with anti-Jewish activities, one should destroy them to avoid their falling into the hands of the enemy" (ibid., p. 406).

37. For a very clear presentation of the essential place of Hitler's anti-Semitism within his ideology, see Eberhard Jäckel, *Hitlers Weltanschauung* (Tübingen, 1969). See also Andreas Hillgruber, "Die 'Endlösung' und des deutsche Ostimperium als Kernstück des rassenideologischen Programms des Nationalsozialismus," in Hillgruber, *Deutsche Grossmacht und Weltpolitik im 19 und 20 Jahrhundert* (Düsseldorf, 1977), pp. 252 ff.

38. About Himmler, see Josef Ackerman, *Heinrich Himmler als Ideologe* (Göttingen, 1970).

39. Karl Dietrich Bracher, *The German Dictatorship* (London, 1971) (German edition, p. 464).

40. See Hannah Arendt, *The Origins of Totalitarianism* (New York, 1958).

41. We will discuss this problem at greater length further on. See *infra*, pp. 18 ff.

42. In an early version of this paper, I made a distinction between those historians who stress the continuity of Nazi policies and those who place the accent on their discontinuous character: the former would be the "intentionalists" and the latter the "functionalists." Cf. Saul Friedländer, "De l'Antisémitisme à l'Extermination: Esquisse historiographique," *loc. cit.* The current definitions allow for more precision. Although the contending positions were developed since the 1960s, the currently used concepts were coined, in their present context, by British historian Tim Mason. Cf. Tim Mason, "Intention and Explanation: A Current Controversy about the Interpretation of National-Socialism," in Gerhard Hirschfeld and Lothar Kettenacker, eds., *Der Führerstaat, Mythos und Realität* (Stuttgart, 1981), pp. 23–41.

43. Quoted by Tim Mason, "Intention and Explanation," p. 29 (Hildebrand's definition is given without exact reference). For the same position, see also Klaus Hildebrand, "Monokratie oder Polykratie? Hitlers Herrschaft und das Dritte Reich," in Gerhard Hirschfeld and Lothar Kettenacker, *op. cit.*, pp. 73 ff.; see particularly Karl Dietrich Bracher, *Zeitgeschichtliche Kontroversen um Faschismus, Totalitarismus, Demokratie* (München, 1976), p. 85.

44. Many of these points had already been made in one form or another quite independently of the systematic development of the functionalist school in West Germany. The best known example is A. J. P. Taylor's *Origins of the Second World War*

(London 1961); see also Edward N. Peterson, *The Limits of Hitler's Power* (Princeton, 1969), or the study of Heinz Höhne on the internal "pulling and hauling" within the SS itself: Heinz Höhne, *Der Orden unter dem Totenkopf: Die Geschichte des SS* (Gütersloh, 1968). In Germany the controversy actually started after the publication of Fritz Tobias's book on the Reichstag fire (Fritz Tobias, *Der Reichstagsbrand: Legende und Wirklichkeit*, [Rastatt, 1962]), with Hans Mommsen's "functionalist" appraisal of the issue: Hans Mommsen, "Der Reichstagsbrand und seine Folgen," *VfZ* 12, no. 3 (1964), pp. 351 ff. Functionalism implies, of necessity, a polycratic view of the Nazi system. For a classical statement about the Nazi regime as a polycracy or as "anarchic authoritarianism," see Martin Broszat, *Der Staat Hitlers: Grundlegung und Entwicklung seiner inneren Verfassung* (München, 1969).

45. According to Ernst Nolte, "Auschwitz was as directly included in the principles of the racial doctrine of the Nazis as the fruit in its seed." E. Nolte, *Three Faces*, p. 400.

46. Eberhard Jäckel, *Hitlers Weltanschauung*, 2nd ed. (Stuttgart, 1981), pp. 71–72.

47. Gerald L. Fleming, *Hitler und die Endlösung* (München, 1982), pp. 13–14.

48. Karl Dietrich Bracher, *The German Dictatorship*, p. 252; the same author presents his thesis of the direct unfolding of Nazi extermination plans and policies in a more detailed and forceful way in the same book on pp. 399–401. For Raul Hilberg, the successive stages of Nazi policies were: definition, expropriation, concentration, extermination.

49. Ino Arndt and Wolfgang Scheffler, "Organisierter Massenmord an Juden in nationalsozialistischen Vernichtungslagern," *VfZ* 2 (1976), p. 112. It should be mentioned, within this context, that Jewish inmates of clinics were considered a special category and were killed whatever their degree of illness. Cf. Eugen Kogon et al., eds., *Nationalsozialistische Massentötungen durch Giftgas* (Frankfurt am Main, 1983), p. 53. The significance of such a decision should not be underestimated, but even if it is difficult to ascertain that the euthanasia killings were considered as a technical preparation for the extermination of the Jews, there is little doubt that the killing by gas of small groups of Soviet war prisoners at Auschwitz in the fall of 1941 was meant to test different gas killing techniques with a view to the start of the "Final Solution." For the killing by gas of Soviet prisoners of war, see Christian F. Streit, *Keine Kameraden: Die Wehrmacht und die sowjetischen Kriegsgefangenen 1941–1945* (Stuttgart, 1978), p. 397, n. 32.

50. Helmut Krausnick et al., *Anatomy of the SS State* (London, 1968), p. 60.

51. Ibid., pp. 60, 67. Recent research shows that there are some contradictions concerning the nature, place, and time of the orders given to the heads of the Einsatzgruppen about the extermination of Soviet Jewry. However, the overall evaluation of this material still indicates that a verbal order about the wholesale extermination of Soviet Jews must have been given at some stage just before or just after the launching of Operation Barbarossa. Cf. Helmut Krausnick and Hans-Heinrich Wilhelm, *Die Truppe des Weltanschauungskrieges: Die Einsatzgruppen der Sicherheitspolizei und des SD 1938–1942* (Stuttgart, 1981), pp. 162, 539, and esp. p. 627.

52. Raul Hilberg, *The Destruction of the European Jews*, p. 262.

53. Martin Broszat, "Soziale Motivation und Führer-Bindung des Nationalsozialismus," *VfZ* 18, no. 4 (1970), p. 403.

54. Ibid., pp. 405, 408.

55. Hans Mommsen, "Die Realisierung des Utopischen: Die 'Endlösung der Judenfrage' in 'Dritten Reich,'" *Geschichte und Gesellschaft* 9, no. 3 (1983), p. 386.

56. Ibid.

57. Ibid., p. 387.

58. Karl A. Schleunes, *The Twisted Road to Auschwitz: Nazi Policy Towards the German Jews 1933–1939* (Urbana, Ill., 1970), p. 257.

59. Uwe Dietrich Adam, *Judenpolitik im Dritten Reich* (Düsseldorf, 1972), p. 357.

325

60. Hans Mommsen, "Die Realisierung," p. 387. We shall come back to this example further on and suggest a course of events somewhat different from the one mentioned by Hans Mommsen.

61. Uwe Dietrich Adam, *op. cit.*, pp. 303–13. See also, for a summary of Adam's position, Uwe Dietrich Adam, "Der Aspekt der 'Planung' in der NS-Judenpolitik," in Thomas Klein, Volker Losemann, and Günther Mai eds., *Judentum und Antisemitismus von der Antike bis zur Gegenwart* (Düsseldorf, 1984), pp. 161 ff.

62. Martin Broszat, "Hitler und die Genesis der 'Endlösung': Aus Anlass der Thesen von David Irving," *VfZ* 25, no. 4 (1977), pp. 752–53. The English translation used here is from *Yad Vashem Studies* 13 (1979), p. 93. Some of Broszat's arguments have been neatly countered in Christopher R. Browning's "Zur Genesis der Endlösung: Eine Antwort an Martin Broszat," *VfZ* 29, no. 1 (1981), pp. 99–109. Further on we shall deal with some of Broszat's main arguments and with Browning's answer. In his recent article, "Die Realisierung des Utopischen . . . ," Hans Mommsen reaches the same conclusion as Broszat about the nonexistence of a Hitler order to exterminate the Jews of Europe; cf. Hans Mommsen, *loc. cit.*, p. 395.

63. Hans Mommsen, "National-Socialism: Continuity and Change," in Walter Laqueur ed., *Fascism: A Reader's Guide* (London, 1979), p. 179. For the earliest presentation of this thesis by the same author, see his "Der Nationalsozialistiche Polizeistaat und die Judenverfolgung vor 1938," *VfZ* 10, no. 1, (1962), p. 76; for the most recent restatement of this position, see his "Die Realisierung" *loc. cit.*, pp. 389–90.

64. Hans Mommsen, "Die Realisierung," p. 390. The author considers Hitler's declarations of January 1939 about the extermination of the Jews of Europe in the event of war as rhetoric. Even Hitler's discussions of April 1943 with Marshal Antonescu of Rumania and Regent Horthy of Hungary, in which extermination is clearly mentioned, are still considered as mostly rhetorical. Ibid., pp. 390, 393.

65. Hans Mommsen, "Die Realisierung," p. 412. In a communication to the author, Hans Mommsen argues that this haziness was meant by Heydrich to leave doubts in the minds of the participants, in order to minimize the basis for possible opposition. My argument is that there was no haziness whatsoever, that the participants in the conference knew exactly what was meant and that anyhow the process of extermination was clear enough to all concerned in case anybody had wished or dared express any opposition. In fact, even a small part of the picture was enough to incite opposition; hundreds of thousands were aware of parts of the picture, but no opposition was voiced. See also n. 111.

66. This is the stand I took in my "De l'Antisémitisme à l'Extérmination," p. 148, thereby approaching the position also expressed in Krausnick and Wilhelm, *Die Truppe des Weltanschauungskrieges*, p. 364.

67. Actually, the opposition between a social-structural historiography and the more traditional "narrative" one is beyond the specific issues at the core of the discussion. It appears clearly in Tim Mason's presentation of the two schools (cf. Tim Mason, *op. cit.*), as well as, for instance, in Wolfgang J. Mommsen's article "Gegenwärtige Tendenzen in der Geschichtsschreibung der Bundesrepublik," *Geschichte und Gesellschaft* XXX, no. 2 (1981), pp. 161 ff. But, in fact, this may well be a misleading dichotomy, as the "intentionalist" position could be set within the conceptual framework of "political religions," in which structural analysis becomes essential and, in many ways, far more sophisticated than the accepted social-structural approach.

68. This is also one of David Irving's arguments. Similarly, he refers to the "weak dictator" and in general uses and misuses some of the salient points of the functionalist position to bolster his own thesis of Hitler's noninvolvement in the Final Solution: "My analysis of this controversial issue [the extermination of the Jews] serves to highlight two broad conclusions: that in wartime, dictatorships are fundamentally weak—the dictator

himself, however alert, is unable to oversee all the functions of his executives acting within the confines of his far-flung empire; and that in this particular case, the burden of guilt for the bloody and mindless massacre of the Jews rests on a large number of Germans, many of them alive today, and not just on one 'mad dictator' whose order had to be obeyed without question." David Irving, *Hitler's War* (London, 1977), p. xiii.

69. Krausnick and Wilhelm, *Die Truppe des Weltanschauungkrieges*, p. 623.

70. Ibid., p. 630.

71. For example, Martin Broszat, "Soziale Motivation," pp. 401–2; and Hans Mommsen, "Die Realisierung," pp. 388–98.

72. Martin Broszat, "Hitler und die Genesis der Endlösung," pp. 770 ff.

73. Hans Mommsen, "Nationalsozialismus," in *Sowjetsystem und demokratische Gesellschaft: Eine vergleichende Enzyklopädie*, Vol. IV (Freiburg, 1971).

74. Hans Mommsen, "Die Realisierung," p. 389.

75. Ibid., p. 397.

76. Ibid., pp. 397–98.

77. Ibid., p. 399.

78. Cf. the order sent on August 1, 1941, by Gestapo Chief Heinrich Müller to the heads of the four Einsatzgruppen: "Regular reports have to be submitted to the Führer concerning the work of the Einsatzgruppen in the East," in Gerald L. Fleming, *Hitler und die Endlösung*, p. 58.

79. Ibid., p. 14.

80. Ibid., p. 141.

81. See Eberhard Jäckel, *Hitlers Weltanschauung*, 2nd ed. (Stuttgart, 1981), p. 78.

82. Cf. *supra*, p. 15.

83. See mainly Christof Dipper, "Der deutsche Widerstand und die Juden," *Geschichte und Gesellschaft* 9, no. 3 (1983), pp. 349 ff.

84. Cf. Otto Dov Kulka, "Public Opinion in Nazi Germany and the Jewish Question," *Zion* 40 (1975), pp. 186 ff. (in Hebrew) and an abridged version in English in the *Jerusalem Quarterly*, no. 25-26 (Fall-Winter 1982), pp. 121 ff. See also Kulka, "Die Nürnberger Rassengesetze und die deutsche Bevölkerung," *VfZ* 33, no. 1, 1985.

85. Ian Kershaw, "The Persecution of the Jews and German Popular Opinion in the Third Reich," *Leo Baeck Institute Year Book* XXVI (1981), p. 288. For earlier studies of German public opinion, which either touch upon attitudes toward the anti-Jewish policies or are devoted to the subject, see Marlis Steinert, *Hitlers Kreig und die Deutschen* (Düsseldorf, 1970); and L. D. Stokes, "The German People and the Destruction of the European Jews," *Journal of Central European History* 6, 1973.

86. See among others Dietrich Orlow, *The History of the Nazi Party*, vol. II, *1933–1945* (Newton-Abbot, 1973), pp. 33, 163–65, 247.

87. Cf. Uwe Dietrich Adam, *Judenpolitik*, pp. 65–66.

88. Orlow, *op. cit.*, pp. 164–65.

89. For a full text of this very important speech, see Hildegard von Kotze and Helmut Krausnick, *Es spricht der Führer: Sieben exemplarische Hitler-Reden* (Gütersloh, 1966), esp. pp. 147–48.

90. Schleunes, *op. cit.*, pp. 245–46.

91. In fact, the noninstrumental, nonmobilizing aspect of Hitler's racial or biological ideology and its direct, nonrhetorical link to policies becomes even more evident when one turns to the little discussed issue of "the destruction of unworthy life" (the so-called euthanasia). Hitler touched upon it in his early writings, proclaimed it as a worthy aim in a public speech at Nuremberg, in 1929, and he gave the secret order for its secret implementation a few days after the beginning of the war. On the whole subject, see Klaus Dörner, "Nationalsozialismus und Lebensvernichtung," *VfZ* 15, no. 2 (April 1967), pp. 121 ff. (for the Nuremberg speech, see p. 131).

92. It is minimized in Schleunes's conclusion and even more so in Hans Mommsen's various texts, particularly in "Die Realisierung," p. 387. Uwe Adam, on the other hand, although stressing the chaotic aspect of Nazi policy toward the Jews, points out that "ultimately the *Reichskanzler* alone decided upon the course of the policy toward the Jews" (*als letzte Instanz allein der Reichskanzler den Gang der Judenpolitik bestimmte*). Uwe Adam, *op. cit.*, p. 196.

93. Ibid., p. 61.

94. Ibid.

95. Cf. p. 22.

96. Cf. p. 16.

97. Kulka, "Die Nürnberger Rassengesetze," n. 128; Cf. n. 84 above. We know that several proposals for such a legislation were discussed within various party and ministerial forums after the Nazis came to power, in particular since the end of 1934 (cf. Lothar Gruchmann, "'Blutschutzgesetz' und Justiz: Zu Entstehung und Auswirkung des Nürnberger Gesetzes vom 15. September 1935," VfZ 31, no. 3 [1983], pp. 418 ff.). Gruchmann's article does not analyze the August 1935 discussions at the ministerial level. The reexamination by Kulka makes obvious that the major source for the spontaneous aspect of the legislation, i.e., Bernhard Lösener's report (Bernhard Lösener, "Als Rassereferent im Reichsministerium des Innern," VfZ no. 3 [1961]), is probably less trustworthy than was thought up to now.

98. Lösener, *loc. cit.*, p. 274.

99. Adam, *op. cit.*, p. 195.

100. During the period 1938–41, one actually can distinguish four different aspects of Nazi policies: (a) Hitler's threats of extermination, which began at the end of 1938 and were expressed in well-known discussions with foreign dignitaries and in public speeches such as that of January 30, 1939, as well as in discussions with close aides after the defeat of Poland; (b) A simultaneous policy of forced emigration and expulsion which in a way includes the Madagascar scheme as well as the expulsions of Jews from Saarpfalz and Baden to unoccupied France, etc.; (c) A policy of concentration in the General Government, including the Nisko project. Concerning Hitler's initiative on the latter, see Arthur Rosenberg's entry of September 9, 1939, in his *Politisches Tagebuch,* Munich, 1964, p. 99; (d) Various limited-scale extermination measures against the Jews or other groups, including the operations of the Einsatzgruppen in Poland and the "euthanasia" program. Moreover, this period of transition becomes even more complex when one notes that at some stage Hitler decided to leave the measures to be taken for the disappearance of the Jews up to his gauleiters. This is clearly stated in Bormann's letter to Lammers of November 20, 1940, in which the latter is informed that the führer expects the gauleiters to see to it that their areas become purely German within a few years, in which case he would not then ask them what methods were utilized to achieve this end. Cf. Helmut Krausnick and Hans-Heinrich Wilhelm, *op. cit.*, p. 626. As stated in the text, this hesitation period was to be expected and it somehow came to an end just before or just after the attack on the Soviet Union.

101. For these various arguments, see Martin Broszat, *loc. cit.*, pp. 746 ff.

102. Christopher R. Browning, *loc. cit.*, pp. 98 ff.

103. Gerald Fleming, *op. cit.*, p. 88.

104. Martin Broszat, *loc. cit.*, p. 749 n. Übelhör's protests against sending deportees from the Reich to Łódź tie in with this kind of reasoning.

105. Gerald Fleming, *op. cit.*, pp. 34–35. It seems that the extermination by gas of the Warthegau Jews was mentioned for the first time in a communication sent to Eichmann on July 16, 1941 by SS *Sturmbannführer* Rolf-Heinz Höppner, belonging to the staff of the Higher SS and Police Leader of the Warthegau. One may assume that Eichmann discussed the matter with Heydrich, but we do not know if Hitler was involved

328

at that stage and gave his assent. As already mentioned, Kommando Lange, which took charge of the exterminations starting in December, came from Berlin. For Heinz Höppner's communication to Eichmann, see Eugen Kogon et al., *Nationalsozialistische Massentötungen*, pp. 110–11.

106. Hans Mommsen, "Die Realisierung," p. 411.

107. Hans Mommsen has presented the following interpretation of the Wannsee Conference. After alluding to Hans Frank's remarks of December 16, 1941, referring to "major measures to be discussed in the Reich [concerning the Jews]," Mommsen writes: "This relates to the forthcoming 'Wannsee Conference' which is generally identified with the immediate commencement of the overall European Genocide, although the 'Initiatives' (*Aktionen*) mentioned by Heydrich in relation to the evacuation of the Jews to the East were presented at alternatives (*Ausweichmöglichkeiten*) aimed at gathering practical experience 'in view of the coming final solution of the Jewish Question.' The liquidation of those Jews who were unable to work was mentioned explicitly. The fiction of compulsory labor (*Arbeitseinsatz*) created the psychological link between the emigration, the reservation solution and the Holocaust itself. At the same time, the chimera of a territorial 'final solution,' which was now to be located beyond the Urals, was still held forth (*schimmerte noch durch*). On the other hand, the formulation concerning 'certain preparatory actions relating to the Final Solution' which had to be taken in the 'territories concerned,' i.e. in the General Government, referred to immediate partial liquidation. . . ." Hans Mommsen, "Die Realisierung," p. 412.

108. The Eichmann Trial, Session 107, July 24, 1961, quoted in Fleming, *op. cit.*, p. 105. For a particularly thorough analysis of the unmistakable meaning of the Wannsee Conference, see Wolfgang Scheffler, "Zur Entstehungsgeschichte der 'Endlösung,'" in *Aus Politik und Zeitgeschichte: Beilage zur Wochenzeitung Das Parlament*, B 43/82, October 1982, pp. 8 ff.

109. Yehuda Bauer, "Auschwitz and the 'Final Solution,'" lecture given at the international conference on the extermination of the Jews of Europe, Stuttgart, May 3–5, 1984.

110. Gerald L. Fleming, *op. cit.*, p. 62.

111. Helmut Krausnick et al., *Anatomy of the SS State*, p. 69.

112. Gerald L. Fleming, *op. cit.*, pp. 65–67. As we have already mentioned in the case of Heydrich at the Wannsee Conference, one cannot imagine that Himmler would have referred to a nonexistent führer order, especially in front of such audiences.

113. Helmut Krausnick et al., *op. cit.*, p. 97.

114. Bernhard Lösener, "Als Rassereferent," p. 311.

115. Gerald L. Fleming, *op. cit.*, p. 77.

116. Ibid., p. 58.

117. Ibid.

118. Josef Ackermann, *Himmler als Ideologe*, p. 166. The word *Abschaffen* is added in red ink. It means that Hitler took the decision during the meeting.

119. For the text of both Korherr reports and the related correspondence, see Serge Klarsfeld, ed., *The Holocaust and the Neo-Nazi Mythomania* (New York, 1978).

120. Gerald L. Fleming, *op. cit.*, pp. 149–52.

121. Cf. Serge Klarsfeld, ed., *op. cit.*

122. Walk, ed., *Das Sonderrecht für die Juden im NS-Staat*, p. 400.

123. For the relevant excerpts of these speeches, see Jäckel, *Hitlers Weltanschauung*, pp. 74–75. The constant repetition of the theme during 1942 seems to indicate, in itself, that Hitler wished to convey that a turning point had been reached, that the extermination he had prophesied had started.

124. In the second conversation with Horthy, on April 17, 1943, Ribbentrop answered first when Horthy asked what should be done with the Jews. According to the

foreign minister, the Jews should either be exterminated or put in concentration camps. Hitler then explained his policies in the clearest possible way: "The Jews are parasites. In Poland one took care of these matters in the most systematic way. If the Jews there did not want to work, they were shot. If they could not work, they had to perish (*Wenn die Juden dort nicht arbeiten wollten, wurden sie erschossen. Wenn sie nicht arbeiten könnten, müssten sie verkommen*). They had to be handled like tuberculosis bacilli, which could contaminate a healthy body. This was not cruel if one took into account that even innocent creatures like deer had to be killed, to avoid their causing damage. Why should one show greater leniency to those beasts which brought us Bolshevism." Cf. Andreas Hillgruber, *Staatsmänner und Diplomaten bei Hitler*, vol. 2 (Frankfurt, 1970), pp. 256 ff.

125. Gerald L. Fleming, *op. cit.*, p. 70.

126. Ibid., p. 37.

127. David Irving, *Hitler's War* (London, 1975).

128. James M. Rhodes, *The Hitler Movement: A Modern Millenarian Revolution* (Hoover Institution Press, Stanford University, 1980), chaps. 2, 8; Uriel Tal, *Political Faith in Nazi Ideology and Policy Prior to the Holocaust*, Annual Lecture of the Jacob M. and Shoshana Schreiber Chair for Contemporary Jewish History (Tel Aviv University, 1978), 53 pp.; idem, "On Structures of Political Theology and Myth in Germany Prior to the Holocaust," in Yehuda Bauer and Nathan Rotenstreich, eds., *The Holocaust as Historical Experience* (New York and London, 1981), pp. 43–74; idem, "Nazism as a Political Faith," *The Jerusalem Quarterly*, no. 15 (1980), pp. 70–90.

129. An interesting example of this paradoxical situation is Andreas Hillgruber's *Endlich, loc. cit.*, where the absolute centrality of Hitler's racial dogma is strongly emphasized ("everything was subordinated to the racial dogma, internal policy as well as foreign affairs," p. 52). However, among the main issues discussed and considered as most relevant to the understanding of nazism, the anti-Jewish policies and the "Final Solution" do not appear.

2 / The Written Matter and the Spoken Word
On the Gap Between Pre-1914 and Nazi Anti-Semitism
SHULAMIT VOLKOV

1. See the recent collection of essays on anti-Semitism from the ancient world to the present, *Antisemitism through the Ages*, ed. S. Almog (Jerusalem, 1980) (in Hebrew). Of special interest in our context is Israel Guttman's "On the Nature of Antisemitism in its Nazi Version," pp. 353–87.

2. Benzion Dinur, "Galuyot ve'Hurbanan" in *Kneset* 8 (1943-44) (in Hebrew), pp. 46–60.

3. See Ettinger's collected essays: *Modern Antisemitism: Studies and Essays* (Tel Aviv, 1978) (in Hebrew).

4. See his "Changing Pattern of Antisemitism: A Survey" in *Jewish Social Studies* XXXVIII, no. 1 (1976), pp. 5–38.

5. See especially the essay on the universal meaning of modern anti-Semitism in Y. Talmon, *The Unique and Universal: Some Historical Reflections* (London, 1965; cited according to the Hebrew edition, Jerusalem, 1965), pp. 299 ff. And compare his comments there, pp. 288–309, with pt. IX of his *Myth of the Nation and the Vision of Revolution: The Origins of Ideological Polarization in the 20th Century* (London, 1981; cited according to the Hebrew edition, Tel Aviv, 1981), pp. 613–49. The quotation, p. 633.

6. George L. Mosse, *The Crisis of German Ideology: Intellectual Origins of the Third Reich* (New York, 1964), pp. 294–311.

7. Yaakov Katz, *Antisemitism: From Religious Hatred to Racial Rejection* (Tel Aviv, 1979) (in Hebrew), p. 306.

8. Compare in this context R. Rürup's and Thomas Nipperdey's essay on anti-Semitism in *Geschichtliche Grundbegriffe: Historisches Lexikon zur politisch-sozialen Sprache*, vol. 1, ed. O. Brunner et al. (Stuttgart, 1972). For a full bibliography, see the appendices to the *Leo Baeck Institute Year Books* (hereafter *LBIY*) annually since 1956. Also Ismar Schorsch, "German Antisemitism in the Light of Post-War Historiography," in *LBIY* XIX (1974), pp. 257–71.

9. Massing's book was first published in New York as early as 1946, and its title is somewhat misleading. The book is considerably more cautious on the matter of continuity than can be presumed from the title. See also Peter Pulzer's book (London, 1964), and Arendt's first ed. (1951), pp. 3–10.

10. See especially Krausnick's Introduction to his part in H. Krausnick et al., *Anatomie des SS-Staates* (Munich, 1965). (English trans.: *The Anatomy of the SS State* [New York, 1968].)

11. Quoted from the 5th ed. (Paris, 1964), pp. 5–6.

12. The quoted phrase, and much of the conceptual apparatus I have used here, is taken from the work of Professor Uriel Tal. See especially his "Political Faith of Nazism Prior to the Holocaust," published separately by the Chair for Contemporary Jewish History, Tel-Aviv University (Tel Aviv 1978). See also my "Antisemitism as a Cultural Code: Reflections on the History and Historiography of Antisemitism in Imperial Germany," in *LBIY* XXIII (1978), pp. 25–46.

13. See the comments in Reginald H. Phelps's introduction to his reprinting of "Hitler's grundlegende Rede über den Antisemitismus," in the *Vierteljahreshefte für Zeitgeschichte*, 1968, pp. 395–99. See also Uwe Lohalm, *Völkischer Radikalismus: Die Geschichte des deutschvölksichen Schutzund Trutz-Bundes 1919–1923* (Hamburg, 1970), esp. pp. 298–301. On Fritsch's influence, see especially R. Phelps, "Theodor Fritsch und der Antisemitismus," in *Deutsche Rundschau* 87 (1961), pp. 442–49.

14. See above all Werner Jochmann's two studies: "Struktur und Funktion des deutschen Antisemitismus," in *Juden im Wilhelminischen Deutschland 1890–1914*, ed. by Werner E. Mosse with the cooperation of Arnold Paucker (Tübingen, 1976), pp. 389–477; and "Die Ausbreitung des Antisemitismus," in *Deutsches Judentum in Krieg und Revolution*, by the same editors (Tübingen, 1971), pp. 409–510.

15. See their works cited above, nn. 1, 3, 5, 7.

16. In *The Origins of Totalitarianism* (New York, 1951), p. 8.

17. Jacob Toury, *Turmoil and Confusion in the Revolution of 1848: The Anti-Jewish Riots in the "Year of Freedom" and their Influence on Modern Antisemitism* (Tel-Aviv, 1968) (in Hebrew). See also Eleonore Sterling, *Judenhass. Die Anfänge des politischen Antisemitismus in Deutschland (1815–1850)* (Frankfurt am Main, 1969).

18. Toury, *op. cit.*, pp. 115–19.

19. See the reprint of these parties' political programs in Fritz Specht, *Die Reichstagswahlen von 1867–1897* (Berlin, 1898), esp. pp. 503–7, and the useful summaries in D. Fricke, *Die Bürgerlichen Parteien in Deutschland: Handbuch der Geschichte der bürgerlichen Parteien und anderer bürgerlicher Interessenorganisationen, vom Vormärz bis zum Jahre 1914*, vol. 1 (East Berlin, 1968), pp. 36–40, 245–55, 429–31, 754–56, 759–62.

20. See esp. Richard S. Levy, *The Downfall of the Antisemitic Political Parties in Imperial Germany* (New Haven, 1975).

21. Despite their emphasis on the transition to racism, the old reliance on the religious, as well as on the socioeconomic and cultural roots of anti-Semitism even in the late nineteenth century is apparent both in Uriel Tal's *Christians and Jews in Germany: Religion, Politics and Ideology in the Second Reich 1870–1914* (Ithaca, 1977), esp. chap. 5; and in Y. Katz, *op. cit.*, chap. 27, and passim.

22. Bloch, *op. cit.*, p. 8.

23. For the controversy over Wagner's racism, see L. Stein, *Racial Thinking of Richard Wagner* (New York, 1950); R. E. Herzstein, "Richard Wagner at the Crossroads of German Antisemitism," *Zeitschrift für die Geschichte der Juden*, no. 2-3 (1967); D. Kulka, "Richard Wagner und die Anfänge des modernen Antisemitismus," in *Bulletin des Leo Baeck Instituts* 16 (1961); Toury, *op. cit.*, pp. 153–60; Y. Katz, *op. cit.*, chap. 15.

24. Quoted in Fritz Stern, *The Politics of Cultural Despair: A Study in the Rise of the Germanic Ideology* (New York, 1961), pp. 91–92.

25. See Eugen Düring, *Die Judenfrage als Rassen-, Sitten- und Kulturfrage* (Karlsruhe, 1880); and in addition, Christoph Cobet, *Der Wortschatz des Antisemitismus in der Bismarckzeit* (Munich, 1973), pp. 82–94.

26. See Wilhelm Marr, *Der Sieg des Judentums über das Germanentum* (Bern, 1879); and Otto Glagau, *Der Bankrott des Nationalliberalismus und die Reaktion*, 8th ed. (Berlin, 1978), passim.

27. Quoted from a 1919 reprint of this edition, p. 20 (emphasis mine).

28. Quotes and phrases from "Unsere Aussichten" (November 15, 1978), reprinted in his *Deutsche Kämpfe: Schriften zur Tagespolitik*, (Leipzig, 1896), pp. 17–28. For Treitschke, see also his collected lectures and essays in *Historische und Politische Aufsätze* (Leipzig, 1886); *Politik* (Leipzig, 1922); and Andreas Dorpalen, *Heinrich von Treitschke* (New Haven, 1957).

29. Cf. Hellmut von Gerlach, *Von Rechts nach Links* (Zürich, 1937), p. 110 ff; and esp. Heinrich Class, *Wider den Strom* (Leipzig, 1932), pp. 15–16, 87.

30. On nationalism at that time, from a different perspective, giving anti-Semitism almost no place at all, see Geoff Eley, *Reshaping the German Right* (New Haven, 1980).

31. See especially Hans Rosenberg, *Grosse Depression und Bismarckzeit: Wirtschaft, Gesellschaft und Politik in Mitteleuropa* (Berlin, 1967). On anti-Semitism in this context, see also Fritz Stern, *Gold and Iron: Bismarck, Bleichröder and the Building of the German Empire* (New York, 1977), esp. pt. III.

32. For further bibliography and more extensive presentation, see my *Rise of Popular Antimodernism: The Urban Master Artisans 1873–1896* (Princeton, 1978), esp. chap. 8.

33. Cf. my "Social and Political Function of Late 19th-Century Antisemitism: The Case of the Small Handicraft Masters," in *Sozialgeschichte Heute*, ed. by H. U. Wehler, (Göttingen, 1974), pp. 416–31. See also H. J. Puhle, *Agrarische Interessenpolitik und preussischer Konservatismus im Wilhelminischen Reich 1893–1914* (Bonn, 1975).

34. On this aspect of anti-Semitism, see my "Antisemitism as a Cultural Code," *loc. cit.*

35. The most comprehensive work on Social Democracy in this context now is Rosemarie Leuchen-Seppel, *Sozialdemokratie und Antisemitismus: Die Auseinandersetzung der Partei mit den konservativen und völkischen Strömungen des Antisemitismus 1871–1914* (Bonn, 1978).

36. Byrnes's vol. I: *The Prologue to the Dreyfus Affair*, was published at New Brunswick, 1950. Particularly instructive are also Pierre Sorlin, *La Croix et les Juifs (1880–1899)* (Paris, 1967); Jeannine Verdes-Leroux, *Scandale financier et antisémitisme Catholique* (Paris, 1969); Pierre Pierrard, *Juifs et Catholiques français* (Paris, 1970). More generally, Zeev Sternhell, *La Droite révolutionnaire 1885–1914* (Paris, 1978); and René Rémond, *La Droite en France: de la Première Restauration à la Vᵉ République* (Paris, 1963) (cited according to the English translation, Philadelphia, 1966). See also Michael R. Marrus and Robert O. Paxton, *Vichy France and the Jews* (New York, 1981). I have benefited greatly from discussions with Mrs. Dafna Schachner, Tel Aviv University, on everything concerning French anti-Semitism.

37. Following the tradition of political geography, however, the study of the geographical distribution of anti-Semitic manifestations is far more advanced in France than in Germany, and is indeed highly suggestive. See the analysis and the maps in Byrnes, *op. cit.*, pp. 251–61; Sorlin, *op. cit.*, pp. 39–55, 219–24; Sternhell, *op. cit.*, pp. 221–24; and esp. Stephen Wilson, "The Antisemitic Riots of 1898 in France," *Historical Journal* XVI (1973); and his "Le Monument Henry: la structure de l'antisemitisme en France 1898–1899," *Annales*, March–April 1977, esp. pp. 266–71.

38. Generally on Drumont, in addition to Byrnes, see Michel Winock, "Édouard Drumont et l'antisémitisme en France avant l'affaire Dreyfus," *Esprit*, May 1971, pp. 1085–1106.

39. Cf. Byrnes, *op. cit.*, pp. 150–154. On the intellectual influence of Drumont see also Zeev Sternhell, "National-Socialism and Antisemitism: The Case of Maurice Barrés," *Journal of Contemporary History* 8 (1973), pp. 47–66; M. Curtis, *Three Against the Third Republic: Sorel, Barrés and Maurras* (Princeton, 1959), pp. 203–20. Also Ernst Nolte, *Der Faschismus in seiner Epoche: Die Action française, der italienischen Faschismus, der Nationalsozialismus* (Munich, 1963), pp. 83–89.

40. Cf. Byrnes, *op. cit.*, pp. 91–92.

41. Cf. Sternhell, *La Droite*, chap. III, pp. 146–76.

42. Ibid., p. 236.

43. For the riots, see esp. S. Wilson, "The Antisemitic Riots," *loc. cit.*; On the Marquis de Morés, see Byrnes, *op. cit.*, pp. 227–50. More in Sternhell, *La Droite*, chap. V, pp. 215–30.

44. Cf. Byrnes, *op. cit.*, pp. 261–80; S. Wilson, "Le Monument Henry," *loc. cit.*, pp. 271–76.

45. This theme is well covered in the literature. See esp. Sternhell, *La Droite*, chap. IV; and Rémond, *op. cit.*, chaps. 6 and 7.

46. Quoted in Sternhell, *La Droite*, p. 177.

47. Rémond, *op. cit.*, p. 224.

48. On the position of the socialists: Byrnes, *op. cit.*, pp. 156–78; Sternhell, *La Droite*, pp. 184–96; 237–41; and the interesting interpretation in J. P. Peter, "Dimensions de l'affaire Dreyfus," *Annales*, 1961. See also H. Arendt's chapter on the "Affair" in her *Origins*, pp. 98–120.

49. On the French Jewish community, see Michael R. Marrus, *The Politics of Assimilation: A Study of the French Jewish Community at the Time of the Dreyfus Affair* (Oxford, 1971); and Paula Heyman, *From Dreyfus to Vichy: The Remaking of French Jewry 1906–1939* (New York, 1979).

50. Cf. Sternhell, *La Droite*, p. 242, and also Marrus and Paxton, *op. cit.*, pp. 31–32.

51. Cf. Richard S. Levy, *op. cit.*, pp. 154–55, 166–72, 206–8.

52. Heinrich Class, *Wider den Strom*, pp. 87–88.

53. Cf. Lohalm, *op. cit.*, pp. 32–54; also D. Fricke, *op. cit.*, pp. 1–26.

54. The book was published under a pseudonym: Daniel Frymann, *Wenn ich der Kaiser wär'—Politische Wahrheiten und Notwendigkeiten* (Leipzig, 1913). On the reactions, see Dirk Stegmann, *Die Erben Bismarcks: Parteien und Verbände in der Spätphase des Wilhelminischen Deutschland* (Cologne, 1970), pp. 295–304.

55. This affair is discussed in detail by Hartmut Pogge von Strandmann in "Staatsstreichpläne, Alldeutsche und Bethmann-Hollweg," in Strandmann and Immanuel Geiss, *Die Erfoderlichkeit des Unmöglichen: Deutschland am Vorabend des ersten Weltkrieges* (Frankfurt am Main, 1965); for the quotes, see pp. 22, 25–26.

56. See Treitschke's "Unsere Aussichten," *loc. cit.*, and again in "Herr Grätz und sein Judentum," pp. 45 ff. For Stöcker, see esp. his *Landtag* speech in *Die Judenfrage: Verhandlungen des preussischen Abgeordnetenhauses . . . am 20. und 22. November 1880*

(Berlin, 1880), esp. p. 126. On the disorientation of the anti-Semites when they came to propose anything of practical significance in the Reichstag, see esp. Richard S. Levy, *op. cit.*, chap. 7. See also Saul Ash, "Antisemitic Schemes for Anti-Jewish Policy in Germany up to the Nazi Rise to Power," in *Yad Vashem Studies* VI (Hebrew ed.), pp. 73–100.

57. Düring, *op. cit.*, chap. V, pp. 113–35.

58. See George Steiner, "The Hollow Miracle" (1959), in *Language and Silence: Essays 1958–1966* (London, 1967), pp. 117–32.

59. See Steiner, again, in "The Language Animal" (1969) in *Extraterritorial: Papers on Literature and the Language Revolution* (London, 1972), esp. sec. IV, pp. 71–88.

60. Stephen Wilson, "Le Monument Henry," *loc. cit.*, pp. 286–87.

61. Munich ed., 1939, p. 525.

62. Ibid., pp. 528–34.

63. For a summary of the forces and ideas which drove Hitler to anti-Semitism, see Joachim C. Fest, *Das Gesicht des dritten Reiches: Profile einer totalitären Herrschaft* (Munich, 1963), pt. I, secs. 1, 2. See also the comments in Reginald H. Phelps, *loc. cit.*, pp. 390–99.

64. For this description and much of the following, see the fascinating book by the philologist Victor Klemperer, *Die Unbewältigte Sprache: Aus dem Notizbuch eines Philologen. LTI* (1st ed., 1946; cited from the 3rd ed., Darmstadt, n.d.), esp. pp. 17–49.

65. R. Phelps, *loc. cit.*, p. 418.

66. Bloch, *op. cit.*, p. 9.

3 / Retracing the Twisted Road
Nazi Policies Toward German Jews, 1933–1939
KARL A. SCHLEUNES

1. Giambattista Vico, *The New Science*, 3rd ed., trans. Thomas Goddard Bergin and Max Harold Fisch (Ithaca, N.Y.: Cornell University Press, 1968), p. 96.

2. Hitler to Gemlich, September 16, 1919. See Ernst Deuerlein, "Dokumentation: Hitlers Eintritt in die Politik und die Reichswehr," *Vierteljahrshefte für Zeitgeschichte* (hereafter *VfZ*) 7 (1959), p. 204.

3. Adolf Hitler, *Mein Kampf* (New York: Stackpole Sons, 1939).

4. Lucy S. Dawidowicz, *The War Against the Jews, 1933–1945* (New York: Holt, Rinehart & Winston, 1975), p. 17.

5. Max Domarus, ed., *Hitler: Reden und Proklamationen, 1932–1945*, 2 vols. (Munich: Süddeutscher Verlag, 1965), vol. 2, p. 1058.

6. Martin Broszat, "Hitler und die Genesis der 'Endlösung': Aus Anlass der Thesen von David Irving," *VfZ* 25 (1977), p. 746. The same argument is made by Yehuda Bauer, *The Holocaust in Historical Perspective* (Seattle: University of Washington Press, 1978), pp. 30–49.

7. Alan Bullock, *Hitler: A Study in Tyranny*, rev. ed. (New York: Harper & Row, 1962), p. 407.

8. Robert Koehl, "Feudal Aspects of National Socialism," *American Political Science Review* 54 (1960), pp. 921–33.

9. Strasser quoted in Udo Kissenkötter, "*Gregor Strasser und die NSDAP*," Schriftenreihe der *VfZ* 37 (Stuttgart: Deutsche Verlagsanstalt, 1978), p. 48.

10. From OA II memorandum of October 20, 1929. Quoted in Wolfgang Horn, *Führerideologie und Parteiorganisation der NSDAP (1919–1933)* (Düsseldorf: Droste Verlag, 1972), p. 381.

11. Dietrich Orlow, *The History of the Nazi Party: 1919–1933*, 2 vols. (Pittsburgh: University of Pittsburgh Press, 1969; 1973), vol. 1, p. 180.

12. Karl Dietrich Bracher, Wolfgang Sauer, and Gerhard Schulz, *Die nationalsozialistische Machtergreifung*, Schriftenreihe des Instituts für Politische Wissenschaft (Cologne: Westdeutscher Verlag, 1960), pp. 411–12; and Uwe Dietrich Adam, *Judenpolitik im Dritten Reich* (Düsseldorf: Droste Verlag, 1972), p. 30.

13. Memorandum in NSDAP Hauptarchiv, Folder 504. Also in Karl A. Schleunes, *The Twisted Road to Auschwitz, Nazi Policy Toward German Jews, 1933–1939* (Urbana, Ill.: University of Illinois Press, 1970), p. 70.

14. Horn, *Führerideologie*, p. 385.

15. Göring's interview of May 27, 1932, with Solari, in NSDAP Hauptarchiv, Folder 504.

16. E. Y. Hartshorne, *The German Universities and National Socialism* (London: Allen & Unwin, 1937), p. 100.

17. Bernhard Lösener, "Als Rassereferent im Reichsministerium des Innern," *VfZ* 9 (1961), p. 267.

18. Shlomo Aronson, *Reinhard Heydrich und die Frühgeschichte von Gestapo und SD*, Studien zur Zeitgeschichte (Stuttgart: Deutsche Verlagsanstalt, 1971), p. 79. Nicolai was replaced in early 1935 by Wilhelm Stuckhart.

19. Schleunes, *Twisted Road*, p. 73.

20. Ibid., p. 75.

21. See Curt Menzel quoted in ibid., p. 88.

22. Helmut Genschel, *Die Verdrängung der Juden aus der Wirtschaft im Dritten Reich* (Göttingen: Musterschmidt, 1966), p. 125.

23. Schleunes, *Twisted Road*, pp. 145–46.

24. Martin Broszat, *The Hitler State*, trans. John W. Hiden (London: Longman, 1981), pp. 264–67.

25. Quoted in Schleunes, *Twisted Road*, p. 115.

26. NSDAP Hauptarchiv, Folder 504. See n. 15.

27. Schleunes, *Twisted Road*, p. 119.

28. Ibid., pp. 118–19.

29. Broszat, *Hitler State*, p. 274.

30. Schleunes, *Twisted Road*, p. 178.

31. Hannah Arendt, *Eichmann in Jerusalem; A Report on the Banality of Evil*, rev. and enlarged ed. (New York: Viking Press, 1963), pp. 32–33.

32. Schleunes, *Twisted Road*, p. 199, table 7.

33. Ibid., p. 193.

34. Ibid., pp. 201–10.

35. Quoted in ibid., p. 207.

36. Quoted in ibid., p. 225.

37. Genschel, *Verdrängung der Juden*, p. 175, n. 159.

38. Helmut Krausnick, Hans Buchheim, Martin Broszat, and Hans-Adolf Jacobsen, *The Anatomy of the SS State*, trans. Richard Barry, Marion Jackson, and Dorothy Long (New York: Walker, 1968), pp. 32–43.

39. Schleunes, *Twisted Road*, p. 224.

40. See "Stenographic Report of the Meeting on 'The Jewish Question' under the chairmanship of Field Marshall [sic] Goering in the Reichs Air Force." Document 1816-PS, *Nazi Conspiracy and Aggression*, vol. 4 (Washington, D.C.: Government Printing Office, 1946), p. 439. See also Rita Thalmann and Emmanuel Feinermann, *Crystal Night: 9–10 November 1938*, trans. Gilles Cremonesi (New York: Coward, McCann & Geohegan, 1974).

41. "Stenographic Report," p. 425.

42. Schumacher Archiv, Folder 240 II. See Schleunes, *Twisted Road*, p. 252.

43. Krausnick et al., *Anatomy*, p. 43. Also Domarus, *Hitler: Reden*, vol. 1, p. 980.

44. Domarus, *Hitler: Reden*, vol. 2, p. 1058.

45. Eberhard Jäckel, *Hitler's Weltanschauung: A Blueprint for Power*, trans. Herbert Arnold (Middletown, Conn.: Wesleyan University Press, 1972), p. 58.

46. Schleunes, *Twisted Road*, p. 253. Krausnick et al., *Anatomy*, p. 46.

47. Heinz Höhne, *The Order of the Death's Head; The Story of Hitler's SS*, trans. Richard Barry (London: Secker & Warburg, 1969), p. 345.

48. Krausnick et al., *Anatomy*, p. 49.

49. Nora Levin, *The Holocaust: The Destruction of European Jewry, 1933–1945* (New York: Schocken Books, 1973), p. 199.

50. Heydrich quoted in Schleunes, *Twisted Road*, p. 256.

51. Dawidowicz, *War*, p. 105. There were some 100,000 Jews in the Czechoslovakia of 1939.

52. Raul Hilberg, *The Destruction of the European Jews* (Chicago: Quadrangle Books, 1969), pp. 260–61.

53. See Gerald Reitlinger, *The Final Solution; The Attempt to Exterminate the Jews of Europe, 1939–1945* (New York: A. S. Barnes, Perpetua Books, 1953), pp. 71–79. Gerald Reitlinger believes the Madagascar project to have been a front for the extermination plan.

54. Joseph Goebbels, *Diaries, 1942–1943*, ed. Louis Lochner (Garden City, N.Y.: Doubleday, 1948), p. 148.

4 / Relations Between Jews and Non-Jews in Eastern Europe Between the Two World Wars
EZRA MENDELSOHN

1. On Romania, see Carol Iancu, *Les Juifs en Roumanie 1866–1919* (Provence, 1978); and Joshua Starr, "Jewish Citizenship in Rumania (1878–1940)," *Jewish Social Studies* 3, no. 1 (January 1941), pp. 57–80. On the situation in Poland, see the article by Alexander Hafftka in *Zydzi w Polsce odrodzonej* II (Warsaw, n.d.), pp. 234–41. On the Soviet Union, see William Korey, "The Legal Position of Soviet Jewry: A Historical Enquiry," in Lionel Kochan, ed., *The Jews in Soviet Russia Since 1917* (London, New York, and Toronto, 1970), pp. 76–98.

2. Ezra Mendelsohn, *Zionism in Poland* (New Haven and London, 1981), p. 107.

3. S. Gringauz, "Jewish National Autonomy in Lithuania (1918–1925)," *Jewish Social Studies* 14, no. 3 (July 1952), pp. 225–46.

4. Thus, many Jews supported the establishment of a Ukrainian state in Eastern Galicia, arguing that in such a state there would be little danger of assimilation. See Mendelsohn, *Zionism in Poland*, p. 98.

5. This was the attitude of the powerful organization of anti-Zionist Orthodoxy, Agudes Yisroel. See Gershon Bacon, *Agudath Israel in Poland, 1916–39: An Orthodox Jewish Response to the Challenge of Modernity* (Ph.D. dissertation, Columbia University 1979), especially pp. 347–455. See also Mendelsohn, "The Politics of Agudas Yisroel in Interwar Poland," *Soviet Jewish Affairs*, no. 2 (1972), pp. 47–60.

6. Mordechai Altshuler, *Ha-yevsektsia be-vrit ha-moatsot, 1918–1930* (Tel Aviv, 1980), esp. pp. 18–40; Zvi Gitelman, *Jewish Nationality and Soviet Politics* (Princeton, 1972).

7. The best one-volume study on this subject is Joseph Rothschild, *East Central Europe Between the Two World Wars* (Seattle and London, 1974). In this part of the world, of course, the influence of nationalism has long been an issue.

8. For Poland, see Mendelsohn, *Zionism in Poland*, pp. 12–17; for a general study, see my book *The Jews of East Central Europe Between the World Wars* (Bloomington, 1983). See also Shmuel Ettinger (intro. by Bela Vago and George Mosse, eds.), *Jews and Non-Jews in Eastern Europe, 1918–1945* (New York and London, 1974), pp. 1–19.

9. Thus, for example, the hostile remarks of the Slovak leader Vávro Šrotár made in 1919 and quoted in Aharon Moshe Rubinowicz, "The Jewish Minority," *The Jews of Czechoslovakia*, vol. I (New York and Philadelphia, 1968), pp. 226–27.

10. For typical accusations that the Jews favored the Bolsheviks, see the memoirs of Wincenty Witos, *Moje wspomnienia*, vol. II (Paris, 1964), pp. 184–85, 307–8, 391–92; and (for a Hungarian example) Cecile Tormay, *An Outlaw's Diary: Revolution* (London, 1923), and *An Outlaw's Diary: The Commune* (Hereford, 1923).

11. For some recent studies of ideologues of modern east European nationalism, see Alvin Marcus Fountain, *Roman Dmowski: Party, Tactics, Ideology, 1895–1907* (New York, 1980); and William Oldson, *The Historical and Nationalistic Thought of Nicholas Jorga* (Boulder, 1973).

12. See the excellent new book by Frank Golczewski, *Polnisch-Jüdische Beziehungen 1881–1922* (Wiesbaden, 1981), pp. 181–245.

13. Nathaniel Katzburg, *Hungary and the Jews, 1920–1943* (Ramat-Gan, 1981), pp. 32–59.

14. Azriel Shohat, "The Beginnings of Anti-Semitism in Independent Lithuania," *Yad Vashem Studies 2* (1958), pp. 7–48; Rabinowicz, "The Jewish Minority," p. 222.

15. Elyohu Cherikover, *Di ukrainer pogromen in yor 1919* (New York, 1965).

16. Quoted in Mendelsohn, *Zionism in Poland*, p. 90.

17. See Katzburg, *Hungary*; William McCagg, *Jewish Nobles and Geniuses in Modern Hungary* (New York, 1972); Yaakov Katz, "Yihuda shel yuhadut hungariya," in *Eanhagat yehude hungariva be-mivhan ha-shoa* (Jerusalem, 1976), pp. 13–24; R. L. Braham, *The Politics of Genocide: The Holocaust in Hungary*, vol. I (New York, 1981).

18. For details, see Katzburg, *Hungary*, and Braham, *The Politics of Genocide*.

19. On Hungarian politics, see the chapter on Hungary in Rothschild, *East Central Europe*, and on the distinction between good and bad Hungarian Jews, see, for example, Nicholas Horthy, *Memoirs* (London, 1956), p. 98.

20. Details on the Jewish laws are available in Katzburg, *Hungary*, pp. 94 ff., and in Braham, *The Politics of Genocide*. See also Raul Hilberg, *The Destruction of the European Jews* (Chicago, 1961), pp. 509 ff.

21. On the reaction of the Jewish leadership, see Bela Vago, "Tmurot be-hanhagat yehude hungariya bi-yeme milhemet ho-olam ha-shniya," in *Hanhagat yehude hungariya*, pp. 61–76.

22. Golczewski, *Polnisch-Jüdische Beziehungen*, passim; for material on Poznań province, see William Hagen, *Germans, Poles, and Jews* (Chicago and London, 1980), esp. pp. 288–319.

23. See esp. Edward Wynot, "'A Necessary Cruelty': The Emergence of Official Anti-Semitism in Poland, 1936–1939," *American Historical Review*, no. 4 (October 1971), pp. 1035–58.

24. Pawel Korzec, "Antisemitism in Poland as an Intellectual, Social, and Political Movement," in Shikl Fishman, ed., *Studies on Polish Jewry, 1919–1939* (New York, 1974), pp. 12–104, and Yeshaye Trunk, "Der ekonomisher antisemitizm in poyln tsvishn di tsvey velt-milkhomes," ibid., pp. 3–98 (Yiddish sec.). See also the surveys by Korzec, *Juifs en Pologne* (Paris, 1980), and Celia Heller, *On the Edge of Destruction: Jews of Poland Between the Two World Wars* (New York, 1977).

25. For the first quotation, see Mendelsohn, "Ha-tsiyonut be-folin ben shte milhamot ha-olam," *Be-tfutsot ha-gola*, no. 3–4 (1972), p. 63; and for an analysis of Jewish youth in the 1930s, Maks Vaynraykh (Weinreich), *Der veg tsu unzer vugnt* (Vilna, 1935).

26. For a list of anti-Jewish disturbances, see Yaakov Leshchinski, "Ha-praot befolin (1935–1937)," *Dapim le-heker ha-shoa ve-ha-mered* 2 (February 1952), pp. 37–92.
27. Mendelsohn, *Zionism in Poland*, pp. 101–4; Gringauz, "Jewish National Autonomy"; Leib Garfunkel, "Maavakam shel yehude lita al zekhuiyot leumiyot," *Yahadut lita*, vol. II (Tel Aviv, 1972), pp. 35–72.
28. Jacob Lestchinsky (Yaakov Leshchinski), "The Economic Struggle of the Jews in Independent Lithuania," *Jewish Social Studies* 8, no. 4 (1946), pp. 267–86.
29. See in general the materials in *The Jews of Czechoslovakia*, vols. I and II (New York and Philadelphia, 1968; 1971). For a relevant study of prewar Czech politics, see Bruce Garber, *The Young Czech Party 1874–1901 and the Emergence of a Multi-Party System* (New Haven and New York, 1978), pp. 141, 302–3. For a different view, see Christoph Stolz, "Zur Geschichte der Böhmischen Juden in der Epoche des modernen Nationalismus," *Bohemia, Jahrhuch des Collegium Carolinum* 14 (1973), pp. 179–221, and 15 (1974), 129–57.
30. Ernest Rychnowsky, ed., *Thomas Masaryk and the Jews* (New York, 1941).
31. This point is emphasized by Stolz. See his article cited above and also, *Katkas böses Böhmen: Zur Sozialgeschichte eines Prager Juden* (Munich, 1975).
32. Solomon Schwarz, *The Jews in the Soviet Union* (Syracuse, 1951), remains the best one-volume treatment of this subject.
33. For the contemporary sociological profile of Soviet Jewry, see Altshuler, *Hakibuts ha-yehudi be-vrit ha-moatsot bi-yamenu* (Jerusalem, 1980). (English trans., *Soviet Jewry since the Second World War* [Westport, Conn., 1987].)
34. In this context, see the remarks of Norman Davies, *God's Playground: A History of Poland*, vol. II (Oxford, 1981), pp. 262–63.

5 / Nazi Actions Concerning the Jews Between the Beginning of World War II and the German Attack on the USSR
UWE DIETRICH ADAM

1. Cf. for the U.K.: Richard Harwood, *Did Six Million Really Die?* (Richmond, 1972). In the Federal Republic of Germany: Thies Christopherson, *Die Auschwitz-Lüge* (Mohrkirch, 1972). And likewise the Frenchman Paul Rassinier, *Die Lüge des Odysseus* (Priester Verlag, 1959). In French, *Le mensonge d'Ulysse*, 1st ed., 1954; 6th ed., 1979. Among the latest pamphleteers, we have to mention Robert Faurisson. Cf. the contribution of Pierre Vidal-Naquet in this volume and the pertinent remarks of Y. Gutman about this kind of "scientific" literature.
2. Marshall Dill, Jr., *Germany—A Modern History* (Ann Arbor: University of Michigan Press, 1961), p. 412. David Irving, *Hitler's War* (London, 1977), esp. pp. xiv, 504 ff. Cf. the excellent reply on the thesis of Irving by Martin Broszat, "Hitler und die Genesis der Endlösung: Aus Anlass der Thesen von David Irving," *Vierteljahrshefte für Zeitgeschichte* (hereafter VfZ) 25, no. 4 (1977), pp. 74 ff.
3. The Allied Military Tribunal in Nuremburg assumed the persecution of the Jews took place in accordance with this "planning-thesis." Cf. Art. 6c of the statute and n. 4.
4. Eberhard Jäckel, *Hitlers Weltanschauung: Entwurf einer Herrschaft* (Tübingen, 1969), esp. p. 57; Lucy L. Dawidowicz, *The War Against the Jews* (New York, 1975), esp. p. 150. For this and the following notes, cf. the contribution of Christopher R. Browning in this volume, who gives us a short and excellent survey of the different interpretations.
5. Helmut Krausnick, "Kommissarbefehl und 'Gerichtsbarkeitserlass Barbarossa,' in

neuer Sicht," *VfZ* 25, no. 4 (1977), p. 682; Raul Hilberg, *The Destruction of the European Jews* (Chicago, 1960), pp. 177, 262; Christopher R. Browning, "Zur Genesis der Endlösung: Eine Antwort an Martin Broszat," *VfZ* 29, no. 1 (1981), p. 97. Cf. also Browning's contribution in this volume.

6. Uwe Dietrich Adam, *Judenpolitik im Dritten Reich* (Dusseldorf, 1978), p. 313. Martin Broszat, "Hitler und die Genesis der Endlösung," *VfZ* 25 (1977), pp. 755 ff.; in this article Broszat even doubts the existence of any "order for the final solution" (p. 753).

7. "Polizeiverordnung über das Auftreten der Juden in der Öffentlichkeit," November 11, 1938, *Reichsgesetzblatt* (hereafter *RGBl*) I, p. 1676.

8. Decree of April 30, 1939, *RGBl* I, p. 864.

9. *RGBl* I, p. 1631. For further measures, see Joseph Walk, *Das Sonderrecht für die Juden im NS-Staat*, (Heidelberg, 1981), pp. 303 ff., nos. 1, 17, 22, 27.

10. Adam, pp. 359 f.; Walk, p. 304, nos. 10, 12.

11. A decree of the minister of transportation (February 23, 1939) which first tried to prohibit also the use of sleeping and dining cars for Jews had been withdrawn by the ministry itself in March 1939.

12. *RGBl* I (1941), p. 547.

13. Cf. Adam, p. 337; Walk, p. 368, no. 326.

14. December 1 and 2, 1939.

15. Walk, p. 387, no. 426.

16. Ibid., p. 310, no. 41.

17. Ibid., p. 326, no. 117.

18. Ibid., p. 309, no. 34.

19. These benefits referred, for example, to an additional salary on holidays, special gratuities, and special allowances in certain cases. Cf. Adam, pp. 285 ff.

20. Adam, p. 288.

21. *Reichsarbeitsblatt* I, p. 195.

22. Adam, p. 289.

23. Adam, p. 289; Walk, pp. 336 ff., nos. 174, 177.

24. Adam, p. 290, n. 265.

25. *RGBl* I, p. 681.

26. Adam, pp. 290 ff.

27. Walk, p. 360, no. 290.

28. The decree was signed September 1, published on the fifth, and got legal force on the nineteenth of September.

29. Conference of November 12, 1938, document 1816-PS, *JMT* XXVIII, p. 536.

30. Adam, p. 217.

31. Ibid., p. 334.

32. Ibid., p. 335.

33. Adam, p. 335.

34. Ibid., p. 336.

35. Conference on August 15, 1941, ibid., p. 336.

36. Bernhard Lösener: "Als Rassereferent im Reichsministerium des Innern," *VfZ* 9 (1961), pp. 305 ff.

37. It is significant that the Jewish merchant Hugo Lowenstein "in the name of the Führer and Reichskanzler" received an honor medal as former soldier of the First World War on January 1, 1935. See Lilli Zapf, *Die Tübingen Juden* (Tübingen, 1974), p. 86.

38. *Reichssteuerblatt*, 1940, p. 225.

39. *RGBl* I (August 5, 1940), p. 1077.

40. *RGBl* I, p. 1666.

41. *RGBl I*, p. 1547.
42. "Richtlinien für das Verfahren in Entschädigungssachen," February 12, 1941, *Reichsministerialblatt*, pp. 277 ff.
43. "Verordnung über die Behandlung von Kriegsschäden von Juden," *RGBl* I, (July 20, 1941), p. 437.
44. Adam, p. 200.
45. "Zehnte Verordnung zum Reichsbürgergesetz," *RGBl* I, (July 4, 1939), p. 1097.
46. For examples, cf. Adam, pp. 192 ff.
47. Cf. *Mein Kampf* (Munich, 1941), pp. 211, 350, 359, 585.
48. Walk, p. 308, no. 32.
49. Ibid., pp. 319 ff., no. 323.
50. Ibid., p. 321, nos. 96, 97; p. 325, nos. 114, 119.
51. Secret letter of May 17, 1940; Walk, p. 321, no. 95.
52. Walk, p. 331, no. 150.
53. Nuremberg document NG 3104.
54. Adam, pp. 256, 304.
55. Walk, p. 347, no. 227.
56. Ibid., p. 353, no. 256.

6 / The Decision Concerning the Final Solution
CHRISTOPHER R. BROWNING

1. Martin Broszat, "Hitler und die Genesis der 'Endlösung': Aus Anlass der Thesen von David Irving," *Vierteljahrshefte für Zeitgeschichte* (hereafter VfZ) 25, no. 4 (1977), p. 753.
2. Tim Mason, "Intention and Explanation: A Current Controversy about the Interpretation of National Socialism," in *Der Führerstaat: Mythos und Realität*, ed. Gerhard Hirschfeld and Lothar Kettenacker (Stuttgart, 1981), pp. 21–40.
3. For the intentionalist view, see Karl Dietrich Bracher, "Tradition und Revolution in Nationalsozialismus," in *Hitler, Deutschland und die Mächte*, ed. Manfred Funke (Duesseldorf, 1978), pp. 17–29; and "The Role of Hitler: Perspectives of Interpretation," in *Fascism: A Reader's Guide*, ed. Walter Laqueur (Berkeley, 1976), pp. 211–28. Klaus Hildebrand, "Monokratie oder Polykratie? Hitlers Herrschaft und das Dritte Reich," in *Der Führerstaat*, pp. 43–70; and *Das Dritte Reich* (Munich, 1979).
For the functionalists, see Martin Broszat, "Soziale Motivation und Führer-Bindung des Nationalsozialismus," *VfZ* 18, no. 4 (1970), pp. 392–409; and *The Hitler State: The Foundation and Development of the Internal Structure of the Third Reich* (London, 1981); Hans Mommsen, "National Socialism," in *Marxism, Communism, and Western Society*, vol. VI, ed. C. D. Kernig (New York, 1973), pp. 65–74; "Hitlers Stellung im national-sozialistischen Herrschaftssystem," *Der Führerstaat*, pp. 43–70; and "National Socialism—Continuity and Change," *Fascism: A Reader's Guide*, pp. 179–210.
4. Lucy Dawidowicz, *The War Against the Jews* (New York, 1975), esp. pp. 150–63. The psychohistorians also support the 1919 date. See Robert Waite, *The Psychopathic God* (New York: Signet, 1978), and Rudolph Binion, *Hitler and the Germans* (New York, 1976).
5. Martin Broszat, "Hitler und die Genesis der 'Endlösung,'" pp. 740–75.
6. Eberhard Jäckel, *Hitler's Weltanschauung* (Middletown, Conn., 1972), p. 57.
7. Karl Dietrich Bracher, *The German Dictatorship* (New York, 1970), pp. 366–68.
8. Klaus Hildebrand, *Das Dritte Reich*, pp. 83, 178. Andreas Hillgruber, "Die Endlösung und das deutsche Ostimperium als Kernstück des rassenideologischen Programmes des Nationalsozialismus," *VfZ* 20, no. 2 (1972), pp. 133–53; and "Die ideologisch-

dogmatische Grundlage der nationalsozialistischen Politik der Ausrottung der Juden in den besetzten Gebieten der Sowjetunion und ihre Durchführung 1941–1944," *German Studies Review* II, no. 3 (1979), pp. 263–96. Gerald Reitlinger, *The Final Solution* (New York, Perpetua, 1961), and Nora Levin, *The Holocaust* (New York, Schocken: 1973), are not explicit but also imply a prewar date.

9. Léon Poliakov, *Harvest of Hate* (London, 1958), p. 110; Robert Kempner, *Eichmann und Komplizen* (Zurich, 1961), pp. 96–97; Helmut Krausnick, "The Persecution of the Jews," in *Anatomy of the SS State* (New York, 1968), p. 67.

10. Raul Hilberg, *The Destruction of the European Jews* (Chicago, 1961), pp. 177, 262. Hilberg argued for this date only against the then prevailing presumption of an earlier date. Since then, arguments for a later date emerged. I have supported the Hilberg date against the thesis of a later date in my "Zur Genesis der 'Endlösung': Eine Antwort an Martin Broszat," *VfZ* 29, no. 1 (1981), pp. 97–109.

11. Uwe Dietrich Adam, *Judenpolitik im Dritten Reich* (Düsseldorf, 1972), pp. 303–316.

12. Sebastian Haffner, *The Meaning of Hitler* (New York, 1979), pp. 142–43.

13. H. R. Trevor-Roper, ed., *Hitler's Secret Conversations* (New York: Signet, 1961), pp. 238, 260. Entries of January 23 and 28, 1942.

14. Broszat, "Soziale Motivation und Führer-Bindung des Nationalsozialismus," *loc. cit.*

15. Mason, "Intention and Explanation," p. 33.

16. For psychological assessments of Hitler's anti-Semitism, see Robert Waite, *The Psychopathic God*, and Rudolph Binion, *Hitler and the Germans*.

For anti-Semitism and Hitler's ideology, see Jäckel, *Hitler's Weltanschauung*, and the articles of Andreas Hillgruber, n. 8 above. The most graphic of Hitler's murderous fantasies is cited in Waite, p. 440: "As soon as I have the power, I shall have gallows after gallows erected, for example in Munich on the Marienplatz. . . . Then the Jews will be hanged one after another, and they will stay hanging until they stink. They will stay hanging as long as hygienically possible. As soon as they are untied, then the next group will follow and that will continue until the last Jew in Munich is exterminated. Exactly the same procedure will be followed in other cities until Germany is cleansed of Jews!" This dates from 1922.

17. See for instance Hitler's support for continuing the Haavara agreement despite considerable internal opposition and his support of Schacht's negotiations over Ribbentrop's objections, as well as his backing of Göring, Himmler, and Heydrich over Goebbels and his encouragement to the Madagascar planners. Christopher R. Browning, *The Final Solution and the German Foreign Office* (New York, 1978), pp. 14, 17–18, 38, 41.

18. Dawidowicz, *The War Against the Jews*, pp. 93, 158. Bracher, *The German Dictatorship*, p. 366. Bracher declares that the Final Solution "was merely a matter of time and opportunity."

19. Helmut Krausnick and Hans-Heinrich Wilhelm, *Die Truppe des Weltanschauungskrieges* (Stuttgart, 1981); Christian Streit, *Keine Kameraden* (Stuttgart, 1978); Andreas Hillgruber, *Hitlers Strategie: Politik und Kriegsfuehrung 1940–1* (Frankfurt, 1965); Hans-Adolf Jacobsen, "The Kommissarbefehl and Mass Executions of Soviet Prisoners of War," in *Anatomy of the SS State*, pp. 505–35; Helmut Krausnick, "Kommissarbefehl and 'Gerichtsbarkeitserlass Barbarossa' in neuer Sicht," *VfZ* 25, no. 4 (1977), pp. 682–738; Jürgen Förster, "The Wehrmacht and the War of Extermination Against the Soviet Union," *Yad Vashem Studies* XIV (1981), pp. 7–34.

20. I am persuaded by the conclusions of Krausnick and Wilhelm, *Die Truppe des Weltanschauunskrieges*, pp. 159–64, 533–39, rather than Christian Streit, *Keine Kameraden*, pp. 127 and 356, that the extermination order was made known to the Einsatzgruppen before the invasion. Streit's attempt to make a major distinction between the

destruction of "all" Jews and the "as complete as possible" (*möglichst umfassende*) destruction of Jews in Russia strikes me as specious.

21. Cited in Norman Rich, *Hitler's War Aims: The Establishment of the New Order* (New York, 1974), p. 6.

22. L-180 (Stahlecker report) in *Trials of the Major War Criminals Before the International Military Tribunal* (Nuremburg, 1947-49), vol. XXVII, pp. 687, 702. Hereafter cited as *IMT*.

23. Cited in Krausnick and Wilhelm, *Die Truppe des Weltanschauungskrieges*, p. 534. "*Das Ziel, das dem Einsatzkommando 2 von Anfang an vorschwebte, war eine radikale Lösung des Judenproblems durch die Exekution aller Juden.*"

24. Streit has argued for the latter interpretation, i.e., the readiness of the army to cooperate in Hitler's *Ausrottungspolitik* in itself contributed to radicalizing this policy. *Keine Kameraden*, p. 126. Hillgruber, on the other hand, has argued that the attacks upon Russia, bolshevism, and the Jews were inseparable in Hitler's mind.

25. Krausnick and Wilhelm, *Die Truppe des Weltanschauungskrieges*, p. 137.

26. Cited in Kempner, *Eichmann und Komplizen*, p. 97. "*Was ich heute nicht niederschreiben will, aber nie vergessen werde.*"

27. Cited in Michael Marrus and Robert Paxton, *Vichy France and the Jews* (New York, 1981), p. 10.

28. Browning, *The Final Solution and the German Foreign Office*, pp. 43–44, 46.

29. Hilberg, *The Destruction of the European Jews*, p. 177.

30. 710-PS, in *IMT*, vol. XXVI, pp. 266–67.

31. Broszat, "Hitler und die Genesis der 'Endlösung,'" p. 747; Adam, *Judenpolitik im Dritten Reich*, 308-9.

32. Adoph Eichmann, *Ich, Adolf Eichmann: Ein historischer Zeugenbericht*, ed. Dr. Rudolf Aschenauer (Leoni am Starnberger See: Druffel-Verlag, 1980), p. 479. "Meine Memoiren," manuscript, Bundesarchiv Koblenz, All. Proz. 6/199, pp. 112-3.

33. National Archives, Wi/ID 1420 (old Wi/ID 2.139), "Anlage zu: Verb. St. D. OKW/Wi Ru Amt beim Reichsmarschall v. 14.8.41," I am grateful to Prof. Dr. Helmut Krausnick for sending me a copy of this document.

34. Politisches Archiv des Auswärtigen Amtes (hereafter PA), Inland IIg 177, Heydrich to Ribbentrop, June 24, 1940 (NG-25886-J). Browning, *The Final Solution and the German Foreign Office*, p. 38.

35. Rudolf Höss, *Commandant of Auschwitz* (New York, 1959), pp. 135–38, 173–36, 197. Höss's earlier testimony before the International Military Tribunal was clearly confused and ran together events of 1941 and 1942. See *IMT*, vol. XI, pp. 396 ff., and vol. XXXIII, pp. 275–79.

36. "Eichmann Tells His Own Damning Story," *Life* magazine (November 28, 1960); Eichmann, *Ich, Adolf Eichmann*; transcripts of Eichmann's interrogations by the Israeli police, Bundesarchiv Koblenz (hereafter BA), All. Proz. 6/1–6; Eichmann's handwritten "Meine Memoiren," BA, All. Proz. 6/119; Eichmann's handwritten notes to his attorney, BA, All. Proz. 6/169; Eichmann, Adolf, defendant, in the District Court of Jerusalem, Criminal Case No. 40/61; Bernd Nellessen, *Der Prozess von Jerusalem* (Düsseldorf, 1964). As in the case with Höss, Eichmann's testimony is not without contradictions. His recollections in Argentina dating from the late 1950s are the basis of the *Life* magazine account and the recent memoirs edited by Rudolf Aschenauer. In the former, Eichmann states that he learned of the *Führerbefehl* in 1941 at a time when the Russian campaign was not going as quickly as planned and that he first saw actual preparations for the annihilation program in the "latter part of 1941." The memoirs refer consistently—indeed, all too consistently for anyone who has tried to follow all of Eichmann's accounts—to Eichmann's initiation into the Final Solution at "year's end 1941/

42." That such a dating occurs in no other account, including the *Life* article based on the same notes and tapes, leads to the strong suspicion that Aschenauer has resolved the many ambiguities of Eichmann's testimony in a way that is comforting to his own thesis (which he ceaselessly intrudes upon the reader) but is of little use for the historian. Eichmann's various accounts while in Israeli custody (interrogation, court testimony, handwritten memoirs, and notes to his defense attorney) all place his meeting with Heydrich in the late summer of 1941. In the same meeting, according to Eichmann, Heydrich also informed him that Globocnik was going to use "antitank ditches" (*Panzer-gräben*) and that Eichmann was to go to Poland and report on the preparations. However, according to Eichmann, he passed through Prague on his way, where he informed Hans Günther, and he vividly remembered the bright fall colors during his visit to the camp (he could not remember the name, though it must have been Bełżec). As Eichmann was in Prague on October 10 and the peak of fall colors would be expected at this time, the dating of Eichmann's trip to Bełżec to mid-October seems reasonably certain. If Aschen-auer's version is dismissed (and I think it should be), the major contradiction is not between Eichmann's accounts, but within them. If his first meeting with Heydrich took place in late summer, he was not immediately sent to Bełżec. If he was immediately sent to Bełżec, the Heydrich meeting did not take place in late summer but presumably in late September or early October. Several factors argue for the former interpretation, i.e., that considerable time passed between Eichmann's meeting with Heydrich and the Bełżec trip. At that meeting Heydrich spoke of Globocnik's plans to use antitank ditches, and Eichmann was clearly under the impression that the Einsatzgruppen method of firing-squad execution at the edge of mass graves was intended. This would have made Bełżec a logical site; located on the Ribbentrop-Molotov line, it had earlier been the site of a Jewish labor camp for digging antitank ditches. (Zentrale Stelle der Landesjustizverwal-tungen, Ludwigsburg, 8 AR-Z 252/59, vols. I, pp. 24–31, and II, pp. 200.) But when Eichmann arrived in Bełżec, he learned for the first time of plans to use gas chambers instead of shooting. That such a fundamental change in German planning could have taken place between Eichmann's meeting with Heydrich in Berlin and an immediate trip to Poland, or that Globocnik had decided upon gas chambers without Heydrich's knowl-edge, seems highly unlikely. That Eichmann learned of Hitler's order for the destruction of the Jews in late August, that is, one and one-half months before the Bełżec trip, is also suggested by Eichmann's letter of August 28, 1941, which speaks for the first time of an "imminent final solution *now in preparation.*" (Emphasis mine.) (See n. 37 below.) In conclusion, the Eichmann testimony cannot exactly date the point at which Himmler and Heydrich were fully conscious of their mission to murder the European Jews, but like that of Höss it strongly suggests the summer of 1941. Eichmann's own awareness cannot be postponed beyond the end of September or the beginning of October, and *probably* dates from late August.

The change in Eichmann's testimony regarding his visit to Auschwitz is less prob-lematic, for the motivation behind his courtroom denial of a fall visit to Auschwitz is highly suspect. In the *Life* account Eichmann said that he had visited Auschwitz "re-peatedly," though he did not specify the time of his first visit. He characterized Höss then as "an excellent comrade and a very proper fellow. . . . I was on close comradely terms with Höss. . . . I liked to visit him." He subsequently told the Israeli interrogator of his visit to Auschwitz "at the beginning," where Höss showed him the hut in which Zyklon B pellets had been tested on Russian prisoners. After excerpts of Höss's autobi-ography were read by the Israeli police interrogators to Eichmann, passages which in the latter's mind attempted to shift too much responsibility from the WVHA to the RSHA and to Eichmann personally, both his account and his opinion of Höss changed. He now claimed that he had not visited Auschwitz until the spring or summer of 1942. He provided his defense attorney with many notes to support this contention, "because," he frankly admitted, "I must prove Höss the arch-liar, that I have had nothing to do with him and his gas chambers and his death camp. . . ."

37. PA, Inland II A/B 47/1, Eichmann to D III, August 28, 1941: "*Im Hinblick auf die kommende und in Vorbereitung befindliche Endlösung. . . .*"

38. PA, Pol. Abt. III 246, Luther memoranda of October 13 and 17, 1941.

39. *Akten zur Deutschen Aussenpolitik, 1918–1945* (hereafter ADAP), series D, XIII, pt. 2 (Göttingen, 1970), pp. 570–72.

40. PA, Inland II A/B 59/3, Wurm to Rademacher, October 23, 1941.

41. NO-365, NO-996, and NO-997.

42. The difficulty in procurement and production of gas vans in the desired numbers is confirmed by testimony in the gas-van trial (Landgericht Hannover 2 Ks 2/65: Strafsache gegen Pradel und Wentritt) and by surviving documents of the automotive section (II D 3) of the RSHA (BA, R 58/871).

43. H. G. Adler, *Theresienstadt 1941–1945*, 2nd ed. (Tübingen, 1960), pp. 720–22. The day following Heydrich's meeting in Prague, Stahlecker informed the *Generalkommissar* of Latvia, Dr. Drechsler, that a concentration camp near Riga was to be set up for Jews from the Reich and Protectorate. On November 8 SS Captain Lange of Einsatzgruppe A confirmed that 25,000 Jews were coming to the new camp at Salspils near Riga and another 25,000 to Minsk. When Dr. Trempedach of the RK Ostland wrote to Berlin to urge that the transports be stopped, Dr. Leibbrandt of the Ostministerium replied that there was no cause for worry since the Jews would be sent "further east." Hilberg, *Destruction of the European Jews*, p. 232.

44. 2718-PS, in *IMT*, vol XXXI, p. 84.

45. 126-EC, in *IMT*, vol. XXXVI, pp. 141, 145.

46. National Archives, Wi/ID 1420 (old Wi/ID 2.139), "Anlage zu: Verb. St. D. OKW/Wi RU Amt beim Reichsmarschall, v. 14.8.41."

47. PA, Inland II g 177, Reichssicherheitshauptamt Madagaskar Projekt.

48. Zentrale Stelle der Landesjustizverwaltungen Ludwigsburg (hereafter ZStL): V 203 AR-Z 69/59 (Urteil der Landgericht Bonn 8 Ks 3/63 gegen Gustav L. u. 11 a.), pp. 24, 28, 92; 203 AR-Z 69/59, vol. IV, pp. 624–43 (testimony of Walter B.).

49. ZStL, 203 AR-Z 69/59, vol. 7a, pp. 1262–65 (testimony of Nelli L.), 1266–69 (Else S.), 1270–77 (Herbert W.), 1281-86 (Erhard M.) and 1288–93 (Konrad S.).

50. ZStL, 8 AR-Z 252/59, vol. VI, pp 1117–20 (testimony of Eustachy U.), 1129–30 (Stanislaw K.), 1150 (Michael K.), 1156 (Jan G.), and 1222 (Edward F.).

51. ZStL, 8 AR-Z 252/59, vol. I, p. 133, and vol. IX, p. 1680–85.

52. ZStL, 8 AR-Z 252/59, vol. V, pp. 974–75.

53. Landgericht Hannover 2 Ks 2/65, vol. III, pp. 64–68. ZStL, 8 AR-Z 252/59, vol. V, pp. 981–89.

54. Browning, *The Final Solution and the German Foreign Office*, pp. 72–76.

55. Felix Kersten, *The Kersten Memoirs 1940–45* (New York, 1957), p. 119.

56. PA, Pol. XIII, VAA Berichte, text of Rosenberg speech of 18.11.41. T 120/270/339/198808-21.

57. 1517-PS, in *IMT*, vol. XXVII, p. 270.

58. 3666-PS, in *IMT*, vol. XXXII, p. 437.

59. Werner Präg and Wolfgang Jacobmayer, eds., *Das Diensttagebuch des deutschen Generalgouverneurs in Polen 1939–1945* (Stuttgart, 1975), pp. 457–58; *IMT*, vol. XII, pp. 68–69; Hilberg, *The Destruction of the European Jews*, p. 263.

60. NG-2586 C. Photocopy in Kempner, *Eichmann und Komplizen*, pp. 127–28.

61. ADAP, E, vol. I, pp. 267–76. Photocopy in Kempner, *Eichmann und Komplizen*, pp. 133–47.

62. Nellessen, *Der Prozess von Jerusalem*, p. 206.

63. Bernhard Lösener, "Als Rassereferent im Reichsministerium des Innern," *VfZ* 9, no. 3 (1961), p. 303; Broszat, "Hitler und die Genesis der "Endlösung,'" p. 750.

64. PA, Inland II g 194, Rademacher marginalia of September 13 on Benzler letter of September 12, 1941.

65. H. G. Adler, *Der Verwaltete Mensch: Studien zur Deportation der Juden aus Deutschland* (Tübingen, 1974), pp. 173–77.

66. Adler, *Theresienstadt*, pp. 720–22.

67. In addition to Himmler's assurances to Greiser and Eichmann's statement to that effect recorded by Wetzel (NO-365), see n. 43 above.

68. Lösener, "Als Rassereferent im Reichsministerium des Innern," pp. 303–5; Adam, *Judenpolitik im Dritten Reich*, p. 337.

69. Louis Lochner, ed., *The Goebbels Diaries 1942–43*, (Garden City, N.Y., 1948), pp. 115–16.

70. Browning, *The Final Solution and the German Foreign Office*, pp. 79–81.

71. Lochner, ed., *The Goebbels Diaries 1942–43*, pp. 147–48.

72. Browning, *The Final Solution and the German Foreign Office*, loc. cit.

73. See n. 13 above. See also the entry for October 25, 1941, pp. 108–9.

7 / The Bureaucracy of Annihilation
RAUL HILBERG

1. These four hierarchical structures, and their roles as independently operating conglomerates, were first recognized by Franz Neumann, *Behemoth* (New York and London: Oxford University Press, 1942; 2d ed., 1944), pp. 467–70. The U.S. prosecution at Nuremberg classified its evidentiary material under four headings: NG, NOKW, NO, and NI, corresponding to the four groups identified by Neumann.

2. Negotiations (by the Foreign Office and SS representatives attached to German embassies and legations) were conducted with Vichy France, Italy, Croatia, Slovakia, Bulgaria, Romania, and Hungary, not always successfully. For characteristic criticism of a Slovak law defining the term "Jew," see *Donauzeitung* (Belgrade), December 10, 1941, p. 3.

3. Dokumentationsdienst der DB, *Dokumentarische Enzyklopädie V—Eisenbahn und Eisenbahner zwischen 1941 und 1945* (Frankfurt am Main: Redactor Verlag, 1973), p. 110.

4. Eugen Kreidler, *Die Eisenbahnen im Maththereich der Achsenmächte während des Zweiter Weltkrieges* (Göttingen: Musterschmid Verlag, 1975), pp. 278–89.

5. Ibid., pp. 205–6. Albert Speer, *Inside the Third Reich* (New York: Macmillan, 1970), pp. 222–25. Prosecution at Düsseldorf to Landgericht Düsseldorf, March 16, 1970, transmitting indictment of Ganzenmüller, File No. 3 Js 430/67, in Zentrale Stelle der Landesjustizverwaltungen, Ludwigsburg, and in Landgericht Düsseldorf. Statement and answers to questions by Ganzanmüller, October 7, 1964, Case Ganzenmüller, vol. 5, pp. 216–27.

6. See the annual *Verzeichnis der obersten Reichsbahnbeamten*, particularly for 1941 and 1943.

7. Statement by Franz Novak, October 19, 1966, Strafsache gegen Novak 1416/ 61, Landesgericht für Strafsachen Wien, vol. 16, p. 33.

8. See *Verzeichnis* and undated statement by Philipp Mangold, Verkehrsarchiv Nürnberg, collection Sarter, folder aa. Generalbetriebsleitung West was involved in processing transports from France, Belgium, and Holland. Leibbrand to West, Ost, Wehrmachtverkehrsdirektionen Paris and Brussels, Plenipotentiary in Utrecht, and

Reichsbahndirektion Oppeln (arrival jurisdiction for Auschwitz), June 23, 1942, Case Ganzenmüller, vol. 4, pt. 3, p. 57.

9. Directives by Jacobi, August 8, 1942, and January 16, 1943, Institut fur Zeitgeschichte, Munich, Fb 35/2, pp. 217 and 206.

10. For example, Reichsbahndirektion Königsberg, timetable instruction no. 62, July 13, 1942, ibid., p. 260, and Generaldirektion der Ostbahn, timetable instruction no. 567, March 26, 1943, Zentrale Stelle Ludwigsburg, Polen 167, Film 6, 192–93.

11. Summary of Reich Main Security Office IV B 4 conference in Düsseldorf, under chairmanship of Eichmann, March 1942, Case Novak, vol. 17, p. 203–07.

12. Report by Lt. Col. Ferenczy (Hungarian gendarmerie), July 9, 1944, Case Novak, vol. 12, p. 427.

13. Reserve lieutenant of Schutzpolizei (Wessermann?) to Kommandeur of Ordnungspolizei for Galician district in Lvov, September 14, 1942, Zentrale Stelle Ludwigsburg, UdSSR, vol. 410; pp. 508–10. About 200 of the Jews were dead on arrival.

14. Affidavit by Walter Schellenberg (Security Police), November 21, 1945, Nuremberg document PS-3033. Kurt Daluege (chief of Order Police) to Karl Wolff (chief of Himmler's personal staff), February 28, 1943, Nuremberg document NO-2861. Daluege was the only Order Police general who began his career in the SS.

15. Daluege to Wolff, February 28, 1943, NO-2861.

16. Order Police strength report (Stärkenachweisung) of Schuma for July 1, 1942, Bundesarchiv R 19/266. Firemen and auxiliaries not included in the figures. Year-end data given by Daluege to Wolff, February 28, 1943, NO-2861. By December, the Schuma (without firemen or auxiliaries) was well over 100,000.

17. Gendarmeriegebietsführer in Brest-Litovsk (Lt. Deuerlein) to Kommandeur of Gendarmerie in Lutsk, October 6, 1942. National Archives microfilm T 454, roll 102.

18. SS Sturmbannführer Zöpf to Judenlager Westerbork, May 10, 1943, Israel Police Eichmann trial document 590. Otto Bene to Foreign Office, June 25, 1943, NG-2631.

19. The 304th Battalion, replaced in 1941 by the 61st. Zentrale Stelle, Ludwigsburg, Polen 365 d and e, passim.

20. Instructions by Captain Kompa, June 22, 1942, T 459, roll 21. The original force was larger. Instructions by Major of Schutzpolizei Quasbarth, April 24, 1942, T 459, roll 21. The men belonged to the 20th Latvian (Guard) Battalion.

21. The German battalion was set up in Berlin for this purpose. Schuma included the 4th, 7th, and 8th Lithuanian battalions, the 17th, 23d, 27th, and 28th Latvian battalions. Hans-Joachim Neufeldt, Jürgen Huck, and Georg Tessin, Zur Geschichte der Ordnungspolizei 1936–1945 (Koblenz, 1957), pt. II (by Tessin), pp. 51–68, 101–9. Daluege to Wolff, February 28, 1943, NO-2861.

22. Order by Daluege, October 24, 1941, PS-3921.

23. Tessin, Ordnungspolizei, p. 97. Helmut Krausnick and Hans-Heinrich Wilhelm, Die Truppe des Weltanschauungskrieges (Stuttgart: Deutsche Verlagsanstalt, 1981), pp. 146–47.

24. Reich Main Security Office IV A 1 Operational Report USSR no. 101, October 2, 1941, NO-3137.

25. Text of Soviet interrogation of Friedrich Jeckeln (Higher SS and Police Leader in Ostland), December 14 and 15, 1945, Krausnick and Wilhelm, Truppe, pp. 566–70.

26. Strength Report of Schutzmannschaft, July 1, 1942, R 19/266, and Friedrich-Wilhelm Kruger to Himmler, July 7, 1943, Himmler Files, folder no. 94, Library of Congress.

27. Adalbert Rückerl, NS-Vernichtungslager (Munich: Deutscher Taschenbuch Verlag, 1977), pp. 262–64.

28. Orchestration of the killings remained in the hands of the Security Police,

whose representatives would usually appear on the local scene a few days before an operation. See Deuerlein report, October 6, 1942, T 454, roll 102. Also, statement by Zeev Sheinwald (survivor of Luboml, Ukraine), Yad Vashem Oral History document 0-3/2947.

29. Stangl's life was reconstructed in detail by Gitta Sereny, *Into that Darkness* (New York: McGraw-Hill, 1974).

30. On Eberl, see Sereny, *Darkness*, pp. 77, 85, 86, and 160, and Lothar Gruchmann, "Euthanasie und Justiz in Dritten Reich," *Vierteljahrshefte für Zeitgeschichte* 20 (1972), p. 250.

31. See for example report by Richard Turk (Population and Welfare Division, Lublin District) for March 1942, Jüdisches Historisches Institue Warschau, *Faschismus-Getto-Massenmord* (Berlin: Rutten & Loening, 1960), pp. 272–73.

32. Note the career of the architect Walter Dejaco. See Friedrich Brill, "Sie hatten nichts gewusst!" *Aufbau* (New York), March 17, 1942, p. 5. Dejaco was body disposal expert in Auschwitz. Report by Untersturmführer Dejaco, September 17, 1942, NO-4467.

33. One of the most telling examples is the attitude of Italian officials and army officers. See Daniel Carpi, "The Rescue of Jews in the Italian Zone of Occupied Croatia" (with documents), Proceedings of the Second Yad Vashem International Historical Conference 1974, *Rescue Attempts during the Holocaust* (Jerusalem: Yad Vashem, 1977), pp. 465–525.

34. Uwe Dietrich Adam, *Judenpolitik im Dritten Reich*, Tübinger Schriften zur Sozial- und Zeitgeschicht I (Düsseldorf: Droste Verlag, 1972), esp. pp. 108–13, 240–46, 292–302.

35. Order dated December 5, 1938, in *Völkischer Beobachter*, PS-2682. Also Adam, *Judenpolitik*, pp. 213, 244.

36. The issuance of an oral order from Hitler to Himmler is reported by Eichmann in his autobiography, *Ich, Adolf Eichmann* (Leoni am Starnberger See: Druffel-Verlag, 1980), pp. 176–79, 229–31. See also affidavit by Albert Speer, June 15, 1977, facsimile in Arthur Suzman and Denis Diamond, *Six Million Did Die* (Johannesburg: South African Jewish Board of Deputies, 1977), pp. 109–12.

37. Göring to Heydrich, July 31, 1941, PS-710.

38. Eichmann, *Ich*, p. 479.

39. Organization plan of Reichskommissar Ostland II (Finance), August 17, 1942, T 459, roll 2. His deputy was Bruns.

40. Hans Umbreit, *Der Militärbefehlshaber in Frankreich 1940–1942* (Boppart am Rhein: Harald Boldt Verlag, 1968), pp. 243–44. On that date the Reichsbahn took over civilian traffic. Directive of Transport Minister (Dorpmüller), June 13, 1942, in Kreidler, *Eisenbahnen*, pp. 356–57.

41. Text in Serge Klarsfeld, ed., *Die Endlösung der Judenfrage in Frankreich* (Paris, 1977), pp. 36–37.

42. Land transfer conferences, November 3 and December 17–18, 1942, under chairmanship of Oberfinanzpräsident Dr. Casdorf, PS-1643.

43. Speer to Himmler, April 5, 1943, Himmler Files, folder no. 67. On gas, see affidavit by Dr. Gerhard Peters, October 16, 1947, NI-9113, and testimony by Joachim Mrugowski, Nuremberg doctors case (*U.S. v. Brand*), transcript 5403-4.

44. Correspondence in T 175, roll 60.

45. Durrfeld (*Dezernat* 3 of German city administration in Warsaw) to SS and Police Leader von Sammern, August 10, 1942, and memorandum by Kunze (*Dezernat* 4), August 13, 1942, Zentrale Stelle Ludwigsburg, Polen 365 d, pp. 275–77.

46. Neuendorff to Generalkommissar/Trusteeship (Kunska), June 4, 1942, T 459, roll 21.

47. Deutsche Reichsbahn/Verkehrsamt, Łódź, to Gestapo in city, May 19, 1942, enclosing bill for twelve trains, facsimile in *Faschismus-Getto-Massenmord*, pp. 280–81, and directive of Reichsverkehrsdirektion Minsk, January 27, 1943, Fb. 82/2, among others.

48. Paul Treibe (E 1) to Reichsbahndirektionen, copies to Generaldirektion der Ostbahn, Protectorate railways, and Mitteleuropäisches Reisebüro, July 26, 1941, Case Ganzenmüller, special vol. 4, pt. 3, pp. 47–55.

49. Reichsbahndirektion Vienna (signed Dr. Bockhonn) to Slovak Transport Ministry, copies in house and to Dresden, Oppeln, and Mitteleuropäisches Reisebüro, April 27, 1942, Yad Vashem document M-5/18 (1).

50. Luther (Foreign Office/Division Germany) via Trade Political Division to Staatssekretar Weizsäcker, January 29, 1943, NG-5108. Ludin (German minister in Slovakia) to Foreign Office, April 18, 1942, NG-4404. Representative of Transport Ministry in Slovakia to Slovak Transport Ministry, March 1, 1945, M-5/18 (I).

51. Reichsvereinigung directive of December 3, 1941, Israel Police document 738.

52. Mädel to Mayer and Kallenbach (all in Finance Ministry), December 14, 1942, Bundesarchiv R 2/12222.

53. Rau (E 1/17) to High Command of the Army, March 1, 1944, and subsequent correspondence in Bundesarchiv R 2/14133.

54. SS Standartenführer Dr. Siegert (budget specialist in the Reich Main Security Office) to Finance Ministry, August 17, 1942, Bundesarchiv R 2/12158. The precipitating factor was the heavy transport cost from France to Auschwitz.

55. Entry by Czerniaków in his diary, December 2, 1941, in Raul Hilberg, Stanislaw Staron, and Josef Kermisz, eds., *The Warsaw Diary of Adam Czerniaków* (Briarcliff Manor, N.Y.: Stein & Day, 1979), p. 304.

56. In Eichmann's office there were ca. 200,000 open and 30,000–40,000 secret folders. He states that destruction of the records was ordered at the end of January 1945. Eichmann, *Ich*, pp. 155, 449. On Stange's files, see statement by Reichsbahn specialist Karl Heim, April 18, 1969, Case Ganzemüller, vol. 18, pp. 98–103. In their very nature, such records were filled with Jewish affairs.

57. Armament Inspectorate Netherlands (Vizeadmiral Reimer), War Diary, summary for 1942, Wi/IA 5.1. German records located in Alexandria, Virginia, during postwar years.

58. Statement by Erich Richter, June 11, 1969, Case Ganzenmüller, vol. 19, pp. 5–12. Interrogation of Walter Stier, March 16, 1963, Case Novak, vol. 16, pp. 355 ff. Richter and Stier were Reichsbahn specialists in Krakow.

59. Notation by Kunska (Generalkommissar of Latvia/Trusteeship), June 27, 1942, on copy of directive from Reichskommissar's Trusteeship Office, April 30, 1942, T 459, roll 21.

8 / The Gas Chambers
UWE DIETRICH ADAM

1. Dachau, Sachsenhausen, Buchenwald, Mauthausen, Flossenbürg, Ravensbrück, Neuengamme, Gusen, Natzweiler-Struthof, and Arbeitsdorf were the concentration camps, even if certain among them had scheduled gassings. The extermination camps were Chełmno (Kulmhof), Bełżec, Sobibór, and Treblinka. Auschwitz and Lublin-Majdanek were at first concentration camps, then altered later to do duty as extermination camps. On the terminology problems, see Oswald Pohl's letter to Himmler dated April 30, 1942, reprinted in R. Kühnl, *Der Deutsche Faschismus in Quellen und Doku-*

menten (Cologne, 1979), pp. 375 ff.; see also Martin Broszat, "Nationalsozialistische Konzentrationslager," in *Anatomie des SS-Staats*, 2 vols., DTV 462/463, vol. 2 (Munich, 1967), p. 63.

2. These publications have roughly the same arguments. Cf. Paul Rassinier, *Le Mensonge d'Ulysse*, 6th ed. (Paris, 1979); Robert Faurisson, *Réponse à Pierre Vidal-Naquet* (Paris, 1982); Richard Harwood, *Did Six Million Really Die?: The Truth at Last* (Richmond, 1971); Thies Christopherson, *Die Auschwitz-Lüge* (Mohrkirch, 1972). See also Martin Broszat, "Zur Publizistik des rechtsextremistischen Antisemitismus," in *Aus Politik und Zeitgeschichte*, supplement to *Das Parlament*, B 14/1976.

3. Adolf Hitler, *Mein Kampf* (Munich, 1941), pp. 588–92.

4. Ibid., p. 772.

5. See the organizational chart of the RSHA (Reich Main Security Office) of October 1, 1943, in *International Military Tribunal, Nuremberg* (42 vol.), vol. XXXVIII, p. 80, document 219-L.

6. On the firms producing Zyklon B and its distribution circuits, see Raul Hilberg, *The Destruction of the European Jews* (Chicago, 1960), (or p. 237 of the German ed., [Berlin, 1982]); on the gases, see Georges Wellers, "Die zwei Giftgase," in Eugen Kogon, ed., *Nationalsozialistische Massentötungen durch Giftgas* (Frankfurt, 1983), p. 282. The references in this work lead back to the German text, except for precise details that are inconsistent (NdE).

7. A facsimile of this text is in H. Kühnrich, *Der KZ-Staat 1933–1945*, 3rd ed., (East Berlin, 1983), p. 89.

8. On the Chancellery, see F. K. Kaul, *Die Psychiatrie im Strudel der "Euthanasie"* (Frankfurt, 1979), pp. 52 ff. On "euthanasia for children," which was later extended to young persons up to the age of sixteen and, unlike euthanasia for adults, was never interrupted, see E. Klee, *Euthanasie im SS-Staat: Die Vernichtung "lebensunwerten Lebens"* (Frankfurt, 1983), pp. 77 ff.; and see K. Dorner, "Nationalsozialismus und Lebensvernichtung," in *Vierteljahrshefte für Zeitgeschichte* (hereafter *VfZ*) 15 (1967), pp. 133 ff.

9. Manifestly, Brack personally requested the secrecy of a large part of the personnel. Cf. Klee, *op. cit.*, pp. 74 and 109. Franz Stangl, future commandant of Sobibór and Treblinka, was impressed by T4. See Gitta Sereny, *Am Abgrund: Eine Gewissenserforschung* (Frankfurt, 1980), p. 48. For example, it was only in July 1940 that Gürtner, the minister of justice, was informed of these murderous operations, which had begun six months earlier. Cf. Lothar Gruchmann, "Euthanasie und Justiz im Dritten Reich," *VfZ* 20 (1972), pp. 88 ff.

10. Klee, *op. cit.*, p. 84. It is certain that Nebe did not receive this order from Brack, as this author states; it would have been impossible for administrative and hierarchical reasons.

11. Ibid., see also Kaul, *op. cit.*, pp. 63 ff.

12. Deposition of Dr. Becker, in Kaul, *op. cit.*, pp. 77 ff.; deposition of Private Heyde, in Klee, *op. cit.*, p. 110. See also Kogon, *op. cit.*, pp. 46 ff.

13. Klee, *op. cit.*, pp. 111, 146.

14. For this detail, see the judgment against Dr. Widmann, Stuttgart Superior Tribunal, in Klee, *op. cit.*, pp. 85, 146; see also Kogon *op. cit.*, p. 52. In November 1944, T4 sold a group of bottles to I. G. Farben. See Klee, *op. cit.*, p. 446.

15. On the crematoria, see Klee, *op. cit.*, pp. 146–150; and Kaul, *op. cit.*, p. 115. Dr. Becker's declaration, that through Brack's efforts both the ovens and special stretchers meant to carry the dead were constructed, is absolutely false. Brack had no workers under his command who would have been qualified to do these things.

16. Klee, *op. cit.*, p. 149.

17. Numbers cited in Kogon, *loc. cit.*, p. 55 of the French ed.

18. Kaul, *op. cit.*, p. 97.

19. Cf. Klee, *op. cit.*, p. 259; Kogon, *op. cit.*, p. 53; and Kaul, *op. cit.*, p. 99.

20. Moreover, the operation was profitable, as in certain cases the families continued paying the costs of asylum stays well after the deaths of the patients. This happened in the case of the Neustadt asylum: the invalids were gassed on September 23, 1940, in Brandenburg. Still, the living expenses were charged until March 31, 1941. See Kogon, *op. cit.*, p. 54.

21. For more details, see Kaul, *op. cit.*, p. 101.

22. Kogon, *op. cit.*, pp. 53 ff.

23. Gerald Reitlinger, *Die Endlösung: Hitlers Versuch der Ausrottung der Juden Europas* 4th ed. (Berlin, 1961), p. 124. (In English, *The Final Solution: The Attempt to Exterminate the Jews of Europe*, 1st ed. [London, 1953].)

24. Declaration of Franz Suchomel, a member of the personnel of T4 at Hartheim. See Sereny, *op. cit.*, p. 53.

25. He was definitively named to this post on March 21, 1941. Cf. Wirth's personal dossier, Hauptstaatsarchiv, Stuttgart.

26. Nevertheless, it is astonishing that Wirth was present at other euthanasia institutions. Thus, he was at Hadamar in August 1941 on the day when the cremation of the ten thousandth cadaver was celebrated. It is improbable that he undertook this trip just for that single occasion. Certain indices allow us to presume that Wirth played an equally important role in the gassing of Jewish mentally ill patients and that he was the "inventor" of the "Cholm Asylum." See M. Tregonza, "Bełżec Death Camp," in the *Wiener Library Bulletin* XXX, nos. 41-42 (1977). Moreover, in a departmental note dated March 22, 1939, from the Stuttgart Prefect of Police, it is mentioned that "he [Wirth] is called upon, even outside the domains of his commisariat's activities, . . . each time that a delicate and important affair needs clarifying and particularly clever and energetic action is needed." Wirth's personal dossier, *loc. cit.*

27. Numbers cited by Klee, *op. cit.*, p. 340.

28. See Helmut Krausnick and Hans-Heinrich Wilhelm, "Die Truppe des Weltanschauungskrieges: Die Einsatzgruppen der Sicherheitspolizei und des SD 1938–1942," in *Quellen und Darstellungen zur Zeitgeschichte*, vol. 22 (Stuttgart, 1981), pp. 88 ff.

29. The mobile gas chamber was in reality a tractor upon which a steel bottle of gas was mounted, pulling an airtight trailer that bore the inscription "Kaisers Kaffeegeschaft," a popular chain of German stores. Cf. Kogon, *op. cit.*, p. 63; and Klee, *op. cit.*, pp. 106 ff., 112 ff., and 190 ff.

30. Shooting executions took place in the forest of Piasnicz. Cf. Klee, *op. cit.*, pp. 95 ff.

31. The details concerning this mission order were only given by Heydrich on July 2, 1941, in a letter to the heads of the regional SS and of the police. Cf. Krausnick and Wilhelm, *op. cit.*, p. 157.

32. A. Streim, *Die Behandlung sowjetischer Kriegsgefangener im "Fall Barbarossa": Eine Dokumentation* (Heidelberg, 1981), p. 86.

33. For the date, see Streim, *op. cit.*, pp. 92 ff. On the details of these killings, see Hilberg, *op. cit.*, pp. 237 ff.

34. Ibid.; see also Krausnick and Wilhelm, *op. cit.*, p. 543.

35. From the judgment pronounced on September 15, 1967, by the Stuttgart Assize Court against Dr. Widmann; Krausnick and Wilhelm, *op. cit.*, pp. 543-50. There remain points of uncertainty about the different means of killing the victims and the chronology of the killings. Thus, these two authors, Krausnick and Wilhelm, in what is the most recent and most serious monograph on the Einsatzgruppen, state that at first

euthanasia was practiced with exhaust gas and only later with carbon monoxide from bottles.

36. Rauff died in April 1984 in Chile. Chile had refused to extradite him to West Germany. On Heydrich and Himmler's role, see text below.

37. Cf. his speech on October 4, 1943, to the SS chiefs, also his speech on October 6, 1943, to the Reichsleiter and the gauleiter at Posen (Poznán). These speeches are reprinted in B. F. Smith and A. Peterson, *Heinrich Himmler, Geheimreden 1933–1945* (Frankfurt, 1974), pp. 169 ff., as well as in the *International Military Tribunal of Nuremberg*, vol. XXIX, pp. 110 ff., document 1919-PS.

38. Declarations by Pradel and Rauff, in Kogon, *op. cit.*, p. 82.

39. Ibid., for other technical details. Also see Krausnick and Wilhelm, *op. cit.*, p. 551.

40. Deposition of Dr. Leidig, who, in his role as a member of the KTI, attended this trial attempt: Kogon, *op. cit.*, pp. 83 ff.

41. It remains difficult to say whether the Saurer and the Diamond were available at the same time. The only sure thing is that the Diamond was put into service later. Ibid., p. 86.

42. Ibid., pp. 93 ff.

43. Ibid., pp. 98, 107. Consult the operation chart at the end of this chapter.

44. Ohlendorf's declaration at the Einsatzgruppe trial. Ibid., p. 98. There are numerous examples in this work, pp. 89–102.

45. Ibid., pp. 93, 104.

46. Doctor Becker's letter to Walter Rauff, ultrasecret document dated May 16, 1942, quoted by Léon Poliakov and J. Wulf, *Das Dritte Reich und die Juden* (Ullstein-Buch 33036) (Frankfurt, 1983), p. 141.

47. Krausnick and Wilhelm, *op. cit.*, pp. 189 ff.

48. Turner's letter to SS Obergruppenführer Wolff dated April 2, 1942, in Kogon, *op. cit.*, p. 107.

49. Ibid., and Hilberg, *op. cit.*, pp. 474 ff.: see also Christopher Browning, "The Final Solution in Serbia: The Samlin Judenlager—a Case Study," in *Yad Vashem Studies* XV (1983), pp. 55–59; and by the same author, "Wehrmacht Reprisal Policy and the Mass Murder of the Jews in Serbia," in *Militärgeschichtliche Mitteilungen* 1 (1983), pp. 31–47.

50. Martin Gilbert, *Die Vertreibung und Vernichtung der Juden: Ein Atlas* (Reinbeck, 1982), p. 104. The commander in chief of the Security Police and of the SD of Riga wrote a request that stated that he did not have enough trucks. This request was dated June 15, 1942. Rauff's response is dated June 22, 1942. Cf. Poliakov and Wulf, *op. cit.*, p. 142.

51. Ibid. See also n. 46.

52. Kogon, *op. cit.*, p. 333.

53. Ibid., p. 85.

54. Ino Arndt and Wolfgang Scheffler, "Organisierter Massenmord an Juden in den nationalsozialistischen Vernichtungslagern," in *Aus Politik und Zeitgeschichte*, supplement to *Das Parlament* B 19 (1976), from May 8, 1976, pp. 10 ff. These authors establish clearly that in sum, thirty trucks had probably been made, but they are not able to prove this number. What is known for certain is that there were fifteen trucks in the USSR, two or three at Chełmno, one at Lublin, and a temporary one at Mauthausen.

55. For the management and the topography of the camp, see Adalbert Rückerl, ed., *NS-Vernichtungslager im Spiegel deutscher Strafprozesse* (Munich, 1977), pp. 259–66.

56. Ibid., p. 268; and Kogon, *op. cit.*, p. 120.

57. Cf. J. von Lang, *Das Eichmann Protokoll: Tonbandaufzeichnungen der israeil-ischen Verhöre* (Berlin, 1982), pp. 71 ff. It is better not to rely on the author's commentaries, which contain some errors.

58. Testimonies in Kogon, *op. cit.*, pp. 122–30.

59. See Gilbert's maps, *op. cit.*, pp. 82, 97, 113.

60. Uwe Dietrich Adam, *Judenpolitik im Dritten Reich*, 2nd ed. (Düsseldorf, 1979), p. 289.

61. Kogon, *op. cit.*, pp. 110 ff. See also M. Broszat, "Hitler und die Genesis der 'Endlösung': Aus Anlass der Thesen von David Irving," in *VfZ* 25 (1977), p. 748.

62. In *Faschismus, Getto, Massenmord: Dokumentation über Ausrottung und Widerstand der Juden in Polen während des zweiten Weltkriegs*, 2nd ed. (East Berlin, 1961), p. 278.

63. RSHA note dated June 5, 1942, reproduced in facsimile in Kogon, *op. cit.*, pp. 333 ff; see also p. 114 on the replacement of one of the drivers.

64. If we may believe the testimonies at hand, there were three gas trucks at Chełmno, a Starer and two smaller Renaults. Most of the time the latter were used, which could hold up to forty persons. When the trucks were used at their full capacities, with two generally working at the same time, the number of victims was between 700 and 1000 per day. See Rückerl, *op. cit.*, p. 272, and Kogon, *op. cit.*, pp. 128, 132, where we find in table form the number of victims for the year 1942. From January 16 to January 29, there was 10,003 victims. From February 22 to April 4 there were 34,073 victims. From May 4 until May 15, 11,680. From September 5 to September 12, 15,859 victims. The latter number corresponds to a daily average of 1,050 persons killed, which is only possible if the three trucks were all working at the same time.

65. Rückerl, *op. cit.*, pp. 280 ff.

66. Ibid., pp. 284 ff.; cf. also Kogon, *op. cit.*, pp. 136 ff.; and Arndt and Scheffler, *op cit.*

67. There are very precise estimates of the assize court in Bonn in Rückerl, *op. cit.*, pp. 288–95.

68. Ibid., p. 287, declarations of the adjunct commandant of the camp, Walter Piller, condemned to death and executed in Poland. Cf. also Kogon, *op. cit.*, pp. 143 ff.

69. Rückerl, *op. cit.*, p. 248.

70. To use the name of the dead chief of the RSHA would have been a choice that was not only improper but also irreverent. Besides, what connection could there have been between the killing of Polish Jews and the Czech perpetrators of outrages? The name refers more probably to the state secretary for finances, Fritz Reinhardt, a spelling that one finds in several documents about the Reinhard(t) Operation. The present writer is preparing a monograph on the Reinhard(t) Operation.

71. For plans and commentaries on Sobibór, see Rückerl, *op. cit.*, pp. 158 ff.; and on Treblinka, see Sereny, *op. cit.*, pp. 154 ff.

72. It is rather unlikely that the Jews in the first convoys were all exterminated with bottled gas, as Joseph Oberhauser, Wirth's assistant, stated (Rückerl, *op. cit.*, p. 136), even though the indications of the number of victims are inexact. However, it is certain that the tribunal reached a false conclusion when they stated that Bełzec "used Zyklon B during the first weeks, and later, for reasons of economy, diesel motor exhaust gas."

73. In his testimony an SS soldier said that there had been no gas chamber at Bełzec. This, considering the number of victims, seems very unlikely. According to the testimony of a Polish laborer, the barracks measured 12 meters by 8 meters and were divided into three sections. Kogon, *op. cit.*, p. 152.

74. Ibid., pp. 165 ff.; and Rückerl, *op. cit.*, pp. 135 ff.

75. Repairs were made in Berlin, according to Oberhauser's statement; Rückerl, *op. cit.*, pp. 136 ff.

352

76. Declaration of Kurt Bolender; Kogon, *op. cit.*, p. 175.

77. A specialist, Dr. Scheffler, drew up a statement on the convoys arriving at Sobibór, which the court of assizes at Hagen took into account during their deliberations; Rückerl, *op. cit.*, pp. 155–57.

78. Franz Stangl reported that during the construction of Sobibór Wirth was infuriated because the gas chamber doors did not close perfectly; see Sereny, *op. cit.*, p. 118.

79. Cf. Klee, *op. cit.*, pp. 376 ff.

80. Sereny, *op. cit.*, p. 165. See also Kogon, *op. cit.*, p. 175.

81. The Munich assize court's indications on the "output" of Bełzec were certainly false. Its estimations were based on the idea that there was only one gas chamber at Bełzec with a capacity of 100 to 150 persons. Rückerl, *op. cit.*, p. 133; Arndt and Scheffler, *op. cit.*, p. 13; see also n. 73. After four weeks of functioning, there were 80,000 victims at Bełzec. That works out to an average of 2,600 killed every day. If one allows only sixty minutes for each collective asphyxiation, that would mean it would have been necessary to repeat the process seventeen times a day. In the information we have about Treblinka, the number of gas chambers varies between six and ten (Arndt and Scheffler, *op. cit.*, p. 16, n. 31), the only sure thing being that the newer installations had a capacity twice as large as the previous ones. Because the older installations continued to function as well, it was possible to gas between 1,500 and 2,000 persons at Treblinka daily. The assertion by Kogon (*op. cit.*, p. 185) that the newer gas chambers were able to kill 4,000 persons at once, is not documentable. See also the statement by Stangl in Sereny, *op. cit.*, p. 174. Rudolph Höss indicated, in the course of the interrogations he went through, that Treblinka had ten gas chambers that could hold a total of 2,000 persons; Poliakov and Wulf, *op. cit.*, p. 129.

82. Hilberg, *op. cit.*, p. 603.

83. Poliakov and Wulf, *op. cit.*, pp. 113 ff.; see also Saul Friedländer, *Kurt Gerstein ou l'Ambiguïté du bien* (Paris, 1967).

84. "Gerstein's Report of May 4, 1945," *Dokumentation zur Massenvernichtung: Schriftenreihe der Bundeszentrale für Heimatdienst* (Documents Relating to Mass Exterminations) (Bonn, 1962), pp. 6 ff.; see also Rückerl, where Gerstein's report of April 2, 1945, is reproduced, *op. cit.*, pp. 61 ff.

85. Kogon, *op. cit.*, p. 171, erroneously placed this episode in the first period of Bełzec's functioning. Gerstein's indications about the number of victims killed at Bełzec are so unlikely that even the uninitiated might immediately recognize it: Gerstein speaks of 700 to 800 persons gassed in an area of 25 square miles. Faurisson, *op. cit.*, bases himself on this absurd error in order to cast worldwide doubt upon Gerstein's testimony. But an error of this type, on the contrary, reinforces the credibility and good faith of the witness.

86. "Gerstein's Report," p. 9.

87. J. von Lang, *op. cit.*, p. 77.

88. Kogon, *op. cit.*, p. 190. Letter from the head of the Lublin SS and Police to the central director of personnel of the SS, dated April 13, 1945, *Faschismus, Getto, Massenmord*, pp. 301 ff.

89. On this subject, see also the declaration by a Jewish prisoner concerning the reaction of members of a special Jewish commando to the fact that the convoys were not arriving; Sereny, *op. cit.*, pp. 156 ff.

90. Gilbert (*op. cit.*, p. 170) erroneously places this event on September 2, 1943. See Rückerl, *op. cit.*, pp. 74 ff.; and the description of the uprising witnessed by Stangl, in Sereny, *op. cit.*, pp. 224 ff.

91. Report of the Order Police detachment of the Lublin district, dated October 15, 1943, *Faschismus, Getto, Massenmord, op. cit.*, p. 365.

92. "Letter on the Industries of the Eastern Territories." "Ostindustrie" or "Osti,"

created in March 1943, was an SS industrial enterprise. Its principal activity was to exploit Polish Jewish manpower (*NdT*). The letter was signed by Globocnik on August 31, 1943; ibid., p. 417.

93. Letter of November 4, 1943, in Poliakov and Wulf, *op. cit.*, pp. 44 ff.

94. *Auschwitz: Geschichte und Wirklichkeit des Vernichtungslagers*, Rororo 7330 (Reinbek, 1980), pp. 35 ff.

95. Ibid., p. 118.

96. Ibid., p. 27.

97. Circular of the chief of the Security Police and of the SD, dated January 2, 1941, in Martin Broszat, *NS Konzentrationslager*, p. 107.

98. *Auschwitz*, pp. 118 ff.; a map of the camp is printed on p. 36.

99. Ibid., pp. 17 ff.; see also Broszat, *op. cit.*, pp. 97 ff.

100. Cf. testimony by SS Perry Broad, in Kogon, *op. cit.*, p. 207. See also Broszat, ed., *Kommandant in Auschwitz: Autobiographische Aufzeichnungen von Rudolf Höss* (Stuttgart, 1958), p. 160.

101. Hilberg, *op. cit.*, p. 597; and *Auschwitz*, p. 122.

102. Kogon, *op. cit.*, pp. 210 ff.

103. Hilberg, *op. cit.*, p. 597.

104. Other details in *Auschwitz*, p. 124; Kogon, *op. cit.*, p. 227; and *Kommandant in Auschwitz*, *op. cit.*, p. 225.

105. *Auschwitz*, p. 125; and Hilberg, *op. cit.*, p. 595 and table 76.

106. Following Kogon, *op. cit.*, chap. VII of the French edition (*NdE*).

107. Hilberg, *op. cit.*, pp. 601 ff.; and Poliakov and Wulf, *op. cit.*, pp. 111 ff.

108. According to the latest research of Georges Wellers, the number of persons gassed at Auschwitz has been raised to at least 1,334,700, of whom 1,323,000 were Jews, 6,430 Gypsies, 1,065 Soviet prisoners of war, and 3,665 other nationalities, the majority Polish. These numbers are only those for which traces of established evidence remain. Doubtless, according to Wellers, these numbers are very much less than the actual sums. See *Le Monde juif*, no. 112 (October–December 1983) (*NdE*).

109. H. Lichtenstein, *Majdanek: Reportage eines Prozesses* (Frankfurt am Main, 1979), p. 21.

110. Note of an employee in the service of the governor general, dated March 17, 1942, in *Fascismus, Getto, Massenmord*, p. 269; see also on this subject the testimony of Jan Nowak in Lichtenstein, *op. cit.*, p. 64.

111. Cf. n. 1 above.

112. In the documentation we have on Majdanek, the number of gas chambers varies from five to seven, but the indications concern different periods. See J. Marszalek, *Majdanek: Geschichte und Wirklichkeit des Verninchtungslagers* (Hamburg, 1982), p. 144. See also Lichtenstein, *op. cit.*, p. 22.

113. Kogon, *op. cit.*, p. 242.

114. The crematorium was built in the spring of 1943. See one of the plans reprinted in Poliakov and Wulf, *op. cit.*, p. 138.

115. Clothes and other objects gathered at Bełżec, Sobibór, and Treblinka were sorted, packed, and warehoused at Majdanek. Moreover, there were interactions of personnel between the camps, which Höfle seems to have maintained.

116. Statement of SS officer Erich Muhsfeld in 1945 in Kogon, *op. cit.*, p. 243. See also the depositions of witnesses during the trial relating to Majdanek, reprinted in Lichtenstein, *op. cit.*, p. 62.

117. Kogon, *op. cit.*, pp. 244 ff.

118. Hilberg, *op. cit.*, p. 594.

119. Kogon, *op. cit.*, p. 242.

120. Hilberg, *op. cit.*, p. 604; Hilberg puts the number of victims at 50,000 per-

sons. The Düsseldorf assize court put the number at 250,000. Cf. Lichtenstein, *op. cit.*, p. 25. Probably Hilberg's figure is much too small.

121. Kogon, *op. cit.*, p. 243.

122. For information about the SS work camps situated in the area of Lublin, see Hilberg, *op. cit.*, p. 372. Hilberg proposes the idea that these Jews had to be got rid of because the camps fell under the control of the WVHA (SS Main Economic-Administrative Office). However, this hypothesis is hardly plausible. For numbers emanating from the report of a Polish resistance group, see *Faschismus, Getto, Massenmord*, p. 366. These numbers agree with the official statistics; Hilberg, *op. cit.*, p. 594, n. 41. The operation was directed by Globocnik's successor, SS Brigadeführer Sporrenberg, who was assisted by Höfle.

123. According to testimony by a prisoner who was forced to distribute the bottles of Zyklon B, this distribution continued until March 1944. See Lichtenstein, *op. cit.*, p. 67.

124. For the reaction of the Polish territories after the revelations by the Russians, see Hilberg, *op. cit.*, p. 663.

125. On all these camps, see Kogon, *op. cit.*, pp. 222–55. On Neuengamme, see also W. Johe, *Neuengamme: Zur Geschichte der Konzentrationslager in Hamburg*, 2nd ed. (Hamburg, 1981), pp. 34 ff.

126. On this point, see *Auschwitz*, p. 117; see also Kogon, *op. cit.*, pp. 58–71 of the French ed. (*NdE*).

127. For example, see E. Calic, *Reinhard Heydrich, Schlüssfigur des Dritten Reichs* (Dusseldorf, 1982), pp. 511 ff., and the polemic that this author engaged in with Martin Broszat.

128. Christophersen, *Die Auschwitz-Lüge*, provides a good example of this attitude. As a member of the SS, he visited Auschwitz in January 1944, at a moment when massive exterminations were not taking place. Even when he declares that he saw no sign at Auschwitz I of any massive executions by gassings, he is not lying, because those killings took place in Auschwitz II. What is more, the author describes these camps as rather agreeable camps for habitation, where the occupants were hardly worse off than inmates of a sanitarium in terms of clothing and food. As for Faurisson, the very essence of logic, he refuses to recognize that Zyklon B was used to exterminate human beings. Zyklon B is for Faurisson merely a necessary step in his "demonstration." Certainly, he admits the existence of a place called the "mortuary depot," but this was only a cold room. Surely, when this "cold room" was examined later, residues of hydrocyanic acid were found, but this acid served only as a disinfectant, etc., etc.; Faurisson, *op. cit.*, p. 35.

9 / The Statistic
RAUL HILBERG

1. Affidavit by Wilhelm Höttl, November 26, 1945, Nuremberg document PS-2738.

2. Judgment, International Military Tribunal, *Trial of the Major War Criminals*, vol. XXII, p. 496.

3. The same number was given in June 1944 by a Jewish emissary, Joel Brand, who had been sent out by Eichmann from Hungary for ransom negotiations with the Allies, to the Jewish Agency's Moshe Shertok. "Preliminary Report" by Moshe Shertok, June 27, 1944, Weizmann Archives, Rehoboth, Israel.

4. Affidavit by Dieter Wisliceny, November 29, 1945, in Office of United States

Council for Prosecution of Axis Criminality, *Nazi Conspiracy and Aggression*, vol. VIII, p. 610.

5. Testimony by Eichmann, July 7 and 20, 1961, Eichmann trial, English transcript, Session 88, p. H 1, and Session 105, pp. L1 1, Mm 1. See also Eichmann's memoirs, *Ich, Adolf Eichmann* (Leoni am Starnberger See: Druffel-Verlag, 1980), pp. 460–61, 472–76.

6. Testimony by Eichmann, July 6, 1961, Session 87, p. Y 1.

7. Institute of Jewish Affairs, "Statistics of Jewish Casualties During Axis Domination," August 1945, in the library of the institute.

8. Jakob Leszczynski, "Bilan de l'extermination," Congrès Juif Mondial (Brussels, Paris, and Geneva, June 1946).

9. See consolidated "excess of deaths over births" calculated by the Jewish councils for the Reich, Austria, and the Protectorate of Bohemia-Moravia for the period of Nazi domination to November 14, 1941. The material was requested by the Reich Main Security Office. Leo Baeck Institute, New York City, microfilm, roll 66. Note also reports for Vienna, with statistics, in archive of Yad Vashem, Jerusalem. In 1942, for example, the Viennese Jews counted 2,319 deaths and 19 births in a population that declined with deportations during the calendar year from 43,013 to 7,989. Report by Council Chairman Löwenherz for 1942, Yad Vashem document O 30/3.

10. For Warsaw, see monthly reports by Jewish council from 1940 through 1942, including detailed statistics in report of Council Chairman Adam Czerniaków to ghetto Kommissar Heinz Auerswald of February 12, 1942, Zentrale Stelle, Ludwigsburg, Akten Auerswald, Polen 365. With a cumulative population of ca. 470,000, deaths during the eighteen-month period from January 1941 through June 1942 were 69,355. In the course of the roundups for summer deportations in 1942, deaths from "bullet wounds" (*Schusswunden*) exceeded "natural deaths." The total for the Warsaw ghetto from its creation at the end of 1940 to the onset (but not including) the Warsaw ghetto battle of 1943 was about 83,000. For Łódź, see compilation of detailed statistics in page proofs for May 1940 to June 1942, prepared by Łódź ghetto Jewish council, YIVO Institute, New York City, Łódź ghetto collection no. 58. See also a monthly statistic from January 1940 through August 1944 in the statistical office of the city of Łódź, Yad Vashem document O 6/79. With a cumulative population of ca. 200,000, the Łódź ghetto had more than 45,000 dead.

11. Report by Jäger (commander of Einsatzkommando 3), December 1, 1941, Institut für Zeitgeschichte (Munich), Fb 85/2.

12. Reich Main Security Office (German abbreviation: RSHA) IV-A-1, Operational and Situation Report USSR no. 135 (60 copies), October 13, 1941, Nuremberg document NO-2832. Report by Feldkommandantur 240/VII covering September 15, 1941 to October 10, 1941, dated October 19, 1941, Yad Vashem document O 53/6.

13. For example, reports by Jewish Council in Slovakia/Division of Special Tasks (signed Hochberg), June 12 and 14, 1942, Yad Vashem document M-5(18)7.

14. Name list of Jews deported from Belgium in Serge Klarsfeld and Maxime Steinberg, *Mémorial de la déportation des Juifs de Belgique* (Brussels and New York, 1982). Name lists for France in Serge Klarsfeld, *Le Mémorial de la déportation des Juifs de France* (Paris, 1978). Name lists for Rome in Liliana Picciotto Fargion, *L'Occupazione tedesca e gli ebrei di Roma* (Rome: Carucci Editore, 1979).

15. For Macedonia and Thrace, there are several sets of statistics, ranging from 11,343 to 11,459: Hoffmann to RSHA/April 5, 1943, Nuremberg document NG-4144. Memorandum by Wagner (Foreign Office), April 3, 1943, NG-4180. Report by Korherr (SS statistician), NO-5193. Also, Bulgarian figures in Frederic B. Chary, *The Bulgarian Jews* (Pittsburgh: University of Pittsburgh Press, 1972), pp. 144–27.

For Hungary, a total of 437,402 deportees, including those from areas annexed by Hungary, were reported by Veesenmayer (German envoy) to Foreign Office in Berlin on June 13, 1944, NG-5619; June 30, 1944, NG-2263; and July 11, 1944, NG-5614. A Hungarian figure is 434,351. Ferenczy (Hungarian gendarmerie) to Hungarian Inspector of Gendarmerie Endre, July 9, 1944, Eichmann trial Israel Police document 1322.

16. For example, Generaldirektion der Ostbahn (signed Glas) instructions for Częstochowa–Treblinka transport, September 21, 1942, and Generaldirektion der Ostbahn (signed Schmidt) instructions for transports from Reich to Treblinka, March 26, 1943, Zentrale Stelle, Ludwigsburg, Polen film 6.

17. For example, Białystok–Treblinka transports in order of Generaldirektion der Ostbahn (signed Meyer), February 1, 1943, Zentrale Stelle, Ludwigsburg, Polen film 6; and Viennese transport to Sobibór in report by Lieutenant Josef Frischmann of Viennese Order Police, June 20, 1942, Yad Vashem document DN/27-3

18. For example, in the statistical compilation of the Łódź ghetto Jewish council, YIVO Institute, Łódź ghetto collection no. 58.

19. For example, the shootings of Reich Jews in Kaunas (Kovno), reported by Jäger (Einsatzkommando 3), December 1, 1941, Fb 85/2.

20. Report by SS and Police Leader Stroop in Warsaw to Higher SS and Police Leader Krüger, May 16, 1943, PS-1061.

21. Cover letter by Korherr to Obersturmbannführer R. Brandt (Himmler's adjutant), March 23, 1943, indicating transmission of report, NO-5195. Himmler to RSHA, April 9, 1943, confirming receipt of report, NO-5197. Brandt to Korherr, April 10, 1943, passing on Himmler's requests for changes in phraseology, NO-5196. Korherr to Brandt, April 19, 1943, noting that the draft of a supplement, for inclusion in a shortened version intended for presentation to Hitler, had been sent out to the RSHA, NO-5193. Cover letter by Korherr to Hauptsturmführer Meine (in Himmler's adjutant's office), April 28, 1943, stating that he was returning the report with editing as requested in the letter of April 10, NO-5193. Text of edited long report in NO-5194. Text of supplement with deportation data to March 31, 1943, in NO-5193. Since the long report and its supplement overlap in contents and language, they will be referred to here as the Korherr report without further distinction between them. A summary, typed with special large lettering in Eichmann's office for submission to Hitler, is not extant. Eichmann, Ich, p. 475.

22. Entry in diary of Gerhard Engel (army adjutant in Hitler's headquarters) of December 19, 1942, in Hildegard von Kotze, ed., Heeresadjutant bei Hitler (Stuttgart: Deutsche Verlags-Anstalt, 1974), pp. 141–42.

23. Korherr to Brandt, March 23, 1943, NO-5195.

24. Brandt to Korherr, April 10, 1943, NO-5196.

25. Statement by Korherr, July 13, 1951, Amtsgericht Regensburg, in Zentrale Stelle, Ludwigsburg, 202 AR 72/60, pp. 207–21; his statement of May 26, 1962, for prosecution of Landgericht Hamburg, 141 Js 573/60, Zentrale Stelle, 202 AR 74/60, pp. 2214–17; and his statement of January 22, 1965, before prosecution in Regensburg, 9 Js 121/62, Zentrale Stelle, 412 AR 536/61, pp. 49–52.

26. Eichmann, Ich, pp. 474–75. Eichmann does not mention Korherr by name. Korherr states that he had a deputy, Dr. Roderich Plate, and an administrative assistant, Hauptsturmführer Hofmann.

27. Testimony by Eichmann, July 6, 1961, Eichmann trial English transcript, session 87, p. Y 1.

28. Czerniaków's entry in his diary of July 24, 1941, in Raul Hilberg, Stanislaw Staron, and Josef Kermisz, The Warsaw Diary of Adam Czerniaków (Briarcliff Manor: Stein & Day, 1979), p. 261.

29. RSHA IV-A-1, Operational Report no. 67, August 29, 1941, NO-2837. For Romanian contribution, see estimate by Matatias Carp, *Cartea Neagra*, vol. 3 (Bucharest, 1946–48), pp. 29–36.

30. Romanian Commission of Inquiry into Irregularities of Chisinau Ghetto (signed by G. Niculescu and five other officials), December, 1941, in Carp, *Cartea Neagra*, vol. 3, pp. 61–65.

31. See Einsatzgruppe D to Eleventh Army, September 2, 1941, Rumänien 29222, in German records located in Alexandria, Virginia, during postwar years.

32. Crossings in September–November 1941 were 118,847. Report by Brosteanu (inspector of gendarmerie in Transnistria), for December 15, 1941 to January 15, 1942, in Carp, *Cartea Neagra*, vol. 3, pp. 319–20. Carp estimated an additional 5,000 people deported in 1942. Ibid., pp. 321–32.

33. Report by inspector general of gendarmerie (Tobescu), September 16, 1942, and undated subsequent report by Interior Ministry/Police (General Vasiliu), ibid., pp. 438–42, 447–51. In addition, there were several hundred "Communist" Jews in a special camp.

34. There were 131,641 deportees. Randolph Braham, *Genocide and Retribution* (Boston and The Hague: Kluwer-Nijhoff, 1983), p. 233. The official Romanian estimate of Jewish population in ceded portion of Transylvania as of 1940 is 148,573; the Hungarian census figure of 1941, which included converts, is somewhat higher.

35. In his report Korherr understates the population of the Białystok district and overstates that of Galicia, but the reason is an apparent failure to translate old Polish provincial boundaries into new German administrative frontiers. There is no error for either of the two regions as a whole.

36. See statistical table of Łódź ghetto in YIVO Institute Łódź ghetto collection no. 58.

37. Report by Stroop, May 16, 1943, PS-1061.

38. Report by Katzmann, June 30, 1943, Nuremberg document L-18. In addition a small number were in hiding.

39. Records of the statistical office of Łódź list 61,086 departures of Jews during January through May 1940, including 51,739 in January, February, and March. Yad Vashem O 6/79. Destinations are not indicated, but the first three months coincide with mass expulsions. See additional statistics in Wlodzimierz Jastrzebski, "Nazi Deportations of Polish and Jewish Populations from Territories Incorporated into the Third Reich," paper for Main Commission for Investigation of Nazi Crimes in Poland/International Scientific Session on Nazi Genocide, Warsaw, April 14–17, 1983.

40. Some additional adjustments are necessary for war dead. Shootings in the Białystok district and, during 1941, also in Galicia, were probably placed under the rubric "excess of deaths." Births and normal deaths, if not completely balanced, may constitute another complication. In view of these problems, it may be tempting to calculate the privation deaths from the available Łódź and Warsaw ghetto data alone. The two communities lost about 19% of their combined cumulative populations under ghettoization. For all of Poland (without war dead and those who escaped) that percentage would spell out a toll of nearly 600,000. Warsaw and Łódź, however, were not sufficiently typical. Some of the smaller, so-called "open ghettos" were less harsh, and other ghettos did not last as long.

41. RSHA IV-A-1, Operational Report no. 21, July 13, 1941, NO-2937, and RSHA IV-A-1, Operational Report no. 67, August 29, 1941, NO-2837.

42. Report by Einsatzkommando 3, December 1, 1941, Fb 85/2. There were additional thousands in a small ghetto (Swieciany) and in hiding.

43. Wehrwirtschafts-Aussenstelle in Vilna, report for October, 1943, Wi/ID 3.26, in Alexandria during postwar years.

44. RSHA IV-A-1, Operational Report No. 178, March 9, 1942, NO-3241, and RSHA IV-A-1, Operational Report no. 184, March 23, 1942, NO-3235.

45. Kube to Reichskommissar Lohse, July 31, 1942, PS-3428. Acting Gebietskommissar Haase of neighboring Wilejka reported on April 8, 1943, that 3,000 Jews were still alive in his area. Record of meeting of Gebietskommissare, FB 85/1.

46. Hauptkommissar in Baranovichi to Generalkommissar of White Russia (Kube), August 27, 1942, NG-1315.

47. Brigadeführer von Gottberg to Gruppenführer Herff, December 21, 1942, NO-1732. In April 1943, Gebietskommissar Hanweg of Lida (in Baranovichi Hauptkommissariat) reported 4,419 Jews still alive in his area. Fb 85/1.

48. RSHA IV-A-1, Operational Report no. 28, July 20, 1941, NO-2943. RSHA IV-A-1, Operational Report no. 43, August 5, 1941, NO-2949. RSHA IV-A-1, Operational Report no. 56, August 18, 1941, NO-2848. RSHA IV-A-1, Operational Report no. 58, August 20, 1941, NO-2846. RSHA IV-A-1, Operational Report no. 66, August 28, 1941, NO-2839.

49. RSHA IV-A-1, Operational Report no. 143, December 8, 1941, NO-2827.

50. Himmler to Hitler, December 20, 1942, NO-1128.

51. See, for example, Armament Command in Lutsk to Armament Inspectorate Ukraine, report for October 1–December 31, 1942, dated January 21, 1943, Wi/Id 1.101, in Alexandria during postwar years.

52. A total of 61 Jews were caught between February 21 and April 21, 1943. Report by Generalkommissar in Volhynia-Podolia, April 30, 1943, EAP 99/77, in records at Alexandria during postwar years. On March 21, 1944, the Gebietskommissariat of Brest-Litovsk (in Volhynia) reported that the area was free of Jews. EAP 99/85, in Alexandria during postwar years.

53. Report of the Anglo-American Committee of Enquiry regarding the problems of European Jewry and Palestine, April 20, 1946, London, Cmd. 6808, pp. 58–59. Philip Friedman, *Roads to Extinction* (New York and Philadelphia: Conference on Jewish Social Studies and Jewish Publication Society, 1980), pp. 211–43. Annual postwar volumes of the *American Jewish Year Book.*

54. The official Polish estimate is consistent with the assumptions that between 1931 and 1939 the Jewish population increased at a lower rate than that of non-Jews and that emigration of Jews exceeded immigration. The estimate does not include converts. In the tabulation, births between 1939 and 1945-46 are assumed not to have been higher or lower than normal deaths. Some survivors were not registered, but others were counted twice.

55. Albert Speer, *Infiltration* (New York: Macmillan, 1981), p. 283.

56. Einsatzgruppe A draft report (undated), PS-2273. Report of Einsatzgruppe B, September 1, 1942, EAP VIII 173 g 1210/1, in Alexandria during postwar years. Kommandos 4a and 5 in RSHA IV-A-1, Operational Report no. 156, January 16, 1942, NO-3405. Einsatzgruppe D in RSHA IV-A-1, Operational Report no. 195, April 8, 1942, NO-3359.

57. RSHA IV-A-1, Operational Report no. 164, February 4, 1942, NO-3399.

58. Kislovodsk proclamation in Nuremberg document USSR-IA(2-4).

59. Statement by Korherr, July 31, 1951, Zentrale Stelle, 202 AR 72/60, pp. 215–16.

60. A total of 55,000 Jews, killed in the summer of 1942 in the area of White Russia (mainly within prewar Polish territory) were probably credited to the toll of Einsatzgruppe A. It is also possible that the Commandos of the General Government Security Police, styled an Einsatzgruppe for Special Purposes, and operating in newly occupied areas of eastern Poland in 1941, may have been included. For analysis of Einsatzgruppen figures, see Helmut Krausnick and Hans-Heinrich Wilhelm, *Die Truppe des*

Weltanschauungskrieges (Stuttgart: Deutsche Verlags-Anstalt, 1981), pp. 605–09, 618–22.

61. Killings by formations of the Higher SS and Police Leaders operating in the areas of the Einsatzgruppen in 1941 are generally reported in the daily RSHA summaries. See, in particular, RSHA IV-A-1, Operational Report no. 94, September 25, 1941, NO-3146.

62. Director of German armed forces intelligence (Abwehr) in Romania (signed Rodler) to Eleventh Army/Intelligence, and intelligence sections of German army, navy, and air force missions in Romania, November 4, 1941, U.S. National Archives microfilm T 501, roll 278. Other materials in Carp, *Cartea Neagra*, vol. 3, pp. 199–209.

63. Extract from indictment of Romanian defendants before Bucharest People's Court, in Carp, *Cartea Neagra*, vol. 3, 225–26.

64. Note, probably by Triska (German Foreign Office), May 16, 1942, NG-4817.

65. See the detailed report by Jewish commission (signed Fred Saraga), January 31, 1943, Yad Vashem M 20.

66. See the analysis, with statistical tables, by Ivor Millman, "Diaspora Jewish Populations," in U. O. Scmelz, P. Glikson, and S. J. Gould, eds., *Studies in Jewish Demography* (New York: KTAV, 1983), pp. 99–109.

67. Ibid.

68. The figures were discovered by Zvi Griliches in vol. 4 of the USSR 1970 population census. He published them in *Near Eastern Report* 17 (July 23, 1973), p. 118.

69. The Soviet census of 1959 reveals 37,830,000 women and 25,829,000 men in the significant age group of thirty to fifty-four. (An eighteen-year-old in 1945 would have been thirty-two in 1959; a thirty-six-year-old in 1941 would have been fifty-four in 1959.) The gap, which consists of 12,000,000 men, may be attributed to the following: one-half to Red Army battle deaths and deaths among Soviet prisoners of war; roughly a quarter to purges; and the remaining quarter to the difference of natural mortality among middle-aged men and women, and to such smaller factors as killings of Soviet partisans, deaths of slave laborers in Germany, and the de facto emigration of Soviet collaborators in German service. The only known number is that of dead Soviet prisoners of war, which passed the 2 million mark in 1944, according to German records. See Christian Streit, *Keine Kameraden* (Stuttgart: Deutsche Verlags-Anstalt, 1978), pp. 245–49. The Jewish percentage of the Soviet population in 1939 was 1.76. The Jewish share of Soviet Red Army dead may have been under 1.5%, given the lower mobilization rate in the western territories of the USSR, which were overrun by the Germans. The Jewish share of the purge victims might also have been under 1.5%, due to the decline of Jewish population in the Holocaust.

10 / The Nazis and the Jews
in Occupied Western Europe, 1940–1944
MICHAEL R. MARRUS and ROBERT O. PAXTON

1. Western Europe is taken to include France, Belgium, Holland, Denmark, Norway, and Italy.

2. We have accepted the statistical estimates for Jewish population losses conveniently found in Lucy Dawidowicz, *The War Against the Jews, 1939–1945* (New York and Philadelphia, 1975), p. 403, with important corrections for France and Belgium. See n. 60 below.

3. *Mein Kampf*, trans. Ralph Manheim (Boston: Sentry, 1943), p. 654.

4. Study prepared by Werner Best, August–September 1941, microfilm series, U.S. National Archives, Washington, D.C., Microcopy T-501/101/1367.

5. The Jewish populations of the various countries occupied in 1940 are approximately as follows: France, 350,000 (including Jewish refugees from Belgium, Holland, and Luxembourg); Belgium, 58,000; Holland, 140,000; Denmark, 8,000; Norway, 1,800.

6. *Mein Kampf*, p. 307. For an interesting recent discussion of Nazi anti-Semitism, see Fred Weinstein, *The Dynamics of Nazism: Leadership, Ideology and the Holocaust* (New York, 1980), esp. chaps. 3 and 4.

7. Arieh Tartakower and Kurt R. Grossman, *The Jewish Refugee* (New York, 1944), p. 32. See Herbert A. Strauss, "Jewish Emigration from Germany: Nazi Policies and Jewish Responses," *Leo Baeck Institute Year Book* XXV (1980), pp. 313–61 and XXVI (1981), pp. 343–409, for the most recent survey of this subject.

8. See Michael R. Marrus and Robert O. Paxton, *Vichy France and the Jews* (New York, 1981). For details on Jewish emigration during 1939–41, see Yehuda Bauer, *American Jewry and the Holocaust: The American Joint Distribution Committee, 1939–1945* (Detroit, 1981), chap. 2 and passim.

9. Luther memorandum, August 21, 1942, Nuremberg document (hereafter ND) : NG-2586-J, in *Trials of War Criminals Before the Nuremberg Military Tribunal*, 13 vols. (Washington, 1951–52), vol. XIII, p. 243; Christopher Browning, *The Final Solution and the German Foreign Office: A Study of Referat D III of Abteilung Deutschland, 1940–1943* (New York, 1978), p. 43.

10. Schellenberg to Foreign Office, May 20, 1941, ND: NG-3104.

11. See Goshen, "Eichmann und die Nisko-Aktion im Oktober 1939: Eine Fallstudie zur NS-Judenpolitik in der letzten Etappe vor der 'Endlösung,'" *Vierteljahrshefte für Zeitgeschichte* (hereafter *VfZ*) 29 (January 1981), pp. 74–96; Philip Friedman, "The Lublin Reservation and the Madagascar Plan: Two Aspects of Nazi Jewish Policy During the Second World War," in Joshua A. Fishman, ed., *Studies in Modern Jewish History* (New York, 1972), pp. 354–80.

12. Rademacher memorandum, July 3, 1940, ND: NG-2586-B.

13. Browning, *op. cit.*, pp. 35–43.

14. "Zentrales Judenamt in Paris," January 21, 1941, Centre de documentation juive contemporaine (hereafter CDJC): CV-59.

15. Best to MBF, April 4, 1941, in Henri Monneray, ed., *La Persécution des Juifs en France et dans les autres pays de l'Ouest presentée par la France à Nuremberg* (Paris, 1947), pp. 137–138.

16. Auswärtiges Amt (hereafter AA): Inland IIg 189, passim.

17. Leni Yahil, "Methods of Persecution: A Comparison of the 'Final Solution' in Holland and Denmark," *Scripta Hierosolymita* 23 (1972), p. 288.

18. Monneray, *op. cit.*, p. 205.

19. Marrus and Paxton, *op. cit.*, chap. 1.

20. Paul M. Hayes, *Quisling: The Career and Political Ideas of Vidkun Quisling, 1887–1945* (Newton Abbot, England, 1971), pp. 271, 274, 288; Lise Lindbaek, "Persecution of the Jews in Norway," *Inter-Allied Review* I (August 15, 1941), pp. 10–11.

21. See Marrus and Paxton, *op. cit.*, chaps. 3 and 4.

22. Raul Hilberg, *The Destruction of the European Jews* (Chicago, 1967), pp. 366–71, 384–86; Louis de Jong, "Jews and Non-Jews in Nazi-Occupied Holland," in Max Beloff, ed., *On the Track of Tyranny* (London, 1960), pp. 146–47.

23. Müller to SS headquarters in Belgium and France, October 23, 1941, CDJC: XXVb-7.

24. See Best to MBF, April 4, 1941, CDJC: LXXV-145; Schellenberg to Foreign Office, May 20, 1941, ND: RF-1201, RF-1202 in Monneray, *op. cit.*, pp. 165–67; Uwe Dietrich Adam, *Judenpolitik im Dritten Reich* (Düsseldorf, 1972), pp. 306–10; AA: Inland IIg 189, "Verhaftungen ausländischen Juden in Frankreich, 1941," 8/1.

361

25. Dannecker memorandum, July 1, 1941, ND: RF-1207, in Monneray, *op. cit.*, p. 85, 113.

26. Zeitschel to Abetz, August 22, 1941, CDJC: V-15.

27. Note to Michel, December 12, 1941, CDJC: LXXV-41, in Joseph Billig, *Le Commissariat général aux questions juives (1941–1944)* 3 vols. (Paris, 1955–60), vol. I, p. 215.

28. On this point see Martin Broszat, "Hitler und die Genesis der 'Endlösung': Aus Anlass der Thesen von David Irving," *VfZ* 25 (1977), pp. 739–75. But cf. Christopher Browning, "Zur Genesis der 'Endlösung': Eine Antwort an Martin Broszat," ibid., 29 (1981), pp. 97–109.

29. See Andreas Hillgruber, "Die 'Endlösung' und das deutsche Ostimperium als Kernstück des rassenideologischen Programs des Nationalsozialismus," ibid., 20 (1972), pp. 133–53; Helmut Krausnick and Hans-Heinrich Wilhelm, *Die Truppe des Weltan-schauungskrieges: Die Einsatzgruppen der Sicherheitspolizei und des SD* (Stuttgart, 1981).

30. ND: PS-710, printed in Raul Hilberg, *Documents of Destruction: Germany and Jewry, 1933–1945* (Chicago, 1971), pp. 88–89. The figure of 300,000 is extrapolated from Einsatzgruppe reports discussed in Browning, *Foreign Office*, pp. 72–74. Cf. Walter Laqueur's estimate for the same period of 600,000, which includes Jews killed by the Romanians in Transnistria (*The Terrible Secret* [London, 1980], p. 12), and the data discussed in Krausnick and Wilhelm, *op. cit.*, pp. 618–22.

31. ND: NG-2586-E, printed in Hilberg, *Documents*, pp. 89–99.

32. Note of Dannecker, March 10, 1942, ND: RF-1216, in Monneray, *op. cit.*, pp. 124–25.

33. See Hilberg, *Destruction*, p. 374; Monneray, *op. cit.*, pp. 232–33; Jacob Presser, *The Destruction of the Dutch Jews*, trans. Arnold Pomerans (New York, 1969).

34. On the imposition of the star, see Adam, *op. cit.*, 334–38; Léon Poliakov, *L'Étoile jaune* (Paris, 1949); Philip Friedman, "The Jewish Badge and the Yellow Star in the Nazi Era," *Historia Judaica* XVII (1955), pp. 41–70.

35. Dannecker's account of the meeting is in ND: RF-1217, in Monneray, *op. cit.*, pp. 126–27.

36. Note of Dannecker, June 15, 1942, ND: RF-1217, in Monneray, *op. cit.*, pp. 126–27 and June 16, 1942, ND: RF-1218; Hilberg, *Destruction*, p. 406.

37. See Browning, *Foreign Office*, p. 101; A. de Jonghe, *La Lutte Himmler-Reeder pour la nomination d'un HSSPF à Bruxelles (1941–1944)*, pt. I: *La Sicherheitspolizei en Belgique, Cahiers d'histoire de la Seconde Guerre mondiale*, 3 (October 1974).

38. De Jonghe, *op. cit.*, passim; Heinz Höhne, *The Order of the Death's Head: The Story of Hitler's SS*, trans. Richard Barry (London, 1972), p. 380.

39. Jacques Delarue, *Histoire de la Gestapo* (Paris, 1962), pp. 365–69; Léon Polia-kov, "A Conflict Between the Germany Army and Secret Police over Bombings of Paris Synagogues," *Jewish Social Studies* XVI (1954), pp. 253–66.

40. Delarue, *op. cit.*, pt. IV, chap. 3, "La Gestapo l'emporte sur l'armée"; Marrus and Paxton, *op. cit.*, chap. 6; Höhne, *op. cit.*, p. 380.

41. Hans Buchheim, "Die höheren SS- und Polizeiführer," *VfZ* 11 (1963), pp. 362–91; Werner Warmbrunn, *The Dutch Under German Occupation, 1940–1945* (Stanford, 1963), pp. 33–34, 62–63.

42. Von Bargen to Foreign Office, July 9, 1942, ND: NG-5209, quoted in Hilberg, *Destruction*, p. 387.

43. Michael R. Marrus, "Les Apatrides: réfugiés sans passeports pendant les annés trente," *L'Histoire*, forthcoming.

44. On Eichmann's visit, see note of Eichmann and Dannecker, CDJC: XXVb-45; Marrus and Paxton, *op. cit.*, pp. 206, 218–19.

45. Quoted in Browning, *Foreign Office*, p. 83.

362

46. Willy Bok, "Considérations sur les estimations quantitatives de la population juive en Belgique," in *La Vie juive dans l'Europe contemporaine* (Brussels, 1965), pp. 94–95.

47. Wladimir Rabi, "De 1906 à 1939," in Bernhard Blumenkranz, ed., *Histoire des Juifs en France* (Paris, 1972); Presser, *op. cit.*, p. 221; Leni Yahil, *The Rescue of Danish Jewry*, trans. Morris Gradel (Philadelphia, 1969), p. 20. On the French offer, see Marrus and Paxton, *op. cit.*

48. Hilberg, *Destruction*, p. 356.

49. Browning, *Foreign Office*, p. 145. See Maxime Steinberg, *Extermination, sauvetage et résistance des Juifs de Belgique* (Brussels, 1979).

50. *Les Crimes de guerre commis sous l'occupation de Belgique Persecution antisemite* (Liege, 1947), p. 28; Gerald Reitlinger, *The Final Solution: The Attempt to Exterminate the Jews of Europe* (New York, 1961), p. 343.

51. Meier Michaelis, *Mussolini and the Jews: German-Italian Relations and the Jewish Question in Italy, 1922–1945* (Oxford, 1978), chap. V.

52. Marrus and Paxton, *op. cit.*, pp. 290–95; Léon Poliakov and Jacques Sabille, *Jews Under the Italian Occupation* (Paris, 1955).

53. See Michaelis, *Mussolini and the Jews*, chap. X.

54. Browning, *Foreign Office*, pp. 160–61.

55. Yahil, *Rescue*, pp. 138–46.

56. Ibid., chap. 5.

57. Ibid., xviii. Cf. idem, "The Uniqueness of the Rescue of Danish Jewry," in Yisrael Gutman and Efraim Zuroff, eds., *Rescue Attempts During the Holocaust: Proceedings of the Second Yad Vashem International Historical Conference, 1974* (Jerusalem, 1977), pp. 617–24.

58. Hannah Arendt, *Eichmann in Jerusalem: A Report on the Banality of Evil* (New York, 1965), p. 175.

59. Yahil, "Methods of Persecution," p. 299.

60. With a survival rate among deportees of between 2% and 3%, there is a slight discrepancy between the numbers of deportees and the numbers who were actually killed. For detailed calculations of these totals, see Serge Klarsfeld, *Le Mémorial de la déportation des Juifs de France* (Paris, 1978); and idem, "Tableau des convois de déportation des Juifs de Belgique," *Le Monde juif* 32 (July–September 1976), pp. 108–9. For a careful recent discussion of the number killed in all European countries, see Georges Wellers, *Les Chambres à gaz ont existé: des documents, des témoignages, des chiffres* (Paris, 1981), pt. 2.

61. Helen Fein, *Accounting for Genocide: National Responses and Jewish Victimization During the Holocaust* (New York, 1979).

62. Warmbrumm, *op. cit.*, pp. 161–62; Presser, *op. cit.*, p. 148; B. A. Sijes, "Several Observations Concerning the Position of the Jews in Occupied Holland During World War II," in Gutman and Zuroff, eds., *op. cit.*, p. 550.

63. Klarsfeld, *Mémorial*, no pagination; idem, "Tableau des convois," pp. 108–9; Presser, *op. cit.*, p. 483; *Deportazione degli ebrei dall'Italia: Ricerca condotta da Giuliana Donati*, Centro di Documentazione Ebraica Contemporanea (Milan, 1975), p. 1; Michaelis, *op. cit.*, pp. 390–91.

11 / The Reaction to the Nazi Anti-Jewish Policy in East-Central Europe and in the Balkans
BELA VAGO

1. See Josef Kermisz's "Postscript" in Emanuel Ringelblum, *Polish-Jewish Relations During the Second World War* (ed. Josef Kermisz and Shmuel Krakowski) (Jerusalem: Yad Vashem, 1974), p. 245; about collaboration with the Nazis against the Jews, ibid., p. 263.

2. Ringelblum, *op. cit.* (Kermisz's "Postscript"), pp. 298–99; anti-Jewish manifestations, ibid., pp. 40–45, 50–51. About the "Shmaltsovnikes," see Yitzhak Arad, Yisrael Gutman, and Abraham Margaliot, eds., Yad Vashem, *Documents on the Holocaust* (Jerusalem, 1981) (hereafter *Documents on the Holocaust*), pp. 330–31. A Polish authoritative criticism of Polish anti-Semitism during the Holocaust is quoted in Ringelblum, *op. cit.* ("Postscript"), p. 279.

3. See the thorough analysis in Shmuel Krakowski's "The Fate of Prisoners of War in the September 1939 Campaign" in *Yad Vashem Studies* XII (1977), pp. 297–334. See also Ringelblum, *op. cit.*, pp. xxxvii (Introduction) 53–56.

4. About pogroms, see Ringelblum, *op. cit.*, ("Postscript"), pp. 276–307. About the increase of anti-Semitism, see Yisrael Gutman's "Selected Aspects of the Relations Between the Poles and the Jews During the Second World War—Against the Backdrop of Historiography" (in Hebrew) in *Proceedings of the Seventh World Congress of the Jewish Studies*, vol. I (Jerusalem, 1980), pp. 57–62.

5. Ringelblum, *op. cit.*, p. 264–66, 273; cf. Shmuel Krakowski, "Policy of the Third Reich in Conquered Poland," *Yad Vashem Studies* IX (1973), pp. 229, 231, 241, 243.

6. See Yisrael Gutman, "Jews in General Anders' Army in the Soviet Union," *Yad Vashem Studies* XII (1977), pp. 231–96.

7. Despite references to "Christian compassion" (Ringelblum, *op. cit.*, p. 257), and "Christian morality" (*Documents on the Holocaust*, p. 328), there is no evidence of any organized activity on the part of the Catholic Church.

8. Kermisz's "Postscript" in Ringelblum, *op. cit.*, p. 328; cf. *Documents on the Holocaust*, p. 305. See also Yisrael Gutman, "A Report of a Member of the Polish Underground on Polish-Jewish Relations in Occupied Poland," *Michael* VI (Tel Aviv, 1980), pp. 102–114.

9. E.g., Shmuel Krakowski ("Policy of the Third Reich in Conquered Poland").

10. Kermisz, *Rescue Attempts During the Holocaust* (Jerusalem, 1977), p. 371.

11. Gutman, "Jews in General Anders' Army": see also his "Report," p. 111, n. 1.

12. See for example Gutman, "The Polish People and the Extermination of the Jews" (in Hebrew), *Molad*, nos. 35–36 (1975), pp. 77–90.

13. Ringelblum, *op. cit.*, pp. 77–78: Kermisz's "Postscript," ibid., pp. 290–91.

14. Kermisz's "Postscript," ibid., pp. 305–6.

15. In the summer months of 1944, when the bombing of Auschwitz preoccupied the Allies, the Polish government-in-exile (e.g., Tadeusz Romer) was instrumental in providing maps and data to the British. (In order to avoid contradictions because of former allegations, cf. n. 12 above.)

16. Josef Kermisz, "The Activities of the Council of the Aid of Jews (Żegota) in Occupied Poland," in *Rescue Attempts During the Holocaust*, pp. 367–98.

17. Kermisz, "Postscript," *op. cit.*, p. 297.

18. Kermisz, *Rescue Attempts During the Holocaust*, p. 373.

19. "The blind folly of Poland's anti-Semites . . . has been responsible for the death of hundreds of thousands of Jews who could have been saved despite the Germans"; Ringelblum, *op. cit.*, p. 247.

20. *Documents on the Holocaust,* document 117.
21. Dr. Ladislav Lipscher quoted in *ICJC Newsletter* XIII, no. 1 (66) (1982), p. 3.
22. Ludin to the Auswärtiges Amt, April 13, 1943, in *Akten zur deutschen Auswärtigen Politik* (hereafter *Akten*), series D, vol. V, no. 299.
23. E.g., *Akten,* vol. V, no. 299.
24. See Yeshayahu Jelinek, *The Parish Republic: Hlinka's Slovak People's Party* (New York and London, 1976), pp. 52, 76; and Livia Rothkirchen, *The Destruction of Slovak Jewry: A Documentary History* (in Hebrew) (Jerusalem: Yad Vashem, 1961), pp. xxvii–xxix.
25. Jelinek, *op. cit.,* p. 75.
26. About the controversy on who initiated the deportations, see Yeshayahu Jelinek, "The Vatican, the Catholic Church, the Catholics and the Persecution of the Jews during World War II: The Case of Slovakia" in *Jews and Non-Jews in Eastern Europe, 1918–1945,* ed. Bela Vago and George L. Mosse (New York, Toronto, and Jerusalem, 1974), pp. 228–29.
27. Jelinek, *The Parish Republic,* p. 75, and Rothkirchen, *op cit.,* p. xxiv. See also Ludin to the Auswärtiges Amt on April 13, 1943, in *Akten,* vol. V, no. 299.
28. See the relevant letters in the *Archives of the Yishuv Rescue Board in Istanbul,* vol. 3: *Register to the Slovakian Files, 1942–1944* (Institute for Research on the Holocaust Period, Haifa University, 1982).
29. About Gizi Fleischmann's and Rabbi Weismandel's relations with the Budapest Zionist leaders, there is ample information in the literature about the Holocaust of Hungarian Jewry; e.g., Randolph L. Braham, *The Politics of Genocide: The Holocaust in Hungary* (New York, 1981), vol. II, pp. 701–711.
30. Jelinek, "Catholics and Jewish Persecution," pp. 226, 230, 239–40; see also Rothkirchen, *op. cit.,* p. xxiii.
31. E.g., J. Šivak, the minister of education and culture, and I. Karvaš, the governor of the National Bank.
32. Nuremberg Military Trials, vol. XIII, NG-4407, p. 231.
33. As early as November 1941, the Germans detected a "critical attitude" toward National Socialism among intellectuals (*Akten,* vol. XIII, no. 500, p. 824).
34. See the German report about the pastoral letter in Rothkirchen's *The Destruction of Slovak Jewry,* document 65.
35. About the Vatican's interventions, see ibid., documents 54, 56, 57.
36. See Jelinek, *The Parish Republic,* p. 170, n. 33; and idem, "Catholics and Jewish Persecution," p. 242 and n. 124.
37. Rothkirchen, *op. cit.,* p. xxv.
38. See the rich and reliable documentation about the fate of the Jews in Croatia (and Serbia) in Löwenthal Zdenko, ed., *The Crimes of the Fascist Occupants and Their Collaborators Against the Jews in Yugoslavia* (Belgrade, 1954).
39. Edmond Paris, *Genocide in Satellite Croatia, 1941–1945: A Record of Racial and Religious Persecutions and Massacres* (Chicago: American Institute for Balkan Affairs, n.d.), p. 93.
40. Richard Pattee, *The Case of Cardinal Aloysius Stepinac* (Milwaukee, 1958), document XXVI, p. 301 (cf. Paris, *op. cit.,* p. 217). The Germans objected sometimes to the alleged lack of determination of Croatia to deal with the Jewish question; Hory Ladislaus and Martin Broszat, *Der Kroatische Ustascha-Staat, 1941–1945* (Stuttgart, 1964), p. 132, n. 360, and p. 267, n. 82.
41. Paris, *op. cit.,* p. 127.
42. Ibid., p. 132.
43. Pattee, *op. cit.,* documents XXV, XXVI, XXVIII, XXXII.
44. Among the few writings about the rescue attempts, see Daniel Carpi, "The

Diplomatic Negotiations over the Transfer of Jewish Children from Croatia to Turkey and Palestine in 1943," *Yad Vashem Studies* XII (1977), pp. 109–124.

45. See examples in Rothkirchen's "Czech Attitudes." See also W. Oschlies, "Phases and Faces of Czech Antisemitism," in the *Wiener Library Bulletin*, 1970-71, no. 2, p. 23.

46. Moshe Leshem's recorded testimony, in Historical Documentation Center, Haifa University, Cz 3 b 4, pp. 7, 12, 14, 19. About acts of solidarity, see Rothkirchen, *op. cit.*, pp. 225, 227.

47. Ibid., pp. 19–20.

48. Rothkirchen, *op. cit.*, p. 232.

49. E.g., in providing information about Auschwitz. About the attitude of the Czechoslovak government-in-exile, I got valuable information from Mr. Otto Aria of Reading, England.

50. About the Jews in the resistance, see Livia Rothkirchen, "The Defiant Few: Jews and the Czech 'Inside Front' (1938–1942)" in *Yad Vashem Studies* XIV (1981), pp. 35–88.

51. *DGFP*, vol. XIII, no. 297, pp. 472–73 (Belgrade, September 10, 1941).

52. Ibid., no. 363, p. 582 (Belgrade, September 28, 1941).

53. Paris, *op. cit.*, pp. 188, 203–4.

54. Chaim Hermesh, *Mivtsa Amsterdam* (in Hebrew) (Operation Amsterdam) (Tel Aviv, 1971).

55. See the ample documentation in Zdenko Löwenthal, ed., *The Crimes of the Fascist Occupants and their Collaborators Against the Jews in Yugoslavia* (Belgrade, 1954).

56. Daniel Carpi, "Nuovi documenti per la storia dell-Olocausto in Grecia: L'atteggiamento degli Italiani (1941–1943)" in *Michael* VII (1981), p. 133.

57. See the detailed survey of the anti-Jewish measures in Michael Molho's *In Memoriam: Hommage aux victimes juives des Nazis en Grèce*, 3 vols. (Salonika, 1948).

58. Constantin Tsoucalas, *The Greek Tragedy* (New York, 1969), p. 58.

59. John O. Iatrides, ed., *Ambassador MacVeagh Reports: Greece, 1933–1947* (Princeton, 1980), p. 348.

60. Molho, *op. cit.*, vol. I, pp. 35–36, 51; cf. Carpi, *op. cit.*, pp. 132, 181.

61. About the positive activities of Genadios and of Archbishop Damaskinos and other ecclesiastical personalities, as well as leading intellectuals, see Molho, *op. cit.*, vol. I, pp. 111–12, 118–20. On the protest of Mgr. Damaskinos, see Miriam Novitch, *Le passage des barbares* (Ghetto Fighters' House, 1982); ibid., details about the Jewish resistance in Greece.

62. For the early German pressures on Bulgaria, see Frederick B. Charny, *The Bulgarian Jews and the Final Solution, 1940–1944* (University of Pittsburgh Press), pp. 50–51. Hitler's veiled pressures in Andreas Hillgruber, ed., *Staatsmänner und Diplomaten bei Hitler* (Frankfurt am Main, 1967), p. 385. About the early anti-Jewish laws and decrees, see Marshall Lee Miller, *Bulgarian Jewry During the Second World War* (Stanford, 1975), pp. 96–97; and Wolf Oschlies, *Bulgarien—Land ohne Antisemitismus* (Erlangen: Ner Tamid Verlag, 1976), pp. 116–25, 126.

63. *DGFP*, series D, vol. XIII, document 504 (Berlin, November 27, 1941).

64. Oschlies, *op. cit.*, pp. 127–30, 134, 136. For the early protests, see Frederick B. Charny, "The Bulgarian Writers' Protest of October 1940 Against the Introduction of Anti-Semitic Legislation into the Kingdom of Bulgaria," in *East European Quarterly* 4 (March 1970), pp. 88–93.

65. Miller, *op. cit.*, pp. 89–99. See also Oschlies, *op. cit.*, pp. 131, 133–36.

66. Oschlies, *op. cit.*, pp. 137–38.

67. About King Boris, see among many German documents *Akten*, vol. VI, document 88, p. 151 (Sofia, June 7, 1943); a favorable work about King Boris is Biniamin

Arditti's *Yehudei Bulgaria b'Shnot ha'Mishtar ha'Nazi, 1940–44* (in Hebrew) (Tel Aviv, 1962); less unequivocal about the king's positive role is Nissan Oren in his "The Bulgarian Exception—A Reassessment of the Salvation of the Jewish Community," *Yad Vashem Studies* VII (1968), pp. 83–106. See also Miller, *op. cit.*, p. 102; and Charny, *op. cit.*, pp. 186–88.

68. Alexander Matkovsky, "The Destruction of Macedonian Jewry," in *Yad Vashem Studies* III (1959), and "On the Catastrophe of the Thracian Jews," recollections by Nadejda S. Vasileva in *Yad Vashem Studies* III (1959), pp. 295–302. I also relied on Jenny Löbl's recorded lecture (Historical Documentation Center, Haifa University, Y 3 h 2). See also Oschlies, *op. cit.*, documents 7, 9, 10; and Miller, *op. cit.*, p. 103.

69. *Akten*, vol. V, document 159 (Sofia, February 27, 1943).

70. About the strong popular pressure against the anti-Jewish measures, see *National Archives*, Report of Services de Renseignements, no. 2951/R.G. (Alger, August 2, 1943), RG 226, OSS, 43035; see also Oschlies, *op. cit.*, document 8.

71. Oschlies, *op. cit.*, pp. 153–57; Charny, *op. cit.*, pp. 42–56. Among the Church personalities who opposed the Nazi policy were Metropolitan Stefan, the head of the Orthodox Church, and Metropolitans Kiril and Neofit.

72. *Akten*, vol. VI, document 88, p. 15 (Sofia, June 7, 1943). See also *Akten*, vol. V, pp. 523–25 (Berlin, April 13, 1943) and (Berlin, April 7, 1943).

73. Oschlies, *op. cit.*, documents 6, 12; also see Miller, *op. cit.*, p. 104.

74. Quoted by Miller, *op. cit.*, p. 97; about the German pressure, see *Akten*, vol. VI, document 266 (Berlin, August 31, 1943).

75. For valuable information about the "Kaylaka" concentration camp and the burning down of the camp, I am indebted to Mrs. Yvette Mashiah (Historical Documentation Center, Haifa University, B 3 H 6).

76. Miller, *op. cit.*, p. 102.

77. "Septemvri," ed., *Le Sauvetage des Juifs en Bulgarie, 1941–1944* (Sofia, 1977). About the part of the Jews in the Bulgarian partisan struggle, see Josif Ilel, "Pages from the Life of 'Anton Ivanov' Partisan Detachment," *Annual* (Sofia) XVI (1981), pp. 181–206).

78. The best comprehensive work about the Jews during the Second World War is Randolph L. Braham's *The Politics of Genocide: The Holocaust in Hungary*, 2 vols. (New York, 1981). For the Kamenets-Podolsk deportations and for the Délvidék massacres, see vol. I., pp. 199–215.

79. For Kállay's Jewish policy, see my "Germany and the Jewish Policy of the Kállay Government" in Randolph L. Braham, ed., *Hungarian Jewish Studies*, vol. II (New York, 1969), pp. 183–210.

80. For the labor service, see Randolph L. Braham, *The Hungarian Labor Service System, 1938–1945* (New York, 1977).

81. Two early books referring also to the attitude of the Hungarian people are Jenő Lévai's *Fekete könyv a magyar zsidóság szenvedéseiről* (Black Book on the Suffering of Hungarian Jewry) (Budapest, 1946), and his *Zsidósors Magyarországon* (Jewish Fate in Hungary) (Budapest, 1948).

82. See my "Budapest Jewry in the Summer of 1944," *Yad Vashem Studies* VIII (1970), pp. 81–105.

83. A comprehensive work about the suffering of the Jews in Bessarabia and in Northern Bukovina is included in *Pinkas ha'Khilot* (Encyclopedia of Jewish Communities), vol. II (Jerusalem: Yad Vashem, 1980).

84. An apologetic work about the massacres is A. Karetki and M. Covaci, *Zile însîngerate la Iasi: 28–30 iunie 1941* (Bucharest, 1978).

85. Alexander Safran, "The Rulers of Fascist Romania Whom I Had to Deal With," *Yad Vashem Studies*, 1967.

86. See my "The Ambiguity of Collaborationism: The Center of the Jews in Romania (1942–1944)," in *Patterns of Nazi Leadership in Europe, 1933–1945* (Jerusalem: Yad Vashem, 1979), pp. 287–309).

12 / Jewish Resistance and Passivity in the Face of the Holocaust
A Balance
YEHUDA BAUER

1. Himmler's response to General von Ginant's memo (of September 9, 1942), October 9, 1942, NO-1611.
2. Henri Michel, *The Shadow War* (London, 1965), p. 297.
3. Abraham Rosenberg (Adam Rutkowski), "Dos Drayzentl," *Bleter far Goszichte* 5, nos. 1–2 (1952), pp. 187–225; 5, no. 3, pp. 116–48.
4. See Joseph Kermisz's "Postscript," in Emmanuel Ringelblum, *Polish-Jewish Relations During the Second World War* (New York, 1976), pp. 275–315; Helen Fein, *Accounting for Genocide* (New York, 1979), pp. 257–61; Yehuda Bauer, *The Holocaust in Historical Perspective* (Seattle, 1978), pp. 50–61.
5. Israel Gutman, *The Jews of Warsaw, 1939–1943* (Bloomington, 1982), pp. 297–301, 320–23, 355–63; Ringelblum, *op. cit.*, p. 218 n. (By Shmuel Krakowski); Bauer, *op. cit.*, p. 58.
6. Shmuel Krakowski, *Jewish Armed Resistance in Poland, 1942–1944* (in Hebrew) (Jerusalem, 1977), pp. 17–45.
7. Ibid., pp. 22; 340–41.
8. Ireneusz Caban and Zygmunt Mankowski, *Zwiazek Walki Zbrojnej i Armia Arajowa Okregu lubelskim*, pt. 2, Lublin, Dokumenty, pp. 60, 504–5.
9. AK order no. 116 of September 15, 1943, by Tadeusz Bor-Komorowski, quoted by I. Gutman and S. Krakowski in their forthcoming book, *Polish-Jewish Relations* (New York: Holocaust Library), chap. 6. Source: *Polski Sily Zbrojne w Drugiej Wojnie Swiatowej* vol. 3, (London, 1973), p. 431.
10. Gutman, *op. cit.*, Ringelblum, *op. cit.*; Kazimierz Iranek-Osmecki, *He Who Saves One Life* (New York, 1971).
11. Gutman, *op. cit.*, pp. 265, 355–56.
12. The literature on this aspect is largely in Hebrew, but cf. Gutman, *op. cit.*, pp. 132–44; Yitzhak Arad, *Ghetto in Flames* (Jerusalem, 1980), pp. 221–38; and Lucy Dawidowicz, *The War Against the Jews* (London, 1975), pp. 261–340.
13. Yehuda Bauer, *A History of the Holocaust* (New York, 1982), p. 256.
14. Ibid., p. 258.
15. Ibid.
16. Ibid., pp. 258–59.
17. Ringelblum, *op. cit.*, p. 173 n.
18. Bauer, *A History of the Holocaust*, pp. 262–64.
19. Shalom Cholawsky, *The Jews in Belorussia During World War II* (in Hebrew) (Tel Aviv, 1982), p. 338; Shmuel Spector, "The Holocaust of Volhynian Jews" (in Hebrew) (Ph.D. thesis, Hebrew University, June 1982).
20. Bauer, *A History of the Holocaust*, pp. 268–70; cf. also Arad, *op. cit.*
21. Zvi Brown and Dov Levin, *The Story of an Underground* (in Hebrew) (Jerusalem, 1962).
22. Bauer, *A History of the Holocaust*, pp. 265–68.
23. Shalom Cholawsky, "The *Judenrat* in Minsk," in Israel Gutman and Cynthia J. Raft, eds., *Patterns of Jewish Leadership in Nazi Europe* (Jerusalem, 1979), pp. 113–32; also Bauer, *A History of the Holocaust*, pp. 166–67.

24. Bauer, A History of the Holocaust, pp. 272–74; Yuri Suhl, They Fought Back (New York, 1967), pp. 7–50, 128–135, 219–25.

25. Krakowski, Jewish Armed Resistance in Poland, pp. 269–309; Bauer, A History of the Holocaust, p. 273.

26. Cf. Jacques Rabine, La Résistance organisée des Juifs en France (Paris, 1973).

27. Jasa Romano, Jevrei Jugoslavije 1941–1945: Zrtve Genocida (Belgrade: Jevrejski Istorijski Muzej, Savez Jevrejskih opstina Jugoslavije, 1980).

28. A. Benček et al., Osvobozeni Ceskoslovenska Rudou Armadou (Prague, 1965), pp. 86–87; Ladislav Lipsher, "Helkan shel hayehudim bemilchemet hamagen ha'anti-fashistit be'Slovakia," in Yalkut Moreshet 14 (1972), pp. 117–42.

29. Bauer, A History of the Holocaust, p. 170.

30. Isaiah Trunk, Judenrat (New York, 1972), pp. 468–69.

31. Yehuda Bauer and Nathan Rotenstreich, eds., The Holocaust as Historical Experience (New York, 1981), pp. 95–108.

32. Cf. Abraham I. Katsh, ed. and trans., The Warsaw Diary of Chaim A. Kaplan (New York, 1973).

13 / The Jewish Councils
An Overview
RANDOLPH L. BRAHAM

1. The SS, and the Germans generally, alternately referred to the council as the Judenrat (Jewish council) or Ältestenrat (council of elders).

2. Trials of this kind were actually held in many parts of liberated Europe, reflecting to some extent the triumph of leftist politics. During the anti-Nazi euphoria of the first postwar years, it was quite fashionable to identify the activities of all Jewish council members as collaborationist. Jewish council members and leaders, as well as ghetto policemen, were tried in regular and Jewish courts of honor in a number of countries, including Greece, Holland, Israel, Hungary, Poland, and Romania. For some details, see Patterns of Jewish Leadership in Nazi Europe, 1933–1945 (hereafter PJL) (Jerusalem: Yad Vashem, 1979), passim.

3. Hannah Arendt, Eichmann in Jerusalem: A Report on the Banality of Evil (New York: Viking, 1963), p. 104.

4. Shalom Cholawsky, "The Judenrat in Minsk," in PJL, p. 118.

5. For details on the Final Solution in Serbia, see Raul Hilberg, The Destruction of the European Jews (Chicago: Quadrangle Books, 1961), pp. 433–42.

6. Maxine Steinberg, "The Trap of Legality: The Association of the Jews of Belgium," in PJL, p. 361.

7. Yitzhak Arad, "The Judenräte in the Lithuanian Ghettos of Kovno and Vilna," in PJL, p. 99.

8. In Italy and in the Italian-occupied territories of Greece, Slovenia, and southern France, the communal leaderships reflected the prewar customs and arrangements. The Italians did not call for the establishment of special Jewish councils. Jacob Robinson, "The State of Research into the Judenräte: A Report," in Imposed Jewish Governing Bodies Under Nazi Rule (New York: YIVO Institute for Jewish Research, 1972), p. 32.

9. Randolph L. Braham, The Politics of Genocide: The Holocaust in Hungary (New York: Columbia University Press, 1981), p. 372.

10. Hannah Arendt claims that Finland "was the one country the Nazis never even approached on the Jewish question." See her Eichmann in Jerusalem, p. 153. For documentation relating to the deportation of the refugees and "Jewish criminals," consult Walter Laqueur, The Terrible Secret (Boston: Little, Brown, 1980), pp. 35–37.

11. The Romanians were, however, involved in a number of massacres. For details, see Braham, *The Politics of Genocide*, pp. 901–5.

12. Professor Raul Hilberg emphasizes that "in no territory . . . was German dependence upon native administration so great as in France." See his *Destruction of the European Jews*, p. 389. For a succinct description and analysis of the antecedents of Xavier Vallat's role in the establishment and operation of the UGIF, see Michael R. Marrus and Robert O. Paxton, *Vichy France and the Jews* (New York: Basic Books, 1981), pp. 108–12.

13. For a documented evaluation of the relationship between the Consistory and the UGIF, see Yerahmiel (Richard) Cohen's "French Jewry's Dilemma on the Orientation of Its Leadership: From Polemics to Conciliation: 1942–1944," in *Yad Vashem Studies* XIV (1981), pp. 167–204.

14. Leni Yahil, "The Jewish Leadership in France," in *PJL*, p. 324.

15. Hilberg, *The Destruction of the European Jews*, pp. 480–83.

16. For details, see Braham, *The Politics of Genocide*, pp. 201–7.

17. On this point, see Lucy S. Dawidowicz, *The War Against the Jews* (New York: Holt, Rinehart & Winston), 1975, pp. 341–53. This point is also correctly stressed by Lucjan Dobroszycki in his perceptive article titled "Jewish Elites Under German Rule," in Henry Friedländer and Sybil Milton, eds., *The Holocaust: Ideology, Bureaucracy, and Genocide* (Millwood, N.Y.: Kraus International Publications, 1980), pp. 221–30.

18. *PJL*, pp. 351–52.

19. 3363-PS. The document is reproduced in *Nazi Conspiracy and Aggression*, vol. 6 (Washington, D.C.: Government Printing Office, 1946), pp. 97–101. See also Isaiah Trunk, *Judenrat* (New York: Macmillan, 1972), pp. 1–3.

20. Trunk, *loc. cit.*

21. For the text of the decree in English translation, see Leni Yahil, *Readings on the History of the Holocaust* (Jerusalem: Hebrew University, n.d.), p. 58. See also Trunk, *Judenrat* pp. 3–7.

22. For details, see Cholawsky, "The Judenrat in Minsk," pp. 126–32; Yahil, "The Jewish Leadership of France," pp. 321, 327; Steinberg, "The Trap of Legality: The Association of the Jews of Belgium," p. 365; and Braham, *The Politics of Genocide*, pp. 448–62.

23. For some details on this point, see Allan Mitchell, "Polish, Dutch, and French Elites Under the German Occupation," in *The Holocaust: Ideology, Bureaucracy, and Genocide*, pp. 231–41.

24. The Jewish leaders, of course, rationalized their actions as being the best that could be done for the community. Nevertheless, as Yitzhak Olshan, the chief justice of the Supreme Court of Israel, declared in a case involving the members of the Jewish council of Będzin, Poland, "no matter how the *Judenrat* acted, they served the Nazis. . . . Even those who served the interests of the Jewish communities assisted the Nazis. . . ." The judgment in this case was handed down on May 22, 1964. *New York Times*, May 23, 1964.

25. Joseph Kermisz, "The Judenrat in Warsaw," in *PJL*, p. 84. On the origins and composition of the Jewish Councils in Eastern Europe, see also Trunk, *Judenrat*, pp. 14–42.

26. For details on the economic, social-welfare, judicial, and educational-cultural activities of the councils in the ghettos of eastern Europe, see Trunk, *Judenrat*, pp. 61–258.

27. For details on the role played by the Jewish police in many of the ghettos of eastern Europe, see ibid., pp. 475–547.

28. For samples of the minutes recorded in Białystok and Lublin, see Lucy S. Dawidowicz, ed., *A Holocaust Reader* (New York: Behrman House, 1976), pp. 259–87.

29. The change in the quality of the wartime Jewish elites is emphasized by Lucjan Dobroszycki as an important factor. See his "Jewish Elites Under German Rule," *op. cit.*

30. According to most accounts, of the slightly more than 300,000 Jews living in France at the time of the German occupation, close to 250,000 survived the war. Hannah Arendt claims that there were no more than 6,000 French nationals among the victims (see her *Eichmann in Jerusalem*, p. 149.) Serge Klarsfeld, however, insists that the number of Jews deported from France was over 75,000. Of the approximately 70,000 Jews deported to Auschwitz, he claims, 23,000 were French nationals and all but a few thousand died. See the introduction to his *Le mémorial de la déportation des Juifs de France* (Paris, 1978).

31. Arendt, *Eichmann in Jerusalem*, p. 150.

32. Ibid., p. 152.

33. Yisrael Gutman, "The Concept of Labor in Judenrat Policy," in *PJL*, p. 162.

34. The questions pertaining to the wartime attitude of the leaders of the free world are beyond the scope of this paper. For details, see Braham, *The Politics of Genocide*, pp. 691–731; Arthur D. Morse, *While Six Million Died* (New York: Random House, 1968); and Laqueur, *The Terrible Secret*.

35. On the issue of colloboration, see also Lucy S. Dawidowicz, *The Holocaust and the Historians* (Cambridge: Harvard University Press, 1981), pp. 135–39.

36. For a thorough evaluation of this subject, see Gutman, "The Concept of Labor in Judenrat Policy," pp. 151–80.

37. This was the case in Kovno, Vilna, and Warsaw, among others. For further details on "rescue-through-work" strategy, see Trunk, *Judenrat*, pp. 400–13.

38. NO-1611, as cited in Gutman, *op. cit.*, p. 167. For the text of Himmler's circular memorandum of October 9, 1942, see also *A Holocaust Reader*, pp. 103–4.

39. For details on the council-member moral dilemma, consult Braham, *The Politics of Genocide*, pp. 718–24.

40. For specific examples of favors enjoyed by the council leaders of various countries, see ibid., pp. 426–28; Michman, "The Controversy Surrounding the Jewish Council of Amsterdam," p. 251; and Ben, "Jewish Leadership in Greece During the Holocaust," pp. 341–42.

41. See his *Notes from the Warsaw Ghetto* (New York: McGraw-Hill, 1958), p. 245. See also Trunk, *Judenrat*, pp. 368–87.

42. In Warsaw, for example, the ZOB (Zydowska Organizacja Bojowa; the Jewish Fighting Organization) executed Jacob Lejkin, the deputy commander of the Jewish Police, on October 29, 1942, and Israel Furst, the council representative on the deportation staff, on November 29, 1942. The campaign against the "agents of the enemy" was intensified just before the Warsaw Ghetto Uprising in April 1943. Similar campaigns against collaborators were undertaken in many other countries in Nazi-occupied Europe. Kermisz, "The Judenrat in Warsaw," p. 88.

43. Steinberg, "The Trap of Legality: the Association of the Jews of Belgium," p. 364.

44. For details, see Braham, *The Politics of Genocide*, p. 432.

45. For a succinct evaluation of the relationship between the resistance groups and the Jewish Councils, see Yehuda Bauer's "Jewish Leadership Reactions to Nazi Policies," in Yehuda Bauer and Nathan Rotenstreich, eds., *The Holocaust as Historical Experience* (New York: Holmes & Meier, 1981), pp. 182–86. See also Trunk, *Judenrat*, pp. 451–74.

46. For details, see Don Levin, "The Fighting Leadership of the Judenräte in the Small Communities of Poland," in *PJL*, pp. 133–47. See also Yehuda Bauer, "Jewish Leadership Reactions to Nazi Policies," pp. 186–87.

14 / Theological Interpretations of the Holocaust
A Balance
AMOS FUNKENSTEIN

1. Joel Taitlbaum, *Vajoel Moshe* (New York, 1952; 2nd ed., 1957).
2. Bab. Talmud, *Ketubot* 111a; *Cant. Rabba* 2,7. Literally, the formula is an oath, but a playful imitation of one: wherefore the invocation of God (*el Shaddai, el Tseva'ot*) is replaced by a phonetical simile (*aylot ha'sade tsviot*). Cf. R. Gordis, "The Song of Songs," in Mordechai M. Kaplann, *Inbille Volume* (New York, 1953), pp. 281–397, esp. 308–9.
3. Menachem M. Kasher, *Hatekufa hagdola* (Jerusalem, 1969); it contains explicit polemics also against Taitlbaum.
4. U. Z. Greenberg, *Rehovot hanabar, Sefer hailiot veha'koah* (Tel Aviv, 1957), p. 7; "father of the superior race," p. 31 and passim. *Geza* is the accepted modern Hebrew term for "race"; a racial ideology will be called *torat geza*. In 1957 it had other connotations than in 1920, when Zabotinsky promised: "With blood and with sweat / A race will be formed for us / proud, magnanimous, and cruel."
5. A. Funkenstein, "Maimonides: Political Theory and Realistic Messianism," *Miscelanea Medievalia* II (1977), pp. 81–103.
6. R. Levi ben Habib, *Responsa* (Venice, 1565), appendix (*kuntres hasmicha*); on the ideological background cf. J. Katz, "Mahloket hasmicha ben Jacob Berab veha Raloah," *Zion* 17 (1951), pp. 34 ff.; Funkenstein, *op. cit.*, p. 102.
7. R. Hilberg, *The Destruction of the European Jews* (Chicago: Quadrangle Books, 1967). We elaborated some of the following remarks elsewhere (*The Passivity of Diaspora Jewry: Myth and Reality*, Aran Lecture 11, Tel Aviv, 1982).
8. Bab. Talmud, *Nedarim* 28a; *Gittin* 10b; *Baba Kama* 111; *Baba Batra* 54b–55a; Cf. Sh. Shiloh, *Dina demalchuta dina* (in Hebrew) (Jerusalem, 1974).
9. J.-P. Sartre, *Réflexions sur la question juive* (Paris, 1947).
10. E. Fackenheim, *God's Presence in History* (New York, 1970); *The Jewish Return into History* (New York, 1978). E. Berkovits, *Faith After the Holocaust* (New York: Ktav, 1973).
11. George Steiner, *The Portage to St. Christobel of A.H.* (New York: Simon & Schuster, 1982).
12. Primo Levi, *Survival in Auschwitz* (orig. title, *Se questo è un uomo*), trans. S. Woolf, (New York: Macmillan, 1961), pp. 151–52.
13. The following chapter repeats and enlarges my remarks in the *Jerusalem Quarterly* 19 (1981), pp. 56–72; from there I also borrowed the nn. 15–46.
14. J. H. Levi, *Olamot Nifgashim* (Jerusalem, Bialik Institute, 1960), pp. 115–89; A. Tcherikover, *Hellenistic Civilization and the Jews*, trans. S. Appelbaum (Philadelphia: Jewish Publication Society of America, 1959).
15. For the following, see M. Stern, ed., *Greek and Latin Authors on Jews and Judaism*, vol. 1: *From Herodotus to Plutarch* (Jerusalem: Israel Academy of Sciences and Humanities, 1976), pp. 62–86 (Manetho) and 389–416 (Apion); I. Heinemann in Pauli-Wissowa, *Encyclopédie*, Supplementband V, s.v. 'Antisemitismus' (coll. 3–43); J. H. Levi, *op. cit.*, pp. 60–196.
16. Tacitus, *Hist.*, V, 4.
17. P. Berger and K. Luckmann, *The Social Construction of Reality* (Garden City, N.Y.: Doubleday/Anchor, 1967), pp. 166–67. It is a curious coincidence that the authors chose as their example a putative leper colony.
18. W. W. Jaeger, *Die Theologie der frühen griechischen Denker* (Stuttgart, 1964), pp. 1 ff., 50 ff. (Xenophanes). (English trans., W. W. Jaeger, *The Theology of the Early Greek Philosophers* [Oxford, 1948]).

372

19. Augustinus, *De civitate Dei*, X, 9 ff. (in *Corpus Christianorum: Series Latina*, vol. 47, pp. 281 ff.).

20. Tractate *Abodah Zarah* 55ᵃ, in I. Epstein, ed., *The Babylonian Talmud*, sec. 4: *Seder Nezikin*, vol. 7 (London: Soncino Press, 1935), p. 281.

21. See H. Chadwick, *Origen: Contra Celsum*, trans. and with an introduction and notes by H. Chadwick (Cambridge: Cambridge University Press, 1965), p. 199. See Andresen, *Logos und Nomos: Die Polemic des Kelsos wider das Christentum, Arbeiten zur Kirchengaschichte* 30 (1955), pp. 266 ff.

22. J. H. Levi, *op. cit.*; M. Stern, *op. cit.*

23. Rule of Qumran, I, 10–11; see J. Licht, *The Rule Scroll* (IQS, IQSa, and IQSb), text, introduction, and commentary (in Hebrew) (Jerusalem: Bialik Institute, 1965), p. 61. See G. Vermes, *The Dead Sea Scrolls in English* (Harmondsworth: Penguin, 1962), p. 72. Also available: Theodore H. Gaster, trans., *The Dead Sea Scriptures* (Garden City, N.Y.: Doubleday/Anchor, 1956); J. Licht, "The Plant Eternal and the People of Divine Deliverance," in C. Rabin and Y. Yadin, eds., *Essays on the Dead Sea Scrolls* (in Hebrew) (Jerusalem: Reuben Mass, 1961), pp. 49–75; D. Flusser, *Jewish Sources in Early Christianity: Studies and Essays* (in Hebrew) (Tel Aviv, 1979).

24. IQPHab VII, 1–5, (G. Vermes, ibid., p. 239).

25. Tractate (Mishnah) *Sotah* IX, 15, in H. Danby, trans., *The Mishnah* (London: Oxford University Press, 1933), p. 306. See M. Avi-Yonah, *The Jews of Palestine: A Political History from the Bar-Kokhba War to the Arab Conquest* (London: Basil Blackwell, and New York: Schocken, 1976), chap. IV, "Judaism and Christianity to the Accession of the Emperor Constantine," pp. 137–57, esp. pp. 145–50.

26. E. G. von Grunebaum, *Medieval Islam* (Chicago, 1953), pp. 174–85.

27. Joachim de Flore, *Tractatus super quattuor evangelia*, 105, ed. E. Buonaiuti (Rome, 1930). See H. de Lubac, *Exégèse médiévale, Les quatre sens de l'Écriture*, Études publiées sous la direction de la faculté de théologie de Lyon-Fourvière, vol. III (II, 1) (1961), p. 144, n. 2.

28. Hugo de Sancto Victore, *De sacramentis Christianae fidei*, II, 6, 4, in Migne, *Patrologie latine*, vol. 176, col. 450A; idem, *De vanitate mundi et rerum transeuntium usu*, IV, in Migne, *op. cit.*, vol. 176, col. 740C. See A. Funkenstein, *Heilsplan und natürliche Entwicklung: Formen der Gegenwartsbestimmung im Geschichtsdenken des hohen Mittelalters* (Munich, 1965), pp. 52 and 165, n. 5. Hugo may have been influenced by Rashi in Hen. 6:9.

29. B. Blumenkranz, *Die Judenpredigt Augustine* (Basel, 1946).

30. F. Kern, *Recht und Verfassung in Mittelalter* (Darmstadt, 1958), pp. 23 ff.

31. Erich Caspar, ed., *Das Register Gregors VII, Epistolae selectae in usum scholarum*, vol. II, fasc. I: *Gregorii VII registrum libri, I-IV* (Berlin, 1920; 1967), pp. 202 ff. (see p. 203).

32. For this and for the following, see A. Funkenstein, "Changes in the Patterns of Christian Anti-Jewish Polemics in the Twelfth Century" (in Hebrew), *Zion* 33 (1968), pp. 125–44.

33. Rimbertus, *Vita Anskari*, 4, in G. Waltz, ed., *Vita Anskari* (MGH, SCY, Germ. in usum scholarum) (Hannover, 1884), p. 24.

34. B. Smalley, *The Study of the Bible in the Middle Ages* (Oxford, 1952); H. Hermann, *Rashi and the Christian Scholars* (Pittsburgh, 1963).

35. Petrus Venerabilis, *Tractatus adversus Iudaeorum inveteratam duritiem*, V, in Migne, *op. cit.*, vol. 189, col. 649 ff. See my article (above, n. 32).

36. Y. Baer, "The Disputation of R. Yechiel of Paris and of Nachmanides" (in Hebrew), *Tarbitz* 2 (1931), pp. 172–87; J. Rosenthal, "The Talmud on Trial 1240," *Jewish Quarterly Review* 47 (1956–57), pp. 58 ff; S. Grayzel, *The Church and the Jews in the XIIIth Century* (Philadelphia, 1933), pp. 29 ff; Ch. Merchavia, *The Church Versus Tal-*

mudic and Midrashic Literature (500–1248) (in Hebrew) (Jerusalem: Bialik Institute, 1970); Jacob Katz, Exclusiveness and Tolerance: Studies in Jewish-Gentile Relations in Medieval and Modern Times (Oxford: Oxford University Press, 1961; and New York: Schocken, 1962), pp. 106–33.

37. J. Trachtenberg, The Devil and the Jews: The Medieval Conception of the Jews and its Relation to Modern Antisemitism (New York, 1961) is an excellent anthropological study but lacks historical analysis.

38. Thomas of Monmouth, De vita et passione Sancti Willelmi martyris Norwicensis, II, 9, in A. Jessop and M. R. James, eds., The Life and Miracles of St. William of Norwich by Thomas of Monmouth (Cambridge, 1896), pp. 93 ff. (Latin and English).

39. N. Cohn's study Warrant for Genocide (London: Eyre & Spottiswoode, 1967) traces the literary affiliations of the Protocols but not the genesis of its topoi.

40. Ch. Wirszubski, Three Studies in Christian Kabbala (in Hebrew) (Jerusalem: Bialik Institute, 1975); idem, A Christian Kabbalist Reads the Law (in Hebrew) (Jerusalem: Bialik Institute, 1977).

41. For the following, see Shmuel Ettinger, Modern Anti-Semitism: Studies and Essay (in Hebrew) (Tel Aviv, 1978), esp. pp. 29 ff.; idem, in Dispersion and Unity 9 (1970), pp. 17–37.

42. H. H. Ben-Sasson, "Jews and Christian Sectarians," Viator 4 (1973), pp. 369–85.

43. See Ettinger, op. cit.; A. Hertzberg, in The French Enlightenment and the Jews: The Origin of Modern Anti-Semitism (New York, 1968), did not realize the older genesis of the motifs he discusses.

44. Cf. J. Katz, Antisemitism: From Religious Hatred to Racial Rejection (in Hebrew) (Tel Aviv: Am Oved, 1979); J. J. Schudt, Jüdische Merkwürdigkeiten (Frankfurt am Main and Leipzig, 1714).

45. For the following, see U. Tal, Judaism and Christianity (Ithaca and London: Cornell University Press, 1975).

46. On Sartre's explanation, in his famous Réflexions sur la question juive, see Menachem Brinker, "Sartre on the Jewish Question: Thirty Years Later," Jerusalem Quarterly 10 (Winter 1979), pp. 117–32. Sartre vividly confronted the anti-Semite and the Jews as dialectically intertwined forms of inauthentic existence. His description of the anti-Semitic mentality is the best I have ever read. His assumption that Jews persist by virtue of being seen as such revives Spinoza's contention in his Tractatus Theologico-Politicus (III). It also translates a psychoanalytical category from Being and Nothingness into terms of historical analysis: the basic situation of "être vue." But Sartre knew only the postemancipatory and assimilation-oriented Jews of his biographical experience.

47. Eva Fleischner, ed., Auschwitz: Beginning of a New Era? (New York, 1974), p. 75. I owe the reference to my student, Priscilla D. Jones, with whom I had repeated discussions on the subject of this chapter.

48. G. G. Baum, Christian Theology After Auschwitz (Robert Waley Cohen Memorial Lecture) (London, 1976), esp. pp. 7–15.

49. E. Berkovits, op. cit. (see above, n. 10).

50. Maimonides, Mishne Tora, Hilchot Shoftim.

51. Franklin H. Little, The Crucifixion of the Jews (New York, 1975).

52. Cf. Funkenstein, above, n. 5. The expression "nations restricted by the ways of religion," which J. Katz ascribes to Hameiri, is actually borrowed from Maimonides' Guide for the Perplexed III, 50; cf. J. Katz, op. cit., p. 115.

53. Baum, op. cit.

54. Ibid., p. 19.

55. M. Heidegger, Sein und Zeit (Tübingen, 1957), p. 12.

56. Ibid., p. 175: "Der Titel (Das Verfallen, etc.), der keine negative Bewertung ausdrückt . . ."

57. Primo Levi, *op. cit.*, pp. 100–103.

15 / Theses on Revisionism
PIERRE VIDAL-NAQUET

1. This essay should be considered as a complement to my study "Un Eichmann de papier," first published in *Esprit*, September 1980, then in my book *Les Juifs, la mémoire et le présent*, with an appendix by P. Bloch (Paris: Maspero, 1981), pp. 193–289. An abridged version appeared in English in *Democracy 2* (April 1981), pp. 70–95. I presume that these texts are known. I thank all those who helped me in preparing this chapter, notably P. Moreau, who knows the German far right very well, Jacques Tarnero, P. A. Targuieff, D. Fourgous, J. Svenbro, Shmuel Krakowski, and Arno J. Mayer. Since the colloquium of July 2, 1982, I have made only a few changes in this essay. However, I was made aware of several studies thanks to colleagues participating in the colloquium.

2. Cf. H. Dutrait-Crozon, *Joseph Reinach Historien: Révision de l'histoire de l'affaire Dreyfus*, with a preface by Charles Maurras (Paris: A. Savaète, 1905).

3. See the place accorded him by K. Stimley, *1981 Revisionist Bibliography: A Select Bibliography of Revisionist Books Dealing with the Two World Wars and Their Aftermaths* (Torrance, Calif.: Institute for Historical Review, 1980). See also H. E. Barnes, *Revisionism: A Key to Peace and Other Essays*, with a preface by J. J. Martin (San Francisco: Cato Institute, 1980).

4. For example, see his preface to L. Hamilton Jenks, *Our Cuban Colony* (New York: Vanguard Press, 1928).

5. See the classic work by Lord A. Ponsonby, *Falsehood in Wartime* (in numerous editions).

6. W. Roscoe Thayer, *Volleys from a Non-Combatant* (New York: Doubleday, 1919).

7. A letter reproduced in *Mouvement social*, January-March 1982, pp. 101–2. I thank Madeleine Rebérioux for bringing this text to my attention.

8. A text reproduced in the *American Historical Review*, April 1951, pp. 711–12; cf. H. E. Barnes, *Revisionism*, p. 131.

9. H. E. Barnes, *The Genesis of the World War* (New York: Knopf, 1929), trans. L. Laurent, with a preface by G. Demartial (Paris: Marcel Rivière, 1931).

10. Ibid., p. 306.

11. *Un débat historique: 1914: Le problème des origines de la guerre* (Paris: Rieder, 1933), p. 224.

12. Barnes, *Genesis*, pp. xi–xiii, 103, 333–35.

13. One might add to these references. See for example the republication of Bernard Lazare's book *l'Antisemitisme, son histoire et ses causes* (Paris: Éditions de la Différence, 1982), printed under the auspices of the Vieille Taupe group, the principal purveyors of French revisionism. Or see the brochure by J. G. Burg, a German Jewish revisionist, entitled, as blithely as you please, *J'accuse (Ich Klage an)* 2nd ed. (Munich: Ederer, 1982). See also Burg's *Zionnazi Zensur in der BRD* (Munich: Ederer, 1980), pp. 48–49.

14. See *Sur l'antisemitisme*, trans. M. Pouteau (Paris: Calmann-Lévy, Diaspora Collection, 1973), p. 195–260.

15. In America and France, that is. It goes without saying that German revisionists, who mainly come from the neo-Nazi far right, hardly seek to "revise" the German nationalist view of World War I.

16. The title of one of Arthur Butz's books, one of the bibles of revisionism, is *The*

Hoax of the Twentieth Century. See the 4th ed. (Torrance, Calif.: Institute for Historical Review, 1979).

17. On Rassinier, see "Un Eichmann de papier," in *Les Juifs*, pp. 236–244. Jean-Gabriel Cohn-Bendit and some of his friends express themselves in *Intolérable intolérance* (Paris: Éditions de la Différence, 1982).

18. A Finkielkraut, *L'Avenir d'une négation: Réflexion sur la question du génocide* (Paris: Éditions du Seuil, 1982), p. 121. In American revisionism today, anti-Semitic propaganda is sometimes cloaked and gussied up with references to World War I. See for example the *Journal for Historical Review* I, no. 2 (1980) for the reprinting of a chapter from Lord Ponsonby's book, cited above (see n. 5). Recall that this is the organ of the American revisionist sect.

19. Cf. H. E. Barnes, *Revisionism*, p. 6, where Paul Rassinier is quoted along with A. J. P. Taylor, Maurice Bardèche, Alfred Fabre-Luce, and some others. But only Paul Rassinier is called "courageous."

20. See "Un Eichmann de papier," *loc. cit.*, and Georges Weller's book, *Les chambres à gaz ont existé* (Paris: Gallimard, Témoins Collection, 1981). The recent publication, through the efforts of Robert Faurisson, of a brochure entitled "Réponse à Pierre Vidal-Naquet" (distributed by La Vieille Taupe, Paris, 1982) calls forth no new discussion from me. I shall simply indicate that the text attributed to me by the author of the preface, P. Guillaume, at the bottom of page 4, is not by me. This error has been rectified in a later edition and has been replaced with new lies.

21. "The conclusion precedes the proofs." I borrow this expression from an unpublished text by Jean-Claude Milner. In speaking of a "total lie," I do not wish to suggest a complete inversion, in which everything the revisionists write is false down to the smallest detail. Instead, it is the sum total that makes up a mendacious system.

22. *Sur l'antisemitisme*, p. 31.

23. Walter Laqueur, *Le Terrifiant secret: La solution finale et l'information étouffée*, trans. A. Roubichou-Stretz (Paris: Gallimard, 1981). (In English, *The Terrible Secret* [London: Weidenfeld & Nicolson, 1980]) See also, more detailed and chronologically extensive but less acute, Martin Gilbert's exposé *Auschwitz and the Allies* (London & New York: Holt, Rinehart & Winston, 1981). It goes without saying that Laqueur's book has been quickly exploited by revisionists: if the Allies themselves did not believe in the genocide, it was because there was nothing to believe. See the articles by Robert Faurisson and P. Guillaume in *Jeune Nation solidariste*, December 1981.

24. Martin Gilbert, *op. cit.*, pp. 190 ff.; and above all, Randolph L. Braham, *The Politics of Genocide: The Holocaust in Hungary*, 2 vols. (New York: Columbia University Press, 1981), vol. II, pp. 708–24, pp. 1109–12.

25. Randolph L. Braham, *op. cit.*, vol. II, pp. 1095–1120.

26. One or the other expression, sometimes both at once, are found in revisionist literature. See for example Arthur Butz, *The Hoax*, esp. pp. 53–100; Robert Faurisson, *Le Monde*, December 29, 1978, reprinted in Serge Thion, *Vérité historique ou vérité politique* (Paris: Vielle Taupe, 1980), pp. 104–5; Wilhelm Stäglich, *Der Auschwitz Mythos: Legende oder Wirklichkeit?* (Tübingen: Grabert, 1979), pp. 146–51.

27. There are some myths that accompanied the great massacre like the religious phenomena which followed it, yet do not suppress its existence. This elementary truth entirely escaped the anthropologist J.-L. Tristani. See his "Supplique à MM. les magistrats de la cour d'appel de Paris," in *Intolérable intolérance*, pp. 161–72, a text that is nevertheless hardly anti-Semitic, although definitely underdeveloped intellectually.

28. F. H. Hinsley, ed., *British Intelligence in the Second World War*, vol. II (London: Her Majesty's Stationery Office, 1981), p. 673.

29. N. Blumental, *Dokumenty, Marterialy z Czasów Okupacji Niemieckiej w Polsce i Obozy* (Łódź, 1946), p. 118.

376

30. Walter Laqueur, *Le terrifiant secret*, pp. 97–98. It is also discussed by revisionist authors such as Arthur Butz; see *The Hoax*, pp. 60–62.

31. Martin Broszat, "Hitler und die Genesis der 'Endlösung,'" *Vierteljahrshefte für Zeitgeschichte* (hereafter *VfZ*) 25, (1977), pp. 729–75. (translated into English in *Yad Vashem Studies* XIII [1979], pp. 73–125); Christopher Browning, "Eine Antwort auf Martin Broszats Thesen zur Genesis der Endlösung," *Yad Vashem Studies* XXIX (1981), pp. 97–109. Christopher Browning's work here corrects some of his earlier work.

32. David Irving, *Hitler's War* (New York: Viking Press, 1977).

33. References may be found in *Les Juifs, la mémoire et le présent*, p. 236, n. 66; in addition, concerning Adolf Eichmann, a document of capital importance, the manuscript written by him in Argentina and published by a neo-Nazi revisionist, Dr. Rudolf Aschenauer, *Ich, Adolf Eichmann: Ein Historicher Zeugenbericht* (Leoni am Starnberger See: Druffel Verlag, 1980), p. 178. Despite Eichmann's categoric affirmation before his capture, the editor still calmly states that Eichmann refers to a nonexistent order (p. 178, n.). I would observe a slight difference between Eichmann's manuscript and his testimony given in Jerusalem. In the former his conversation with Heydrich takes place toward the end of 1941. In the latter it takes place at the end of the summer of 1941. Cf. *Eichmann par Eichmann* (Paris: Grasset, 1970), p. 110.

34. See for example H. Härtle, *Freispruch für Deutschland* (Göttingen: Verlag K. W. Schütz, 1968), pp. 201–4; Burg, *Zionnazi Zensur in der BRD*, pp. 173–76, uses the existence of monetary and postal units in the ghettos of Łódź and Theresienstadt to show that all was normal.

35. I was able to do this in the beginning of April 1982, at the Yad Vashem Library in Jerusalem.

36. The record-breaker apparently was the famous brochure by Richard E. Harwood (the pseudonym of the British neo-Nazi R. Verall), *Did Six Million Really Die?* (Richmond, 1979), a tiny monument of imaginary erudition.

37. For example, the Institute for Historical Review, located in Torrance, California, publishes a complete collection of works, apart from the *Journal* of the same name.

38. One of the most exact studies on this Internationale is P. A. Taguieff's "L'Héritage nazi," in *Nouveaux cahiers* 64 (Spring 1981), pp. 3–22.

39. I draw this information from the biography of this personage published in the *Journal of Historical Review* I, no. 2 (1980), p. 187. I have used the indications provided by J. Jakubowski in the *Expressen* (Stockholm) of July 17, 1981.

40. Its first number in 1979 was a subscription campaign aimed at all the members of the American Historical Association.

41. I have at hand one of the issues published in 1981. On the first page some hairs are glued under the heading "Please Accept This Hair from a Gassed Victim."

42. L. Marschalko, *The World Conquerors: The Real War Criminals*, translated from the Hungarian by A. Suranyi (London: Joseph Sueli, 1958; reprinted by the Christian Book Club, New York, 1978). I have read Jean-Claude Milner's remarkable work. A typical example of his erudition is his claim that the Jewish nationalist journal *Shem*, published clandestinely in France, stated on July 8, 1944, that conditions in the camps were generally good and that Jewish children aged two to five frequented Berlin kindergartens (p. 115). One of Milner's French sources is the work of Maurice Bardèche.

43. Thus the Vieille Taupe published in *Intolérable intolérance*, alongside inept but hardly anti-Semitic texts, a highly anti-Semitic (through its anti-Zionism) text by Vincent Monteil.

44. Cf. *Le Monde* of June 2, 1982, quoting from Rabat's *L'Opinion*, the organ of Istiqlal, Mr. Bougenaa Amara: "Nazism is a creation of Zionism. The historic reality of the camps has yet to be authenticated. Some doubts still remain as to their existence, even."

45. The most singular book that I know on this theme is Hussein Ahmad's *Palästina meine Heimat: Zionismus—Weltfeind der Völker* (Frankfurt am Main: E. Bierbaum Verlag, 1975); every form of anti-Semitism and revisionism is assembled herein.

46. See, for example, in the *Revue d'études palestiniennes*, no. 1 (Autumn 1981), Maxime Rodinson, "Quelques idées simples sur l'antisémitisme," pp. 5–21. See p. 17 for a denunciation of the Arab use of anti-Semitic classics.

47. The best-known case is that of J. G. Burg (né Ginzburg), who experienced Europe under Hitler and Stalin, then Israel before moving to Germany. His autobiography, *Schuld und Schicksal* (Oldendorf: K. W. Schütz, 1962; K. G. Preuss, 1979), is therefore interesting and only on the margins of revisionism. The book's subtitle may be translated as "European Jewry Between the Hangmen and the Hypocrites." Since then, Burg has slid from revisionism to German nationalism. See, apart from the books already cited, *Maidanek in alle Ewigkeit?* (Munich: Ederer, 1979) (confiscated); *Sündenböcke, Grossangriffe des Zionismus auf Papst Pius XII und auf die deutschen Regierungen*, 4th ed. (Munich: Ederer, 1980). All of these books were published by a specialty house. Burg also published a collection of Jewish stories, *Jüdische Anekdotiade* (Munich: Ederer, 1970).

48. The most fecund author in this domain is Erich Kern. I shall mention only two of Kern's works, *Meineid gegen Deutschland* (2nd ed. 1971) and *Die Tragödie der Juden* (1979), both published by a specialized house of the Preussich Oldendorf—Schütz. The French reader will note with interest in the latter book, pp. 289–99, the ardent praise of Robert Faurisson. A collection of ten writers, including the Englishman David Irving, along with biographies, is *Verrat und Wiederstand im Dritten Reich* (Coburg: Nation Europa, 1978). Finally, the efforts of U. Walendy, a specialist in the use of retouched photographs for propaganda purposes, should be noted. See the first issue of the *Journal of Historical Review* I, no. 1 (1980), pp. 59–68. Walendy's books include *Wahrheit für Deutschland* (1965) (Vlotho am Weser: Verlag für Volkstum und Zeitgeschichtsforschung, 3rd ed., 1976); and *Auschwitz im I. G. Farben Prozess*, same publisher, 1981.

49. See, for example, Kern, *Die Tragödie der Juden*, p. 83; Stäglich, *Der Auschwitz Mythos*, pp. 82–85, with reference, for example on p. 83, to the *American Hebrew* (New York) of May 24, 1934, and to the *Youngstown* (Ohio) *Jewish Times* of April 16, 1936.

50. See, for example, Stäglich, *Der Auschwitz Mythos*, p. 82, and p. 395, n. 103, which refers to all of the revisionist authors. The first mentioned is the Frenchman Paul Rassinier, who used this same document.

51. "Les redresseurs de morts," *Temps modernes*, June 1980, pp. 2150–2211.

52. For example, Stäglich, *Der Auschwitz Mythos*, pp. 38–65; Kern, *Die Tragödie der Juden*, pp. 122–33. Butz, *The Hoax*, pp. 211–14, only hold the latter interpretation.

53. I have provided the main references in "Un Eichmann de papier," pp. 209 and 249–50.

54. Stäglich, *Der Auschwitz Mythos*, p. 94, quoting and commenting on the discourse of Posen (Poznań) of October 6, 1943. But the quotation on pp. 89–103, is the author's only "demonstration." One might also mention an anthology page on Himmler's "bragging" in a brochure from the Parisian far left, "De l'Exploitation dans les camps à l'exploitation des camps," a supplement to the third issue of *La Guerre sociale*, May 1981, pp. 27–28; also Robert Faurisson's *Réponse à Pierre Vidal-Naquet*, pp. 14–17.

55. One might refer here to a number of works by Paul Rassinier, such as *De Drame des Juifs européens* (Paris: Sept Couleurs, 1964), pp. 79–91. I have already cited the astonishing book by L. Marschalko, but the masterpiece of this type of material is the work of H. Härtle, *Freispruch für Deutschland*, esp. pp. 204–74.

56. Irving, *Hitler's War*, pp. 332, 393. This so-called order is in fact the result of a little intellectual swindle, which was summarily denounced by Martin Broszat in "Hitler und die Genesis der 'Endlösung,'" p. 760, and by Gitta Sereny and L. Chester in the

Sunday Times (London) of July 10, 1977. It is a question of the telephone calls made by Himmler to Heydrich on November 30, 1941. The führer's QG spoke of a planned convoy of Berlin Jews and the order was not to exterminate this specific convoy (*keine Liquidierung*).

57. See the important testimony of H. J. Klein, *La Mort mercénaire*, with a preface by D. Cohn-Bendit (Paris: Editions du Seuil, 1980).

58. I have myself contributed to disseminating this legend in an early version of this text, following Jacques Tarnero, *Nouveaux Cahiers* 64 (Spring 1981), p. 28. My friend Diego Lanza made me aware that the often cited text from the *Frankfurter Allgemeine Zeitung of* December 15, 1972, p. 6, simply proves that the journalist understood nothing about Ulrike Meinhof.

59. For exact, verifiable information on this lobby, which edits the weekly *Spotlight* (which rather closely follows the formula of *Minute* but is even more directly racist), see *Facts* (published by B'nai B'rith) 26, no. 5, 1 and 2 (June 1980). For certain recent episodes in the life of the Institute for Historical Review, see also R. Chandler in the *San Francisco Chronicle* of May 5, 1981. W. A. Carto presided over the Revisionist conference of 1981; see his contribution, "On the Uses of History," in the *Journal of Historical Review*, 3, no. 1 (1982), pp. 27–30.

60. In the United States there have been several discussions on the more or less "libertarian" character of revisionism, particularly of H. E. Barnes and his crew. See the letters published in the *Village Voice* on July 1, 1981.

61. See for example, A. Rabinbach, "Anti-Semitism Reconsidered," *New German Critique* 21 (Autumn 1980), pp. 129–41, esp. p. 141, n. 21.

62. A complete polemic has been published in the press during 1981. For examples, see Myrdal's articles in the *Svenska Dagbladet* of March 5, 1981, and the *Expressen* on April 13, 1981. I myself responded to these articles (*Expressen*, July 16 and 17, 1981), which led to new articles from Jan Myrdal (*Expressen* of July 28 and 29, 1981). One of Myrdal's texts is an attack on French intellectuals and their role in the Faurisson Affair. This was reprinted in Myrdal's book *Dussinet fullt Skriftställining 12* (Stockholm: Norstedts, 1982), pp. 221–29. However, in this text Jan Myrdal does not truly express his fundamentally favorable feelings about Faurisson. These appear in *Tidskrift för Folkets Rättigheter* I (1982).

63. For some indications, see "Un Eichmann de papier," p. 267–68, and esp. what Bennett himself says about his action and the polemics that resulted, in "In the Matter of Robert Faurisson," the *Journal of Historical Review* 1, no. 2 (1980), pp. 115–20.

64. Robert Faurisson gave an interview to the Italian periodical *Storia illustrata* 261 (August 1979), reprinted with corrections in Serge Thion's *Vérité historique ou vérité politique?* pp. 171–212. The Gruppo Communista Internazionalista Autonomo, a small Marxist sect, published a brochure in March 1981 entitled *Il Caso Rassinier*. I am grateful to Robert Paris for sending me this item.

65. *Mémoire en défense contre ceux qui m'accusent de falsifier l'histoire: La question des chambres à gaz* (Paris: Vieille Taupe, 1980).

66. Lothar Baier, "Die Weisswäscher von Auschwitz: Robert Faurisson und seine Genossen," *Transatlantic*, July 1981, pp. 14–26; Paul L. Berman, "Gas Chamber Games: Crackpot History and the Right to Lie," *Village Voice*, June 10, 1981: Lucy S. Dawidowicz's article, "Lies About the Holocaust," *Commentary*, December 1980, pp. 31–37, is more international in scope but confines itself to French-language references.

67. "Hitler never ordered or allowed anyone to be killed because of his race or religion": this formula made Faurisson notorious and has disseminated since 1978, it appears. The neo-Nazi revisionist W. D. Rothe ended his book *Die Endlösung der Judenfrage* (Frankfurt am Main: E. Bierbaum, 1974) by affirming the same statement: "Dass es nicht einen einzigen Juden gegeben hat, der mit Wissen und Billigung der Regierung des

Dritten Reiches, des damaligen Führers Adolf Hitler oder gar des Deutschen Volkes umgebracht worden wäre, weil er Jude war."

68. Such trials have taken place in America without creating much publicity.

69. In the above-mentioned work, *Vérité historique ou vérité politique?*

70. See for example, in the *Journal of Historical Review* I, no. 2 (1980), p. 153–62, the letters exchanged by various revisionists and the directors of London's *New Statesman*. According to Gitta Sereny, the highest moral and legal authorities debated the question in England's press, finally refusing the right to reply.

71. The Faurisson Affair really began with the publication in *Le Monde* on December 29, 1978, of an article by Robert Faurisson, followed by a response from Georges Wellers. Certainly, *Le Monde* was clearly opposed to Faurisson, but one may read, for example, in *Le Monde* of June 30, 1981, an article about a trial by Ch. Colombani entitled "Universities Confront One Another over the Faurisson Case." The discussion was more intense in *Libération* (I participated there in a conversation with Didier Eribon on January 24–25, 1981); it was rounded off with an article by F. Paul-Boncour on July 11–12, 1981, entitled "Putting an End to the Faurisson Affair."

72. For example, apart from the books by Bardèche and Rassinier, there is the work by G. A. Amaudruz, a Swiss Nazi, *Ubu justicier au premier procès de Nuremberg* (Paris: Charles de Jonquière, 1949).

73. See my "Un Eichmann de papier," pp. 236–44.

74. I provide some details concerning La Vieille Taupe in the second part of my study "Un Eichmann de papier." Noam Chomsky allied himself with the French group La Vieille Taupe based on what he knew, or thought he knew, about Paul Rassinier. Chomsky himself has never totally adhered to revisionist theses.

75. These themes appear with an absolute clarity in a tract disseminated by these groups in October 1980, entitled *Notre royaume est un prison*. It was reproduced in the above-mentioned brochure (see n. 54) "De l'Exploitation dans les camps à l'exploitation des camps."

76. On Édouard Drumont and the influence he exerted, see Zeev Sternhell, *La Droite révolutionnaire, 1885–1914: Les origines françaises du fascisme* (Paris: Éditions du Seuil, 1978); and also, Michel Winock's collection, *Drumont et Cie* (Paris: Éditions du Seuil, 1982).

77. Édouard Drumont, *La France Juive*, vol. II (Paris: Marpont-Flammarion, 1886), pp. 408–9.

78. See my text, "Des musées et des hommes," preface to Richard Marienstras, *Être un peuple en Diaspora* (Paris: Maspero, 1975), reprinted in *Les Juifs, la mémoire et le présent*, pp. 110–25.

79. Lucy S. Dawidowicz's book *The Holocaust and the Historians* (Cambridge: Harvard University Press, 1981) is a basic work on historiographic practices and, in general, on all of the historiography on the great massacre. Unfortunately, this work too often gives way to the reverse excess of those it correctly denounces for banalizing the great massacre. Instead, Professor Dawidowicz falls into Judeo-centrism. However, the book contributes valuable information on the USSR and Poland.

80. Essentially, C. Simonov, in *Maïdanek, un camp d'extermination*, follows the findings of the Polish-Soviet Commission of Inquiry (Paris: Éditions Sociales, 1945) and V. Grossman, *L'Enfer de Treblinka* (Paris: Arthaud, 1945; reprinted 1966). Neither work has any real documentary value. See, apart from the guidelines in Lucy S. Dawidowicz, *The Holocaust*, pp. 69–79, the brief study by Erich Goldhagen, "Der Holocaust in der Sowjetischen Propaganda und Geschichtsschreibung," *VfZ* 28 (1980), pp. 502–7.

81. There exists a good Polish documentary guide for the entire period before 1962, which does not treat the pure extermination camps such as Treblinka, but does include Auschwitz: Wanda Kiedrzyńska, *Materialy do Bibliografii Hitlerowskich obosów Koncen-*

tracyjnych, *Państwowe Wydawnictwo Naukowe 1934–1962* (Warsaw, 1964). Works in twenty-one languages are abstracted here, including Russian. One sees quickly that the works in Russian are insignificant. The Russian translation of the classic work on Auschwitz by the Pole Jean Sehn is given the number 1,382 in this bibliography; it was published in Warsaw in 1961.

82. I quote the German translation presented and commented upon by Andreas Hillgruber and Hans-Adolf Jacobsen: *B. S. Telpuchowski: Die Sowjetische Geschichte des Grossen Vaterländischen Krieges (1914–1945)* (Frankfurt am Main: Bernard & Graefe, 1961); on the Jews, see p. 272; on the camps. see pp. 422–24. The German editors do not remark on the author's discretion on the genocide of the Jews, although their introduction and notes are highly critical. Some years later a record of the 1944–45 campaign was published: I. Konev et al., *The Great Campaign of Liberation by the Soviet Army* (Moscow: Progress Editions, n.d. [1975]); mentioned on p. 71 is the "giant extermination factory" of Auschwitz, along with absurd statistics, but not a word anywhere about the Jews. For more details, and more significantly, the role of anti-Zionism in Soviet historiography, see the essay by Saul Friedländer in the present volume.

83. Martin Broszat writes in "Holocaust und die Geschichtswissenschaft," *VfZ* 27 (1979), pp. 285–98 (see esp. pp. 294–95) that the *Zeitschrift für Geschichtswissenschaft* of East Berlin, between 1953 and 1972, published a grand total of one article on this subject, that this solitary study appeared in 1961, on p. 1681, and that it amounted to no more than a review of works published in the West. This is not true. See, for example, in 1962, pp. 954–57, the review of a Polish book; in 1963, pp. 794–96, the review of the *Hefte von Auschwitz* series; in 1964, pp. 5–27, the article by L. Berthold on the fascist terror in Germany and its victims, etc. But it is true that such articles are basically rare, unequal in quality or quantity to those published in Munich. Plus, the polemic emphasis against West Germany is highly characteristic. A collective study that treats in depth the East German historiography on this subject, which has the great merit of distinguishing the diverse chronological sequences, is K. Kwist's "Historians of the German Democratic Republic on Antisemitism and Persecution," *Leo Baeck Institute Year Book* XX (1976), p. 173–98. I am grateful to Saul Friedländer for bringing this reference to my attention.

84. See, for example, F. K. Kaul and J. Noack, *Angeklagter Nr. 6. Eine Auschwitz-Dokumentation* (Berlin: Akademisches Verlag, 1966). This provides complementary documentation on Perry Broad, one of the accused at the Auschwitz trial at Frankfurt.

85. I have given some examples of these qualities and drawbacks of Polish historiography in "Un Eichmann de papier," pp. 223, 229–30, 264–65.

86. For some aperçus on the Polish work (notably by the historians Kazimierz Iranek-Osmecki of London and C. Luczak of Poznań), see the articles by Shmuel Krakowski, "The Slaughter of Polish Jewry—A Polish Reassessment," *Wiener Library Bulletin* XXVI, nos. 3–4 (1972–73), pp. 13–20; "The Jewish Fight Against the Nazis in Poland, according to Jewish and Polish Literature" (in Hebrew), *Seventh World Congress on Jewish Sciences: Research on the History of the Holocaust* (Jerusalem, 1980), pp. 45–49; "The Shoa for Polish Jews," in the book by the Polish researcher C. Luczak, *Yalkut Morekhet* (Historical Heritage Collection) (Jerusalem, 1980), pp. 193–98. It is hard for me to give a personal judgment on an historiography in a language I do not know. A friend whose judgment I trust, to whom I sent Shmuel Krakowski's articles, states that the author tends to place the enemies at opposite poles, each one easily perceiving the other's chauvinism. Still, it remains true that absolute symmetry cannot be found in nature.

87. See, for example, M. Teich, "New Editions and Old Mistakes" (about Reitlinger), *Yad Vashem Studies* VI (1967), pp. 375–84; N. Eck, "Historical Research or Slander?" (on Bruno Bettelheim, Hannah Arendt, and Raul Hilberg), ibid., pp. 385–430;

381

and above all (on Hannah Arendt), Jacob Robinson, *La Tragédie juive sous la croix gammée à la lumière du procès de Jérusalem: Le Recit de Hannah Arendt et la réalité des faits*, trans. L. Steinberg (Paris: CDJC, 1969). It is only fair to say that a number of Israeli contributions to the present colloquium, such as those of Amos Funkenstein and Shulamit Volkov, indicate a break with this tradition.

88. One noticed it at the time of the colloquium that later became this book, particularly during the debate following the exposition by Arno J. Mayer. Mayer's work is now available in book form (*Why Did the Heavens Not Darken?* [New York: Pantheon Books, 1989]).

89. See the courageous article by the Israeli journalist Boaz Evron, "Les interprétations de l'holocauste, un danger pour le peuple juif," translated in *Revue d'études palestiniennes* 2 (Winter 1982), pp. 36–52. The original appeared in Hebrew in *Yiton* 77 (May–June 1980).

90. The Yad Vashem Institute is at the same time a scientific institution, a museum, and a central repository for collections, all of which roles it fulfills admirably. But one also finds in Jerusalem, in the offices of the Bureau of Tourism, leaflets inviting tourists to visit a "Holocaust cave" on Mount Zion which is better left undescribed.

91. Theodor Wiesengrund Adorno, *Dialectique négative* (Paris: Payot, Collection "Critique de la Politique," 1978), pp. 283–86. I quote from pp. 283–84.

92. Today it is necessary to make an effort to remember, but in the years after World War II, the symbol of the concentration-camp world was not Auschwitz but Buchenwald. In referring to the above-mentioned Polish bibliography (see n. 81), we verify that in 1962 the number of books published on Buchenwald clearly exceeded the number of those on the great Silesian slaughterhouse.

93. The notion of absolute crime as justifying relative crimes is, alas, operational in Israel and even elsewhere.

94. Apropos of Dachau, see the letter by Martin Broszat, *Die Zeit*, August 19, 1960, often reproduced since, and often misprinted in the revisionist press and in revisionist literature. That said, we must not push too far the differences between concentration camps and extermination camps. In the case of Dachau specifically, the personnel trained there were then largely used at Auschwitz and other murder sites. See the recent restatement of the case by H. G. Richardi, *Schule der Gewalt: Die Anfänge des Konzentrationslager Dachau 1933–1934: Ein Dokumentarischer Bericht* (Munich: Beck, 1983), pp. 241–48. For *The Diary of Anne Frank*, see, for example, Robert Faurisson, in Serge Thion, *Verité historique ou verité politique?* pp. 213–300, a study reprinted in English in the *Journal of Historical Review* III, no. 2 (1982), pp. 147–209. On the Crematorium I of Auschwitz, see Stäglich, *Der Auschwitz Mythos*, pp. 77, 137. I have received photographic documentation on this point that leaves no doubt about the retouchings.

95. I borrow this expression from Jean-Claude Milner, *Ordre et raisons de la langue* (Paris: Éditions du Seuil, 1982), pp. 323–25.

96. See Pierre Vidal-Naquet, "Un Eichmann de papier," sec. II.

97. It is a question here of a domain little studied in France; the study by Frederick Raphael presented at the colloquium constitutes a first approach. In Germany recent revisionist literature is often in reaction to the television film *Holocaust* (1979); this is also true in the United States. See the articles by J. Herf, by A. S. Markovitz and R. S. Hayden, and by S. Zielinski, in *New German Critique* 19 (Winter 1980), pp. 30–96, which present a highly complete tableau of the television series' reception in Germany. An example of revisionist reaction is H. Härtle, *Was Holocaust verschweigt; Deutsche Verteidigung gegen Kollektiv-Schuld-Lügen* (Leoni am Starnberger See, 1979).

INDEX OF NAMES

Bismarck, Otto von, 42
Blobel, Paul, 140, 141
Bloch, Marc, 35–36, 39, 53
Böckel, Otto, 38
Boris, King, 206, 224, 226
Bormann, Martin, 7, 29–30, 66, 88, 91
Börne, Ludwig, 51
Bothmann, Hans, 143, 144
Bouhler, Philip, 136
Bracher, Karl Dietrich, 8, 10–11, 98
Brack, Viktor, 108, 136
Bradfisch, Otto, 27
Braham, Randolph L., 252–74
Brandt, Karl, 136
Brandt, Rudolf, 29
Broszat, Martin, 14–17, 19–20, 21, 24–25, 56, 85, 96, 97–98, 105, 115, 309
Browning, Christopher R., 10, 24, 25, 85, 96–118, 309
Bühler, Joseph, 113, 144
Bullock, Alan, 56
Butz, Arthur, 313, 318
Byrnes, Robert, 44

Canaris, Karl, 187
Carol, King, 203
Carto, W. A., 313
Celsus, 283
Chamberlain, Houston Stewart, 34, 38, 44, 291
Chomsky, Noam, 313
Christiansen, Friedrich Christian, 188
Chvalkovsky, Frantisek, 68
Class, Heinrich, 37, 49
Cohn-Bendit, Jean-Gabriel, 306
Czerniaków, Adam, 131, 253

Daluege, Kurt, 124
Damaskinos, Métropolite, 258
Dannecker, Theodor, 128, 180, 182, 185, 186
Darré, Walther, 57
Dawidowicz, Lucy, 55, 85, 97–98
de Lagarde, Paul, 37, 40, 51
de Pellepoix, Darquier, 256
Descartes, René, 54

Deutscher, Isaac, 4
Dilli, Gustav, 122
Dinur, Benzion, 34
Donati, Angelo, 192
Doriot, Jacques, 190
Dorpmüller, Julius, 122
Dreyfus, Alfred, 48, 304, 306
Drumont, Édouard, 44–45, 46, 47, 314
Dühring, Eugen, 36, 40, 50–51

Eberl, Irmfried, 127, 146
Ehlers, Ernst, 187
Eichmann, Adolf, 10, 24, 27, 29, 64, 65, 66, 68, 91, 94, 105, 106–108, 109, 110, 111, 113, 114, 115, 122, 128, 132, 142, 147, 155, 159, 178, 182, 185, 186, 189, 309, 317
Eimann, Kurt, 138
Esau, 277
Ettinger, Shmuel, 34

Fackenheim, E., 279
Falkenhausen, Alexander von, 176, 187, 191
Faurisson, Robert, 313, 314
Felderer, Dietlieb, 310
Feuerbach, Ludwig, 282
Filipovic-Majstrovic, 217
Filov, Bogdan, 207, 223, 224, 225
Fleming, Gerald L., 12, 23, 26, 27
Fontane, Theodor, 51
Förster, Paul, 38
Frank, Anne, 318
Frank, Hans, 57, 89, 113, 176, 260
Frank, Karl-Hermann, 91
Franz Josef, Emperor of Austria, 80
Fresco, Nadine, 311
Freud, Sigmund, 282, 312
Frick, Wilhelm, 57, 59, 63, 67
Friedländer, Saul, 3–31
Fritsch, Theodor, 37, 40, 51
Fröhlich, Wilhelm, 123
Fromm, Bella, 66
Fromm, Friedrich, 158
Funk, Walther, 67
Funkenstein, Amos, 275–303

INDEX OF PLACES